AF724031

Albrecht Mendelssohn Bartholdy
Graduate School of Law

Schriften der Albrecht Mendelssohn Bartholdy
Graduate School of Law

edited by

Prof. Dr. Stefan Oeter,
Lehrstuhl für Öffentliches Recht, Völkerrecht und ausländisches öffentliches Recht, Universität Hamburg

Prof. Dr. Tilman Repgen,
Lehrstuhl für Deutsche Rechtsgeschichte, Privatrechtsgeschichte der Neuzeit und Bürgerliches Recht, Universität Hamburg

Prof. Dr. Hans-Heinrich Trute,
Lehrstuhl für Öffentliches Recht, Medien- und Telekommunikationsrecht, Universität Hamburg

Band 6

Xenofon Kontargyris

IT Laws in the Era of Cloud Computing

A Comparative Analysis between EU and US Law on the Case Study of Data Protection and Privacy

Nomos

Gefördert durch einen Druckkostenzuschuss der Albrecht Mendelssohn Bartholdy Graduate School of Law.

Funded by a print subsidy from Albrecht Mendelssohn Bartholdy Graduate School of Law.

The Deutsche Nationalbibliothek lists this publication in the Deutsche Nationalbibliografie; detailed bibliographic data are available on the Internet at http://dnb.d-nb.de

a.t.: Hamburg, Univ., Diss., 2018

Original title: "ICT LAWS IN THE ERA OF CLOUD COMPUTING – A comparative analysis between EU and US law on the case study of data protection and privacy"

ISBN 978-3-8487-5362-8 (Print)
978-3-8452-9562-6 (ePDF)

British Library Cataloguing-in-Publication Data
A catalogue record for this book is available from the British Library.

ISBN 978-3-8487-5362-8 (Print)
978-3-8452-9562-6 (ePDF)

Library of Congress Cataloging-in-Publication Data
Kontargyris, Xenofon
IT Laws in the Era of Cloud Computing
A Comparative Analysis between EU and US Law on the Case Study of Data Protection and Privacy
Xenofon Kontargyris (ed.)
378 p.
Includes bibliographic references and index.

ISBN 978-3-8487-5362-8 (Print)
978-3-8452-9562-6 (ePDF)

1st Edition 2018
© Nomos Verlagsgesellschaft, Baden-Baden, Germany 2018. Printed and bound in Germany.

This work is subject to copyright. All rights reserved. No part of this publication may be reproduced or transmitted in any form or by any means, electronic or mechanical, including photocopying, recording, or any information storage or retrieval system, without prior permission in writing from the publishers. Under § 54 of the German Copyright Law where copies are made for other than private use a fee is payable to "Verwertungsgesellschaft Wort", Munich.

No responsibility for loss caused to any individual or organization acting on or refraining from action as a result of the material in this publication can be accepted by Nomos or the author and editors.

To my parents, who have been my greatest supporters even at times that I did not believe so strongly in myself.
Στους γονείς μου, που πιστεύουν πάντα σε μένα ακόμα κι όταν ο ίδιος δεν πιστεύω τόσο δυνατά στον εαυτό μου.

To my brother, who made sure that over the past three years no emergency would distract me from my goal.
Στον αδερφό μου, που τα τρία αυτά χρόνια δεν επέτρεψε σε απρόοπτα να με αποσπάσουν από το στόχο μου.

Foreword

I do not consider myself a genius. Over the course of my studies I have had the good fortune to meet and collaborate with colleagues and teachers who have razor sharp minds for science; I certainly do not feel I am one of them. Therefore, I am not one of those researchers who had been confident that they would sit down and conduct a PhD since their first day at University. Nevertheless, I have been lucky enough to be inspired and encouraged in the course of my academic life by friends, colleagues and teachers who saw potential in me and made me believe that everything is possible with hard, systematic work. Through this note, I would like to express my heartfelt gratitude firstly to Prof. Trute for giving me the chance to undertake this particular project despite the interdisciplinary challenges it posed for a lawyer; to Prof. Schulz for being an excellent second supervisor helping me to maintain the dual approaches between law and IT and between EU and US law that the challenge I had set up for myself necessitated; to Prof. Papadopoulou from my alma mater, the Aristotle's University of Thessaloniki, for offering me as much help and support as possible in order to remain academically sharp while I was looking for a suitable opportunity to conduct a project as demanding as an interdisciplinary PhD; to my ex-colleagues at Apogee Information Systems, my first full-time employer and at the Directorate General for Media at the European Commission for facilitating my curiosity to get to know the real meaning of terms such as 'software', 'data processes', 'cloud-based systems' etc., which are always intriguing for an IT lawyer but require a lot more than a strong legal background in order to tackle regulatory challenges associated to them. And last but not least, I wish to cordially thank all those classmates and teachers from my school years and the colleagues, friends and teachers from my university years who helped me build the confidence it took to make it from high school to my LLB study, then on to my LLM and further onwards to my PhD term. Regardless of degrees and titles, all these people and experiences have taught me that everything is possible if you are determined to fight for it. And this is a lesson I will cherish for life!

This work has been finalized on 27 September 2017. All its contents and arguments should be read in light of the legal status quo applicable at that time.

PS: Grandma, I know you are happy about this. I promise you I will not stop here!

Hamburg, 27. September 2017

Table of Contents

List of abbreviations

(in alphabetical order)

Amazon Web Services	AWS
Application Programming Interface	API
Application Service Provision	ASP
Artificial Intelligence	AI
Asian-Pacific Economic Cooperation	APEC
Binding Corporate Rules	BCR
Charter of Fundamental Rights of the European Union	CFREU
Chief Executive Officer	CEO
Cloud Service Provider	CSP
Communication as a Service	CaaS
Communications Decency Act	CDA
Community Based Participatory Research	CBPR
Customer Relationship Management	CRM
Data as a Service	DaaS
Data Protection Directive (European)	DPD
Digital Millennium Copyright Act	DMCA
Electronic Communications Privacy Act	ECPA
European Convention on Human Rights	ECHR
European Economic Area	EEA
European Union	EU
Fair Credit Reporting Act	FCRA
Federal Trade Commission (US)	FTC
Foreign Intelligence and Surveillance Act	FISA
General Data Protection Regulation (European)	GDPR
Hardware as a Service	HaaS
Health Insurance Portability and Accountability Act	HIPAA
Information & Communications Technology	ICT
Information Technology	IT
Infrastructure as a Service	IaaS

Internet Corporation for Assigned Names and Numbers	ICANN
Internet of Things	IoT
Internet Service Provider(s)	ISP(s)
Local Area Network	LAN
National Institute of Standards and Technology	NIST
Official Journal (of the European Union)	OJ
Operating System	OS
Organization for Economic Co-operation and Development	OECD
Platform as a Service	PaaS
Platform for Privacy Preferences Project	P3P
Privacy Enhancing Technologies	PETs
Remote Computing Service	RCS
Secure Sockets Layer	SSL
Service Oriented Architecture	SOA
Service as a Service	SaaS
Software as a Service	SaaS
Stored Communications Act	SCA
Terms of Service (agreement)	ToS (agreement)
Transport Layer Security	TLS
Treaty on the European Union	TEU
United Nations Commission on International Trade Law	UNCITRAL
United Nations Universal Declaration of Human Rights	UDHR
United States (of America)	US(A)
United States of America: Uniting and Strengthening America by Providing Appropriate Tools Required to Intercept and Obstruct Terrorism Act	USA PATRIOT Act
Virtual Machine(s)	VM(s)

CHAPTER 1. Introduction

a. Reasoning of the project and current state of affairs

Since the cloud has started gaining popularity, one of the catch-phrases used about it by supporters and adversaries alike and which can indeed be read in a positive or negative manner, depending on one's predisposition, has been: "There is no cloud. It's just someone else's computer."[1] Cloud computing made its entry in the IT industry as a revolution which was meant to profoundly alter the way most of IT and digital data business had been done till then[2]. Indeed, despite the partial loss of control over data that comes immediately with its use, cloud computing has been massively successful and, apart from average users' data, a great variety of critical records are also being entrusted to it, generating ever-growing concerns about their integrity, privacy and security.

In the face of these trends around the cloud and its uses, privacy and security have grown into two somewhat competing forces attempting to balance opposing needs: privacy focuses on the need to use information against the need to protect personal data, while security is centered on the need to provide access to records against the need to stop unauthorized access[3]. The importance of these competing goals has led to a plethora of legal and regulatory ventures to strike a balance and, ultimately, to achieve a certain level of trust in digital records and their storage in the cloud[4]. A particular challenge to the whole effort has come to be the fact that different jurisdictions approach privacy in substantially different manners while an in-depth understanding of what a jurisdiction's laws may aim at, or under the rules of what particular jurisdiction certain data may be governed,

1 Tom Geller, *In privacy law, it's the U.S. vs. the world*, 59 Commun. ACM 21–23 (2016.)

2 See also Chapter 2.

3 Luciana Duranti, Trust in online records and data. Integrity in Government through Records Management: Essays in Honour of Anne Thurston.

4 D. Hofman, Duranti L. & E. How, *Trust in the Balance. Data Protection Laws as Tools for Privacy and Security in the Cloud*, 10 Algorithms 47 (2017.)

requires a tremendous analytical effort. Nonetheless, in order to protect privacy and enhance security, this effort is unavoidable.

Should one look for a single phrase to summarize why cloud computing does make a difference in the way we are handling digital information and why we should regulate all this information processing having cloud computing in our focus, a suitable passage could be the following: …"preserving information in the cloud may be a black box process in which we know, at least ideally, what we put in for preservation, and we know what we want to access and retrieve—essentially the same things we put in—but often we do not know what technology is used by cloud service providers to manage, store, or process our information"[5].

Even in the ideal case in which there was no intended malice by actors involved in the cloud, data record keeping and processing done via cloud computing poses a number of unanswered questions. As Duranti and Rogers have most recently categorized them[6], those challenges broadly refer to: managing trans-jurisdictional data flows, attributing liability for and resolving data breaches, and establishing the chain of custody when a cloud service provider goes dark[7]. Given these risks, one might wonder why people continue to trust the cloud so strongly and at such a growing pace. The answer, as it will be demonstrated soon[8], is that, from a technological efficiency point of view, there is no better option in the realm of the internet-driven world right now and the cloud stands out by far from all other available technologies. Of course, the greatest ally in dealing with such risks is constant technological innovation itself, which tries hard to keep pace with malicious and innocent challenges of the cloud alike and ensure the trustworthiness of records stored on it. However, approaches based solely on technical means cannot solve the problems that arise from technology and its maluses; besides, there is no technical solution to determined human misuse of technology, to say the least[9]. In fact, technological tools need support from legal, social, and business structures that set the

5 Luciana Duranti, Adam Jansen, Giovanni Michetti, Mumma Courtney, Daryll Prescott, Corinne Rogers & Thibodeau Kenneth, *Preservation as a Service for Trust*, in Security in the private cloud, 47–72 (John R. Vacca ed., 2017.)

6 *Id.*

7 This issue does not form part of this analysis which solely focuses on the public law aspects of cloud computing regulation, leaving civil or criminal law issues aside for future research.

8 See Chapter 2.

9 Luciana Duranti (note 3).

bar for minimum expectations from cloud service providers. While some users (particularly those heavily based on data storage and processing from their core operation model already) might indeed thoroughly analyze the "reputation, performance, competence, and confidence"[10] of cloud service providers to verify their trustworthiness and robustness, experience and market data show that the majority continue to be quite instinctive with the choice of whom they entrust with their data[11]. It is precisely for those cases – which probably constitute the majority anyway – where consumers rely upon a service without having sought assurances of its quality beforehand that the law must step in to provide the certainty and trust users cannot or did not bother to obtain on their own[12]. The typological diversity of records kept in cloud environments is forcing the law to modernize existing regulatory tools and improvise on new ones. Combined together, these tools aim to strike the balance described earlier: between long-standing concerns, namely access, control, security, and trust and a world where data have got considerably detached from the physical bonds that traditionally kept them within the borders of a single jurisdiction and the control of an identified and trusted custodian.

Discussing "privacy" as a legal pursuit is challenging to say the least; according to Solove, "Privacy seems to be about everything, and therefore it appears to be nothing"[13]. The very conception of privacy is widely contextual; as it has been argued, "our conceptions of privacy result from our juridified intuitions—intuitions that reflect our knowledge of, and commitment to, the basic legal values of our culture"[14].

On a broader basis, Americans' use of the term 'privacy' typically refers to "privacy as an aspect of liberty, the right to freedom from intrusions by the state"[15]. Consequently, American privacy laws tend to focus on the freedom to determine who and to what extent has access to one's

---

10 Luciana Duranti & Corinne Rogers, *Trust in digital records. An increasingly cloudy legal area*, 28 Computer Law & Security Review 522–531 (2012.)

11 Frank B. Cross, *Law and trust*, 93 The Georgetown Law Journal 1457–1545 (2005.)

12 Huaiqing Wang, Matthew K. O. Lee & Chen Wang, *Consumer privacy concerns about Internet marketing*, 41 Commun. ACM 63–70 (1998.)

13 Daniel J. Solove, *A Taxonomy of Privacy*, 154 University of Pennsylvania law review 477–560 (2006.)

14 James Q. Whitman, *The Two Western Cultures of Privacy. Dignity versus Liberty*, 113 The Yale Law Journal 1151–1221 (2004.)

15 For further analysis, see Chapter 3.

private life, particularly to the category of private information generally quoted as "personally identifiable information"[16]. From that perspective, gravity primarily lies with the possibility for a data subject to consent to their loss of privacy, while in laws developed under this prism the need for privacy is often juxtaposed by the need to use personally identifiable information for data subjects for countless different purposes. In contrast, the European concept of privacy views the term "as an aspect of dignity"[17]. The "juridified intuitions" on the foundations of European understandings of privacy cannot bear human dignity as a commodity. As a result, the American concept of 'privacy' coincides much better with the European notion of 'data protection'[18]. Both these policy areas on the two sides of the Atlantic seek to draw boundaries around information and records, putting up effective protection mechanisms for them from public or unauthorized private scrutiny. Such laws set off from the predicament that not all people can be trusted with all information[19]. In the pre-internet, offline era, this was operatively translated in controlling access to and, if necessary, retracting paper records containing sensitive information. However, under the profound impact of information and communications technologies on data and record keeping, along with an intensifying blur between "data" and "records," personally identifiable information can today be regarded as just a small subset of data[20], about which it cannot be said with certainty whether it is the original record or just an archived copy. However, this is a precarious approach as it strips the data off its context; an immediate effect is, for example, that we are no longer able to determine whether the data is 'private' for a particular purpose. Instead, by moving the protection focus at record, rather than data level, we could achieve better results. What is more, data mining and other big data techniques are increasingly rendering data-level privacy protection ineffective[21].

---

16 Paul M. Schwartz & Daniel J. Solove, *The PII Problem: Privacy and a New Concept of Personally Identifiable Information*, 86 New York University Law Review 1814–1894 (2011.)

17 James Q. Whitman (note 14).

18 *Id.*

19 Luciana Duranti (note 3).

20 Paul M. Schwartz & Daniel J. Solove (note 16).

21 Daniel J. Weitzner, Harold Abelson, Tim Berners-Lee, Chris Hanson, James Hendler, Lalana Kagal, Deborah L. McGuinness, Gerald Jay Sussman & K. Krasnow

Based on these two poles, i.e. the European versus the American legal thinking about data protection and privacy, this study aims to take the decisive step and look into the matter from the broader perspective of technologies facilitating data processing and archiving of all kinds instead of the acts of processing and archiving per se. Those technologies are beyond doubt those collectively termed as 'cloud computing'. And because of the fact that legal research which aims to build up on an existing regime and provide better answers to tangible problems, which have nevertheless been around for a long time (with several laws that have already tried to tackle them thus making any new approach conditional to cohesion and not just innovative spirit), cannot set off from nowhere but needs to have one firm foot on actual acquis before it can take the leap forward, the starting point of endeavors of this study will largely, though not exhaustively, be privacy and data protection laws from Europe and the US.

i. The European state of affairs

The latest development out of deployment of cloud computing technologies, i.e. big data decision-making algorithms, are by nature meant to discriminate, to make distinctions based on voluminous data of a wide variety. An immediate challenge of algorithmic discrimination is the loss of judgment[22]. "The machine is incapable of determining whether a distinction is ethical or not. Unless we come up with a comprehensive theory of discrimination that can be represented algorithmically, we have no rigorous way of distinguishing between ethical and non-ethical machine-based discrimination [... however,] some of our ethical and moral criteria are so fragile, nuanced, and culturally dependent that it is not clear that the machine will ever be capable of appropriately weighing them"[23]. Still the data-driven approach to regulation of personally identifiable information runs on the assumption that by redacting or pseudonymizing the most sensitive kinds or parts of data set, we can prevent the algorithm from filling in missing information using the vast amounts of other data, quite possibly

---

Waterman, Transparent Accountable Data Mining: New Strategies for Privacy Protection (2006.)

22 Omer Tene & Jules Polonetsky, *Judged by the Tin Man: Individual Rights in the Age of Big Data*, 11 J. on Telecomm. & High Tech. L. 351–368 (2013.)

23 *Id.*

even from the same data subject, that has at its disposal. However, sealing certain bits of data which have been labeled as personally identifiable information while leaving all other data available and open to whatever techniques resourceful data holders can devise, is a lost battle. The current data-centric approach to privacy will be less and less effective in building up or maintaining trust in cloud-based records[24].

The brand new European General Data Protection Regulation (GDPR)[25] explicitly recognizes these challenges, and seeks to establish a higher standard of trust and security for EU citizens[26]. And while it does not categorically solve all big data challenges to privacy, it does provide a much firmer ground for European citizens to expect that their privacy will not be breached by resourceful data processors. Furthermore, the European Union provides a second line of legal protection for its citizens, as the GDPR directly cites Article 8(1) of the Charter of Fundamental Rights of the European Union (CFREU)[27] which has already been repeatedly interpreted as providing robust protection for the online version of the right to privacy[28]. However, the GDPR largely remains a technology agnostic

---

24 Jiahong Chen, *How the best-laid plans go awry. The (unsolved) issues of applicable law in the General Data Protection Regulation*, 6 International Data Privacy Law 310–323 (2017.)

25 Regulation (EU) 2016/679 on the protection of natural persons with regard to the processing of personal data and on the free movement of such data, and repealing Directive 95/46/EC (General Data Protection Regulation); (OJ) L119, 4/5/2016, p. 1–88.

26 Recital 26 of the GDPR explicitly notes that, even though personal data may have undergone pseudonymization, "account should be taken of all of the means reasonably likely to be used [...] to identify the natural person directly or indirectly," distinguishing between pseudonymized data and anonymous data.

27 Charter of Fundamental Rights of the European Union, 26 October 2012, 2012/C 326/02.

28 Recital 73 of the GDPR reads: "Restrictions concerning specific principles and the rights of information, access to and rectification or erasure of personal data, the right to data portability, the right to object, decisions based on profiling, as well as the communication of a personal data breach to a data subject and certain related obligations of the controllers may be imposed by Union or Member State law, as far as necessary and proportionate in a democratic society to safeguard public security, including the protection of human life especially in response to natural or manmade disasters, the prevention, investigation and prosecution of criminal offences or the execution of criminal penalties, including the safeguarding against and the prevention of threats to public security, or of breaches of ethics for regula-

legislation[29], one that follows on the long path of data-focused EU privacy legislation, which is developed having specific existing or foreseeable applications of data-related technologies in sight instead of the specifications, present and foreseeable ones, of those technologies.

ii. The US state of affairs

The regulatory plateau in the US regarding phenomena occurring in the cloud, most prominently regarding the issue of how to gain access to data hosted on cloud environments, is substantially different to the one in Europe; not so much as to the aims it pursues or the genre of protection it wishes to grant to data subjects but rather on the way it has developed over the years and how it looks today[30]. Owing to the endemic differences of legal tools between Europe and America, in the US there is no central legislation regarding cloud data but rather several legal resources (from provisions of the US constitution, to Acts, to case law) which provide legal basis for regulating cloud-related phenomena. The global clouds on which the greatest part of the IT world operates today pose challenging questions regarding the scope of traditional legal tools governing these phenomena and, most importantly, the issue of access to data stored in cloud facilities outside the United States. The far from settled landscape on the issue can be observed even through latest case law with regard to the Stored Communications Act (SCA)[31]. Different decisions expose numerous unan-

---

ted professions, other important objectives of general public interest of the Union or of a Member State, in particular an important economic or financial interest of the Union or of a Member State, the keeping of public registers kept for reasons of general public interest, further processing of archived personal data to provide specific information related to the political behavior under former totalitarian state regimes or the protection of the data subject or the rights and freedoms of others, including social protection, public health and humanitarian purposes. Those restrictions should be in accordance with the requirements set out in the Charter and in the European Convention for the Protection of Human Rights and Fundamental Freedoms.".

29 For more extensive analysis on the GDPR and its shortcomings as well as the innovations it introduces refer to Chapter 4.

30 For a comparative analysis on the development of data protection and privacy law in Europe and the US refer to Chapter 3.

31 The Stored Communications Act (SCA), 18 U.S.C. Chapter 121 §§ 2701–2712. For more refer to Chapter 3.

swered questions about the conditions under which parties can obtain cloud data. Specifically, in litigation involving extra-territorial data requests under the SCA US courts have at times focused on where the requested data is located, and on other instances on where the search or seizure of it will take place[32]. In addition to the SCA, there are further statutory authorities that grant government and private parties the permission to make extra-territorial data requests, creating additional unresolved issues as well. What is more, American academia is also far from settled about the meaning of territoriality for data access[33]. This scattered playing field produces equally varying legal outcomes which themselves demonstrate how disconcerted existing US laws applying to the cloud are, their most alarming effect being that they powerfully incentivize international data localization[34]. Mandatory data localization is already a legal requirement in a number of countries such as Brazil and Russia, while there is additionally another important trend of voluntary data localization[35]. Both of them are, to a significant degree, fueled by concerns about US rules for data access, which make more and more non-US companies to choose to bind themselves to national or regional protections which recognize or demand data localization for cloud networks. However, in the long run, this trend risks seriously disrupting the Internet and undermining one of its fundamental characteristics, the lack of boundaries in the circulation of da-

32 For an overview of the latest trends and developments in US law and jurisprudence regarding data and access to them, especially in relation to the cloud and information hosted on facilities abroad, refer to: Jennifer C. Daskal, *The Un-Territoriality of Data*, 125 Yale Law Journal 326–398 (2015); Andrew Keane Woods, *Against Data Exceptionalism*, 68 Stanford Law Review 729–789 (2016); Orin S. Kerr, *The Fourth Amendment and the Global Internet*, 67 Stanford Law Review 285–329 (2014); Orin S. Kerr, *The Next Generation Communications Privacy Act*, 162 University of Pennsylvania law review 373–419 (2014); David Cole & Federico Fabbrini, *Bridging the Transatlantic Divide? The United States, the European Union, and the Protection of Privacy Across Borders. iCourts Working Paper Series, No. 33, 2015* International Journal of Constitutional Law (2015); Damon C. Andrews & John M. Newman, *Personal Jurisdiction and Choice of Law in the Cloud*, 73 Md. L. Rev. 313–388 (2013.)

33 Paul M. Schwartz, Legal Access to Cloud Information. Data Shards, Data Localization, and Data Trusts.

34 For a thorough analysis on the issue of mandatory and voluntary data localization, refer to: Anupam Chander & Uyen P. Le, *Breaking the Web. Data Localization vs. the Global Internet* Emory Law Journal, Forthcoming 53 (2014.)

35 *Id.*

ta and overall traffic[36]. Therefore, it is high time for the US to work with other jurisdictions, primarily with the EU, towards developing internationally harmonized rules for access to cloud information.

iii. Current state of affairs in other countries

In response to growing concerns about security and privacy of data in the cloud, regulators in jurisdictions around the world are turning to data localization measures[37]. These regulatory tools include laws, regulations, and policies designed to make sure that data and records are accessed, processed, and stored within a specific jurisdiction[38]. Data localization measures are conceptualized with the aim of fortifying the privacy rights of data owners whose records cross jurisdictional borders[39].

Briefly, data localization laws are based on the assumption that, if the jurisdictions in which records and data can be accessed, processed, and stored are limited, those records will be sealed against bad actors for whom laws from other jurisdictions would provide no effective recourse. Realistically speaking though, this is a problematic assumption[40]. Any records and data made available at some point online can eventually be accessed and harmed by malicious actors in almost any jurisdiction. And, of course, whether or not the jurisdiction in which the records are located can provide effect remedy in such an instance depends on more than just localization laws. Secondly, data localization laws assume that records hosted locally are by default more secure[41]. However, there is no guarantee for that; everything depends on adequate technical solutions and expertise being available within the jurisdiction where cloud services are provided. To put it plainly, it should not be taken for granted that there are actual data centers and hardware facilities by all cloud providers within the area of every single jurisdiction. In addition, data localization laws assume that local custody is a preferable means of protecting records and data and as-

36 Paul M. Schwartz (note 33).
37 Anupam Chander & Uyen P. Le (note 34).
38 *Id.*
39 *Id.*
40 Paul M. Schwartz (note 33).
41 Y. Tian, *Current Issues of Cross-Border Personal Data Protection in the Context of Cloud Computing and Trans-Pacific Partnership Agreement. Join or Withdraw*, 34 Wisconsin International Law Journal 367–408 (2016.)

suring their trustworthiness. However, this predicament invalidates the very important element of evaluation of trustworthiness that any cloud service provider, regardless of their size, should undergo in order to survive on the market according to internationally accepted market practice[42]. The last assumption is that data localization laws provide augmented stability should cloud services prove untrustworthy or insecure, because, at least, they provide clarity as to which jurisdiction's laws will apply in resolving the disputes that may arise. In reality, however, there is no better safeguard for security of records and data in the cloud than the trust mechanisms of the international cloud market, only by taking part in which can a cloud service provider, regardless of size, survive and remain competitive; thus, all CSPs will do whatever it takes to make sure they remain part of it[43].

b. Research question and structure of the project

Given the state of affairs described above, this project is going to look for ways for achieving better coordinated regulation of the cloud and the issues arising from using it. The stated aim will not be pursued though having in mind the establishment of an international regulatory framework for the cloud, let alone the introduction of some other type of supranational jurisdiction for cloud and IT-related phenomena. Instead, in an attempt to be realistic in the way the research question is approached in conjunction with the regulatory state-of-the-art across jurisdictions, the project's focus will be on pinpointing and bringing together best practices regardless of their origin which, if combined and taken into consideration as the foundations for the future development of cloud regulation laws by law makers from all legal orders will lead to a more coherent governance scheme for cloud computing. Logically, some of the suggestions put forward in the course of this analysis may not sound as ground-breaking for all readers, depending on whether each one of them is more familiar with the European or US legal thinking on the matter. However, the originality of this analysis lies precisely on drawing for the first time the best each and every school of thought has to offer under the same roof.

---

42 Nicholas Platten, *Protectors of Privacy: Regulating Data in the Global Economy – By A.L. Newman*, 48 JCMS: Journal of Common Market Studies 453–454 (2010.)
43 *Id.*

The forthcoming analysis should be read in light of the following understandings:

- Although from a technical point of view it is always easier to discern between cloud computing per se and specific applications made possible thanks to the cloud, this distinction has not yet been unquestioningly achieved on the regulatory front. Therefore, while the technical parts of this research invariably refer to cloud computing generically, in the parts of legal analysis it is mandatory to begin discourse from the laws currently applicable in order to understand how the current status has been consolidated and how steps forward could be taken. Therefore, in parts of this project where the legal dimension of the research question is dealt with the starting point is mostly, but not exclusively, existing laws about privacy, data protection and data transfers on the cloud. It is hoped that by applying the findings and suggestions presented throughout this study, current laws will move forward towards a more generic and less case-based direction, grasping the cloud phenomenon per se and not limiting their understanding to specific cloud applications.
- With regard to the jurisdictions and the origins of scholarly opinion that form part of this comparative analysis, it needs to be pointed out right from the beginning that there is a similar distinction between resources and literature of a technical and those of a legal nature. in particular, given that, from a technological perspective, the cloud is viewed in the same manner worldwide, this study utilizes relevant resources from a variety of origins (e.g. from European, American, Chinese and Canadian academics, to name a few). However, due to the greatly varied ways in which the cloud has been viewed so far from a legal point of view, only the laws and regulations of the EU and the US form part of this study. The two jurisdictions together account for the biggest part of the ways in which law makers currently deal with the cloud[44]. Moreover, this choice was also made due to practical factors, namely ease of access to resources, linguistic capabilities of the researcher (these two are the main reasons why the Chinese jurisdiction is left out of the scope of the project altogether) as well as time constraints for the completion of the project.

44 For more on the significance EU and US laws and markets play with regard to cloud computing refer to Chapter 3.

With the above understandings in mind, the chapters of the analysis that follow deal with these groups of challenges[45] regarding the prospect of a more consolidated regime on cloud computing regulation:

- The jurisdictional challenge, mainly dealt with in Chapter 6;
- The privacy and security challenge, mainly dealt with in Chapter 7;
- The convergence challenge, mainly dealt with in Chapters 8, 9 and 10.

45 Y. Tian (note 41).

CHAPTER 2. Cloud computing; a historical and technical overview

a. Introduction – scope of this chapter

Cloud computing technologies have been rapidly expanding over the past ten to fifteen years to be today the standard enabling technology for most of the applications and aspects of the internet as we know it. Cloud-based systems and cloud computing, as such, were not an invention, nor a pioneering discovery when they started to be widely commercialized in the beginning of 2000s. They had actually been around long before, as technically feasible arrangements for the handling of data and the execution of computational tasks. However, the growing appetite for processing power that an increasing e-economy necessitated, the commoditization of more and more internet-based services related to data handling and the equally fast rate at which consumers adopted these services led to a rapid commercialization of cloud technologies[46]. Yet, despite the fact that the cloud, as a technical feasibility, had been around since long before, its true meaning and the ways in which it did things differently than before had not been adequately realized or examined for many years after its popularization as a commodity. In order to understand what cloud computing is all about and, eventually, demonstrate what it does differently in comparison to previous technical arrangements for data handling tasks, a review of the history of the cloud is the first step.

Getting familiar with the essence of the technical aspects of cloud computing is the aim of this chapter of the study.

---

46 For more information on the history and technical evolution of cloud computing refer to: M. Arif, A history of cloud computing, available at: http://www.computerweekly.com/feature/A-history-of-cloud-computing (18 February 2015); Hongji Yang & Xiaodong Liu, Software reuse in the emerging cloud computing era (2012); Thomas Erl, Richardo Puttini & Zaigham Mahmood, Cloud computing. Concepts, technology, & architecture (2013); Antonio Regalado, Who Coined 'Cloud Computing'?, available at: https://www.technologyreview.com/s/425970/who-coined-cloud-computing/ (11 January 2017); Inc. Gartner, Cloud Computing Confusion Leads to Opportunity (2008).

b. A brief history of the cloud

Cloud computing has evolved to be the technology that we so extensively use today through a number of phases that included concepts like client-server arrangements[47], grid[48] and utility computing[49], application service provision (ASP)[50] and, more recently, Software as a Service (SaaS)[51].

On a visionary level, the idea of an "intergalactic computer network"[52] was for the first time formulated in the 1960s by Joseph Carl Rob-

47 The client–server model of computing is a distributed application structure that partitions tasks or workloads between the providers of a resource or service, called servers, and service requesters, called clients. At most times, clients and servers communicate over a computer network on separate hardware, but both client and server may reside in the same system. (https://www.techopedia.com/definition/18321/client-server-model; last accessed on 01/11/2017.)

48 Grid computing is a collection of computer resources from multiple locations that are dedicated to reaching a common goal. The grid can be thought of as a distributed system with non-interactive workloads that involve a large number of files. (https://www.techopedia.com/definition/87/grid-computing; last accessed on 01/11/2017.)

49 Utility computing is a service provisioning model in which a service provider makes computing resources and infrastructure management available to the customer as needed, and charges them for specific usage rather than a flat rate. (https://www.techopedia.com/definition/14622/utility-computing; last accessed on 01/11/2017.)

50 Application Service Provisioning (ASP) is the business of providing computer-based services to customers over a network, such as access to a particular software application using a standard protocol (such as HTTP). (https://www.techopedia.com/definition/2476/application-service-provider-asp; last accessed on 01/11/2017.)

51 Software as a service (SaaS) is a software licensing and delivery model in which software is licensed on a subscription basis and is centrally hosted. (https://www.techopedia.com/definition/155/software-as-a-service-saas; last accessed on 01/11/2017.)

52 Intergalactic Computer Network or Galactic Network was a computer networking concept similar to today's Internet. The term was used for the first time in the early 1960s to refer to a networking system as an electronic commons open to all, 'the main and essential medium of informational interaction for governments, institutions, corporations, and individuals.' (https://en.wikipedia.org/wiki/Intergalactic_Computer_Network; last accessed on 01/11/2017.)

nett Licklider[53], who was responsible for facilitating the development of ARPANET[54] in 1969.

Licklider's vision was for everyone to be interconnected and able to access programs and data hosted at any site, from anywhere. "It is a vision that sounds a lot like what we are calling cloud computing"[55].

Another popular view is that the cloud concept was first envisaged by computer scientist John McCarthy who proposed the idea of computation being delivered as a public utility[56].

From a technical point of view, several decades went by with the know-how related to today's cloud-based systems already existing. Literally, cloud technologies were no invention and did not come as a result of a ground-breaking discovery. They were simply the outcome of better or, at least, different exploitation of existing knowledge related to IT systems[57]. One of the first milestones in cloud computing history was the arrival of

53 Joseph Carl Robnett Licklider was an American psychologist and computer scientist who is considered one of the most important figures in computer science and general computing history. He is particularly remembered for being one of the first to foresee modern-style interactive computing and its application to all kinds of activities; and also as an Internet pioneer with an early vision of a worldwide computer network long before it was built. (https://en.wikipedia.org/wiki/J._C._R._Licklider; last accessed on 01/11/2017.)

54 The Advanced Research Projects Agency Network (ARPANET) was an early packet switching network and the first network to implement the protocol suite TCP/IP. Both technologies became the technical foundation of the Internet. ARPANET was initially funded by the Advanced Research Projects Agency (ARPA, later Defense Advanced Research Projects Agency, DARPA) of the United States Department of Defense. (https://www.techopedia.com/definition/2381/advanced-research-projects-agency-network-arpanet; last accessed on 01/11/2017.)

55 J. Locke, The Roots of Cloud Computing, available at: http://www.servercloudcanada.com/2013/10/the-roots-of-cloud-computing/ (11 January 2017); last accessed on 01/11/2017.

56 John McCarthy was an American computer scientist and cognitive scientist. McCarthy was one of the founders of the discipline of artificial intelligence. He coined the term "artificial intelligence" (AI), developed the Lisp programming language family, significantly influenced the design of the ALGOL programming language, popularized timesharing, and was very influential in the early development of AI. (https://en.wikipedia.org/wiki/John_McCarthy_(computer_scientist); last accessed on 01/11/2017.)

57 M. Arif (note 46).

Salesforce.com[58] in 1999, which pioneered the concept of delivering enterprise applications via a simple website. The services firm paved the way for both specialist and mainstream software firms to deliver applications over the internet.

The next important step was Amazon Web Services[59] in 2002, which provided a suite of cloud based services including storage, computation and even human intelligence.

Another big milestone came in 2009, with the advent of Web 2.0[60], when Google and others started to offer browser-based enterprise applications through services such as Google Apps[61].

c. The NIST definition of cloud computing; a starting point

It has been so far impossible among stakeholders, namely, regulators, the IT industry etc., to agree on a universally acceptable definition of cloud computing. However, for the purposes of this study when reference is made to 'cloud computing' this is to be understood under the definition published in 2011 by the US National Institute of Standards and Technology (NIST); so far, this definition is generally heralded as the most preva-

58 Salesforce.com is a cloud computing company headquartered in San Francisco, California. Though its profits come basically from a customer relationship management (CRM) product, Salesforce also tries capitalizing on commercial applications of social networking through acquisition. (https://en.wikipedia.org/wiki/Salesforce.com; last accessed on 01/11/2017.)

59 Amazon Web Services (AWS) is a collection of remote computing services, also called web services, that make up a cloud computing platform offered by Amazon.com. These services are based in 11 geographical regions across the world. The most central and well-known of these services are Amazon Elastic Compute Cloud and Amazon S3. These products are marketed as a service to provide large computing capacity more quickly and cheaper than a client company building an actual physical server farm. (https://en.wikipedia.org/wiki/Amazon_Web_Services; last accessed on 01/11/2017.)

60 Web 2.0 describes World Wide Web sites that emphasize user-generated content, usability, and interoperability. Although Web 2.0 suggests a new version of the World Wide Web, it does not refer to an update to any technical specification, but rather to cumulative changes in the way Web pages are made and used. (https://en.wikipedia.org/wiki/Web_2.0; last accessed on 01/11/2017.)

61 Google Apps is a suite of cloud computing productivity and collaboration software tools and software offered by Google. (https://en.wikipedia.org/wiki/Google_Apps_for_Work; last accessed on 01/11/2017.)

lent[62] in explaining the 'cloud' and it reads as follows: "Cloud computing is a model for enabling ubiquitous, convenient, on-demand network access to a shared pool of configurable computing resources (e.g., networks, servers, storage, applications, and services) that can be rapidly provisioned and released with minimal management effort or service provider interaction. This cloud model is composed of five essential characteristics, three service models, and four deployment models"[63].

The most essential characteristics of cloud computing technologies and of the services developed based on them are[64]:

- **On-demand self-service**: A consumer can unilaterally calculate and preorder or buy in real time computing capabilities, such as server time and network storage, as needed, automatically without requiring human interaction with a salesperson or service provider;
- **Broad network access**: Services are available over the network and accessed through standard mechanisms that promote use by heterogeneous client platforms (e.g., mobile phones, tablets, laptops, and workstations);
- **Resource pooling**: The provider's computing resources are pooled to serve multiple consumers using a multi-tenant model, with different physical and virtual resources dynamically assigned and reassigned according to consumer demand. There is an impression of location independence owing to the fact that the customer generally has no control or knowledge over the exact location of the provided resources but may be able to specify location at a higher level of abstraction (e.g., country, state, or datacenter). Examples of resources include storage, processing, memory and network bandwidth;
- **Rapid elasticity**: Resources can be elastically provisioned and released, in some cases automatically, to scale rapidly outward and inward in accordance with demand. To the consumer, the resources available for provisioning often appear to be unlimited and can be appropriated in any quantity at any time;

62 Bill Williams, The economics of cloud computing (2012.)

63 Peter Mell & Timothy Grance, The NIST Definition of Cloud Computing. Recommendations of the National Institute of Standards and Technology, available at: http://csrc.nist.gov/publications/nistpubs/800-145/SP800-145.pdf (4 November 2015.)

64 Thomas Erl, Richardo Puttini & Zaigham Mahmood (note 46).; Peter Mell & Timothy Grance (note 63); Bill Williams (note 62).

- **Measured service**: Cloud systems automatically control and optimize use of resources by leveraging a metering capability at some level of abstraction appropriate to the type of service (e.g., storage, processing, bandwidth and active user accounts). Resource usage can be monitored, controlled and reported, providing transparency for both providers and consumers of the utilized service.

Cloud computing services come in several different genres. These broad categories under which cloud-based applications fall are typically called 'service models' and they are the following[65]:

- **Software as a Service (SaaS):** The consumer can use the provider's applications running on a cloud infrastructure. The applications are accessible from various client devices through either a thin client interface, such as a web browser (e.g. web-based email), or a program interface (e.g. a Dropbox installation on the user's laptop). The consumer does not manage or control the underlying cloud infrastructure including network, servers, operating systems, storage, or even individual application capabilities, with the possible exception of limited user-specific application configuration settings;
- **Platform as a Service (PaaS):** The capability provided to the consumer is to deploy onto the cloud infrastructure consumer-created or acquired applications built using programming languages, libraries, services, and tools supported by the provider. The consumer does not manage or control the underlying cloud infrastructure including network, servers, operating systems, or storage, but has control over the deployed applications and possibly configuration settings for the application-hosting environment;
- **Infrastructure as a Service (IaaS):** The capability provided to the consumer is to provision processing, storage, networks and other fundamental computing resources where the consumer is able to deploy and run arbitrary software, which can include operating systems and applications. The consumer does not manage or control the underlying cloud infrastructure but has control over operating systems, storage and

65 Christof Weinhardt, Arun Anandasivam, Benjamin Blau, Nikolay Borissov, Thomas Meinl, Wibke Michalk & Jochen Stößer, *Cloud Computing – A Classification, Business Models, and Research Directions*, 1 Bus. Inf. Syst. Eng. 391–399 (2009); Bill Williams (note 62); Norman Pelzl, Methodische Entwicklung von zukunftsorientierten Geschäftsmodellen im Cloud-Computing, Band 88 (2016.)

deployed applications; and possibly limited control of select networking components (e.g., host firewalls).

According to the different types of users that use a given cloud infrastructure, these are the major cloud deployment models[66]:

- **Private cloud:** The cloud infrastructure is provisioned for exclusive use by a single organization comprising multiple consumers (e.g., business units). It may be owned, managed and operated by the organization, a third party or some combination of them, and it may be situated on or off premises;
- **Community cloud:** The cloud infrastructure is provisioned for exclusive use by a specific community of consumers from organizations that have shared concerns (e.g., mission, security requirements, policy, and compliance considerations). It may be owned, managed and operated by one or more of the organizations in the community, a third party or some combination of them, and it may be located on or off premises;
- **Public cloud:** The cloud infrastructure is provisioned for open use by the general public. It may be owned, managed and operated by a business, academic or government organization or some combination of them. It is located on the premises of the cloud provider;
- **Hybrid cloud:** The cloud infrastructure is a composition of two or more distinct cloud infrastructures (private, community or public) that remain unique entities, but are bound together by standardized or proprietary technology that enables data and application portability (e.g., cloud bursting for load balancing between clouds).

d. The technologies that preceded cloud computing; a brief overview and comparison

i. Cloud computing compared to traditional IT – Their main differences and why the cloud matters

In attempting to answer whether cloud computing is fundamentally different from IT technologies that had existed before, the prime question to answer is what it means for an organization to "do" cloud computing. The response to this question will give us in the end an estimate as to whether

66 Christof Weinhardt, Arun Anandasivam, Benjamin Blau, Nikolay Borissov, Thomas Meinl, Wibke Michalk & Jochen Stößer (note 65).

the cloud is a revolution or simply a 'version 2.0' of a continuous series of innovations.

In this debate, Oracle's CEO Larry Ellison[67] has a history of discounting cloud computing as no more than a new name for what has already been in place since long ago. Actually, in a 2009 interview that has become somewhat of a web cult classic, he declared: "All the cloud is, is computers in a network… Our industry is so bizarre. I mean, they just change a term and they think they've invented technology."[68].

From certain aspects, this statement is correct. Many of cloud computing's most common features – namely, virtualization, pay-as-you-go, reduced cost and moving IT responsibility to third parties – have been around much longer than "the cloud". Yet there are also those who argue that despite the similarities to what had already existed before, cloud computing is fundamentally different.

One of the most outright supporters of this opinion has been Salesforce.com's CEO Marc Benioff[69]. In a keynote speech at the Oracle OpenWorld 2010 conference, Benioff outlined his own definition of cloud computing: "Our definition of cloud computing is multi-tenant, it's faster, half the cost, pay as you go, it grows as you grow or shrinks as you shrink. It is extremely efficient. We're not going to show you computers taller than you. We're not going to show you a cloud in a box because clouds don't come in a box. They never have. That's the whole idea"[70].

---

67 Lawrence Joseph "Larry" Ellison (born August 17, 1944) is an American programmer, internet entrepreneur, businessman and philanthropist. He has been the chief executive officer of the software company Oracle Corporation from its foundation in 1977. (https://en.wikipedia.org/wiki/Larry_Ellison; last accessed on 01/11/2017.)

68 Larry Ellison, Larry Ellison on cloud computing (2009.)

69 Marc Russell Benioff (born September 25, 1964) is an American internet entrepreneur, author and philanthropist. He is the founder, chairman and CEO of salesforce.com, a cloud computing company. (https://en.wikipedia.org/wiki/Marc_Beni off; last accessed on 01/11/2017.)

70 C. Tuna, *Ellison and Benioff Spar Over Cloud Credentials* Wall Street Journal (2010.)

In the end, cloud computing offers a breakthrough in at least four main areas in comparison to the past[71]:

- Virtualization, i.e. the ability to increase computing efficiency
- Democratization of computing, by bringing enterprise scale infrastructure to small and medium businesses
- Scalability and fast provisioning, by bringing web scale IT at a rapid pace
- Commoditization of infrastructure, by enabling IT to focus on the strategic aspects of its role.

Although any of these areas may not qualify as a computing revolution by itself, one could persuasively argue all of them, put together, have fundamentally changed computing.

ii. Cloud computing environments compared to client-server systems

Client-server is a method where information processing is split between a client and a server[72]. Back in the days, time share computers[73] were used that were accessed by terminals that only handled the display of information without doing any processing.

An easy-to-grasp example of a client/server service is the email. The email client[74] processes incoming email and then presents it to the user. The mail server[75] processes email messages and figures out where they go next.

---

71 2009 ICSE Workshop on Software Engineering Challenges of Cloud Computing.

72 M. Arif (note 46).

73 Time share computing: A technique permitting many users simultaneous access to a central computer through remote terminals. (https://www.britannica.com/technology/time-sharing; last accessed on 01/11/2017.)

74 An email client, email reader or more formally mail user agent (MUA) is a computer program used to access and manage a user's email. (https://en.wikipedia.org/wiki/Email_client; last accessed on 01/11/2017.)

75 A mail server, or e-mail server is a computer within a network that works as a virtual post office. A mail server usually consists of a storage area where e-mail is stored for local users, a set of user definable rules which determine how the mail server should react to the destination of a specific message, a database of user accounts that the mail server recognizes and will deal with locally, and communications modules which are the components that actually handle the transfer of messages to and from other mail servers and email clients. (http://www.webopedia.com/TERM/E/e_mail_server.html; last accessed on 01/11/2017.)

Cloud computing is a different story altogether. Cloud computing embodies the ideas that you can abstract the software from the hardware, have applications that can scale up and down based on factors such as demand, time, etc. The act of services provisioning in the cloud is automated and requires no user intervention. Cloud services are also on-demand and can be metered meaning that you are only charged for the resources that you eventually use. Ultimately, cloud computing can be more precisely described as a consumption model[76].

As it has been already demonstrated, a cloud can be a public one, where someone else manages the hardware and infrastructure and the user just puts his operating systems and apps into. There can also be a private cloud, where the same entity owns the hardware and infrastructure and out of them derives a scalable, automated, metered service. And, lastly, there is hybrid cloud which is when one has apps that reside in both.

In other words, the 'client server' concept describes how applications are modeled. Cloud computing, on the other hand, describes and focuses on the environment that applications reside in.

iii. Cloud computing compared to outsourcing – The key differences

Before the emergence of cloud computing, computational and data processing needs of organizations and individual users were largely covered through outsourcing[77]. As a result, initial IT laws envisaged traditional outsourcing and the stand-alone databases that had been in use when they were drafted. In addition, it needs to be pointed out that this inspiration coming mainly from the outsourcing model still prevails across a wide range of IT legislation given the difference in pace in which technical standards have evolved compared to the respective evolutionary cycles of IT legislation.

Traditional outsourcing of data processing involved commissioning agents, who were provided with data and tasked with processing that data actively for the user according to the user's mandate. The agent had the possibility to engage sub-processors to assist with this processing[78]. With

---

76 Bill Williams (note 62).

77 W. Kuan Hon & C. Millard, *Cloud Computing vs. Traditional Outsourcing – Key Differences*, 23 Computers & Law (2012.)

78 *Id.*

today's public cloud services[79], users 'rent' pre-packaged IT resources from providers and then process data themselves in a self-service manner, using infrastructure and/or resources supplied by the provider.

With traditional outsourcing, a user would hire a processor to meet its specific processing needs. The processor might then engage sub-processors to help fulfil this contract with the user. Successive contracts down the chain of processors could therefore be easily tailored, from both timing and control perspectives. With cloud computing, however, the sequence of events and direction of travel of data are quite the opposite. Many cloud services are pre-packaged standardized commoditized services, which may be built on existing sub-provider services on the sub-provider's standard terms. The sub-service in turn may be based on other existing services. Users choose the provider and pre-built package that they think that best meets their specific processing and other needs. Public cloud computing providers use standardized, shared infrastructure/environments, often using relatively cheap commodity hardware, rather than tailoring to each customer. Similarly, some traditional outsourced processing might have used standardized infrastructure, sometimes at large scale, but it is unlikely that it was shared to such a degree as in cloud computing[80].

With traditional outsourcing, the user had control over its processor through the contract and its instructions to the processor. With cloud computing, while it is commonly thought cloud users lose control, much depends on the type of service and exact nature and design of individual services. A 'one size fits all' approach to cloud is common, but would not be wise, because there are significant differences between services and, respectively, many different cloud arrangement versions through which to provide those services.

---

79 The same largely applies also for community and hybrid cloud arrangements. Private clouds also share these characteristics but, due to their 'secluded' nature, they also differentiate on certain aspects from what applies to public, community or hybrid cloud installations.

80 For more extensive analysis and comparison between cloud computing and traditional outsourcing of computational tasks, refer also to: Bill Williams (note 62)., as well as to a comparative presentation of the two alternatives from a prominent tailored cloud services provider, GetCloud Services, under http://www.getcloudservices.com/blog/cloud-computing-vs-traditional-outsourcing/ (last accessed on 01/12/2017.)

e. Data handling needs and the parallel technological evolution – How developing computational requirements led to technological progress

At this point, it is worth briefly summarizing the sequence of innovations related to computing technologies parallel to the evolution of the volume of computational needs. When widespread corporate computing initially occurred, it was based on a shared resources model where massive computer facilities took up acres of space within dingy warehouses and users would book time for both the machines themselves and the skilled technicians who knew how to operate them. Their standard use was narrow business analysis and hence computing had a very limited sphere of influence[81].

Later, the introduction of mini computers[82] and the personal computer[83] in the 1970s meant the ability to utilize the benefits of technology extended to a much broader audience. While still relatively expensive and functionally basic machines, personal computers put computing onto (almost) any desktop in a reasonably well resourced organization.

The arrival of the Internet, however, changed things for good, both from the perspective of the network and that of individual computers. The increased reliability and reduced cost of the internet (in comparison to older proprietary networks) along with the decreasing cost of computers, led to increased use of web based applications. This, along with the demand for application access via multiple devices, led to a rapid growth for cloud computing[84] – at an infrastructure, a platform and an application level.

81 M. Arif (note 46).

82 A minicomputer, or colloquially mini, is a class of smaller computers that were developed in the mid-1960s and sold for much less than mainframe and mid-size computers from IBM and its direct competitors. In a 1970 survey, the New York Times suggested a consensus definition of a minicomputer as a machine costing less than 25,000 USD, with an input-output device such as a teleprinter and at least four thousand words of memory, that is capable of running programs in a higher-level language, such as Fortran or BASIC. The class formed a distinct group with its own software architectures and operating systems. (https://en.wikipedia.org/wiki/Minicomputer; last accessed on 01/12/2017.)

83 A personal computer is a general-purpose computer whose size, capabilities and original sale price make it useful for individuals, and is intended to be operated directly by an end-user with no intervening computer operator. (https://en.wikipedia.org/wiki/Personal_computer; last accessed on 01/12/2017.)

84 Bill Williams (note 62).

f. Explaining cloud computing and its predecessors – what did the cloud replace and what is now done different than before?

Having gone through the history and evolution of the cloud, through the most predominant theory and policy approaches currently on the table about it and the fields where it is mostly used, it is now time to examine what cloud computing did actually replace. Further to that, it is also in order now to explain what the technological and business differences between cloud computing and the precedent technological status quo actually are.

In a nutshell, one could say that the cloud itself is not an out-of-nowhere invention nor did it come to replace anything in particular. As it has already been demonstrated[85] cloud computing was not invented or discovered; it simply evolved out of pre-existing technologies that matured over time as the possibilities they offered were better understood and been taken advantage of. Naturally, cloud did not take over from one day to the other but it gained ground, and at a faster and faster pace, because it was becoming clearer that it offered competitive advantages over its predecessors, mainly in the field of economies of scale and ease of use[86]. However, as the economic aspects of the cloud phenomenon are beyond the scope of this study, the overview that follows will focus on how the cloud evolved from a technological point of view and what it does differently when applied and not so much on what differences it brings about in the economic factors of the sectors where it is applied.

The technologies that cloud computing replaced could be generically described as based on a Service Oriented Architecture (SOA)[87]. In other words, they were technological arrangements which had been primarily developed not so much with efficiency or economies of scale in mind but mostly with fulfilling particular service needs as primary goal. In layman's terms, what defined SOA-focused arrangements was not how to do the job in the most economically and resources-efficient manner but, merely, how to get the job done. Therefore, from the simplest SOA system [i.e. the Local Area Network (LAN)] to the most complex data handling systems

85 Chapter 2.a.

86 *Id.*

87 D. Linthicum, MSDN Documentation. Service Oriented Architecture (SOA), available at: https://msdn.microsoft.com/en-us/library/bb833022.aspx (4 November 2015.)

based on the SOA perspective, one can always recognize the predominantly linear connections between different building parts of the network, be them servers, computers, printers etc.

A generic definition of service oriented architecture (SOA) would be: "Loosely coupled services with well-defined interfaces that provide business functionality and can be shared or reused across and beyond the network's constituting parts. These services can be discovered through a registry/repository or other directory, and can be assembled and disassembled to meet current business process demands"[88].

Generally observing the SOA logic, hereunder are the main technologies that pre-existed the cloud and whose revisited use led to what we know nowadays as cloud computing technologies:

i. File hosting

"File hosting services provide a broad range of services to businesses, including building an intranet and managing an overall internal network"[89]. File hosting and the enabling technologies have existed for decades, ever since businesses turned to the Internet for storage solutions and project management. Yet, while file hosting is more localized and focused on an internal aspect of getting everyone in an office or organizational complex on the same page, cloud computing goes far beyond this.

ii. Clustering

"A cluster is a group of independent IT resources that are interconnected and work as a single system."[90] Clusters were developed in an effort to re-

---

88 *Id.*

89 R. Peeva, File Hosting vs. Cloud Computing, available at: http://www.websitepulse.com/blog/file-hosting-vs-cloud-computing (4 November 2015.)

90 A cluster server is a group of independent servers working together as a single system to provide high availability of services for clients. When a failure occurs on one computer in a cluster, resources are redirected and the workload is redistributed to another computer in the cluster. You can use server clusters to ensure that users have constant access to important server-based resources. Server clusters are designed for applications that have long-running in-memory state or frequently updated data. Typical uses for server clusters include file servers, print servers, data-

duce system failure rates and, at the same time, increase availability and reliability; these were made possible thanks to redundancy and failover features inherent to clusters. In terms of hardware used to build cluster installations, a general prerequisite was that its component systems had reasonably identical hardware and operating systems so that similar performance levels could be achieved when one failed component was to be replaced by another. Component devices forming a cluster were kept continuously synced through dedicated, high speed communication links.

Stemming from clusters, this basic concept of built-in redundancy and failover was carried out today to be in the core of cloud platforms.

iii. Grid Computing

"A computing grid (or 'computational grid') provides a platform in which computing resources are organized into one or more logical pools. These pools are collectively coordinated to provide a high performance distributed grid, sometimes referred to as a 'super virtual computer'."[91] Grid computing was different from clustering in that grid systems were much more loosely coupled and distributed, already allowing for greater flexibility and reallocation of resources of the network to ensure the best possible efficiency at all times. As a result, grid computing systems were the first to involve computing resources of heterogeneous nature and geographically dispersed, which was generally not possible with the preceding cluster computing-based systems.

Grid computing was firstly conceptualized in the early 1990s and has been constantly under review and further research ever since[92]. The technological advancements achieved through that research into grid computing projects have influenced various aspects of cloud computing platforms and mechanisms, particularly in relation to feature sets such as networked access, resource pooling, scalability and resiliency. These features were

---

base servers, and messaging servers. A more detailed description of the cluster server is available at https://technet.microsoft.com/en-us/library/cc785197(v=ws.10).aspx; last accessed on 01/12/2017.

91 Thomas Erl, Richardo Puttini & Zaigham Mahmood (note 46).

92 Ian Foster, Yong Zhao, Ioan Raicu & Shiyong Lu, *Cloud Computing and Grid Computing 360-Degree Compared," IEEE Grid Computing Environments (GCE08) 2008, co-located with IEEE/ACM Supercomputing 2008* 2012 ACM/IEEE 13TH INTERNATIONAL CONFERENCE ON GRID COMPUTING 1–10.

initially introduced via grid computing systems. Today, they have been incorporated in cloud computing arrangements with updated distinctive approaches.

iv. Virtualization

"Virtualization represents a technology platform used for the creation of virtual instances of IT resources. A layer of virtualization software allows physical IT resources to provide multiple virtual images of themselves so that their underlying processing capabilities can be shared by multiple users. Prior to the advent of virtualization technologies, software was limited to residing on and being coupled with static hardware environments. The virtualization process made redundant this software-hardware dependency, as hardware requirements can be simulated by emulation software running in virtualized environments."[93]

Elements of virtualization technologies can be traced in several cloud computing mechanisms and they have also inspired many of the core features of modern cloud systems. As cloud computing evolved, it brought along a new generation of modern virtualization technologies, which, based on the know-how from the past, have now managed to overcome the performance, reliability and scalability limitations of traditional virtualization platforms. In other words, lying at the foundations of contemporary cloud technology, modern virtualization concepts provide a variety of virtualization types and technology layers that have facilitated optimization of cloud platforms to the flexible, adaptable systems we know today.

g. Cloud computing: its core philosophy and structural features

Bringing together features and functionalities of all main IT concepts that preceded it, cloud computing rose to be today's standard technology for data handling. But before pointing out what it does differently from past solutions and IT systems, it is essential to describe the founding features upon which it has been built to become what we know and extensively use today as possibly the most popular way of handling and processing data.

---

93 Thomas Erl, Richardo Puttini & Zaigham Mahmood (note 46).

i. The cloud's business model

The prevalent cloud-based business model[94] has the customer paying the provider on a consumption basis. In effect, use of cloud solutions is charged under the same principle applied by utility companies when they charge for basic utilities such as electricity, gas, and water. This arrangement relies on economies of scale in an effort to drive prices down for users and maximize profits for providers[95].

ii. The architecture of cloud computing systems

Cloud-based technologies have been developed to be able to address Internet-scale computing problems; this actually means that some of the key assumptions of the data handling tasks clouds are expected to carry out are essentially different from those of the technologies that the cloud succeeded[96]. The term 'clouds' is usually understood to refer to "a large pool of computing and/or storage resources, which can be accessed via standard protocols via an abstract interface"[97]. Cloud systems have actually been built on top of many pre-existing protocols such as Web Services[98] or other advanced Web 2.0 technologies[99].

In line with the observation that cloud computing is actually not an out-of-nowhere technology but the result of continuous evolution of pre-existing IT tools, its architecture is not a linear one but, rather, includes elements of all technologies upon which the cloud is based. As a rule, the cloud's architecture is divided in four layers, in particular, the fabric, unified resource, platform, and application layers[100].

---

94 Christof Weinhardt, Arun Anandasivam, Benjamin Blau, Nikolay Borissov, Thomas Meinl, Wibke Michalk & Jochen Stößer (note 65).

95 Bill Williams (note 62); Norman Pelzl (note 65).

96 Liang-Jie Zhang & Qun Zhou, CCOA: Cloud Computing Open Architecture (2009.)

97 Ian Foster, Yong Zhao, Ioan Raicu & Shiyong Lu (note 92).

98 Thomas Erl, Richardo Puttini & Zaigham Mahmood (note 46).

99 *Id.*

100 In addition to this structural analysis of cloud's architecture, in Chapter 8 there is an analytical presentation of the internal organization of cloud networks, which, combined, serve as the basis for the regulatory proposals contained in this study.

The fabric layer contains all raw hardware level elements, such as compute, storage and network resources. The unified resource layer contains resources that have been abstracted/encapsulated (usually by virtualization) so that they can be exposed to upper layer and end users as integrated resources, for instance, a virtual computer/cluster, a logical file system, a database system, etc[101]. The platform layer is where a collection of specialized tools, middleware and services on top of the unified resources are categorized; for example, a Web hosting environment or a scheduling service. These elements are necessary in order to facilitate the development and/or deployment of the cloud platform. Finally, the application layer contains the applications that would run on this cloud-based system[102].

h. The resource management aspects of the cloud

i. The cloud's compute model

The cloud's compute model is fundamentally different from that of its preceding technologies, with resources in the cloud being dynamically shared by all users at all times; in contrast to that, technologies previous to cloud systems were governing resources in a queuing manner, assigning to them the execution of computational tasks in the order that these tasks were given to the system[103].

101 *Id.*

102 One could easily recognize these layers if the architecture of a widely known service such as Dropbox is brought to mind; a. fabric layer is Dropbox's server farms and infrastructure (either privately owned or sublet); b. the unified resource layer corresponds to Dropbox's way of organizing the content of its users' folders content, the way it arranges their files into parent folders, sub-folders etc.; c. the platform layer is Dropbox's backend, the environment from which Dropbox stuff can control and make sure that their service runs smoothly towards the users; finally, d. the application layer, which contains all the editing tools and applications that Dropbox makes available to users to work with the files they host on the service.

103 *Id.*

ii. Virtualization[104]

Virtualization has preceded the cloud and was deeply incorporated in cloud systems to become a quasi-indispensable ingredient for most of them in order to enhance their abstraction and encapsulation. Virtualization is the tool thanks to which clouds, which need to run vast numbers of user applications, make it appear as if all these applications were running simultaneously and had ready for use all the available resources in the cloud facility[105]. Virtualization offers to the cloud all necessary abstraction so that the underlying elements of a cloud system (storage, network resources etc.) can be unified to resemble a pool of resources so that then resource overlays (e.g. web hosting environments) can be built on top of them. Virtualization also permits each cloud application to be encapsulated so that it can be configured, deployed, migrated, suspended, stopped, etc., and thus provides better security, manageability, and isolation.

One can reasonably argue that virtualization is the technology from which the cloud borrowed more features than any other from those that it succeeded. There are indeed many valid reasons that support such a claim[106]:

- virtualization offers to cloud systems the server and application consolidation they need in order to be able to run as many applications as needed on the same server by making use of available resources in the most efficient manner possible;
- high degree configurability is also possible thanks to virtualization: as resource requirements for the various applications running on a cloud facility differ significantly, virtualization is necessary in order to dynamically configure and aggregate resources for these varying needs, given that this is not achievable at the hardware level;
- optimized application availability; virtualization permits quick recovery from unplanned outages, as virtual environments can be backed up and migrated without interruption in service;
- last but not least, virtualization has offered to the cloud improved responsiveness, as resource provisioning, monitoring and maintenance

---

104 *Id.*

105 Christof Weinhardt, Arun Anandasivam, Benjamin Blau, Nikolay Borissov, Thomas Meinl, Wibke Michalk & Jochen Stößer (note 65).

106 Liang-Jie Zhang & Qun Zhou (note 96).

can be automated, while common or residual resources can be cached and reused.

Virtualization with all these features has actually been the basis for cloud systems to meet the stringent requirements of the tasks they are carried out through them.

iii. Monitoring[107]

The extensive use of virtualization technology in cloud environments caused as a side-effect the difficulty in maintaining control over the monitoring of resources of the system. When utilizing applications hosted on the cloud, different levels of services can be offered to each end user; nevertheless, every user is only exposed to a predefined API[108] while lower level resources are invisible to them. Apart from interacting with the standard API users do not have the liberty to deploy their own monitoring mechanisms over the cloud resources of the platform, while the limited information returned to them most commonly does not provide adequate level of details that would permit them to figure out what the resource status is at any given moment[109]. Essentially, monitoring a cloud facility is a quite complicated process requiring a fine balance of business application monitoring, enterprise server management, virtual machine monitoring, and hardware maintenance[110]. It is worth mentioning, however, that, as technology evolves, it is already possible that, in the near future, user-end monitoring might become less important as cloud systems become more sophisticated, more self-maintained and self-healing[111].

107 *Id.*

108 In computer programming, an application programming interface (API) is a set of routines, protocols, and tools for building software applications. (https://en.wikipedia.org/wiki/Application_programming_interface; last accessed on 01/12/2017.)

109 Larry Ellison (note 68).

110 Liang-Jie Zhang & Qun Zhou (note 96).

111 Benoit Dupont, *Cybersecurity Futures: How Can We Regulate Emergent Risks?* Technology Innovation Management Review 6–11 (2013); Willcocks, Leslie P., Venters, Will and Whitley, Edgar A., Cloud and the future of business: from costs to innovation: part two: challenges (2012.)

iv. Provenance

"Provenance refers to the derivation history of a data product, including all the data sources, intermediate data products, and the procedures that were applied to produce the data product. Provenance information is vital in understanding, discovering, validating, and sharing a certain data product as well as the applications and programs used to derive it"[112]. In some disciplines, such as finance and medicine, this provenance path is also mandatory to provide and it is called an 'audit trail' at all times so that a thorough audition over the course the data has followed is at all times possible. Cloud platforms are becoming the new standard playground for modern scientific research and, consequently, provenance management is extremely important in order to track the processes and support the reproducibility of scientific results. What is more, this provenance feature can also serve as the key to overall efficient regulation of cloud computing: when coupled with the teleological principle, provenance mechanisms can very effectively serve the crucial issue of regulating cloud computing no matter for what purpose it is utilized[113].

i. The application model of the cloud

Cloud computing could in principle cater to the whole set of applications most commonly needed by the average user who needs to perform data computational processing. This is not of course to be understood as implying that all other technologies are bound to cease to exist. Most probably, there will always be tasks and specific data processing queries that, for reasons of security (or other similar grounds) will preferably continue to run in non-cloud environments and on platforms based on the technologies that pre-existed the cloud. However, given that already these exceptions are an ever-dwindling minority and, also, due to the undeniable power of the comparative advantages of the cloud, it should not come as a surprise if, eventually, the cloud unquestionably prevails over all other options[114]. Therefore, a timely regulation of the cloud is necessary as soon as possible

112 Ian Foster, Yong Zhao, Ioan Raicu & Shiyong Lu (note 92).
113 See also Chapter 10.
114 Liang-Jie Zhang & Qun Zhou (note 96).

if we are to be able to handle all issues that may arise out of it and call for settlement.

j. The security model of the cloud

Cloud systems today usually comprise dedicated data centers belonging to the same organization. In each of these data centers, hardware and software configurations along with supporting platforms are in general more homogeneous as compared with those in data environments built on technologies prior to cloud computing[115]. Interoperability is clearly one of the most serious issues for cross-data center, cross-administration domain interactions[116]. Currently, the security model for clouds typically relies on Web forms (over SSL[117]) that allow creation and easy management of account information for end-users, whom they also permit to reset their old and receive new elements of these accounts (such as passwords) even in unsafe and unencrypted communication channels (for example, via emails). As a rule, new users can use cloud-based services more easily and almost instantly (most of the times, it is possible to create a profile just with a credit card and/or an email address). On the contrary, data environments based on technologies prior to cloud computing were usually stricter about security but, of course, at the same time, were readily addressed only to a limited and very specific pool of users (for example, the members of the organization which a grid-based data center belonged to)[118].

Security has been and still is one of the greatest concerns regarding the adoption of cloud computing[119]. To give a thorough catalogue of all secu-

115 Ian Foster, Yong Zhao, Ioan Raicu & Shiyong Lu (note 92).

116 Sean Marston, Zhi Li, Subhajyoti Bandyopadhyay, Juheng Zhang & Anand Ghalsasi, *Cloud computing — The business perspective*, 51 Decision Support Systems 176–189 (2011.)

117 Transport Layer Security (TLS) and its predecessor, Secure Sockets Layer (SSL), both of which are frequently referred to as 'SSL', are cryptographic protocols designed to provide communications security over a computer network. (https://en.wikipedia.org/wiki/Transport_Layer_Security; last accessed on 01/12/2017.)

118 Ian Foster, Yong Zhao, Ioan Raicu & Shiyong Lu (note 92).

119 For an analytical overview of the security parameter as one of the main determinant factors for growth and further adoption of cloud computing, refer to: W. K. Hon, C. Millard & I. Walden, *The problem of 'personal data' in cloud computing:*

rity questions surrounding the cloud, it would be extensively technical and beyond the scope of this paper. However, here is a list of the seven most common (and potentially affecting most users) security threats coming with the adoption of cloud computing:

- **Privileged user access**[120]: whenever cloud-based services users need to perform computational tasks involving sensitive data on a cloud system from which they lease resources, it is very common that they ask for assurances that any processing done to those data will only be accessible by those privileged users;
- **Regulatory compliance**[121]: customers who decide to turn to cloud services commonly ask to verify if their cloud provider has external audits and security certifications and if they truly comply to the awarded security certificates they demonstrate;
- **Data location**[122]: this is one the most fervently debated and contested issues regarding cloud technology. Extensive discourse will be made over data location and cloud computing in the course of this study. However, at this point one could briefly mention that currently, since a

---

what information is regulated?--the cloud of unknowing, 1 International Data Privacy Law 211–228 (2011); Dara Hallinan, Michael Friedewald, Paul McCarthy, *Citizens' Perceptions of Data Protection and Privacy in Europe*, 28 Computer Law and Security Review 263–272 (2012); M. Friedewald & R. J. Pohoryles, Privacy and Security in the Digital Age: Privacy in the Age of Super-Technologies (2016); Neil Robinson, Lorenzo Valeri, Jonathan Cave, Tony Starkey, Hans Graux, Sadie Creese & Paul P. Hopkins, The Cloud: Understanding the Security, Privacy and Trust Challenges. Prepared for Unit F.5, Directorate-General Information Society and Media, European Commission (2012); S. Subashini & V. Kavitha, *A survey on security issues in service delivery models of cloud computing*, 34 Journal of Network and Computer Applications 1–11 (2011); Hassan Takabi, James B. D. Joshi & Gail-Joon Ahn, *Security and Privacy Challenges in Cloud Computing Environments* IEEE Security & Privacy 24–31 (2010); A. van Cleeff, W. Pieters & R. J. Wieringa, Security Implications of Virtualization: A Literature Study, vol. 3; A. E. Whitley, P. L. Willcocks & W. Venters, *Privacy and Security in the Cloud: A Review of Guidance and Responses*, 22 Journal of International Technology and Information Management 75–92 (2013); M. Zhou, R. Zhang, W. Xie, W. Qian & A. Zhou, Security and Privacy in Cloud Computing: A Survey; Kirstin Brennscheidt, Cloud Computing und Datenschutz.

120 Christof Weinhardt, Arun Anandasivam, Benjamin Blau, Nikolay Borissov, Thomas Meinl, Wibke Michalk & Jochen Stößer (note 65).

121 Liang-Jie Zhang & Qun Zhou (note 96).

122 Sean Marston, Zhi Li, Subhajyoti Bandyopadhyay, Juheng Zhang & Anand Ghalsasi (note 116).

customer does not immediately know where data are stored, it is not uncommon for mid- and big-scale users of cloud services to ask their providers for reassurances regarding storing and processing data in specific jurisdictions and under pre-defined privacy requirements on behalf of the customer;

- **Data segregation**[123]: mid- to big-scale users often ask for reassurances that their data is fully segregated from data belonging to other users of the same cloud facility;
- **Recovery**[124]: it is a pressing request from the market that cloud providers have an efficient replication and recovery mechanism to restore data if a disaster occurs;
- **Investigative support**[125]: Cloud services are especially difficult to investigate but not at all impossible. Right now, if this is important for a customer, it is usually concretized in the contractual agreement between the customer and the cloud service provider. However, in the future and as investigative mechanisms for the cloud will become more and more efficient, they can actually be among the cornerstone of an efficient regulatory mechanism for cloud computing;
- **Long-term viability**[126]: obviously, it is already a pressing demand from users that data remain viable even when the cloud provider is acquired by another company.

k. What is cloud computing after all and why does it merit a new regulatory approach?

In conclusion, it can now be said without hesitation that cloud computing is an operations model, not a technology[127]. What makes cloud computing stand out from other data handling technologies is the fact that the physical resources of a cloud facility are operated to deliver abstract IT resources on-demand, at scale, and (almost always) in a multi-tenant envi-

123 Christof Weinhardt, Arun Anandasivam, Benjamin Blau, Nikolay Borissov, Thomas Meinl, Wibke Michalk & Jochen Stößer (note 65).

124 W. K. Hon, C. Millard & I. Walden (note 119).

125 *Id.*

126 Liang-Jie Zhang & Qun Zhou (note 96).

127 See also Chapter 9.

ronment[128]. In a nutshell, cloud computing as a term should be understood to signify the way in which available technologies for data handling are involved to maximize efficiency, economies of scale and ease of use.

Cloud borrows much from long established technologies and from various long standing operation models. However, the combination of all these technologies and models in an on-demand, at scale and multi-tenant infrastructure is relatively unique for the post client-server era, and is the main reason why cloud computing has had such an impact on the standards of data handling industry, rather than being another passing fad.

Consequently, cloud computing is the evolutionary climax of several decades of technological progress in the field of computational data processing. It is a 'revolution', since it fundamentally simplified and optimized the processes involving digital data but, at the same time, it is not a 'revolution' in the sense of a phenomenon coming out of nowhere. The cloud has firm roots to almost all technological steps that preceded it, it borrows features from most of them yet it rearranges them in an entirely new spectrum. This new arrangement results in different processes, problems and challenges that will ensure that the processes carried out through it are flawless and respectful of the rights and duties of all the actors involved (from data subjects to data owners to data controllers and regulators). Nevertheless, the fact that it happened so gradually and in a rather 'natural evolution' pattern has resulted in ignoring, to some extent, its gravity and differentiation from the previous status quo. As it will be demonstrated immediately after, this has resulted in a current situation where the cloud is attempted to be regulated with pre-existing norms and rules, which were produced in the era of its preceding technologies[129]. However, things in the cloud era are essentially different and they merit a new regulatory approach which will be explored over the course of this study.

---

128 Software Multitenancy refers to a software architecture in which a single instance of a software runs on a server and serves multiple tenants. A tenant is a group of users who share a common access with specific privileges to the software instance. With a multitenant architecture, a software application is designed to provide every tenant a dedicated share of the instance including its data, configuration, user management, tenant individual functionality and non-functional properties. Multitenancy contrasts with multi-instance architectures, where separate software instances operate on behalf of different tenants. (https://en.wikipedia.org/wiki/Multitenancy; last accessed on 11/4/2015.)

129 See Chapter 2.e.

CHAPTER 3. EU vs. US: the two major schools of thought regarding internet and privacy regulation and why they took divergent paths. Can this distance be bridged in the context of a regulatory framework for the cloud?

a. Introduction – scope of the chapter

It is commonly accepted and can be also verified through figures[130] that the EU and the US have been the two most important players when it comes to the issue of internet and privacy regulation[131]. The EU has managed to influence with its legislation on the fields tens of other national or regional jurisdictions worldwide, which have developed their privacy and internet laws very much following the essence and cornerstone elements of European legislation[132]. On the other hand, the USA, despite not having been equally successful in 'exporting' their legal approach regarding the above issues, have clearly managed to maintain a gravitas in the field due to their enormous share in the overall market size of the internet, both from the perspective of users and from that of service providers[133]. As it is known, these two jurisdictions have over the course of the years followed distinct paths as to how issues related to the development of applications of information technologies were regulated[134]. The distance between them was never totally bridged and it exists, as far as the issue of cloud computing is concerned, as well. However, given that the genuinely borderless nature of cloud technologies contradicts the fragmented regulatory landscape caused by divergent jurisdictional tendencies, in the context of an

---

130 Graham Greenleaf ed., Global Data Privacy Laws: 89 Countries, and Accelerating. Special Supplement, Issue 115 (2012.)

131 *Id.*

132 Graham Greenleaf, *The Influence of European Data Privacy Standards Outside Europe: Implications for Globalisation of Convention 108*, 2 International Data Privacy Law 68–92 (2012.)

133 Graham Greenleaf, Major Changes in Asia Pacific Data Privacy Laws: 2011 Survey (2012.)

134 For more see Chapter 4.

analysis that seeks to bring together potential points of convergence on the matter between EU and US law, we must agree on a minimum common understanding that will permit not necessarily the convergence of different jurisdictions but most importantly the effective interaction between them. Over the course of this chapter, the different standpoints at which European and American laws about the internet and its subsequent phenomena have been traditionally standing, are summarized and presented. Then, the ground is set for ways in which these two schools of thought (and the numerous others that have been evolving under the influence thereof[135]) could approach each other and govern in a more pragmatic manner a state-of-the-art IT phenomenon, such as cloud computing.

b. How extensive is the influence of European data privacy standards outside Europe? Is it EU law that has been so influencing or is it more the entire European legal thinking?

One of the generally admitted facts about data privacy and regulation thereof worldwide is that a great deal of countries across continents have developed their respective laws by following the patterns and legal notions originally conceived in Europe[136]. However, despite the fact that popular belief usually attributes this wave effect to EU legislation, in reality it is the overall European legal tradition that has succeeded so much in shaping data privacy legislative standards on a global scale[137]. The two major areas and jurisdictions that have been exempt from the influence of the European school of thought in the area of data privacy, are the USA and China. The fact that these two countries have largely maintained their independent path in regulating data privacy related issues along with the economic and political power they both carry requires special consideration in any assessment of global data privacy developments[138]. Neverthe-

135 Graham Greenleaf ed. (note 130).

136 For more see Chapter 4.

137 L. A. Bygrave, *Privacy protection in a global context–a comparative overview*, 47 Scandinavian Studies in Law 319–348 (2004.)

138 Graham Greenleaf, *Global Data Privacy Laws: Forty Years of Acceleration. UNSW Law Research Paper No. 2011-36* Privacy Laws and Business International Report 11–17 (2011) (Significant as China's role may be in the state of affairs regarding privacy and internet regulation on a global scale, it falls outside the scope of this study to assess the Chinese effect on the future of privacy and cloud com-

less, the increasing pressure for change these two jurisdictions face, especially in recent years, must also be pointed out.

In the USA, there are many privacy laws with relevantly effective enforcement, but no comprehensive privacy law in the private sector[139]. What is more, despite the fact that the revelations of latest years have increased pubic outcries for more comprehensive protection of privacy, there is not much real prospect for a comprehensive legislative package on the matter, despite periodic calls for one from major companies or draft Bills introduced into Congress. It is not of course the case that the USA does not have any standards for (private sector) data privacy; the main problem is rather that they must be inferred from many scattered pieces of legislation, while, in various sectors, there is utter absence of any significant legislation[140]. There are also some State constitutional protections along with common law structures[141]. All of the above lead as a fact to a situation that often makes scholars claim that the US approach is incoherent, sectoral-based, and with legislative protections that are largely reactive, driven by outrage and at particularly narrow practices[142].

On the other hand, since everyone admits that 'European standards' for data privacy have been influential on a global scale, we need to devise ways in which we could measure that. It is also essential to check whether the causes of influence can be traced, apart from its effects. With a very small number of exceptions (Israel, public sector laws in some OECD countries, New Zealand) data protection laws outside Europe were adopted in the aftermath of the 1995 Directive[143] (or at least in the aftermath of

---

puting regulation. For structural, as well as practical barriers, e.g. the language barrier, this project focuses on the European and US jurisdictions alone.)

139 Elisa Bertino, Ravi Sandhu, Lujo Bauer & Jaehong Park eds., the third ACM conference.

140 Chris Hoofnagle, COMPARATIVE STUDY ON DIFFERENT APPROACHES TO NEW PRIVACY CHALLENGES, IN PARTICULAR IN THE LIGHT OF TECHNOLOGICAL DEVELOPMENTS. B.1 – UNITED STATES OF AMERICA, available at: http://ec.europa.eu/justice/policies/privacy/docs/studies/new_privacy_challenges/final_report_country_report_B1_usa.pdf (2 May 2016.)

141 *Id.*

142 Graham Greenleaf (note 132).

143 Directive 95/46/EC of the European Parliament and of the Council on the Protection of Individuals with Regard to the Processing of Personal Data and on the Free Movement of Such Data, 24 October 1995, (OJ) L 281, 23/11/1995 P. 0031 – 0050.

the introduction of its draft form in the early 90s)[144]; consequently, they were open to influences from it at their inception. In certain cases, even revised laws (for instance, those of Taiwan, South Korea and New Zealand) have incorporated new elements in their body influenced by the EU Directive[145].

If one would like to present a comprehensive picture about how laws outside Europe have been influenced by the European legal thinking about data privacy regulation, one would need to pinpoint two big pools of influences: (i) those which can be attributed to both the EU Directive and the OECD Guidelines[146]; and (ii) those which are found in the Directive but are not required by the OECD Guidelines[147]. In literature, it has prevailed that the first are called influences with 'global' and the second influences with 'European' origins[148]. All of them put together, they prove that it is not EU law that has had such a profound influence on global standards for data privacy regulation but, in fact, European legal thinking in its entirety.

Those ten plus ten influences offer a comprehensive picture about the most common elements that define data privacy in the online world currently across jurisdictions worldwide. In particular, the ten influences with 'global' origins, i.e. notions that are common to all three major international instruments governing online (data) privacy that have started developing in Europe[149] plus the APEC Privacy Framework[150] of 1998 (which was lastly revised in 2004) are[151]:

---

144 *Id.*

145 *Id.*

146 The comprehensive set of OECD guidelines on privacy and transborder flows of personal data is available here: https://www.oecd.org/sti/ieconomy/oecdguidelinesontheprotectionofprivacyandtransborderflowsofpersonaldata.htm (lastly accessed 02/23/2017.)

147 L. A. Bygrave (note 137).

148 Graham Greenleaf (note 132).

149 These instruments are: the EU Data Privacy Directive of 1995, the Council of Europe Convention for the Protection of Individuals with regard to Automatic Processing of Personal Data of 1981, the OECD Guidelines on the Protection of Privacy and Transborder Flows of Personal Data of 1980 (ETS 108).

150 The APEC Privacy Framework (1998) is available here: http://www.ag.gov.au/www/agd/rwpattach.nsf/VAP/(03995EABC73F94816C2AF4AA2645824B)~APEC+Privacy+Framework.pdf/$file/APEC+Privacy+Framework.pdf (last accessed on 09/11/2017.)

151 Graham Greenleaf (note 132).

- **Collection**, which has to be limited, lawful and conducted by fair means; with consent or knowledge of the data subject [OECD 7; CoE 5(c), (d)]
- **Data quality**, which requires that any data collected need to be relevant, accurate and up-to-date [OECD 8; CoE 5(a)]
- **Purpose specification** at time of collection [OECD 9; CoE 5)]
- **Notice of purpose and rights at time of collection**, which have to be communicated to all data subjects [OECD ambiguous; APEC stronger; CoE not explicit but implied]
- **Uses of collected data have to be limited** (including disclosures) to specified or compatible purposes [OECD 10; CoE 5(b)]
- **Security of data has to be continuously maintained** through reasonable safeguards (OECD 11; CoE 7)
- Personal data and the **practices applied** to them **need to be open and clearly stipulated** at all times [OECD 12; CoE 8(a)]
- **Access**: data subjects need to have individual right of access to their data at all times [OECD 13; CoE 8(b)]
- **Correction**: the data subject needs to have the individual right of correcting the data relevant them [OECD 13; CoE 8(c), (d)]
- **Accountable**: data controllers are to be held accountable for implementation of previous nine points (OECD 14; CoE 8)

Then, there are these ten influences with 'European' origins that may or may not be found in national privacy laws[152]:

- Requirement of an independent Data Protection Authority as the key actor of an enforcement regime (EU Directive, and Additional Protocol to Convention 108)
- Requirement of recourse to courts to enforce data privacy rights (EU Directive, Convention 108 and more explicitly the Additional Protocol to Convention 108)
- Requirement of restrictions on personal data exports to countries that do not meet sufficient standards of privacy protection (defined as 'adequate') (EU Directive, and Additional Protocol to Convention 108)
- Collection of data must at each time be the minimum necessary for the purpose it is executed, not simply 'limited' to this purpose (both EU Directive and Convention 108)

152 *Id.*

- A general requirement of 'fair and lawful processing' (not just collection) (both EU Directive and Convention 108)
- Requirements to notify, and sometimes to provide 'prior checking', of particular types of processing systems (EU Directive)
- Destruction or anonymization of personal data after a certain period (both EU Directive and Convention 108);
- Additional layers of protections for particular categories of sensitive data (both EU Directive and Convention 108)
- Limitations on automated decision-making, along with a right to know the logic of any automated data processing arrangement (EU Directive)
- Requirement to provide 'opt-out' of any direct marketing use of personal data (EU Directive).

c. What is the main difference from Europe in USA's arrangement of their regulatory framework for privacy and the internet?

There are several reasons which serve to explain why the United States have not been anywhere near as successful as Europe in exporting their legal culture on privacy and the Internet to third jurisdictions. However, before moving into seeking the answers to this questions, one observation is essential: There is a fundamental difference in the way the issues of data privacy and internet regulation have been built so far compared to Europe and the European Union, in particular[153]. In fact, the United States continues to lack an omnibus law that would cover, in a comprehensive manner, all these issues in the private sector. At the same time, it has, at best, only a relatively limited omnibus law for part of the public sector[154]. This is in stark contrast to what happens in Europe, where new countries that have joined the EU, have quickly adapted their regulation of information privacy with omnibus laws. Then, they have supplemented these statutes with sectoral ones, wherever further details in regulation where necessary. According to many scholars, this continuing difference between Europe and America can best be explained by the following two factors[155]:

---

153 Elisa Bertino, Ravi Sandhu, Lujo Bauer & Jaehong Park eds. (note 139).

154 Paul M. Schwartz & Daniel J. Solove (note 16).

155 Paul Schwartz, *The EU-U.S. Privacy Collision: A Turn to Institutions and Procedures*, 126 Harvard Law Review 1966–2009 (2013.)

- initial regulatory choices which were then solidified as a pattern by path dependency in each jurisdiction, and
- the usefulness of omnibus laws in multinational systems, such as the European Union, that wish to harmonize their regulations compared to the tendency of federal systems, like the USA, to prefer regulatory arrangements and more multi-layered regulatory structures.

There has been a lot of discussion as to whether a federal US law on privacy would be a good or a necessary thing. It is certain that the consequences from a unifying federal legislation would be both positive and negative. On the one hand, an omnibus law would overcome the inability of sectoral laws to respond adequately to telecommunications convergence, which is one of the most prevalent processes on the Internet[156]. In addition, omnibus laws tend to level the regulatory playing field while sectoral laws can place unequal burdens on industries in closely related areas[157]. Last but not least, an omnibus law is considered by many that it could help convince the EU of the adequacy of US privacy laws, thereby assisting in smoothing data flows between the two markets[158]. However, there is a good deal of people who tend to criticize an eventual movement of the US towards the adoption of omnibus legislation on privacy. They cite as the most important reasons for this criticism the costs that an extra layer of regulation would give rise to, and the risk of an omnibus law's obsolescence due to latency in the pace of its reform cycles[159].

d. The 'privacy collision' between Europe and the USA: a brief historical overview

Having pointed out how the USA, as a legal culture and jurisdiction have traditionally decided to deal with privacy in a diffusible, non-omnibus manner, it is worth briefly examining how Europe has moved through time in dealing with the same issues. At the end of this historical flashback, one will have already discerned some of the causes that made these two impor-

156 Paul M. Schwartz & Daniel J. Solove (note 16).

157 Paul M. Schwartz, *Preemption and Privacy*. UC Berkeley Public Law Research Paper, 118 Yale Law Journal 904-947 (2009.)

158 Paul Schwartz (note 155).

159 *Id.*

tant players in the privacy and internet regulation field follow so divergent paths.

On a European, as well as on a global level, it was the Hessian Parliament that enacted the world's first comprehensive information privacy statute in Wiesbaden, Germany, in 1970[160]. This piece of law was followed by similar ones of other German states[161], and in 1977 a Federal German law on privacy was adopted[162]. Other European countries closely followed suit in 1970s when Sweden (1973)[163], Austria (1978)[164], Denmark (1978)[165], France (1978)[166], and Norway (1978)[167] all enacted data protection statutes.

Europe has been also the stage for some of the most important supranational privacy agreements that were adopted even before the EU Data Protection Directive of 1995. The two most important, as it has already been demonstrated[168], are the Privacy Guidelines of the Organization for Economic Cooperation and Development (OECD) and the Convention on Privacy of the Council of Europe. The OECD principles, despite being non-binding, have had a great influence on numerous national laws.

Simitis, one of the academic forerunners in the field of data protection in Europe, summarizes the prevailing view about privacy in EU law already since its early days, as follows: "Data protection does not stop at national borders. Transfers of information must be bound to conditions that attempt in a targeted fashion to protect the affected parties."[169]

The impact of the Data Privacy Directive had been significant. Apart from shaping the form of numerous laws, inside and outside the EU, it contributed to the evolution and concretization of the well-known substantive EU model of data protection, which has been so highly influential. What is more, given the expressive preference for omnibus privacy laws,

---

160 Peter Gola, Christoph Klug, Rudolf Schomerus & Barbara Körffer, Bundesdatenschutzgesetz. Kommentar (2010.)

161 *Id.*

162 *Id.*

163 Nordic Council of Ministers, Information Security in Nordic Countries (1993.)

164 P. E. Agre & M. Rotenberg, Technology and Privacy: The New Landscape (1998.)

165 Nordic Council of Ministers (note 163).

166 P. E. Agre & M. Rotenberg (note 164).

167 Nordic Council of Ministers (note 163).

168 See also Chapter 4.1.

169 Ulrich Dammann & Spiros Simitis, Bundesdatenschutzgesetz (2014.)

European legal thinking contributed towards the establishment of regulatory standards with a broad scope in contrary to the limited protection guaranteed by sectoral laws.

These developments led to today's status quo with reference to privacy regulation in the US and Europe. Following the sectoral instead of the omnibus legislative route, the United States have different statutes on privacy for the public and private sectors. Within the private sector, they concentrate on the data holder and, in some instances, on the type of data[170]. In certain privacy statutes, there is an even deeper distinction related to the form in which the data is held, or the content of the information[171]. This approach has been thought by scholars to generally give a freer rein to data processors to try new kinds of processing[172]. This has been regarded as a boost to innovation as, particularly enterprises in new business areas, are largely free of regulation under a sectoral regime and thereby able to test innovative new practices; on the other hand, there is the opposite perspective which sees this greater freedom as fertile ground for new ways to violate privacy[173]. Another effect of this approach is the tendency that has been repetitively witnessed in the USA to place heavier data privacy restrictions on established enterprises than on new companies[174].

The two starkly different approaches have met equally diversifying critique from scholarly opinion. For instance, on the one end of the stick we find Joel Reidenberg, who, in a bold move already in 2000, took the view that between the US and the European approach on privacy there is a profound dichotomy. In particular, Reidenberg found that "US information privacy regulation was based on liberal norms and market forces, while the EU's information privacy regulations were based on "social-protection norms," where "data privacy is a political imperative anchored in fundamental human rights protection."[175]

A more positive take was adopted by scholars such as Anne-Marie Slaughter whose opinions are demonstrative of the scholarly thought that

---

170 Paul Schwartz (note 155).

171 *Id.*

172 *Id.*

173 Joel Reidenberg, *Lex Informatica: The Formulation of Information Policy Rules through Technology*, 76 Tex. L. Rev. 553–593 (1997.)

174 Reidenberg, J. R., Schwartz, P. M., Data Protection Law and On-line Services: Regulatory Responses.

175 Joel Reidenberg, *Yahoo and Democracy on the Internet* Jurimetrics 261 (2001.)

took a more insightful perspective on global privacy policymaking. According to Slaughter, "states now relate to each other through their parts and not their whole. States are disaggregated, that is, they interact not only through their foreign offices and state departments, but also through a variety of regulatory, judicial, and legislative channels"[176].

Extensive analysis of how the current EU Data Protection Regulation works are done in other parts of this study[177]. In terms of the evolutionary perspective of EU's data protection policymaking and the need for it to become more accountable and transparent the most promising element is Article 45[178] of the Regulation, which calls for collaboration in data protection on a global basis. For the time being, this is only a wish and encouragement for the future. However, a regulatory field such as the one of cloud computing would be an ideal one for putting this call into practice.

The evolutionary process of data protection laws in Europe and the USA and the point where we are right now, in terms of available technologies, IT applications which have already been or are about to be commercialized and, in particular, the appearance of cloud computing, big data, internet of things and artificial intelligence, not as small sectors of IT activity but as entire industries that have the potential to substitute or, at least, offer all-inclusive alternatives to practically all kinds of data processing and knowledge generation we used to do offline so far, call for much more proactive and generic policymaking and regulatory rules in the future. Both Europe and the US have to work towards laws that will not simply concentrate on a limited set of instances made possible through IT technologies or the cloud but towards legislation that will stand above individual occurrences and will bring the big picture in focus. At the same time, apart from promoting a more generic over a case-based approach, future IT laws need to set the foundations for a regulatory regime that will be able to work independently without the constant need for interventions from executive supervisory bodies such the Data Protection Authorities, in Europe, or the National Security Agency, in the USA. In other words, just as it has been done in other more conventional sectors of regulation, cloud computing and IT laws in general should be constructed in such a manner that they empower the actors in the very system that they regulate to make sure the system will work in a trustworthy manner. Proactivity instead of

176 Anne-Marie Slaughter, A New World Order (2009.)
177 For more see Chapter 4.
178 Art. 45, Regulation (EU) 2016/679 (GDPR) (note 25.)

interventionism is the answer to a sound legislative future for the cloud and this is what regulators need to try to achieve both in Europe and in the USA, even if they have to depart, of course, from the different points where their diversified legal traditions have led them today.

Homogeneity is not sine qua non for such a way forward. In Europe, privacy and data protection are heralded as fundamental rights that deserve erga omnes protection. Conversely, in the United States, the Constitution contains no express right to privacy. Instead, the American conception of privacy is practically synonymous to the 'right to be left alone' – a provision whose constitutional basis can be traced in the Fourth and Fifth Amendments of the Bill of Rights. As it has been put, in the core of the American version of the right to privacy still exists to a great extent 'the form that this took in the eighteenth century: it is the right to freedom from intrusions by the state, especially in one's own home'[179]. In essence, contrary to the path followed in Europe, privacy in the U.S. (as a constitutional right) has materialized as one exclusively assertable against the State[180]. This 'public nature' of the right to privacy still remains prevalent today, even though certain subsequent statutory laws have endorsed a legal right to privacy enforceable also in private affairs on the basis of a 'sectoral approach'[181].

Despite these profoundly differing courses, it is definitely possible and, at the same time, desirable for both EU and US law to move towards a more pragmatic direction with reference to laws for the cloud. An element that would certainly bolster this necessity and would invigorate a regime of governance[182] instead of one of continuous state inspection is self-regulation[183]. This would imply a certain degree of independence from state regulation, as market players would be responsible for regulating themselves by following common rules and self-enforcing them[184]. The consequences, in case of failing to abide by this legal obligation for self-regu-

179 K. S. Ziegler, Human Rights and Private Law: Privacy as Autonomy (2007.)

180 Paul Schwartz (note 155).

181 *Id.*

182 For more see Chapter 5.

183 National Telecommunications & Information Administration (NTIA), PRIVACY AND SELF-REGULATION IN THE INFORMATION AGE, available at: https://www.ntia.doc.gov/report/1997/privacy-and-self-regulation-information-age (4 May 2016.)

184 D. Tambini, D. Leonardi & C. T. Marsden, Codifying Cyberspace: Communications Self-regulation in the Age of Internet Convergence (2008.)

lation, would come at a stage prior to the occurrence of any detrimental incidents for the data hosted on the cloud or the subjects of that data. They will in fact be the repercussions of failing to prove that, as an actor of the cloud environment, one lives up to the duties expected from them, not as a result of allowing a network failure to cause damage to the data or the subjects thereof. In other words, responsibility will be asserted on a proactive instead of a punitive basis. In the actual business of cloud computing, self-regulation can be made more attractive as an approach if it is promoted as a means to increase professional reputation and preserve ethical standards[185]. Practically speaking, self-regulation can be achieved by promoting certain practices (interoperability, privacy-compliant services, etc.), from the one hand, and banning or heavily discouraging others kinds of activities that might negatively affect users (user-profiling, targeted advertising, arbitrary censorship, etc.) on the other[186].

Nevertheless, this is not to imply at all that the State would have no role to play in a future cloud computing regulatory regime. In fact, the very way in which cloud services exist today, along with the dominance of the cloud market by a few large corporations, mean that private regulation amongst market players alone is unlikely to lead to satisfactory results. The state will continue to play a decisive role in the future cloud governance structure as the extra-network actor that will be tasked with intervening in order to push self-regulation towards the right direction[187]. Indeed, despite the fact that self-regulation concerns market players, to the extent that they operate within the boundaries of sovereign states and their respective jurisdictions, they are nonetheless subject to national rules[188]. As a result, state regulation can serve as the necessary backbone and provide the incentives for cloud providers to regulate themselves in a manner that effectively responds to users' demands and expectations[189].

In addition, self-regulation should not be limited to the realm of market players; in response to the sectoral diversification the cloud applications and uses demonstrate, it could be implemented amongst specific communities of users belonging to specific sectors who are eager to autonomous-

185 Andrew Charlesworth, *Clash of the Data Titans? US and EU Data Privacy Regulation*, 6 European Public Law 253–274 (2000.)

186 *Id.*

187 D. Tambini, D. Leonardi & C. T. Marsden (note 184).

188 National Telecommunications & Information Administration (NTIA) (note 183).

189 Andrew Charlesworth (note 185).

ly establish the rules they will have to abide to, rather than observing rules dictated by third party cloud operators[190]. This typology of self-regulation stands out from the self-regulation of cloud operators as it does not primary rely on pre-fabricated contracts or codes of conduct, but rather on technical arrangements (hardware or software) developed by users to tackle what has not been properly addressed by cloud operators[191]. In conclusion, self-regulation rules addressed to users (coming from specific sectors) will act as a form of self-discipline with private origins effected through bottom-up technical regulation[192].

e. Personal data privacy in Europe and the US: a pragmatic and an articulate approach

The evolution of the European and the American doctrine on privacy has led to the current legal approaches of the two jurisdictions on the issue of personal data privacy. Europe has nourished through the years a more pragmatic approach. In particular, Community lawmakers had to bridge the gap between the 'ideal' of the Single Market for unrestricted and unregulated movement of all personal data within the EU Members' area and the requirements of the Council of Europe's (CoE) Convention on the Automated Processing of Personal Data[193], to which all EU Member States are signatories[194]. The latter stipulates that any information about individuals which is to be automatically processed has to be handled in such a manner that the privacy rights of the subjects of this information are protected[195]. At the same time, CoE's Convention encouraged the establishment of a common international standard of protection for individuals[196], with the aspiration that the free flow of information across international boundaries could proceed without interruptions. In the end, EU law had to

190 D. Tambini, D. Leonardi & C. T. Marsden (note 184).

191 Andrew Charlesworth (note 185).

192 *Id.* .

193 Council of Europe, Convention for the Protection of Individuals with Regard to the Automatic Processing of Individual Data (note 148.)

194 C. J. Bennett, Regulating Privacy: Data Protection and Public Policy in Europe and the United States (1992.)

195 Convention for the Protection of Individuals with Regard to Automatic Processing of Personal Data (note 148.)

196 Id.

strike a balance between various country interpretations of this goals: for a number of them, such as Germany, France and the Nordic countries, these issues had been understood as having a significant human rights element. For others, such as the UK, the primary concern turned to be making sure that the minimum standards of protection required by the Convention were ensured so that international trade may not be disrupted[197]. These diversified tendencies were attempted to be abridged by means of the Data Privacy Directive which elevated the concept of personal data privacy into a concrete and enforceable privacy right[198]. As it was stated in Article 1 of the Directive: 'Member States shall protect the fundamental rights and freedoms of natural persons, and in particular their right to privacy with respect to the processing of personal data.'[199] Finally, the currently applicable General Data Protection Regulation is an effort to further concretize the nature of privacy of personal data as a fundamental right mainly by increasing the means or possibilities for individuals to verify or keep under control the circulation of their data[200].

The United States have concretized through the years a more complex approach on the issue of data privacy[201]. Despite the lack of an explicit constitutional provision for a right to privacy, the concept of privacy in the sense of 'the right to be left alone' has traditionally been entertained in principle by the US legal system, despite having been only rarely genuinely supported in practice when it comes to informational privacy.

Nevertheless, the types of privacy issues that federal and state legislators and courts have dealt with so far in the US tend to revolve around physical or decisional privacy[202]. What is more, these US constitutional privacy rights are always exercised against either federal, or state, government, i.e. they prevent the government from degrading individual citizens' rights; they do not require them to protect these rights against third parties. This is by no means to imply that the USA lack personal data privacy

197 Andrew Charlesworth (note 185).
198 For more see Chapter 4.
199 Directive 95/46/EC (DPD) (note 143.)
200 EU General Data Protection Regulation (note 25.)
201 Primavera De Filippi & Internet Policy Review, Foreign clouds in the European sky: how US laws affect the privacy of Europeans (2013.)
202 S. Scoglio, Transforming Privacy: A Transpersonal Philosophy of Rights (1998.)

laws. What the USA lack, however, is a coherent personal data privacy framework and any meaningful enforcement mechanism[203].

In summary, it can be argued that the key differences between the EU and US approaches to privacy are more in the mechanics of achieving data privacy than in the concept itself. The essential difference between them lies with the fact that EU laws provide for a legislatively backed data privacy regime, applicable to both public and private sector, overseen by regulatory authorities and with remedies to individuals whose data privacy rights have been breached. This renders the US strategic choice to leave privacy matters in the private sector untouched as the main obstacle towards a convergence of data privacy laws between the EU and the USA[204].

However, for the comparative presentation of the two approaches to be complete, it is meaningful to also present the arguments against the US adopting a similar regime, which can be summarized to the following points[205]:

- the USA should not comply with the extraterritorial application of another jurisdiction's laws[206];
- trade in personal data in the USA is so advanced that it is too late to provide a data privacy regime[207];
- a centralized government privacy regulator is not trustworthy; at the same time, centralization of data and knowledge about data protection is a graver threat to personal privacy than commercial activity involving data[208];
- the cost of compliance would outweigh the social benefit[209];
- such a radical change of course would hamper information-related businesses and would slow their expansion into global markets[210];

203 Paul Schwartz (note 155).

204 *Id.*

205 Chris Hoofnagle (note 140).

206 Peter P. Swire & Robert E. Litan, None of your business. World data flows, electronic commerce, and the European privacy directive (1998.)

207 Andrew Charlesworth (note 185).

208 Paul T. Jaeger, Jimmy Lin, Justin M. Grimes & Shannon N. Simmons, *Where is the cloud? Geography, economics, environment, and jurisdiction in cloud computing*, 14 First Monday (2009.)

209 Andrew Charlesworth (note 185).

210 Paul T. Jaeger, Jimmy Lin, Justin M. Grimes & Shannon N. Simmons (note 208).

- the way the US Constitution is modeled may prevent the federal government from engaging in European-style regulation of personal data use[211]; and
- deliberate self-regulation is a more effective approach than legal regulation.

f. Cyber challenges and state-of-the-art in Europe and the USA

Before concluding the analytical comparison between Europe and the USA regarding their legal traditions and treatment of online data privacy, the Internet and related phenomena, it is essential to go over the latest and current developments about these issues in the two jurisdictions. In this way, the state-of-the-art picture in the two jurisdictions will lead to evidence about the course future cloud computing laws will need to follow so that an overall efficient regulatory regime for the cloud is achieved among different jurisdictions on a worldwide scale.

i. EU's approach towards cyber challenges

The EU has recently taken a decisive step by introducing the General Data Protection Regulation into force[212]. However, and despite the undoubted novelties that this new piece of legislation introduces in the field of data protection, it largely focuses on just one aspect of the uses of technologies like cloud computing, leaving aside the cloud as a broader regulatory phenomenon per se. Additionally, the GDPR continues on Europe's tradition on regulating privacy from the perspective of a human right that needs to be defended against malpractice. Nevertheless, few, if any, new elements are added that reflect on the true nature of cloud computing, that of a generic IT technology, which regulation-wise cannot be dealt with on a case by case basis but needs laws with a holistic approach. Even if the EU succeeds in creating an abuse-proof environment of cyber security within its borders (which is in itself a very ambitious and not necessarily realistic goal), it can by no means be totally immune to the threat of cyberattack. At the end of the day, when arguing about cyber issues, it is vital to keep

211 Paul Schwartz (note 155).
212 For more see Chapter 4.

in mind that the internet, as a borderless environment, guarantees no protection from outer coming threats. In today's digital environment, a cyber-attack on an EU target will more likely originate from outside the EU than from within.

It is high time for Europe to live up to its role as a global economic and political power and exert its political strength and outreach capacity to the international field as well. Cyber security has an enormous impact on the global economy and can affect the general public in many different ways as it has already been demonstrated. Securing the personal data of consumers and the general public should be of the utmost importance not only for regulators but also for the international private sector and state institutions. However, it is imperative that soon these goals are pursued not only on an ex-post basis but also on a proactive basis by switching their focus from correcting damage when it is done or by adding layers of control that may hinder damage to occur to ensuring that the cloud and cyber environments, in general, are properly built up and continuously run in a manner that upholds these values and effectively eliminates (or seriously limits) the chances of such unfortunate damage to happen.

What is more, although personal data security may be the major, or most common, kind of damage that may occur through cloud computing, it is crucial to understand that data protection is only an element within the broader challenge of "the misuse of technology"[213]. Besides, apart from the fundamental right aspect of data privacy, mishandling personal information can be much more than simply the means of very lucrative accumulation of wealth. The cloud, and the internet that is facilitated thanks to it, can be abused by terrorist organizations, organized crime groups, cyber warfare and espionage on the part of states. Moreover, a cloud based internet can also be manipulated (and, in fact, more effectively than the pre-cloud Web) for the proliferation of cryptocurrencies and the promotion of cyber underground economy. In a nutshell, Europe has done enough to develop a protective shield for the human rights put at risk for its subjects due to the expansive transposition of data-related processes from the offline to the online realm. On a long-term level, what the EU needs to focus on is not changing or substituting its existing data related legal tools but rather on complementing it with laws that will realistically regulate the en-

213 Francesca Bosco, Assessing Europe's cyber challenges, available at: http://policyreview.info/articles/news/assessing-europes-cyber-challenges/355 (4 July 2016.)

vironments where such data damage may occur[214]. The most prominent field of this kind nowadays is probably the cloud.

ii. The US approach towards cyber challenges

In the wake of 9/11 and the threats to national security the USA faced over the last 15 years, the country's legal landscape for the internet and online privacy was not left unaffected. In fact, these incidents led US lawmakers to pass bills that reflected the profound aftermath of those historic attacks -which were to a crucial degree made possible thanks to data or security breaches – both on the internal and on the external affairs of the USA. The two most crucial of these acts were:

- the U.S. PATRIOT Act[215] and,
- The U.S. Foreign Intelligence and Surveillance Act

The USA PATRIOT Act is only one aspect of the problematic landscape regarding privacy that currently exists in the USA. Most of the US safeguards for privacy that have been discussed so far are instantly invalidated when confronted with a much more intrusive (although, interestingly, much less debated) piece of U.S. legislation, the Foreign Intelligence and Surveillance Act (FISA)[216], which provides for special procedures for conducting physical searches and electronic surveillance of individuals allegedly involved in international espionage or terrorism against the United States of America[217].

The landscape that has been displayed above on both coasts of the Atlantic makes imperative the need for an international coordination for the future of IT laws, even those regulating data protection. While the European Data Protection Regulation introduced new safeguards aimed at fur-

---

214 *Id.*

215 United States of America: Uniting and Strengthening America by Providing Appropriate Tools Required to Intercept and Obstruct Terrorism Act of 2001 (USA Patriot Act) [United States of America], Public Law 107-56, 107th Congress, 26 October 2001. For more see Chapter 7.

216 The Foreign Intelligence Surveillance Act of 1978 (FISA), Pub.L. 95–511, 92 Stat. 1783, 50 U.S.C. ch. 36, is a United States federal law. It has been repeatedly amended since the 9/11 attacks.

217 Tridimas, T., & Gutierrez-Fons, J. A., *EU Law, International Law, and Economic Sanctions against Terrorism: The Judiciary in Distress?*, 32 Fordham International Law Journal 660–730 (2008). For more see Chapter 7.

ther reducing the risks of EU citizens' data being handed over to the US or other third countries' governments, concerns are expressed as to whether European authorities will properly address these issues out of fear of not decisively standing up against US authorities[218]. Others point one more danger out: the possibility that European intelligence services may try to circumvent EU law and benefit from the surveillance activities of the U.S. government that has a much wider margin of freedom as it has been demonstrated, in order to obtain information that could not be lawfully collected under European law[219].

As things stand right now, Europeans wishing to enjoy the maximum protection for their online presence, may only achieve that by storing their data exclusively on European cloud computing platforms operated by EU-based service providers. However, except for any setbacks that such a strategy could set on cloud adoption in the EU, it is a viable only for citizens living within the EU. It cannot for work for non-EU residents or EU citizens residing outside the EU, who may ultimately be subject to the laws of the country they live in. Yet, in a global and increasingly connected online world, the EU, as the most influential global legislator on privacy and internet issues, should lead the way and take actual care not only of the privacy of EU citizens but it should pave the path towards the establishment of a more comprehensive framework of international rules when it comes to privacy and data protection. More broadly, the EU needs to take actual steps towards an improved system of internet governance, with more sophisticated models of laws and/or standards which are properly adapted and constantly updated to the latest advancements in cloud computing[220].

g. Can cloud computing be a tipping point for regulating and thinking about privacy in the US or Europe?

Moving towards the concluding observations on how Europe's and USA's legal cultures have evolved through time in relation to the issue of online

---

218 L. Moerel, *Back to basics: when does EU data protection law apply?*, 1 International Data Privacy Law 92–110 (2011.)

219 *Id.*

220 Kristina Irion, *Government Cloud Computing and the Policies of Data Sovereignty*, 4 Policy and Internet 40–71 (2012.)

data privacy, it is time to examine whether up to this point the massive expansion of cloud computing has already initiated any profound processes of change in the two jurisdictions and the way they deal with these issues.

i. Privacy under the effect of the cloud in the US

In the US, the piece of law most relevant to the technological status quo effected by cloud computing is the Stored Communications Act[221]. The privacy protection that a user of cloud services will have the right to enjoy under the Act is currently dependent on the cloud provider's terms of service (ToS) agreement and privacy policy[222]. Actually, whenever the ToS agreement permits to the cloud provider to rely on customer's data in order to determine the contextual advertising it will channel towards him, that cloud service does not qualify as a remote computing service (RCS). Similarly, when the cloud provider in its ToS agreement reserves a general right to access customer's data without setting specific limits for that possibility, this cloud service is also unlikely to qualify as an RCS[223]. It is only when a cloud provider sets expressive limitations to its access to customer's data solely for the purposes of providing computer storage or processing functions that the customer benefits from the Act's RCS provisions, including the protection from compelled disclosure by the government and civil litigants[224].

It becomes evident that the margin for granting protection to a customer's data under the Act is much narrower than that of excluding the said data from protection. However, the consequences of being excluded from the Stored Communications Act privacy protections can be substantially significant for a cloud services user. Experience has shown that the US government have limited restrictions in assessing whether or not they

221 The Stored Communications Act (SCA) (note 31) is a US law that addresses voluntary and compelled disclosure of "stored wire and electronic communications and transactional records" held by third-party internet service providers (ISPs). It was enacted as Title II of the Electronic Communications Privacy Act of 1986 (ECPA).

222 Neil Robinson, Lorenzo Valeri, Jonathan Cave, Tony Starkey, Hans Graux, Sadie Creese & Paul P. Hopkins (note 119).

223 *Id.*

224 *Id.*

have the ability to compel disclosure of a customer's data[225]. A user might try to fight back by revoking a Fourth Amendment privacy right, but such a defense has not prevailed in past cases involving email[226]. These facts suggest that US courts under the current status quo would be unlikely to extend privacy related constitutional protections into the realm of cloud computing. Simultaneously, the only effective limit to the ability to disclose a customer's data to a third party under US law is currently the contractual promises made in the cloud provider's ToS agreement and privacy policy. Unfortunately for users of cloud services, these protections are, as a rule, weak or nonexistent. As a result, cloud providers under the nowadays applicable US law have complete discretion in deciding whether to respond to requests for their customers' data or personal identifying information[227].

As more and more Americans move their personal content to the cloud, a respective upgrade in the privacy regime seems appropriate. There are, however, serious obstacles that would need to be tackled for this new concept of privacy to be made feasible.

ii. Judicial obstacles

Fourth Amendment jurisprudence indicates until today that courts are unlikely to uphold elevated privacy protections for cloud computing users. In the US, courts only rarely act as the initial forum for expanding privacy protections; when they do, it is typically through very reluctant extensions of the Fourth Amendment principles, under the pressing effect of societal or technological change[228]. However, as it has been already demonstrated[229], the Supreme Court has been formulating an ever-narrower view of the Fourth Amendment's provisions and the applicability of them. Lately, the Supreme Court has focused its Fourth Amendment handling on weigh-

225 Susan Freiwald & Patricia Bellia, *The Fourth Amendment Status of Stored E-mail: The Law Professors' Brief in Warshak v. United States* Journal Articles 559–588 (2007.)

226 Neil Robinson, Lorenzo Valeri, Jonathan Cave, Tony Starkey, Hans Graux, Sadie Creese & Paul P. Hopkins (note 119).

227 *Id.*

228 Orin S. Kerr, *The Fourth Amendment and New Technologies: Constitutional Myths and the Case for Caution*, 102 Michigan Law Review 102–183 (2004.)

229 See Chapter 7.

ing the costs and benefits of decisions excluding evidence gathered in breach of the Fourth Amendment and on limiting the range of situations that merit Fourth Amendment protection. Overall, the way the Supreme Court has treated its Fourth Amendment jurisprudence allows for limited hope only as to the chances that it will drastically expand the extent of privacy protections for Internet users[230]. The main argument why it will still be too difficult for such a turn in jurisprudence to happen is that not only would such a shift change the dimensions of the Fourth Amendment's scope but it would also require reassessing core privacy principles, such as the third-party disclosure doctrine[231], that would have extensive repercussions as to how the US treats privacy beyond the digital world.

iii. Legislative obstacles

it is not up to a legal study like this to deal with factors external to the law making and judicial process that could impede (or enhance) evolution of legislature. Nevertheless, a few observations can and should be made as to the legislative and political landscape in the US in which the need for effective regulation of cloud computing has to mature. Although the US Congress has historically been favorable to the calls for enlargement of privacy protections, it is unlikely to lead the way towards expansion of the protective realm in the direction of online privacy[232]. This standstill could possibly be overcome with the right combination of catalysts like political momentum and societal demand. It is beyond the aims of this study to analyze what is the current balance of powers in the US Congress and

---

230 Orin S. Kerr, *The Problem of Perspective in Internet Law*, 91 Georgetown Law Journal 357–405 (2003.)

231 The third-party doctrine is a United States legal theory stipulating that people who voluntarily give information to third parties—such as banks, phone companies, internet service providers (ISPs) etc.—have "no reasonable expectation of privacy." A lack of privacy protection enables the United States government to obtain information from third parties without a legal warrant and without any other formality in compliance with the Fourth Amendment prohibition against search and seizure without probable cause and a judicial search warrant. Libertarians and liberals traditionally call this government activity unjustified spying and a violation of individual and privacy rights. For more, see Orin Kerr, *The Case for the Third-Party Doctrine*, 107 Michigan Law Review 561–601 (2009.)

232 Orin S. Kerr (note 228).

whether this is favorable for online privacy issues or not. However, even if there is societal demand for greater online privacy protections, a certain amount of time is needed before this is observed and realized by elected officials and judges[233]. Unfortunately, the typical age range of members of US Congress and the Judiciary makes it unlikely that they are as responsive as necessary to societal expectations such as those stemming from emerging technologies. Younger populace embrace cloud computing services very fast, but the average age of legislators – as well as that of Justices on the Supreme Court – exposes a noticeable generational gap between law subjects and law makers[234]. It is therefore up to advocates for enhanced online privacy as well as scholars and academia to bridge this gap and convey to legislature the technological state-of-the-art and its implications for individual privacy, which calls for the respective changes or additions in the regulatory status quo.

iv. Societal obstacles

One last obstacle towards US laws adopting a more advanced approach towards online privacy is the changing societal views toward the issue. In general, younger generations have much less concern about online privacy than older generations[235]. This differentiation can to a certain extent be explained by the different ways in which each generation uses the Internet. Older users generally engage into transactional encounters online, such as looking up information from websites, exchanging e-mail, or purchasing goods[236]. On the contrary, users from younger age groups embrace the internet's interconnectivity by engaging in social networking, sharing content, and adopting cloud services[237].

Another important element decisively shaping cloud users' privacy expectations is their growing expectation to receive 'free services' from cloud providers. In fact, especially younger users declare to be comfortable with cloud providers analyzing which websites they visit, what kind

---

233 Susan Freiwald & Patricia Bellia (note 225).

234 *Id.*

235 John G. Palfrey & Urs Gasser, Born digital. Understanding the first generation of digital natives (2010.)

236 Older Adults and Technology Use (2014.)

237 Susan Freiwald & Patricia Bellia (note 225).

of data they store online or other similar data that enable them to deliver targeted advertising[238]. From a market economics perspective, the frequency with which Internet users are willing to expose their online activities or exchange their personal data for free services and content suggests that they assign a low market value to their privacy[239].

h. Europe's combined approach towards the cloud and economic growth

Although the EU has not yet taken serious steps towards analyzing the specific challenges and characteristics of the cloud in order to regulate it, it has already realized its economic significance and the expansive effect it will have on many of the world's economies. This explosive global demand for cloud services, especially in emerging economies, has served as a cornerstone of the European cloud strategy[240]. The European Commission has explicitly addressed the paradox of a growing demand in cloud services as opposed to the slower progress of engineering science in Europe or the lack of a 'cloud-friendly' environment in Europe so that the continent can be at the forefront of global cloud developments. So far, the two main steps taken to amend this situation have been:

- negotiating free trade agreements that contain favorable conditions for EU-based cloud service providers

This method of 'positive conditionality' that the Commission implements in relation to cloud development is not new. It was also utilized by the US in the early 2000s with regard to the regulation of internet service providers (ISPs)[241]. Its reasoning is that third countries that wish to conclude free trade agreements with the European Union are requested to develop a regulatory framework for cloud-related matters that will be in line with Europe's respective regulatory framework so that EU-based cloud service providers can more easily lay foot on those markets.

---

238 William Jeremy Robison, *Free at What Cost? Cloud Computing Privacy Under the Stored Communications Act*, 98 Georgetown Law Journal 1195–1239 (2010.)

239 *Id.*

240 Osvaldo Saldias & Internet Policy Review, Cloud-friendly regulation: The EU's strategy towards emerging economies (2013); Reinhard Posch, *Neue Herausforderungen für eine Informations- und Datensicherungsstrategie*, 2014 Strategie und Sicherheit (2014.)

241 Digital Agenda in the Europe 2020 strategy (2012.)

– deliberations and close contact with key cloud stakeholders

The second pillar of the EU's cloud computing strategy is fostering an intra-European dialogue with key actors of the broader cloud ecosystem[242]. In order to tackle current problems and challenges of cloud computing within the European digital single market, the Commission is fostering several initiatives which aim to bring if in direct contact with key actors of the cloud sector, who through these channels will have the opportunity to express their concerns and propose their ideas for generating solutions to problems or tackling challenges. It remains to be seen, however, to what extent this input from market stakeholders is indeed taken into account in the future handling of the Cloud by the European authorities or not.

i. A close look on how the EU and the US currently handle sensitive consumer data on the cloud. It the current regime adequate and efficient enough?

Before wrapping up this all-inclusive comparison between Europe and the USA and how the two legal cultures currently deal with issues associated or generated out of cloud technologies, as well as how they deal with the cloud itself, one last aspect merits careful presentation: the handling consumer data receive in each of the two legal environments. As individual users are undoubtedly the most powerful driving force behind the cloud's geometric expansion, it is crucial to have a clear picture of how the data generated by this type of users are handled. Answering this question is easier from the EU perspective since the EU Data Protection Regulation contains in itself a precise definition of sensitive data when talking about 'special categories of data' as 'personal data revealing the racial origin, political opinions or religious or other beliefs, as well as personal data on health, sex life or criminal convictions' of natural persons[243]. This definition of special categories of data is, of course, closely connected and affected by the European view that data protection is a fundamental human right. Some EU member states currently include in the term of sensitive data additional categories of personally identifiable data such as informa-

242 European Commission, Unleashing the Potential of Cloud Computing in Europe, available at: http://eur-lex.europa.eu/LexUriServ/LexUriServ.do?uri=COM:2012:0529:FIN:EN:PDF (20 November 2014.)

243 For more see also Chapter 4.

tion about consumers' debts, financial standing, or the payment of welfare benefits[244]. However, this regime is bound to be homogenized once the General Data Protection Regulation enters into full force.

In contrast, there is no clear definition for sensitive data in the United States or one that could serve as an analogous point of reference to the 'special categories' of personal data found in EU legislation. This is reasonable, of course, if one takes into account that, in principle, there is no generally applicable data protection legislation in that legal order. However, a careful analysis of federal privacy legislation in the United States brings forward certain types of consumer data that are entitled to solid data protection[245]; as a result, one could use them as a counter reference to Europe's sensitive data. The most prominent data categories of this nature are:

- data collected by websites that refer to children under the age of thirteen,
- data collected by financial institutions about their customers,
- patient data collected by health care providers and
- data collected by credit reporting agencies about consumers' credit history.

Despite the FTC[246], as the competent agency, not having expressly defined sensitive data, from its practice it can be broadly inferred that the above categories of data are classified under US law as sensitive. At the same time, the FTC also recognizes that whether a particular piece of data is sensitive or not may also depend on certain subjective considerations. Yet, in any case, excluding data related to consumers' protected classifications under discrimination laws from the definition of sensitive data is not uncommon practice. On the contrary, it very well fits the prevalent U.S. view that information privacy law is primarily an instrument aimed at prevent-

---

244 Douwe Korff, EC Study on Implementation of Data Protection Directive 95/46/EC (2008.)

245 Nancy J. King & V. T. Raja, *What Do They Really Know About Me in the Cloud? A Comparative Law Perspective on Protecting Privacy and Security of Sensitive Consumer Data*, 50 Am Bus Law J 413–482 (2013.)

246 The Federal Trade Commission (FTC) is an independent agency of the United States government, founded in 1914 by virtue of the Federal Trade Commission Act. Its principal mission is the promotion of consumer protection and the elimination and prevention of anticompetitive business practices, such as coercive monopoly. In the field of IT, the FTC is mandated with several tasks that make it the US analogous of Europe's Data Protection Authorities.

ing economic harm[247]. This approach is, of course, a juxtaposition from the fundamental human rights approach adopted by EU law, under which consumers are protected from a visibly broader scope of privacy harms.

i. Regulating privacy and security of consumer sensitive data in the cloud; the US current status quo

At present, it could be argued that the cloud computing industry faces limited legal restrictions in the United States, as all activities related to the field are largely permissible or unregulated. This is both a blessing and a curse for the industry. On the one hand, the lack of comprehensive federal legislation that would set minimum requirements regarding the protection of consumers' privacy in the cloud leaves considerable freedom of activity to US cloud businesses[248].

At the same time, the federal laws that define the specific categories of sensitive consumer data that were previously presented, mandate for sensitive data under these four statutes a protection regime analogous to the data protection for sensitive personal data provided for consumers in the EU[249]. However, in the absence of such industry-specific legislation there may be no requirement for businesses offering or using cloud services to guarantee information privacy for consumers' personal data. This leads to the other extreme, where information as crucial as a consumer's name, residence address, e-mail address, mobile phone number, income level, marital status, sex, and race do not qualify as sensitive and, hence, do not receive adequate privacy protection. Of course, before concluding that information privacy management is a matter of unlimited discretion for U.S. cloud businesses, it is important to examine other sources of law that may serve as foundations for privacy and security rights for consumers such as state privacy tort laws and federal or state consumer protection laws[250].

Across several US states there are statutes that require companies to inform consumers in advance about security breaches that may expose consumers' personal data to identity theft or other wrongful uses, despite the

247 Wesley Gee, *Internet Tracking: Stalking or a Necessary Tool for Keeping the Internet Free*, 20 CommLaw Conspectus 223–252 (2011.)

248 Nancy J. King & V. T. Raja (note 245).

249 *Id.*

250 Susan Freiwald & Patricia Bellia (note 225).

lack of a federal data breach notification law[251]. Another source of protection for consumers' privacy rights are state tort laws which may enable consumers to recover their data through the civil litigation process from businesses that misuse them[252]. The applicability of tort law in the field of security for sensitive data is not yet settled; nevertheless, civil lawsuits are increasingly being brought by consumers as a means of redress for such claims[253].

To sum up, although at present there are only few U.S. laws that restrict the growth of cloud computing industry, and the regulatory framework for the cloud heavily relies on contractual agreements between CSPs and their clients or industry self-regulation, issues such as the uncertainty regarding the applicability of the USA Patriot Act and related federal statutes against global CSPs sets legal obstacles to unhindered cross-border provision of cloud service between the United States and the EU.

ii. Regulating privacy and security of consumer sensitive data in the cloud; the EU current status quo

In contrast to the current legal framework in the USA, European rules set high compliance obligations for companies active in the field of cloud computing requiring them to protect the privacy and security of consumers' sensitive data, including such data stored in public cloud facilities. EU laws establish two levels of consumer rights and compliance obligations for businesses dealing with personal data, a basic and a heightened one[254].

On the first level, the EU's Regulation grants to consumers (i.e. data subjects) a number of basic protections with regard to their personal data while it requires data controllers to abide by rules and restrictions with respect to their data processing operations. Additionally, consumers are entitled to receive notification about any data controller that expropriates their data as well as the purposes for which these are being collected or otherwise processed. On an advanced level, increased levels of data protection may also be required under the Regulation. For example, sensitive data

251 Nancy J. King & V. T. Raja (note 245).
252 *Id.*
253 *Id.*
254 *Id.*

that fall within the definition of 'special categories of data'[255] are entitled to increased data protection.

iii. The need for efficient protection of sensitive data also points towards regulatory reform in the cloud

All the above facts point out to the need for a fundamentally different regulatory approach for the cloud, both in Europe and the US. Cloud computing as a generic technology empowering today most variations of the IT economy and applications in the world calls for lawmakers to realize the true extent of the change the introduction of the cloud has signaled for all these areas of human activity[256]. Before drawing some general conclusions, we can now summarize the most important changes or innovations that sensitive data, in particular, call for in the way we will be regulating cloud computing:

– Working out a competent definition for sensitive data on the cloud

Right now, neither U.S. nor EU laws adequately define sensitive consumer data[257]. In the quest for an all-inclusive definition of sensitive data applicable in the global cloud computing industry, each jurisdiction could and should benefit from the other. Future laws governing the cloud should expand regulatory protection of sensitive data in such a way that both goals of encompassing the protection of human rights and avoiding economic and physical harms are effectively pursued. This pluralistic approach would clearly be in better alignment with information systems architecture for the cloud industry, which is largely defiant towards national borders, typically serves clients from every single country and jurisdiction and most often involves the processing and transfer of the personal data of users on a cross-country basis. A competent for current standards definition of sensitive consumer data should aim to prevent both discrimination on the basis of protected classifications as well as serious economic and

255 Andrew Charlesworth (note 185).

256 W. K. Hon, C. Millard & I. Walden, *Who is responsible for 'personal data' in cloud computing? --The cloud of unknowing, Part 2*, 2 International Data Privacy Law 3–18 (2012.)

257 Nancy J. King, V.T. Raja, *What Do They Really Know About Me in the Cloud? A Comparative Law Perspective on Protecting Privacy and Security of Sensitive Consumer Data*, 50 American Business Law Journal 413–482 (2013.)

physical harm[258]. A carefully planned step ahead for both US and EU laws for the cloud would adequately define sensitive consumer data to ensure efficient privacy and security for this kind of data on the cloud. Such a legislation and such a well-articulated definition would support administrative, industry as well as information technology best practices to establish themselves and be decisively mirrored in cloud service agreements thus guaranteeing better protection for customers, particularly since many cloud service agreements are effectively nonnegotiable due to the lack of bargaining power by users[259].

– In the US, moving towards comprehensive cloud computing laws

Even if existing US privacy laws are reformed to adequately clarify issues such as sensitive data and, thus, address the needs and concerns of users and providers of cloud services, they still lack an overall applicable federal information privacy regulation to govern the cloud. It is a historic opportunity for the US to take advantage of the generic nature of cloud computing and work out, for the first time in their legislative history, a robust, federal legislation for cloud computing that will also serve the broader need for a more federal approach on information security and privacy.

– In Europe, producing laws for the cloud that will keep on the continent's tradition of protecting privacy, as a human right, in ways more in line with the technological standards the cloud has established

Europe has an expressed intention of attracting more businesses to invest in cloud infrastructure on its soil, while existing cloud providers also put pressure on Europe to adopt a more business-friendly attitude towards cloud computing. In other words, both sides want the same thing and there has to be found the best way to pursue it. This could be achieved if Europe adopts a more receptive attitude towards technology solutions that could permit it to produce laws regulating the broader landscape the cloud has set. There are already, for instance, advancements in technology[260] that achieve anonymity of data in the cloud. These tools could be the implementing means of future cloud computing laws that would continue to serve Europe's long-held and much-cherished tradition of preserving pri-

258 J. Goldring, *Globalisation, National Sovereignty and the Harmonisation of Laws*, 3 Uniform Law Review – Revue de droit uniforme 435–451 (1998.)

259 Nancy J. King & V. T. Raja (note 245).

260 Response to the UK Ministry of Justice's Call for Evidence on the European Commission's Data Protection Proposals (2012.)

vacy as a fundamental right and, at the same time, make the EU area a much more favorable market for doing cloud business in.

CHAPTER 4. An introduction to the definition of cloud computing under EU law and the challenges it poses

a. Introduction – scope of this chapter

According to European Commission's White Paper on the cloud: "'Cloud computing' in simplified terms can be understood as the storing, processing and use of data on remotely located computers accessed over the internet. This means that users can command almost unlimited computing power on demand, that they do not have to make major capital investments to fulfil their needs and that they can get to their data from anywhere with an internet connection."[261]

Based on this definition, the Commission had recognized back in 2012 certain key areas where regulatory actions were needed: Fragmentation of the digital single market due to differing national legal frameworks and uncertainties over applicable law; digital content and data location, which ranked highest amongst the concerns of potential cloud computing adopters and providers; problems with contracts related to worries over data access and portability; change control and ownership of the data[262]. The current labyrinth of standards generates confusion by, on one hand, a proliferation of standards and on the other hand, a lack of certainty as to which standards provide adequate levels of interoperability of data formats to permit portability.

In its Digital Agenda for Europe[263], the Commission set itself the objectives to achieve the digital single market, enhance interoperability and standards, strengthen online trust and security, simplify copyright clearance, management and cross-border licensing, goals that have gained importance as a result of the prevalence of cloud computing as the standard technology in the field of data processing.

---

261 European Commission (note 242). (last accessed on: 01/18/2017.)

262 *Id.*

263 (note 241).

Adopting the definition of cloud computing which the US National Institute of Standards and Technology (NIST) released in its Special Publication SP 800-145 in September 2011[264], European Commission's Art. 29 Working Party brought out in 2012 a cornerstone document for the treatment of cloud computing in Europe, usually quoted as the 'Sopot Memorandum'[265]. In that paper, Art. 29 WP highlighted the most important issues that the cloud poses for European regulators, which include[266]:

- there is not yet an international agreement on common terminology;
- the development of the technology is still in progress making unclear the precise landscape that needs to be regulated;
- enormous amounts of data are being accumulated and concentrated posing even more challenges that stem from cloud technologies which facilitate these processes;
- cloud technology is boundless and transboundary;
- data processing has become genuinely global;
- transparency is lacking with respect to cloud service provider processes, procedures and practices, including whether or not cloud service providers sub-contract any of the processing and if so, what their respective processes, procedures and practices are;
- this lack of transparency makes it difficult to conduct a proper risk assessment;
- this lack of transparency also makes it more difficult to enforce rules regarding data protection;
- cloud service providers are under great pressure to quickly capitalize significant investment costs;
- cloud customers are under increasing pressure to reduce costs, including those of their data processing; and
- to keep low prices cloud service providers are more likely to offer standard terms and conditions.

264 Peter Mell & Timothy Grance (note 63).

265 International Working Group on Data Protection in Telecommunications, Working Paper on Cloud Computing – Privacy and data protection issues. "Sopot Memorandum", available at: http://ec.europa.eu/justice/data-protection/article-29/documentation/opinion-recommendation/index_en.htm#h2-3 (3 February 2015.)

266 *Id.*

In the same document, Art. 29 WP laid down the major risks associated to the surge of cloud computing[267]:

- breaches of information security such as breaches of confidentiality, integrity or availability of (personal) data that go unnoticed by the controller;
- data being transferred to jurisdictions that do not provide adequate data protection;
- acts in violation of laws and principles for privacy and data protection;
- the controller accepting standard terms and conditions that give the cloud service provider too much leeway, including the possibility that the cloud service provider may process data in a way that contradicts the controller's instructions;
- cloud service providers or their subcontractors using the controllers' data for their own purposes without the controllers' knowledge or permission;
- accountability and responsibility seemingly fading or disappearing in a chain of subcontractors;
- the controller losing control of the data and data processing;
- the controller or its trusted third party (e.g. auditor) being unable to properly monitor the cloud service provider;
- data protection authorities being precluded from properly supervising the processing of personal data by the controller and the cloud service provider; and
- the controller relying on unfounded trust in the absence of insight and monitoring, thereby potentially contravening the data protection legislation in force in the country of establishment.

In light of the above, the aim of this chapter is to present an overview of how cloud computing has been progressively defined under EU law as well as put together the most important critique and arguments regarding the efficiency of the Union's latest cornerstone regulation in the wider area of IT law, i.e. the General Data Protection Regulation. Finally, in the last sections of the chapter analysis will be focused on how a heavily cloud-based IT landscape looks like (or is expected to look like, in a few years' time). This analysis will then serve, along with findings from following chapters, to determine the rate at which existing IT laws applicable when it comes to cloud regulation have achieved the required level of maturity

267 *Id.*

and efficacy with regard to the subject matter they are supposed to settle and how they should evolve in the future.

b. The most important policy views on aspects of cloud computing brought out so far and why they are not yet sufficient

During the last decade, since the cloud started to rapidly gain ground as a data handling technology, actors in the EU and the US market with a direct or indirect interest in the relevant fields have formulated a number of policy manifestos that contain the main current views on the cloud and how it should be dealt with from a regulatory perspective. By summarizing the main principles of these views one can then more easily point out the loopholes in the way the cloud has been treated so far by regulators[268].

Purpose limitation used to be a key concept in the EU's data privacy legislation[269] during the DPD era, which largely served as the basis for any regulatory approach for cloud computing. In particular, purpose limitation protected data subjects[270] by setting limits on how controllers[271] were able to use their personal data[272]. The concept of purpose limitation was built on two main ideas: personal data had to be collected for 'speci-

268 Article 29 Working Party, Opinion 03/2013 on purpose limitation, available at: http://ec.europa.eu/justice/data-protection/article-29/documentation/opinion-recommendation/index_en.htm (3 February 2015.)

269 Hunton Privacy Blog, Article 29 Working Party Clarifies Purpose Limitation Principle; Opines on Big and Open Data, available at: https://www.huntonprivacyblog.com/2013/04/09/article-29-working-party-clarifies-purpose-limitation-principle-opines-on-big-and-open-data/ (5 November 2015.)

270 By 'data subject' in the context of IT and privacy law reference is made to an individual entity who is the subject of personal data.

271 A 'controller' is "the natural or legal person, public authority, agency or other body which, alone or jointly with others, determines the purposes and means of the processing of personal data". Definition as it appears in Regulation (EU) 2016/679 (GDPR) (note 25).

272 'Personal data' is any information relating to an identified or identifiable natural person ('data subject'); an identifiable natural person is one who can be identified, directly or indirectly, in particular by reference to an identifier such as a name, an identification number, location data, an online identifier or to one or more factors specific to the physical, physiological, genetic, mental, economic, cultural or social identity of that natural person. Definition as it appears in Regulation (EU) 2016/679 (GDPR) (note 25).

fied, explicit and legitimate'[273] purposes (purpose specification) and could not be 'further processed in a way incompatible'[274] with those purposes (compatible use). It should be noted that further processing for a different purpose does not necessarily mean that there is a breach of the purpose limitation: compatibility is assessed on a case-by-case basis.

This Art. 29 WP Opinion was meant to apply to all kinds of data transfers, i.e. also to those effected through the use of cloud computing technologies. Given that, so far, European regulators tend to approach the task of regulating the cloud through the prism of already existing legislation for specific uses of it, such as data transfers, several elements of the practical application of the purpose limitation principle lead to a need for an in-depth analysis of this concept, which, after all, decisively defined EU data protection law:

- The way privacy limitation has been implemented in Member States has led to a diversity of interpretations over it[275]. If we are to keep applying it in data transfer related legislations in the future, a clear common understanding of the concept will better ensure its effective application – and that would be, of course, in the interest of all concerned.
- The context of processing activities needs also to be updated and amended to reflect today's standards[276]. The development of new technologies, such as cloud computing, results in increasingly more data being available, for a far wider diversity of purposes.
- Apart from the traditional concept of data transfer, i.e. transferring data between two points of a linear or at least insulated network, there are many more current trends for reuse of data by the private sector ('big data') but also 'open data' and 'data sharing' initiatives proposed by many governments, including EU legislative initiatives[277]. These practices which have been made feasible and are clearly based on the newest technologies in data transfers are of particular relevance and their repercussions need to be meticulously analyzed so that any future legislation can provide realistic answers for them.

273 Article 29 Working Party (note 268).

274 *Id.*

275 Neil Robinson, Hans Graux, Maarten Botterman & Lorenzo Valeri, RAND Europe: Review of the European Data Protection Directive, available at: http://www.rand.org/pubs/technical_reports/TR710.html (13 February 2015.)

276 Borivoje Furht & Armando Escalante, Handbook of cloud computing (2010.)

277 Hunton Privacy Blog (note 269).; European Commission (note 242).

As it has already been pointed out the 'purpose limitation' principle does not stop to the explicitly defined purposes for which a set of given data are collected, transferred or stored but goes one step further to assess also how compatible are the actual uses effected with a particular set of data compared to the stated ones at the moment of collection.

The framework for the compatibility assessment which answers whether uses of data other than the ones stated at the moment of collection are permissible or not is based on the notion of 'further processing'. A generally acknowledged working definition for this notion is: "...any processing following collection, whether for the purposes initially specified or for any additional purposes, must be considered 'further processing' and must thus meet the requirement of compatibility."[278] From here comes another term that needs to be defined, i.e. that of '(in)compatibility'. This notion is understood to suggest that "the fact that the further processing is for a different purpose does not necessarily mean that it is automatically incompatible: this needs to be assessed on a case-by-case basis."[279] A compatibility assessment can be either a purely formal or a substantive one[280]:

- A formal assessment is suggested that it should compare the purposes that were initially provided, usually in writing, by the data controller with any further uses to find out whether these uses were covered by the initially stated purposes (explicitly or implicitly).
- A substantive assessment should go beyond formal statements to identify both the new and the original purpose, taking into account the way they are (or should be) understood, depending on the context and other factors.

When conducting a compatibility assessment several key factors are suggested to be considered, namely[281]:

- the relationship between the purposes for which the data had been originally collected and the purposes of further processing
- the context in which the data had been collected and the reasonable expectations of the data subjects as to the further use of their data that they agreed to submit to the controller for collection

278 Neil Robinson, Hans Graux, Maarten Botterman & Lorenzo Valeri (note 275).
279 *Id.*
280 Siani Pearson & George Yee, Privacy and security for cloud computing (2013.)
281 *Id.*

- the nature of the data and the impact of the further processing on the data subjects
- the safeguards applied by the controller to ensure fair processing and to prevent any undue impact on the data subjects.

The newly arriving GDPR tried to settle the above frictions by introducing the 'legitimate interest' concept[282], which tries to make use and processing of data more flexible and pragmatic in light of the technological standards of today by recognizing wider margins of differentiation in the stated purpose for which data are collected between the time of their collection and the time the processing takes place, without, however, going as far as allowing processing of data for purposes totally alien to those at the time of their collection[283]. Despite the fact that this latest regulatory device is indeed heralded by many as a facilitator for the big data and IoT economy[284], there are just as many scholars who point out to the risk that an arbitrary interpretation of the 'legitimate interest' concept may jeopardize

282 Regulation (EU) 2016/679 (GDPR) (note 25); in particular, perambulatory clause no. 47, which reads: "The legitimate interests of a controller, including those of a controller to which the personal data may be disclosed, or of a third party, may provide a legal basis for processing, provided that the interests or the fundamental rights and freedoms of the data subject are not overriding, taking into consideration the reasonable expectations of data subjects based on their relationship with the controller. Such legitimate interest could exist for example where there is a relevant and appropriate relationship between the data subject and the controller in situations such as where the data subject is a client or in the service of the controller. At any rate the existence of a legitimate interest would need careful assessment including whether a data subject can reasonably expect at the time and in the context of the collection of the personal data that processing for that purpose may take place..."; also, perambulatory clauses 48, 49 and 50, which aims to retain some of the limitations (i.e. protections) offered to data subjects with the old regime of the DPD by stating: "…such transmission in the legitimate interest of the controller or further processing of personal data should be prohibited if the processing is not compatible with a legal, professional or other binding obligation of secrecy.".

283 This precarious balance can be observed throughout GDPR's operative clauses regarding the 'legitimate interest' ground, i.e.: Art. 1(f) ["…processing is necessary for the purposes of the legitimate interests pursued by the controller or by a third party, except where such interests are overridden by the interests or fundamental rights and freedoms of the data subject which require protection of personal data, in particular where the data subject is a child."], art. 13, para. 2(d), art. 35, para. 7(a), to name a few; Regulation (EU) 2016/679 (GDPR) (note 25).

284 Viktor Mayer-Schonberger & Yann Padova, *Regime Change: Enabling Big Data through Europe*, XVII The Columbia Science & Technology Law Review 315–

the protection granted so far to data subjects or, at least, it may cause a lot of confusion before the transit from the old to the new regime is completed[285]. It goes without saying that in the meantime technological advancement may have again bypassed regulatory prudence causing a vicious circle, the exit of which can only be achieved if cloud computing regulation stops being so ad-hoc formulated and takes a more technologically abstract yet intra-jurisdictionally systematic direction. In other words, cloud computing regulation should not serve as a cure to technological implementations that may go wrong but should change its focus on making sure that the margin for accidents from cloud-enabled technological applications (presently known or even forthcoming ones) is limited to the biggest extent possible.

c. The European Data Protection Directive 95/46/EC; an assessment of its effects on the prevalent views about data protection and related IT technologies; are things different under the GDPR?

In April 2016, the European Parliament and the Council finally reached a conclusion after several years of consultations and negotiations and adopted the General Data Protection Regulation, which is set to become, as of 2018 when it enters into force, Europe's law of reference regarding a wide range of privacy and IT affairs. However, prior to the GDPR, Europe had been handling these affairs based on its world-famous Data Protection Directive or the DPD, as it is often quoted. And despite the fact that the DPD

---

335 (2016); W. Gregory Voss, *European Union Data Privacy Law Developments*, 70 Business Lawyer 253–260 (2014/2015.)

285 Dutch Lawyers ed., Privacy for the Homo Digitalis. Proposal for a New Regulatory Framework for Data Protection in the Light of Big Data and the Internet of Things (2016); Olof Nyrén, Magnus Stenbeck & Henrik Grönberg, *The European Parliament proposal for the new EU General Data Protection Regulation may severely restrict European epidemiological research*, 29 European Journal of Epidemiology 227–230 (2014); Menno Mostert, Annelien L. Bredenoord, Biesaart, Monique C I H & Delden, Johannes J M van, *Big Data in medical research and EU data protection law. Challenges to the consent or anonymise approach*, 24 European Journal of Human Genetics 956–960 (2016); Tobias Bräutigam, The Land of Confusion. International Data Transfers between Schrems and the GDPR; Alexander Roßnagel ed., Datenschutzaufsicht nach der EU-Datenschutz-Grundverordnung. Neue Aufgaben und Befugnisse der Aufsichtsbehörden (2017.)

will soon cease to apply, its remarkable lifespan makes it a timelessly significant piece of law, whose functions and effects merit careful analysis in the context of a study on cloud computing regulation.

To begin with, after two decades of continuous application, one could generally say that the impact of the DPD on European perceptions of data protection principles has been largely positive. The Directive can fairly be credited for achieving to harmonize and professionalize a core body of data protection principles within Europe, even if implementation still varies from one Member State to the other. The Directive is also generally recognized as a piece of law that created one of the world's leading paradigms for privacy protection, which has served as an inspiration to legal regimes outside Europe. According to the opinions of many academics but also as statistical data suggests[286], EU's DPD has been the reference for the production of data protection legislation by most third countries, apart from the United States and China that have their very own data protection legal cultures.

However, despite this substantially positive impact and general admittance of the soundness of principles behind the Directive, certain aspects have also received considerable criticism which, for the most part, remains relevant even after the adoption of the GDPR given the dynamism with which cloud computing technology continues to evolve. The main objections voiced from within the EU have often focused on the formalities imposed by the Directive (or by its national transpositions across Member States), the economic costs of compliance to the procedures it prescribes and the unequal enforcement from one EU country to another. Compliance costs largely remain an issue under the GDPR as well, especially considering the introduction of the data protection officer as an essential role in the organigram of a great deal of entities dealing with personal data. The unequal enforcement is an issue that is supposed to be resolved when a piece of EU law is elevated from the status of a Directive to that of a Regulation[287]. However, there are numerous voices warning of the reservations the GDPR makes for national regulators, which can be exploited and undermine equal implementation across all EU member states[288]. Outside Europe, many data protection competent organizations tend to perceive the European regulations as somewhat paternalistic towards the respective

286 Neil Robinson, Hans Graux, Maarten Botterman & Lorenzo Valeri (note 275).

287 P. P. Craig & G. de Búrca, EU law. Text, cases, and materials (2015.)

288 Jiahong Chen (note 24).

laws of third country legal orders or other comparably valid data protection approaches.

One of the most fervently debated points for the DPD was its mechanism for determining and assigning accountability[289]. Overall, it is extremely difficult to infer or even predict how public and private sector bodies that act as data controllers intend to use personal information in the future[290]. Therefore, accountability provisions must be flexible enough to apply in different cases and suit the context in which personal data is used on each occasion. This may be reasonably understood as implying that accountability measures for data controllers with economic drives in mind might need to be different from those for the public sector or individuals, as accountability imposable via economic sanctions can expectedly be more effective in situations where the incentive for personal data processing was generated by pursuance of direct economic benefit. Under the GDPR a step is certainly made towards more efficient accountability allocation not only with economic criteria in mind but also with consideration of the various ways in which data are processed and not just of the entities they run the processing and how financially robust or weak they are, e.g. the possibility to allocate accountability even to algorithms enacting data processing[291]. Nevertheless, the problem of technology-bound regulation persists and further, bolder moves towards more generic rules are necessary.

Just as there have been several pioneering points in the DPD, over the two decades that it has been in force, scholarly opinion and interested bodies have also pointed out certain weaknesses of the Data Protection Directive. The most important ones, which have actually been aggravated with the advancement of new technologies like cloud computing and which pay witness to the need for IT regulation to take the decisive step and more from a perspective anchored to current applications of cloud computing technology to a more generic one that will take into account what the cloud is capable of doing beyond what it is currently doing, were:

- The link between the concept of personal data and the real risks related to data handling, which is no longer clear enough[292]. The DPD was

289 Borivoje Furht & Armando Escalante (note 276).
290 European Commission (note 242).
291 D. Hofman, Duranti L. & E. How (note 4).
292 Siani Pearson & George Yee (note 280).

conceptualized in an era of plainer, more linear data transfers[293]; today's cloud applications and networks, which are characterized by lack of geographical borders, dynamic handling of resources and a true global nature, have fundamentally altered the standards regarding data handling. The risks that data face today are more complicated and multi-layered, just as more multi-layered are the cloud systems used to handle it.

- The application scope of the DPD largely depended on whether or not the data processed can be defined as "personal"[294]. In fact, provisions of the Data Protection Directive set a 'take it or leave it' setting regarding applicability of what they prescribe to each and every collection of data: there is no room for "more or less personal" data (and, respectively, "more or less protection" of them). However, today's economy has already facilitated the emergence of different types of data, such as anonymous or anonymized big data, data related to state and governance etc.[295]. For these subdivisions of data, the DPD did not provide adequate answers anymore and understandably so given that these data species are products of human activity much more recent than the times the DPD was drafted. As it was just pointed out, the GDPR contains specific provisions for these new typifications of data, yet the issue of excessive anchoring to the current state-of-the-art instead of focusing on technological feasibilities as well persists.
- DPD's measures aimed at ensuring transparency of data processing through better information and notification of data regulators had become inconsistent and ineffective in today's data processing landscape[296]. The privacy policies provisioned by the DPD were no longer matching average data practice. The majority of data handling actions are nowadays carried out by plain consumers, yet the processes prescribed to make these actions secure were highly complex, addressed primarily to law professionals and not average individual users who, nevertheless, should have a clear idea of protective measures in effect[297]. As these non-expert individuals are the direct perpetrators of

293 Neil Robinson, Hans Graux, Maarten Botterman & Lorenzo Valeri (note 275).
294 *Id.*
295 Christopher Kuner, Transborder Data Flows and Data Privacy Law (2013.)
296 European Commission (note 242).
297 International Working Group on Data Protection in Telecommunications (note 265).

such a significant amount of data processing, they do need to be able to easily comprehend the protective measures which they need to apply or which are in place to protect them. This unanimity in prescribed privacy policies does not really enhance market differentiation, given its stiff, all-or-nothing nature, while it can also be reasonably argued that it hinders fair competition and consumer choice as it sets up very specific standards for market entry to aspiring new service providers. The notification mechanism that the DPD had foreseen was of an unclear purpose[298]: there were as many as 20 different notification processes, and an equally significant variety of exemption rules; at the same time, much of the process was carried out through paperwork or via an awful load of reporting platforms, which are totally incompatible with the rapidness and efficiency that cloud technologies permit today in all data handling processes[299].

- The rules on data export and transfer to third countries, as they were prescribed in the DPD, are nowadays outmoded and out of line with the technological status quo[300]. First of all, the definition of 'third countries' is perceived as outmoded in light of the fact that technological facilities are no longer restricted within the geographical borders of particular countries, let alone within the geographical borders where a service provider has its headquarters. This, in turn, had caused even more complexities as notions like the 'adequacy of countries' is no longer relevant to business realities or data protection, given that the business or the data processing is not carried out necessarily within one and only country anymore. Last but not least, regulation in some other countries is generally admitted to be even stronger than in the EU; however, given the DPD's stiff criteria in its adequacy mechanism (but also, due to other, mainly political or bilateral reasons) these countries were still, till the very last days of DPD's applicability, not recognized as adequate.
- The tools providing for transfer of data to third countries were cumbersome[301], as it has already been pointed out. At the same time, the length of time and effort required to get Standard Contractual Clauses, Model Contracts or Binding Corporate Rules approved was excessive

298 Neil Robinson, Hans Graux, Maarten Botterman & Lorenzo Valeri (note 275).
299 Christopher Kuner (note 295).
300 Borivoje Furht & Armando Escalante (note 276).
301 Neil Robinson, Hans Graux, Maarten Botterman & Lorenzo Valeri (note 275).

and unrealistic in light of the fast pace at which data handling is carried out via cloud systems today.

- It is beyond the purposes of this paper to examine weaknesses of the current regime that are rooted in factors such as the poor coordination between the Member States, the role of DPAs in accountability and enforcement of the provisions or the uneven implementation of enforcement across Member States or the different criteria for imposing sanctions. However, these too were fair points of criticism against the DPD which should not fail our attention.
- Last but not least, the DPD regime was heavily criticized towards the end of its era on the definition of entities involved in processing and managing personal data it contains as being simplistic and static[302]. Genuinely globalized data transfers[303] and increased re-use of personal data have effectively rendered outmoded the static definitions of data controller and processor of the DPD, calling for a fundamentally new regulatory framework.

As it will be argued immediately after, the GDPR dealt with a fair amount of these shortcomings and criticisms. However, the regulatory challenges posed by cloud computing are from definitively settled with the new Regulation and on the course of this analysis ideas and solutions will be put forward that will hopefully permit a more wholesome take on cloud computing and overall IT regulation in the near future.

d. Focus on the General Data Protection Regulation: is the European Union's brand new law already insufficient to effectively regulate the cloud?

An historical overview on the most important legal texts that have shaped the way EU law is treating the cloud phenomenon today would not be complete without a conclusive reference and analysis on the newly voted and impedingly binding upon all EU Member States General Data Protection Regulation. The GDPR has been adopted recently by the European Union and is expected, as of 2018, to replace the Data Protection Directive. This brand-new piece of EU law deals with all IT applications involving processing of personal data that used to be regulated by way of the

302 *Id.*
303 Christopher Kuner (note 295).

provisions of the DPD and it is the fruit of yearlong negotiations and consultation processes. Therefore, one would reasonably expect that during the preparatory phase for this new law the particularities of the cloud computing phenomenon had been well taken into consideration and that its provisions are structured in such a way that they can tackle all sorts of legal challenges posed by the cloud. True as that may be – and indeed it is not the intention of this study to argue that the GDPR is of little use before it even enters into force – the overall regulatory framework of EU law in the field of IT law remains incomplete. As it will be argued and thoroughly analyzed at a later stage of this paper[304], the main reason for that is the fact that so far IT laws insist on focusing and regulating applications made possible thanks to cloud technologies but not the cloud phenomenon itself. In other words, all the laws that we currently have on our disposal to provide solutions caused by the IT applications that we are using are absolutely useful and welcome but, as long as we continue to produce or update them having the end cloud-enabled applications that exist on the market in mind, they will just be specialized laws. By 'specialized laws' reference is made to the typification of technology-specific laws, which is of paramount importance in the discipline of IT law[305]. Although it extends beyond the scope of this study to analyze under what criteria a piece of IT legislation or regulatory principle classifies as a technology-specific or technology-generic one, the aim of this project is to propose the methodology with which regulators should work to complement the frameworks of their jurisdictions with basic principles on cloud computing of a technology-generic nature.

304 For more see Chapters 8, 9 and 10.

305 For a more thorough introduction on the issue of technology-specific vs. technology-generic IT laws refer to: Xenofon Kontargyris, From effective to efficient regulation of ICT: time to build the backbone of information technology legislation, available at: http://www.juwiss.de/66-2016/. In addition, for more extensive analysis on the issue look in: V. Sharma, Information Technology Law and Practice (2011); N. Cox, Technology and Legal Systems (2016); Jonathan B. Wiener, *The regulation of technology, and the technology of regulation*, 26 Technology in Society 483–500 (2004); R. Brownsword, E. Scotford & K. Yeung, The Oxford Handbook of Law, Regulation and Technology (2017); S. Brenner, Law in an Era of Smart Technology (2007.)

i. Does the GDPR set up a truly universal legal framework for data transfer law?

For starters, it is worth dedicating some attention on the GDPR and discuss some of its inherent deficiencies or failings, which may even undermine its ability to provide for a very long time working solutions to the well-known issues of privacy and security in the field of data transfers, which is its natural field of application anyway. One of the primary points of concern with regard to the efficiency and longevity of the GDPR is the way its makers chose to deal with the issue of territoriality as far as applicable law is concerned. Actually, the Regulation follows a similar pattern to the one implemented by the DPD on this issue; however, unlike the Directive, the issue of applicable national law is no longer addressed at all[306]. On the contrary, the Regulation explicitly permits Member States to deviate from its default rules on a series of specific matters, certain among which have the potential to trigger serious problems concerning the applicability of national data protection laws. What is worse, these potential conflicts of law may be further exacerbated by the tendency of Member State laws to exploit this possibility of unilateral scope definition in incompatible ways, are bound to create legal uncertainties to data subjects, data controllers and data protection authorities[307]. Several scholars are putting forward the idea of resorting to private international law for resolving such conflicts. Nonetheless, handy as it may come in certain cases, private international law can only play a very limited role in this respect due to the unique and bindingly structured nature and objectives of EU data protection legislation. It goes without saying that uncertainties posed by this issue of silence on the topic of territoriality will eventually be clarified by the new European Data Protection Board or the CJEU, but some difficulties are nevertheless bound to persist.

Prima facie, the fact that the GDPR does not contain any reference regarding the relationship between EU and national legislations should sound perfectly reasonable; after all, a Regulation is precisely meant to have direct, universal, and consistent binding force throughout the EU[308]. According to the letter of EU constitutional law, if perfectly implemented,

306 Jiahong Chen (note 24).

307 Ibrahim Hasan, *New EU data protection regulation* Law Society Gazette (2016); Alexander Roßnagel ed. (note 285).

308 P. P. Craig & G. de Búrca (note 287).

the GDPR should lead to a data protection legal framework that is unanimously applied across all Member States, at least in principle. Consequently, the issue of determining applicable national law would no longer exist as the Regulation would be considered the only valid law on the matter in all EU and EEA jurisdictions. It goes without saying that this was the intention of those that drafted the GDPR and, taking this into account, it appears to be beyond necessary to have provisions on conflict of laws, since the main is let only one law take over anyway. This is most likely why the question of applicable national law no longer shows up in the Regulation and no such reference is to be found. But the question remains whether this EU-wide landscape will indeed be achieved.

In reality, early analysis and review of the provisions of the GDPR suggest that there are at least two areas where national data protection laws will remain relevant even after the Regulation's entry into force. Firstly, the Regulation does not prevent Member States from enacting national provisions with regard to particular issues that are unspecified by the GDPR itself. The most common reason why such issues are not explicitly regulated in the text of the Regulation is the fact that, in relation to several topics, the GDPR has maintained the letter and text of the DPD; although the room for national 'originality' will be narrower due to the binding force of the Regulation compared to the Directive, as long as these issues remain vague, nothing can be taken for granted[309].

Secondly, apart from the grey areas where there is silence from the Regulation on specific matters in the way it was just explained, there are some other issues on which, even more importantly, the Regulation explicitly permits Member States to decide whether they wish to deviate from its own provisions on certain aspects. In particular, Recital 8 of the GDPR reads: 'Regarding the processing of personal data for compliance with a legal obligation, for the performance of a task carried out in the public interest or in the exercise of official authority vested in the controller, Member States should be allowed to maintain or introduce national provisions to further specify the application of the rules of this Regulation...

309 An extensive analysis of all concepts and ideas in the field of data protection law that are even somewhat differently defined across different national EU laws can be found in: European Commission, Working Paper No. 2: Data protection laws in the EU: The difficulties in meeting the challenges posed by global social and technical developments (2010.)

This Regulation also provides a margin of manoeuvre for Member States to specify its rules, including for the processing of sensitive data...'[310]

This excerpt reflects then in the provisions of Article 6(1) [in particular, points (c) and (e)] and Article 9 of the operative part of the GDPR. Article 6(1) is where the legal grounds on which processing of personal data can be legitimized are stipulated. Point (c) provides that processing is considered legal if it 'is necessary for compliance with a legal obligation to which the controller is subject'[311]. In the same spirit, point (e) permits processing that 'is necessary for the performance of a task carried out in the public interest or in the exercise of official authority vested in the controller'[312]. Further down, in Article 6(3) the GDPR elaborates that the two previous legal bases must be provided for by either 'Union law' or 'Member State law to which the controller is subject'[313]. As far as Article 9 is concerned, the GDPR therein attempts to set a higher threshold for the processing of sensitive data by imposing a prohibition on operations over these categories of personal data, unless one of the exceptions it stipulates applies[314]. In similarity to what happens in Article 6(1), this provision also gives Member States a sideway regarding a few matters, as it can be verified by reading its text. Each of these provisions could potentially set fertile ground for a conflict of laws between two or more Member States.

ii. What does the spirit of GDPR tell us about the longevity of the current overall EU data protection regime?

It is admittedly a bit early to bring out strong verdicts on how good or bad the GDPR will turn out to be as a piece of legislation. However, while waiting for the new law to enter into force and start producing real regulatory output so that we can evaluate it as positive and efficient or negative and insufficient, we can already draw certain conclusions regarding the dynamism and rejuvenation that this major uplift of EU data protection law, which has been attempted with the adoption of the GDPR, does indeed carry. And, in this context, it has to be pointed out that the GDPR is

310 Regulation (EU) 2016/679 (GDPR), Recital 8 (note 25).
311 Id,, art 6(1)(c) (note 25).
312 Id,, art 6(1)(e) (note 25).
313 Id,, art 6(3) (note 25).
314 Id,, art 9 (note 25).

expected to achieve very little with regard to reviving the long-stagnated data protection regime of Europe. This is so due to the fact that the three main aims that the GRDR sets for itself are based on unrealistic assumptions[315].

The first wrongful impression is the persistent one, at least in Europe, that data protection law can offer to individuals actual control over their data, which it cannot[316]. The second is the popular belief that the recent reform has managed to simplify the law, while in fact it has only made compliance even more complex. And last but not least, comes the assumption that data protection law should be comprehensive, while, as it has also been previously discussed, data protection is an issue raised by specific IT end applications only and, therefore, it can only provide footing for technology-specific legislation. We cannot stretch data protection laws to regulate every single issue raised by IT as a whole, because then we drain the originality out of it causing only confusion and legal uncertainty. In detail:

– Shortcoming no. 1: too much obsession with data self-determination

Although data protection is in no way synonymous with the unequivocal ability to decide alone on the destiny of any kind of data referring directly or indirectly to you, in European legal thinking and practice the two concepts have persistently been brought forward as concurrent. 'Informational self-determination' is the most widely-used term to describe the notion that people should be able to exercise control over what happens with their personal data[317]. This concept implies, on the one hand, that individuals' free and informed consent is an important element towards legitimizing data processing, and, second, that individuals have various and very pluralistic in content rights by which they can exercise control over the data, such as rights to correction or erasure.

Viewed through the prism of today's technological status quo, the idea of consent is largely a fallacy[318]. Yes, consent may be considered within a great number of contexts as a typical way for individual data owners to fa-

315 B.-J. Koops, *The trouble with European data protection law*, 4 International Data Privacy Law 250–261 (2014.)

316 See also Chapter 3.

317 W. K. Hon, C. Millard & I. Walden (note 119); Steffen Kroschwald ed., Informationelle Selbstbestimmung in der Cloud. Datenschutzrechtliche Bewertung und Gestaltung des Cloud Computing aus dem Blickwinkel des Mittelstands (2016.)

318 See also Chapters 2 and 8.

cilitate or block data processing; but in light of today's status quo, this is now largely theoretical and with little practical meaning, if any at all.

For the greatest number of services where personal data are involved, often, there is little room for choice: if you want to use a service, you have to comply with the technical conditions its maker or provider has built it upon — which may well entail giving in certain personal data. Otherwise, access will be simply denied, not because the specific service provider is not interested in profit or increasing the market of their service but because the service simply cannot work otherwise[319]. In addition, it needs to be pointed out that, while it gets more and more popular to work on ever more simplified ways for IT applications users to express consent, this works to the detriment of meaningful consent. The fact that a user of a data-related service ticks a box next to a statement of consent after having viewed some brief and simplified imagery roughly describing the kind of consent they are about to give does not mean, of course, that they have sincere knowledge over the kind of permission they are giving[320].

What is more, technological reality of the 21st century tends to erode or progressively invalidate any giving of consent. Even if a data owner expressly permitted certain uses of their information at some point, technological practices such as databases, profiling, and Big Data make informational self-determination all the more elusive[321].

Last but not least, even if we accept that informational self-determination can function effectively in the context of private relationships and applications or services – and to a very significant degree, it does function – it works poorly or it is not even supposed to apply in many cases when it comes to citizen–government affairs[322]. Citizens exercising control over the fate of their personal data, which is what informational self-determination is all about, contrasts with the character of many data-driven applications from the public sector[323].

---

319 Solon Barocas & Helen Nissenbaum eds., On Notice: The Trouble with Notice and Consent (2009); Alexander Roßnagel ed. (note 285).

320 Solon Barocas & Helen Nissenbaum eds. (note 319).

321 Viktor Mayer-Schönberger & Kenneth Cukier, Big data. A revolution that will transform how we live, work, and think (2013.)

322 A. Froomkin, *Of Governments and Governance*, 14 Berkeley Technology Law Journal 618–633 (1999.)

323 Kristina Irion (note 220).

- Shortcoming no. 2: taking controllers' due diligence too much for granted

The current data protection regime not only relies too much on user permission, but also on the assumption that data controllers are duly fulfilling their duties, either because they feel obliged to do so from the presence of Data Protection Authorities or because they deliberately choose to be diligent[324]. And it is true that, some notorious exceptions aside, for most undertakings and organizations dealing with data, legal compliance is of paramount value. However, even if we assume that all kinds of data controllers want to observe data protection law, it cannot be taken for granted that they are in a realistic position to do so. To begin with, controller compliance is undermined by the fact that data protection law is complex to put from theory to practice. Moreover, the GDPR invests a lot on a priori over a posteriori regulation, which is in principle of course better. Notwithstanding, it still interprets a priori protection as a range of procedures and checklists data controllers have to go through before any specific data processing and not as some clearly formulated, aim-oriented general principles which will make clear the level of protection that is to be maintained at all times during a data processing cycle irrespective of how this will be achieved by any given data controller. In other words, what we need for a data protection regime looking to the future is not more forms or compliance questionnaires; the real challenge is to let everyone know under what quality standards data are expected to be processed and let them then decide how to achieve them, knowing that, should they fail, equally clear repercussions will be faced[325].

- Shortcoming no. 3: excessively outstretching statutory data protection laws to the extent that they become dysfunctional

As it has been analyzed both the GDPR and its predecessor, the DPD, are pure examples of technology-specific laws. They determine how the issues they deal with are to be regulated by focusing on the results data technology has when applied in the context of specific data services or for the completion of particular data-related tasks. This is an understanding we need to keep in mind at all times when reading a statutory law such as the GDPR, which, in addition, has been constructed in light of a particular factual framework (e.g. the reality of transborder data transfers). Very of-

324 B.-J. Koops (note 315); Alexander Roßnagel ed. (note 285).

325 See also Chapters 8, 9 and 10.

ten, expanding the meaning of the provisions of a statutory law, which is, nevertheless, of a technology-specific nature, to such an extent that is can cover more and more novel phenomena caused much more legal confusion and uncertainty than it actually resolves[326]. In other words, what needs to be done is to stop abusing technology-specific IT laws, such as the GDPR and the like, in order to continue being on a relative par with technological advancement and novel IT applications and focus on conceptualizing robust regulatory principles reflecting on the core and heart of modern and future IT, i.e. on cloud computing.

e. GDPR and its readiness to respond to big scale uses of data in the cloud; the case of machine learning

Just as the GDPR was going through its negotiations phase, the cloud was becoming the platform for numerous big scale data-based applications which are becoming increasingly important in several aspects of the internet-based economy[327]. The majority of them are founded on processing of data of massive amounts, typically being referred to as 'big data'[328]. Most, if not all of these uses, are made possible thanks to cloud computing and,

326 Colin S. Diver, *Statutory Interpretation in the Administrative State*, 133 University of Pennsylvania law review 549–599 (1985.)

327 See also Chapter 11.

328 Big data is an evolving term that describes any voluminous amount of structured, semi-structured and unstructured data that has the potential to be mined for information. Big data is often characterized by three qualities, which in relevant technical literature have been established as 'the 3 Vs': extreme **volume** of data, wide **variety** of data types and **velocity** at which the data must be processed. Although big data does not equate to any specific volume of data, the term is often used to describe terabytes, petabytes and even exabytes of data captured over time. Such voluminous data can derive from countless different sources, such as business sales records, harvested results of scientific experiments or real-time sensors used in the internet of things. Data may be raw or preprocessed using separate software tools before analytics are applied. It may also exist in a wide variety of file types such as structured data, e.g. in SQL database stores; unstructured data, e.g. document files; or streaming data from sensors. Moreover, collection of big data may involve multiple, simultaneous data sources, which may not otherwise be integrated. Velocity refers to the speed at which big data must be analyzed. As a rule, every big data analytics project will ingest, correlate and analyze data sources, and then render an answer or result based on an overarching query. This means that for the final product of the processing to be of essence, human ana-

naturally, will clearly be within the field of application of the GDPR. The aim of such massive data processing operations can be greatly diversified but one of the most common purposes they serve is to create patterns that will be able to predict human behavior, choices and decisions[329]. These patterns are then fed to systems such as online marketplaces or software and systems used in tracking health of patients or dissemination patterns of diseases, to name a few. Moreover, the bigger the amount of data collected and processed, the more accurate these patterns are supposed to become and the more precise the predictions they render[330].

It goes without saying that one of the biggest questions surrounding the GDPR is to what extent the new law has managed to be timely enough when it was officially adopted in order for its provisions to regulate these phenomena efficiently for as long as possible. Of course, this question is too broad one for it to merit a mere 'yes' or 'no' answer. However, an as-

---

lysts must have a clear understanding of the available data and possess some sense of the kind of answer they are looking for. Velocity becomes of growing importance as big data analysis expands into fields like machine learning and artificial intelligence, where analytical processes mimic perception by finding and using patterns in the collected data. Achieving such velocity in a cost-effective manner is a major challenge. Even enterprise leaders are reticent to invest in an extensive server and storage infrastructure that might only be used occasionally to complete big data tasks. Consequently, public cloud computing has emerged as a primary vehicle for hosting big data analytics projects. A public cloud provider can store petabytes of data and scale up thousands of servers just long enough to accomplish the big data project. The business only pays for the storage and compute time actually used, and cloud instances can be turned off until they're needed again. For more details and orientation into the concept of big data, refer to: Viktor Mayer-Schönberger & Kenneth Cukier (note 321).; Jonathan Stuart Ward & Adam Barker, Undefined By Data. A Survey of Big Data Definitions, available at: http://arxiv.org/pdf/1309.5821; Amir Gandomi & Murtaza Haider, *Beyond the hype. Big data concepts, methods, and analytics*, 35 International Journal of Information Management 137–144 (2015); Andrea de Mauro, Marco Greco & Michele Grimaldi, *What is big data? A consensual definition and a review of key research topics*, in, 97–104 (2015); Ibrahim Abaker Targio Hashem, Ibrar Yaqoob, Nor Badrul Anuar, Salimah Mokhtar, Abdullah Gani & Samee Ullah Khan, *The rise of "big data" on cloud computing. Review and open research issues*, 47 Information Systems 98–115 (2015).

329 Dimitra Kamarinou, Christopher Millard & Jatinder Singh, Machine Learning with Personal Data (2016.)

330 Andrej Savin, *Profiling and Automated Decision Making in the Present and New EU Data Protection Frameworks* SSRN Journal (2014); Alexander Roßnagel ed. (note 285).

sessment can indeed be driven for the issue of machine learning given the specialized provisions on profiling[331] that form part of the GDPR.

As a rule, automated decision-making[332] often entails profiling, where the profiles gradually constructed through the processing of data guide the decision-making process[333]. Reflecting this technological fact, the GDPR defines profiling as a sub-category of automated processing, and stipulates it as the use of personal data to evaluate certain personal aspects of natural people in an effort to analyze and predict certain aspects of their behavior.

In the era of the DPD already a number of academics had suggested that one of the Directive's underlying principles was that 'fully automated assessments of a person's character should not form the sole basis of decisions that significantly impinge upon the person's interests'[334]. This principle survives in the provisions of the new Regulation, where according to its Article 22 – which also covers profiling of people based on their health, location and movement – data subjects have the right not to be subject to decision-making if that is solely based on automated processing, at all instances that this may significantly affect them in some way. This provision plays a crucial role in relation to machine learning, given that proponents of the specific technology emphasize precisely its ability to automate and facilitate decision making processes.

The rest of protection mechanisms, appeal processes and risk assessment or control procedures of the GDPR can naturally be read through the prism of profiling as well, given its explicit recognition as a form of data processing that falls within its regulatory scope from the GDPR[335]. It is beyond the scope of this study to analyze the entire body of provisions of the new Regulation; however, if one conclusion is to drawn regarding big scale data processing operations which are made possible thanks to cloud

---

331 In particular, Art. 4, para. 4, and Art. 22, Regulation (EU) 2016/679 (note 25).

332 The term 'automated decision making' refers to the use of computers to carry out tasks requiring the generation or selection of options. For further details refer to: McGraw-Hill, McGraw-Hill Dictionary of Scientific and Technical Terms (2003.)

333 Andrej Savin (note 330).

334 Lee A. Bygrave, *Aytomated Profiling*, 17 Computer Law & Security Review 17–24 (2001.)

335 Profiling is explicitly mentioned in all instances of GDPR rules where specific protective measures and tools available to data subjects are stipulated, namely: Art. 13, para. 2f; Art. 14, para. 2g; Art. 15, para. 1h; Art. 21, para. 1 & 2; Art. 35, para. 3a; Art. 47, para. 2e Regulation (EU) 2016/679 (GDPR) (note 25).

computing (such as profiling and, subsequently, machine learning), it can be argued that EU data protection law, in its latest form, still assumes that large scale data applications such as automated decision-making processes are risky and that individuals need to be protected from them. Among the types of protection granted to data subjects are the right to be informed about automated decision-making, including profiling, as well as rights to have a human review a machine decision. While such measures are indeed useful to be in place and uphold Europe's long tradition of empowering the individual against undesirable uses of their data, as much as possible, enthusiasts of relevant technologies (the cloud being one of them) point out that technology should not always be viewed with suspicion[336]. For instance, advances in machine learning research and in cloud networks as the main enabler of machine learning systems, mean that machines can more and more may surpass certain limitations of human decision makers and provide us with decisions that are emphatically fair[337]. How 'ready' is the GDPR to show tolerance and trust towards these technologies and their constantly improved capabilities? Time and actual enforcement practices of the new law by competent authorities will soon tell us.

f. Vision for a cloud-based future

It has already been demonstrated that today data is prevalent everywhere. Sources of data are multiple in comparison to a couple of decades ago, their uses are also many more, their economic value is incomparably higher than it used to be and from the moment they are collected, data venture on an open-ended journey through multiple uses, different formats and several platforms. With this landscape in the field of data in mind, a very different privacy framework for the data age is necessary, one focused less on individual consent at the time of collection and more on continuously holding data users, be them controllers or processors as they are typified for the time being, accountable for what they do with the information they have in their possession[338]. Under such a regulatory regime, entities that have any kind of data in their possession will formally assess any particular use or reuse of them based on the impact it has on the individuals these

336 Jiahong Chen (note 24).; Andrej Savin (note 330).; B.-J. Koops (note 315).
337 Dimitra Kamarinou, Christopher Millard & Jatinder Singh (note 329).
338 For more see Chapter 8.

data originally belong to or come from. This perpetual accountability does not have to be onerously detailed or excessively time-consuming[339]. Future privacy laws should stipulate broad categories of uses and services involving data, certain of which will also be permissible without or with only limited, standardized safeguards. For riskier applications involving data, future regulatory schemes should articulate ground rules for how data users will determine the dangers of a particular data use or service and determine thereafter what measures best avoid or mitigate them. In general, the cloud and the IT environment it fosters call for a regulatory framework that will spur creative services for, uses and reuses of data, while at the same time it will ensure that sufficient measures are taken[340] to make sure individuals, who data belong to or come from, are not hurt.

g. The road from data privacy to cloud computing regulation

i. Privacy and security viewed through the years and across major jurisdictions[341]

Viewed from a European standpoint, privacy has been traditionally regarded as a fundamental human right. Enshrined in the United Nations Universal Declaration of Human Rights (1948)[342], it subsequently became part of the European Convention on Human Rights[343] and numerous national constitutions and charters of rights across Europe but also worldwide[344]. Since

---

339 For more see Chapter 10.

340 For more see Chapters 8, 9 and 10.

341 Siani Pearson & George Yee (note 280).

342 Article 12 of the UN Universal Declaration of Human Rights reads: "No one shall be subjected to arbitrary interference with his privacy, family, home or correspondence, nor to attacks upon his honor and reputation. Everyone has the right to the protection of the law against such interference or attacks.". UN General Assembly, Universal Declaration of Human Rights, 10 December 1948, 217 A (III).

343 Article 8 para. 1 of the ECHR reads: "Everyone has the right to respect for his private and family life, his home and his correspondence.". Council of Europe, European Convention for the Protection of Human Rights and Fundamental Freedoms, as amended by Protocols Nos. 11 and 14, 4 November 1950, ETS 5.

344 For an extensive overview of the basic privacy laws and regulations across most countries around the world, refer to http://privacypolicies.com/blog/privacy-law-by-country/ (last accessed: 01/19/2017.)

at least the 1970s, the primary focus of privacy had been personal information particularly that which was put under question from government surveillance or potential mandatory disclosure in light of the need to set up databases on topics of public security, health or other emergencies.

The 1980s brought along the rise of direct marketing and telemarketing[345] and, consequently, new kinds of concerns were raised related to privacy of personal data and security, while soon after the transposition of buying and commerce on the internet spurred further consideration to the increasing threats of online identity theft and spamming[346].

In the end, one could argue that one way of thinking about privacy is as 'the appropriate use of personal information under the circumstances'[347]. Data protection is the management of such personal information and it is a terminology often used within the European Union with reference to privacy-related laws and regulations. On the contrary, in the USA the term 'data protection' mostly refers to security[348].

The terms 'personal information' and 'personal data' are commonly used within Europe and Asia; in the USA, the respective term is 'Personally Identifiable Information' (PII), but, as convergence of jurisdictions as a result of the globalized structures of today's world moves on, the same terms are generally used also in America to refer to the same (or a very similar) concept[349].

The European Union definition of 'personal data', since long established via the DPD, is that of "any information relating to an identified or identifiable natural person ('data subject'); an identifiable person is one who can be identified, directly or indirectly, in particular by reference to an identification number or to one or more factors specific to his physical, physiological, mental, economic, cultural or social identity"[350].

Traditionally, scholarly views tend to differ about certain types of personal data which are considered more sensitive than others; expectedly, these variations occur as a result of the differences in the definition of

345 Bradley, A. K. (1991). An employer's perspective on monitoring telemarketing calls: Invasion of privacy or legitimate business practice? Labor Law Journal, 42(5), 259. Retrieved from https://search.proquest.com/docview/1290705829?accountid=11262 (last accessed: 01/19/2017.)

346 Huaiqing Wang, Matthew K. O. Lee & Chen Wang (note 12).

347 Siani Pearson & George Yee (note 280).

348 C. J. Bennett (note 194).

349 Borivoje Furht & Armando Escalante (note 276).

350 Directive 95/46/EC (DPD) (note 143.)

what is considered sensitive personal information from one jurisdiction to the other.

As opposed to Europe's, the US approach to privacy legislation is historically sector-based or enacted at the state level (e.g. the State of Massachusetts has set out appropriate security standards for protecting the personal information of residents of that state) and imposes few if any restrictions on transborder data flow[351].

To summarize, privacy is essentially regarded as a human right in Europe; on the contrary, in America, it has been traditionally viewed more as a concept aimed at avoiding harm to people in specific contexts[352]. It is a complex but important notion, and correspondingly, the collection and processing of personal information is subject to regulation in many countries across the world. As a result, any future set of rules for cloud business will need to reflect these varied perspectives and try to balance among or, ultimately, merge them; and this is a policy recommendation that should be taken into account by regulators in both jurisdictions.

ii. Privacy issues particular to cloud computing technologies

The specificities of cloud technologies and the differences they have introduced in the field of data handling have, subsequently, also modified the challenges that privacy faces in today's IT landscape[353].

For starters, handling your data via cloud means a great lack of user control[354]. User-centric control seems essentially incompatible with the cloud: as soon as a SaaS environment is used, the service provider becomes responsible for storage of data, in a way in which visibility and control is limited. As a result, unauthorized secondary usage of data, risks to data integrity owing to complexity of regulatory compliance or the efforts in addressing transborder data flow restrictions are always possible.

Legal uncertainty is one more direct effect of the rapid development of the cloud sector[355]. Since cloud technology has moved ahead of the law,

351 See also Chapter 3.
352 Id.
353 Siani Pearson & George Yee (note 280).
354 Borivoje Furht & Armando Escalante (note 276).
355 Digital Agenda in the Europe 2020 strategy (note 241); Reinhard Posch (note 240).

there is understandably much legal uncertainty about privacy rights in the cloud and it is becoming more and more prevalent that applying existing laws to cloud environments gives insufficient results. Cloud computing poses significant challenges for organizations that need to meet various global privacy regulations at the same time, due to the universal nature of IT as a market and its collision with geographical or jurisdictional borders that exist in the real world.

Security issues are also raised due to the emergence of cloud computing[356]. Security gaps, instances of unwanted access or vendor lock-in, inadequate deletion of data, potential compromise of the management interface that would extend to a degree beyond the average user's control or understanding, backup vulnerabilities, isolation failure, inadequate monitoring are just a few situations that could jeopardize the security of cloud platforms and merit attention.

iii. Why does cloud computing call for a new regulatory framework?

It has been already sufficiently demonstrated that cloud computing, from a technological perspective, is fundamentally different from what existed before[357] as tools to perform computational processing of data tasks. Similarly, there are essential differences on the focus of cloud technologies in comparison to previous environments: while systems based on technologies prior to the cloud where largely one-dimensional and they were built more or less on a linear logic and architecture (in the sense that the processing was easily traceable at all times throughout the system, regardless of whether the resources of the system were all in the same physical location or not), cloud environments obey to a multi-dimensional logic: the processing work can be executed using resources dispersed around the cloud facility and without even being at the same physical location either.

Understandably, this shift in the way data processing environments are constructed resulted also in a shift on the priorities they set: pre-cloud facilities were designed with a primary objective to get the data processing done in a clearly laid-out and secure manner. Cloud-based facilities are constructed with the primary aim of getting data processing done in an as

---

356 Borivoje Furht & Armando Escalante (note 276).
357 See Chapter 2.

user-friendly as possible manner and with a priority on optimizing economies of scale for the provider but also the user of the cloud infrastructure. This change of focus resulted in the security of the processing not being possible to be taken for granted anymore. From a status quo where it was enough to know what role each of the actors participating in a data processing sequence held in order to be able to identify their responsibilities and duties, we are today in a situation where the data processing workflow is geographically and resource-wise dynamic and spread-out across the cloud facility, hence calling for a different approach that will guarantee security and transparency throughout the processing workflow.

In the following parts of this study it will be examined to what degree using the criterion of 'legitimate scope' (teleological perspective) in order to define the justifiable actions of each actor in a data processing workflow facilitated by cloud infrastructure would be a viable norm in order to produce an efficient regulatory framework for cloud computing technologies and the tasks carried out through them. Moreover, recognizing the boundless nature of the cloud, effort will be made to set up this set of regulatory principles with a universal perspective. Consequently, from the one hand, the best possible regulatory approaches will be looked for across the two most predominant markets and jurisdictions where the cloud business thrives, i.e. Europe and the U.S.A. Simultaneously, the proposed scheme will in as much as possible be fit for 'universal applicability', i.e. without being affected by the cross-country or cross-market nature of cloud environments but, instead, by focusing on the cloud infrastructure as a locus in itself, where certain rules should apply and specific regulatory goals and priorities should at all times be respected.

CHAPTER 5. Legal pluralism and harmonization – how can we reach a common minimum understanding on how to regulate the cloud?

a. Introduction – scope of this chapter

As it has been already exposed[358] cloud computing brought about one fundamental change in the standards regarding data handling: it has rendered largely invalid the notion of a specific physical space within which any instance of data processing – or any part thereof – takes place. Of course, exceptions still are – and presumably will always be – technically feasible to exist but the norm nowadays is that the cloud, as the vital space where data 'live' and 'circulate', is a boundless, limitless area, at least in terms of the geographical meaning of boundaries. Clearly, this is not the first time we are faced with such a concept of lack of borders, or more precisely, of lack of clearly manifested borders: the internet itself is a limitless conception, an entity that can be verbally and technically defined but cannot be physically delineated.

It should be made clear from the very beginning that the internet and cloud computing are not the same thing. In fact, cloud computing is, as it has been demonstrated[359], a technological concept for the ultimate use of available tools facilitating computing while, the internet could be described as one of the main constituting parts of this technological concept, as its backbone. Nevertheless, given the internet's pivotal role in facilitating cloud computing applications, it is reasonable to look among the theoretical approaches and patterns used for its regulation for answers and tools that can potentially help also with the challenge of an effective regulation of the cloud.

Regulation of the internet is, of course, an all but settled issue[360]. Still, there are a few clearly prevailing approaches or suggestions that can serve

---

358 See Chapter 2.

359 Id.

360 Dan Jerker B. Svantesson, *Privacy, the Internet and transborder data flows – An Australian perspective*, 4.1 Masaryk University journal of law and technology 1–20 (2010.)

as an efficient starting point in a quest for a unique and dedicated framework for cloud computing regulation. Legal pluralism and harmonization of laws are two juridical norms largely compatible with the particularities of the internet and the challenges its nature poses to any legislator. These two approaches have over the past decades offered some of the boldest propositions in the debate for effective internet regulation, ideas that were clearly in touch with the actual nature of the internet sphere[361]. The solutions constructed on the basis of legal pluralism and harmonization of laws are discussed in this chapter as potential answers or starting points to the challenge of a pragmatic cloud computing regulatory framework.

In this chapter, the legal methodologies that will be the main instruments of this research are presented and put in context. These are legal pluralism and harmonization of regulatory principles in the context of global administrative law, which are argued to be the most suitable approaches in the quest for an efficient regulatory framework for the cloud. In addition, it has been argued that the cloud's universal nature necessitates not a conventional harmonization of laws on a regional level (as harmonization has been traditionally understood until today) but an original process that will aim to bring closer the way regulators worldwide think about and develop rules that govern it. This proposal is also brought in context along with the legal methodologies named above as the instruments with which the following parts of this study are constructed.

b. Internet Regulation: a paramount of unilateralism

The internet has emerged to be one prime example of legal unilateralism[362]. Although the medium itself was by no means defined by limits or boundaries in the traditional sense – with the exception, probably, of some of its earliest versions which still had not reached an adequate level of maturity – early efforts to regulate it followed the traditional pattern of national (or intergovernmental) regulators getting down to set up legal frameworks which would control how the internet 'worked' within the ex-

361 David R. Johnson & David G. Post, *Law And Borders--The Rise of Law in Cyberspace*, 48 Stanford Law Review 1367–1402 (1996.)

362 Y. Benkler, *Internet regulation: a case study in the problem of unilateralism*, 11 European Journal of International Law 171–185 (2000.)

tent of their competence[363]. Unilateralism clearly prevailed over cooperation among nations and, as a result, internet related legislation quickly became fragmented, while it is meant to address one and the same thing[364].

Nevertheless, unilateralism in producing internet laws should not be so effortlessly dismissed as a bad choice[365]. One side of the coin being a fragmented mosaic of laws governing the internet, on the other side of the debating table stand those who believe that unilateralism in internet regulation may have given a boost to the evolution of the net as a medium[366]. In fact, there has been repeatedly suggested that differing legislations may have impeded internet growth and evolution in certain legal orders but may well have accelerated them in others. After one point, these gaps in internet advancement among different jurisdictions have paved the way for two distinct consequences[367]:

- from a technological point of view, this imbalance among internet laws of different legal orders meant that the net developed much faster in certain parts of the world than others. At the same time, though, after a certain point, the universality of the net permitted it to expand also in areas where stricter control and regulations had been responsible for poorer evolution. The economics of scale of internet based activities made it eventually defiant of borders and limitations and served as the driving force behind the emergence of global technological standards. The latter found the way to establish themselves even in jurisdictions where prima facie they were not allowed; yet, consumer demand made them a de facto necessity.
- from a legal point of view, irregularities in internet laws may, from the one side, be responsible for the fragmented legal mosaic with which the internet is governed today. Notwithstanding, these differing legislations mean exactly that there have been specific geographical areas and respective jurisdictions where internet laws became powerful more quickly and robust enough to affect regulatory trends in other jurisdictions as well. Just as technological standards were manifesting themselves more and more as of a truly global nature, so did internet

363 Chris Reed, *How to Make Bad Law: Lessons from Cyberspace*, 73 The Modern Law Review 903–932 (2010.)

364 *Id.*

365 Y. Benkler (note 362).

366 David R. Johnson & David G. Post (note 361).

367 Paul M. Schwartz (note 157).

laws[368]: some of them managed to rise above the others and to dictate pretty much the legal landscape regarding the internet in vast areas of the world[369].

To sum up, a system with imperfectly defined relations between local and global, private and public regulatory processes, and between exceptionalism and harmonization, as is the system of laws regulating the internet, serves as an institutional environment ideal for non-representative commercial or other organizations to embed their values in the regulatory framework that will eventually emerge[370]. This is a tendency we already witness in the field of internet law; more and more non-legislative entities contest a seat on the law-making table and several of them, either directly or representatively, manage to make their voice heard[371]. Similarly, an area which started to develop so recklessly as that of cloud computing, mainly due to the fact that it was not immediately recognized as a distinct phenomenon, might have set off from a unilateral basis regulation-wise but this is not necessarily bad. As long as, from now on, we make sure that we take the best from every cup (i.e. from every national or regional jurisdiction) and end up with a set of rules that will give universal and working answers to handling the cloud, unilateralism can turn out to be a good thing.

As the US Supreme Court stipulated in a landmark judgement of 1997[372]: "law dictates behavior and technology dictates behavior. Efforts to regulate technology usually end up in pushing technological develop-

---

368 Y. Benkler (note 362).

369 Paul M. Schwartz (note 157).

370 Baudouin. Dupret, *Legal pluralism, plurality of laws, and legal practices*, 1 European Journal of Legal Studies (2007.)

371 *Id.*

372 Reno v. American Civil Liberties Union, 521 U.S. 844 (1997); The case in brief: Two provisions of the Communications Decency Act of 1996 (CDA) that criminalized providing obscene materials to minors by on the internet were held unconstitutional by the Supreme Court of the United States (Supreme Court). Synopsis of Rule of Law: Where a content-based blanket restriction on speech is overly broad by prohibiting protected speech as well as unprotected speech, such restriction is unconstitutional. Facts: At issue was the constitutionality of two statutory provisions enacted to protect minors from "indecent" and "patently offensive" communications on the Internet. The District Court made extensive findings of fact about the Internet and the CDA. It held that the statute abridges the "freedom of speech" protected by the First Amendment of the United States Constitution (Constitution).

ment towards the desired direction". Regulating technology in one jurisdiction, although not a matter of clearly unilateral nature, usually prompts technology development towards the desired direction also in other jurisdictions as technological standards today are of a truly global nature[373]. Consequently, the choices regulators, especially those of the prominent legal orders, will make in the path they will shape for the regulation of the cloud in the years to come will play a decisive role in the development of cloud computing on a global scale. Therefore, it is of vital importance to make the best out of what unilateralism has produced so far as regulatory perceptions regarding the cloud and come up with a representative and, at the same time, effective governing scheme.

c. From governments to governance; learning to do laws for a borderless world[374]

Regulating a dynamic phenomenon such as the internet or cloud computing requires a profoundly different approach from legislators. It is not the scope of this study to go on and propose such far-fetched ideas as global laws for cloud computing. Even if this is what cloud computing and IT technologies regulations eventually evolve into, this cannot happen overnight and, certainly, it cannot be proposed at this moment as the next step; there is yet a great distance to be covered till such a development. The need for evolution in law making in such dynamic areas as cloud computing calls, however, for at least two significant changes of perspective:

- regulators need to be more in tune with the borderless nature of more and more constituting parts of today's world[375]. And this not by bringing down borders or homogenizing jurisdictions but by making sure that the laws put in place will take into account that they are meant to give sufficient answers and persuasive solutions to a far greater vital space than that of the geographical area where they are immediately applicable[376].

373 Paul M. Schwartz (note 157).
374 A. Froomkin (note 322).
375 David R. Johnson & David G. Post (note 361).
376 A. Froomkin (note 322).

- law making process has to be more open towards non-legislative bodies and actors and their input[377]. Of course, this is not to mean that existing jurisdictions and their law-processing workflows are ready or should admit non-legislative actors as peers on the table; however, it is imperative to come up with ways in which the key players of an area can provide their crucial first-hand experience, suggestions and proposals and that this input shall be taken into serious consideration when formulating laws for such unconventional phenomena as the cloud.

In order to initiate a transition from laws for governing to laws for governance scholarly opinion has brought forward certain guiding principles that should characterize the new law-making mindset. Without prejudice to other propositions, the ideas that are suggested as the most crucial ones are:

- private sector should lead the debate on how sectors, whose development was spurred primarily by non-state actors, need to be regulated[378]. This proposal should not be understood as a call for a carte blanche to private entities. It goes without saying that the answer to the need for more efficient laws is not laws that would facilitate recklessness. However, legislators need to make sure that private actors, especially those spearheading the way in a specific field, will have considerable autonomy to take their sector one step further at any time and that their ideas about how activity in the sector could be streamlined through laws are carefully heard.
- governments are encouraged to avoid undue restrictions[379]. Experience and history tell us that in dynamic phenomena, such as cloud computing, restrictive approaches usually either hinder progress or are simply rendered invalid via a workaround. Consequently, it does not seem meaningful to try to control what will happen next in a sector by forbidding certain things from happening. The key to better regulation is definitely not greater or unjustified restrictions.

---

377 Dennis D. Hirsch, *In Search of the Holy Grail: Achieving Global Privacy Rules Through Sector-Based Codes of Conduct*, 74 Ohio State Law Journal 1030–1069 (2013.)

378 *Id.*

379 A. Froomkin (note 322).

- the legislators' mindset should be towards fostering a predictable, minimalist, consistent and simple legal environment[380]. In fact, many scholars agree that this should not be just the wish pursued with every new adopted legislation but rather the primary goal future laws should serve: ensuring that the regulated environment in which law subjects will be let to act will be a simple-to-understand and opaque one.
- legislators should recognize the unique qualities of cloud computing[381]. This means that, first of all, the cloud should not be confused with any other neighboring phenomenon and should be clearly defined before regulated. In this manner, we can be more certain that the laws we will end up with will correspond to the actual matters they aim to settle.
- further development of cloud computing should be facilitated in an orchestrated global manner[382]. This call for globalized action does not immediately mean reckless, unimpeded growth that knows and needs to respect no boundaries or particularities. Nevertheless, a minimum common understanding between legislators of different legal orders would definitely foster this globalized growth much more effectively.

As far as the most suitable locus to facilitate this transition from governing to governance is concerned, scholarly opinion largely agrees that international law can be a good first playing field in the progress towards greater harmonization of laws about phenomena such as the internet or cloud computing. By carefully studying what has been happening already on the front of the internet, which is a relatively riper phenomenon than cloud technologies, one could recognize the following forces that facilitate harmonization processes[383]:

- the most decentralized form of harmonization mechanism generally occurs when norms spontaneously develop within a usually specialized transnational community (e.g. lex mercatoria)[384].
- a strong harmonization drive also builds up when one jurisdiction's law becomes the de facto rule also for other places, perhaps due to regula-

380 Paul M. Schwartz (note 157).

381 David R. Johnson & David G. Post (note 361).

382 Ralf Michaels, *Global Legal Pluralism*, 5 Annual Review of Law & Social Science (2009.)

383 Joel Reidenberg (note 173).

384 *Id.*

tory arbitrage (e.g. a country with excellent internet connectivity manages to set the pace in the field of internet regulation globally)[385]
- harmonization may also be accelerated under conditions of regulatory competition. i.e. when one jurisdiction copies elements of another in a race for supremacy in a harmonized field[386]
- participation of governments in communal law reform projects also fosters harmonization forces (e.g. UNCITRAL[387]).
- proven contributors to harmonization are the supranational bodies with a mandate to harmonize national laws of member-states (e.g. the United Nations bodies)
- last but not least, international and, especially, multilateral treaties also serve the harmonization goal.

d. So far, existing laws about cyberspace are bad laws. Lessons learnt?

Excessively complicated legal frameworks tend to prove themselves as bad laws[388]. Classical examples of this rule are laws governing phenomena which are global or borderless by nature but which are dealt with in a conventional jurisdictionally compartmentalized manner. Such over-complex sets of laws have serious disadvantages, particularly a greatly weakened normative effect, and problems of contradiction and over-frequent amendment. One of the most common paradigms is the until now produced cyberspace law.

---

385 David R. Johnson & David G. Post (note 361).; see also Chapter 3.

386 Ralf Michaels (note 382).

387 UNCITRAL is the core legal body of the United Nations system in the field of international trade law. A legal body with universal membership specializing in commercial law reform worldwide for over 40 years, UNCITRAL's business is the modernization and harmonization of rules on international business.
Interpreting trade as meaning faster growth, higher living standards, and new opportunities through commerce, UNCITRAL is formulating modern, fair, and harmonized rules on commercial transactions. These include:
Conventions, model laws and rules which are acceptable worldwide
Legal and legislative guides and recommendations of great practical value
Updated information on case law and enactments of uniform commercial law
Technical assistance in law reform projects
Regional and national seminars on uniform commercial law.

388 Chris Reed (note 363).

In legal theory, it is possible to judge the quality of law as long as, at any such attempt, you adopt a specific legal perspective from which to execute this judgement[389]. Law is broadly defined to be 'a system of rules which a particular country or community or group of subjects recognize as regulating their actions and which may be enforced by the imposition of penalties'[390]. A fundamental aim of any law, inherent in this definition, is to influence its subjects' behavior to some useful end. Thus, when a law fails to achieve such influence, it is necessarily not as good as one which does achieve these aims. This conclusion also applies to whole groups of laws regulating different aspects of the same phenomenon.

The law system which attempts to regulate activities in cyberspace is, taken as a whole and as it currently stands, of a lower quality than of what if could have been had the laws which constitute that system been devised more effectively. One of the reasons for this low quality of the existing corpus legis for the cyberspace is that cyberspace laws have, until present, fixated on the precision of rules to the exclusion of the basic morality, which must underlie all systems of law[391].

The basic morality that any law or system of laws needs to be characterized with in order to prove successful has been greatly discussed and formulated by legal philosopher, Lon Luvois Fuller[392]. Throughout his academic discourse, Fuller went at great lengths to understand what made laws fail. In the end, he proposed his famous 'eight routes of failure of any legal system', a set of principles and conditions which, if met at the heart of a corpus legis or an entire legal system, can answer as for the reasons of their failure[393]. It is worth pointing out that the Fuller routes (or principles as they are commonly alternatively denominated) do not need to be cumulatively traceable in a system of laws for it to be regarded as a failed one; presence of even one of them suffice to explain for failure. These eight principles are:

---

389 Y. Benkler (note 362).

390 Legal Information Institute – an Open Access to Law Project, Conrell University, Faculty of Law; available online at: https://www.law.cornell.edu/wex/legal_systems, last accessed: 03/12/2015.

391 Chris Reed (note 363).

392 Edwin Tucker, *The Morality of Law, by Lon L. Fuller*, 40 40 Indiana Law Journal 270 (1965) 270–279 (1965.)

393 Lon L. Fuller, The morality of law (1965.)

- The lack of rules or law, which leads to ad hoc and inconsistent adjudication.

This is not so relevant in the case of laws on cyberspace. Quite the opposite, for those aspects of cyberspace for which laws have already been put together, they are so numerous and contradictory towards each other that, in the end, failure is due to their abundance.

- Failure to publicize or make known the rules of law.

Although not the most prevalent, this principle can indeed be attributed to the current body of laws governing cyberspace. Especially on the level of international law, there are treaties and conventions dealing with specific aspects of the cyber world which are only on the sidelines of legal attention and remain largely unused as legal tools.

- Unclear or obscure legislation that is impossible to understand.

This is one of the Fuller principles most excessively defining the problematic nature of cyberspace law till today. Cyber laws attempted to regulate technological concepts which had already been considerably advanced and complicated, while, equally frequently, the real life repercussions of these complex technological notions were also perplexed situations. Regrettably, these laws fell victims to this perplexity and, instead of trying to clear out the way and provide simple answers to complicated situations, they went on reiterating this complexity on the regulatory level. This danger is one of the things that needs to be avoided at all costs also in the case of any regulation for cloud computing. The fact that the cloud, its applications and the real life situations it facilitates are already quite advanced should not trick us into believing that the laws governing them need to be equally perplexed.

- Retrospective legislation.

In an effort to bridge the gap between the time when cyberspace had started to matter and affect real life and the time when, finally, laws to regulate it were adopted, legislators tend at times to devise legal instruments with a retrospective nature. However, unless we are talking about aspects of human activity that cannot be left unregulated, even for a short block of time, such as the issues dealt with by criminal law, retrospectivity is not always the way to go. After all, until laws came to exist, areas such as the internet were self-regulated in a de facto sense and it is of little, if any use, to try and arrange otherwise ex post situations that have been settled since long ago in a particular functioning manner.

– Contradictions in the law.

This is the second most prevalent problem with currently existing cyberspace legislation. Given that Fuller was applying these principles not only against individual laws but also against bodies of laws governing one topic across borders and jurisdictions, contradictions are probably the gravest wound on the body of cyberspace law. What is more, this is probably the gravest issue also with frameworks dealing with cloud computing affairs till now: as these laws were developed simply under the mindset and legal traditions prevalent in each and every legal order, forgetful of the fact that they are meant to be applied to issues of purely cross-border nature that call for unanimous response otherwise we can only expect even more complicated situations after than prior to the application of a particular law.

– Demands that are beyond the power of the subjects and the ruled.

When it comes to cyberspace laws, this Fuller principle could be traced to the burdensome procedures some pieces of legislation necessitate from cyber law subjects. For instance, the licensing processes that some national laws impose on entities that wish to execute trans-border data transfers compared to the volume and frequency with which such transfers occur in the course of their business is nowadays clearly counter-productive.

– Unstable legislation (e.g. daily revisions of laws).

It is not so much the case in cyberspace laws. On the contrary, one might say that the delays occurring in the revision processes of cyberspace laws are mostly the problem rather than the very frequent revisions of them.

– Divergence between adjudication/administration and legislation.

This is an often malice across many areas of law, the EU law produced through Directives being prominent among them. Such was the case also with the EU Data Protection Directive and the differentiating applications it came to have across jurisdictions of the EU Member States. This is attempted to be ameliorated with the General Data Protection Regulation, which will be directly applicable across EU jurisdictions and is meant to replace the Directive[394].

In summary, already existing laws for cyberspace issues teach us a thing or two about the reasons that could lead to the production of bad laws, which, if disregarded for long, can cause this body of poor quality

394 However, there are still counterarguments as to the extent in which the GDPR will manage to establish a truly unanimous regulatory space across the EU. For more, see Chapter 4.

legislation to grow exponentially[395]. Since, so far, there has been no concrete cloud regulation, it is a golden opportunity to avoid past mistakes committed in neighboring fields and produce laws that will be effective and to-the-point bearing in mind the particularities of the cloud right from the beginning.

e. Lex informatica: The formulation of policy rules for the web through applied technology. Can it offer any useful insight for the conceptualization of a dedicated cloud computing regime?

The notion of 'lex informatica' was originally introduced in legal discourse over internet affairs around the second half of 1990s, when the web started to gain momentum as a new space or means of human activity. By 'lex informatica' it is to be understood the whole range of interpretations, adaptations and approaches to practices and activities on the web and the norms and generally accepted policy rules that have been concretized thereof[396]. Lex informatica is, one could assert, the de facto way in which participating actors fine-tuned and self-regulated their activities on the internet. A significant amount of these policies and norms have, over the years, transformed into laws or have, at least, influenced the respective law making processes. Of course, there is at the same time an equally great deal of lex informatica that has not yet made it to law status. However, promoters of the notion have constantly suggested that this set of rules for information flows imposed by technology and communication networks call for policymakers to understand, consciously recognize, and encourage them.

It goes without saying that lex informatica is not law, in the conventional sense of the term, because it has certain differences from typical laws. On the other side, it is these very differences that have permitted it to establish itself and serve well the functioning of regulating online activities. To begin with, jurisdictionally, the regime that lex informatica encourages provides overlapping of rule systems. Jurisdiction for conventional legal regulation is primarily based on territory. Legal rules apply only in a well-defined place where a sovereign can exert its power. In contrast, the juris-

395 Chris Reed (note 363).
396 Joel Reidenberg (note 173).

dictional lines for lex informatica do not depend on or necessarily agree with territorial borders[397].

Instead, the jurisdictional space of lex informatica is the network itself because the governing rules apply to information flows across network spheres rather than physical places. Consequently, lex informatica does not contest to replace legal rules. The latter can still apply to each constituent part of the network that is located in a particular physical jurisdiction.

Lex informatica, bearing all basic characteristics of a legal regime, offers both the possibilities of customization of rules and inalienable rules. The most commonplace customization mechanism for lex informatica is the various technological configurations. It has also been attributed with distinct enforcement properties. Legal regulation depends primarily on judicial authorities for rule enforcement. Rule violations are pursued on an ex post basis before the courts. Lex informatica, on the contrary, allows for automated and self-executing rule enforcement. Technological standards can be designed to prevent actions from taking place without the proper permission or authority.

In summary, lex informatica is defined by three sets of particularly valuable characteristics for establishing information policy and rule-making in an information society. First, technological rules do not rely on national borders. Second, lex Informatica permits easy customization of rules through a variety of technical mechanisms. Finally, lex informatica rules may also benefit from built-in self-enforcement and compliance-monitoring capabilities[398].

As already previously stated, lex informatica and legal rules exist both parallel to and overlapping one another. Therefore, legal discourse never suggested that lex informatica should substitute law. Instead, this relationship means that policymakers should add lex informatica to their set of policy instruments and pursue lex informatica norms as an effective substitute for law where self-executing, customized rules are desirable.

In conclusion, lex informatica is a de facto existing complex source of information policy rules on global networks. Lex informatica does not constitute a separate jurisdiction, antagonistic to the conventional ones. It just provides useful tools to formulate rules customized for particular situ-

397 David R. Johnson & David G. Post (note 361).
398 Joel Reidenberg (note 173).

ations, allowing the coexistence of varying information policies in a heterogeneous environment. The pursuit of technological rules that embody flexibility for information flows maximizes public policy options; at the same time, the ability to embed an immutable rule in the architecture of a legal system allows for the preservation of public-order values. These tools can lessen a number of problems that traditional legal solutions face in regulating information society. As it has been pointed out, despite being on the table as a concept, already since about 20 years, lex informatica has not yet been unquestionably recognized as a working supplement to legal regulation. Yet, the numerous instances at which it has proven to be of use can serve as a reference for the perspective we should view cloud computing regulation from.

f. Sectoral codes of conduct: the most dedicated attempt to come up with cloud computing laws so far and how it could be improved

Globalization of commerce and the intensification of cross-border trade were the main driving forces behind a relatively recent effort to regulate affairs in a homogenous and dedicated manner as regards specific business sectors. Sectoral codes of conduct are regulations concluded and agreed by the most prominent actors in a specific sector of (usually) economic activity, which, thanks to the gravitational positions these actors hold within the sector, reach a status of governing principles for the affairs they apply to[399]. A quasi bi-product of the sectoral rules of conduct are the 'binding corporate rules' (BCRs). These are regulations devised and self-imposed by multinational companies active in the field of cross-border data transfers[400]. BCRs were created in response to the need for ensuring adequate and comparable levels of protection to those upheld within the European Union when data is transferred to a third country. BCRs have been the most ad hoc effort till now in the strive to construct regulatory schemes for IT related issues for which currently existing regulations are not concretized enough and deal only in an analogous manner with.

The problem with sectoral codes of conduct so far has been that, although they are concluded precisely in an effort to help the industry work

399 Dennis D. Hirsch (note 377).
400 Christopher Millard, Cloud Computing Law (2013.)

more efficiently in the environment delineated by the laws applicable at the time, they lack the legitimacy of law per se[401]. The minds behind sectoral codes are members of a given sector themselves who, no matter how much gravity they may exert in their sector, they are not in the same institutional position as law makers. A great share of scholarly opinion asserts that if this bridging between sector actors and their working principles and institutional regulators is somehow achieved, then sectoral codes could well be the forerunner of sectoral legislations much more in touch with the specific nature of each sector. Actually, this challenge, i.e. how to shorten the gap between actors of a sector and law makers that are charged with formulating laws that will govern this sector, is at the root of the problem of efficient law making[402]. When it comes to increasing the efficiency of sectoral codes for the IT business, one of the most promising proposals put forward is the adoption of internationally approved industry codes of conduct[403]. This could work as follows: The IT sector would draft a code of conduct on issues such as privacy, cloud computing, big data etc., which would be ensured that it fulfills the core requirements of the main pieces of legislation on the table, at that given time, on a global scale (for instance, the E.U.'s relevant pieces of legislation, the APEC forum's Privacy Principles and, maybe, also other regional privacy regimes). Competent sector representatives would then submit the code to the relevant authority of each regional jurisdiction. If the authority gives the green light for the code, firms that comply with it can know that their activities meet the requirements for that jurisdiction (the E.U., the APEC countries, etc.). In this way, a single industry code, approved in each of the regional jurisdictions, can step-by-step reach a status of a nearly global set of privacy rules for that sector.

So far, all the attempts to develop such codes of conduct were initiatives of a single firm or group of companies, usually of a multinational nature[404]. It goes without saying that this was a factor weakening the efficacy of these efforts. Apart from any discipline it might ensure for the company which self-imposed the code on it, any code of binding corporate rules is, by nature, impractical for the great majority of companies to abide

401 Paul M. Schwartz (note 157).

402 Paul M. Schwartz (note 157); Joseph Raz, *Legal Principles and the Limits of Law*, 81 The Yale Law Journal 823–854 (1972.)

403 Dennis D. Hirsch (note 377).

404 Chris Reed (note 363).

by, expensive for governments to administer and enforce, and difficult for stakeholder groups to track and monitor. By looking into the possibility of developing sector based codes, not only does a profoundly different attempt to regulate effectively such fast developing sectors like cloud computing emerge, but we can also gain significant insights into the collective and synthetic way in which regulators should work when devising new laws for cloud computing or even other similar subject matters.

A sectoral code for cloud computing would need to provide persuasive answers to, among others, the following two pressing questions:

– problems related to privacy protection

Differences among national privacy regimes pose a fundamental challenge for the protection of individual privacy[405]. Some companies may purposely orchestrate their operations in such a way in order to take advantage of "regulatory arbitrage" prevalent in certain jurisdictions. Global data flows, combined with national privacy laws, can result in migration of personal data primarily to nations with the weakest laws or, at minimum, to temporary gaps in privacy protection as the data moves from one jurisdiction to the other. Even in instances when each of the nations a given set of data crosses has implemented meaningful privacy laws, the cross-border nature of a standard data transfer today makes it difficult to track compliance with them.

– problems for the business

This lack of consistency among national laws additionally poses problems for the businesses that engage in cross-border transfers of personal data and wish to be compliant with legal requirements[406]. These companies must closely track the flow of their data in order to know which jurisdiction's rules apply at any given moment, a process that can be quite costly.

As a result, a new framework for privacy protection needs to be constructed bearing in mind this global scale of the phenomenon it is expected to regulate. Through this law, it will be attempted to decrease the cost of doing business globally, provide consumers with consistent levels of protection worldwide, and contribute to global economic growth.

Now that the aims of a new law on privacy and the cloud have been crystallized the big question is how to achieve these goals. This is, of

---

405 Joel Reidenberg, *Resolving Conflicting International Data Privacy Rules in Cyberspace*, 52 Stan. L. Rev. 1315–1371 (1999.)

406 P. Blume, *Transborder data flow: is there a solution in sight?*, 8 International Journal of Law and Information Technology 65–86 (2000.)

course, a question of regulatory design and by consulting regulatory theory we can have answers with respect to the possible approaches. Any question of regulatory design requires the designer to answer two basic questions: Who will regulate? At what level will that entity regulate?

In the case of a sectoral code for the market of cloud computing the regulators need to be clearly more than one and spread out in a horizontal and vertical manner[407]: (1) government will regulate industry (direct government regulation), (2) industry will regulate itself (self-regulation), and (3) government and industry will intentionally and expressly share responsibility for the drafting and enforcement of rules (co-regulation). Regarding the question at what level each of these entities will regulate, there are likewise three possible answers[408]: (1) regulating at the level of the individual company (company-based regulation), (2) regulating at the level of the industry sector (sector-based regulation), or (3) regulating at the level of the economy as a whole (economy-wide regulation). Each of these three levels of regulation presents distinct features:

– direct government regulation[409]

In direct regulation, government bodies create, monitor compliance with, and enforce the regulatory requirements.

The advantages of such an approach are all those commonly associated with direct regulation. Governments are expected to establish relatively uniform sets of rules. Uniformity would make it easier for regulators to monitor compliance with, and enforceability of these rules. Such a regulatory regime would also create a level playing field for business. Nevertheless, direct regulation, in the form of national laws enforcing an international treaty, traditionally face important obstacles and presents significant downsides. At first and from a purely practical perspective, it is extremely difficult to establish an international treaty of any sort, let alone one that will merge together all the differing views existing today around the world on the issue of privacy and IT technologies.

– self-regulation[410]

Because of the concerns pointed out above some question the viability of direct government regulation and consider self-regulation as the most suitable approach to privacy over IT governance. Under this approach, indus-

407 Dennis D. Hirsch (note 377).
408 *Id.*
409 A. Froomkin (note 322).
410 Joel Reidenberg (note 173).

try sets, monitors, and enforces its own standards. Multinational companies could utilize self-regulation to formulate and impose uniform, cross-border privacy rules. To achieve this a specific company, or a sector organization that represents it, would firstly establish a voluntary set of privacy rules. It would then commit itself to following that set of rules throughout its international operations establishing in this manner a single, global set of privacy rules for the company.

Promoters of self-regulation argue that, since the rules developed in this method come from industry itself, they are able to tap into business knowledge and thereby produce more intelligent and effective rules than government regulation[411]. It is further argued that self-regulatory entities, which do not need to comply with notice-and-comment procedures and other such bureaucratic legal requirements, should be able to update their rules far more quickly than government regulators can.

Notwithstanding its promoters' arguments, there are both practical and theoretical reasons to question whether self-regulation is the best choice for international privacy rules. For starters, self-regulation, by definition, does not involve formal government approval[412]. As a consequence, it neither provides the legal safe harbor that companies need to engage confidently in cross-border data transfers, nor saves firms from the costly duty of having to track and comply with multiple national privacy laws.

Regulatory theory suggests additional reasons to be cautious about self-regulation. Businesses have an incentive to draft self-regulatory rules on the surface offer solid protection but are not, in fact, very stringent[413]. Self-regulation accordingly tends to be more lenient than government requirements, and may not achieve public goals like privacy. Theory further indicates that companies may commit to impressive-sounding self-regulatory goals but then fail to subject themselves to the independent monitoring needed to make these claims credible.

– co-regulation

What has been discussed so far may well explain why the greatest focus is lately on "co-regulatory" initiatives in which government and industry expressly share responsibility for drafting, monitoring, and enforcing privacy

---

411 Christopher T. Marsden, Internet Co-Regulation. European Law, Regulatory Governance and Legitimacy in Cyberspace (2011.)

412 Neil Gunningham & Joseph Rees, *Industry Self-Regulation: An Institutional Perspective*, 19 Law & Policy 363–414 (1997.)

413 Christopher T. Marsden (note 411).

standards[414]. Proponents of co-regulation claim that it combines the advantages of self-regulation with those of direct regulation[415]. Like self-regulation, co-regulatory methods such as enforceable codes of conduct allow industry to draft the specific privacy rules. They therefore profit from industry knowledge and expertise in the same way that self-regulation does. They are also more likely to get industry to accept and buy in to rules that they or their peers have drafted. Like direct regulation, co-regulatory strategies generally call on government to establish the privacy framework which all industry-drafted rules must conform to. Co-regulatory schemes also get regulators involved in assessing, monitoring compliance with, and enforcing rules. This governmental involvement increases the guarantees that the rules will truly protect the public interest, and that companies will comply with them. In conclusion, co-regulation promises rules that are stringent, intelligent and up-to-date, that government enforces and industry accepts. This is a promising picture for an area like cloud computing and privacy law where technologies and business models change too quickly for direct regulation, but where the stakes are too high to rely solely on industry self-regulation.

Co-regulation, of course, has its weaknesses too. It envisions a government–industry negotiation over rules. Such regulation through "deal-making" can lead to sweetheart deals that favor industry interests over those of the public[416]. An equally alarming point is that co-regulation can sometimes provide certain companies with an advantage over others, with the chances being, most likely, with those controlling a decisive share of the market. Last but not least, co-regulation will likely be less nimble and adaptive than self-regulation.

g. Efforts undertaken so far on the front of sector-based regulation of IT and their common weakness

The initiatives that have been undertaken so far towards self-regulation in the IT sector — binding corporate rules (BCRs), community based partici-

414 Dennis D. Hirsch (note 377).

415 M. Gillen, *Internet Co-Regulation: European Law, Regulatory Governance and Legitimacy in Cyberspace*, 20 International Journal of Law and Information Technology 147–149 (2012.)

416 Christopher T. Marsden (note 411).

patory research (CBPRs), and the once mighty U.S.–E.U. Safe Harbor Agreement[417]— definitely have shared certain common virtues. They have served as bases for companies (and, in the case of the Safe Harbor Agreement, self-regulatory privacy programs such as TRUSTe[418]) with the means to create an approved, cross-border set of privacy rules by which to do business[419]. They have attempted to do this through co-regulatory mechanisms that utilize industry knowledge to produce intelligent rules. Unfortunately, each of them has worked only with respect to certain regions (i.e. BCRs within the borders of the E.U.; CBPRs among APEC member nations; and the Safe Harbor Agreement between the EU and the United States), and none managed to provide a truly global solution[420].

---

417 The international Safe Harbor Privacy Principles or Safe Harbor Privacy Principles or the Safe Harbor Agreement were principles developed between 1998 and 2000 in order to prevent private organizations within the European Union or United States which store customer data from accidentally disclosing or losing personal information. They were struck down on October 6, 2015 by the Court of Justice of the European Union (CJEU) with its Judgement in the case Maximillian Schrems v Data Protection Commissioner. Under the Safe Harbor Regime, US companies storing customer data could self-certify that they adhered to 7 principles, to comply with the EU Data Protection Directive and with Swiss requirements. The US Department of Commerce developed privacy frameworks in conjunction with both the European Union and the Federal Data Protection and Information Commissioner of Switzerland.
Within the context of a series of decisions on the adequacy of the protection of personal data transferred to other countries, the European Commission made a decision in 2000 that the United States' principles did comply with the EU Directive applicable at the time (the DPD) – the so-called "Safe Harbor decision". However, after a customer complained that his Facebook data were insufficiently protected, the ECJ declared in October 2015 that the Safe Harbor Decision was invalid, leading to further talks being held by the Commission with the US authorities towards "a renewed and sound framework for transatlantic data flows".
Consequently, the European Commission and the United States agreed to establish a new framework for transatlantic data flows on 2nd February 2016, known as the "EU-US Privacy Shield", which governs relevant data transfers between the two jurisdictions since then. See also the CJEU's Judgement in Maximillian Schrems v Data Protection Commissioner, C-362/14, ECLI:EU:C:2015:650.

418 TrustArc (formerly TRUSTe) is a technology compliance and security company based in San Francisco, California. It became famous worldwide thanks to its software and tools were used to help corporations update their technology so that it complies with government laws, or operates using best practices.

419 Paul M. Schwartz (note 157).

420 Dan Jerker B. Svantesson (note 360).

Notwithstanding, each of them has been worthy as an effort toward the goal of broadly applicable, cross-border privacy rules.

At the same time, all three initiatives suffer from the same fundamental weakness: They rely on individual companies, rather than industry sectors, to draft the cross-border privacy rules[421]. In other words, they are company-based rather than sector-based codes, which undermine their contribution to the ultimate goal of universally effective IT regulation. Additionally, company-based codes also frustrate public participation thus enduring reduced accountability.

In light of these observations, it is becoming more and more tempting to switch to the sectoral approach regarding construction of a regulatory framework for the cloud, over company initiated solutions.

h. Seeking the way forward on cloud computing regulation in the field of global administrative law

i. Defining global administrative law

As it has been demonstrated so far, seeking to produce dedicated and in principle harmonized cloud computing regulation, either in the form of concrete laws or just as generic regulatory principles, cannot be achieved via conventional routes of law making (i.e. international law treaties or supervisory bodies) nor via arbitrary ventures such as the construction of an IT-only legal order that will be built on its own foundations, totally separated by other disciplines of law (such as a full-fledged corpus of lex informatica).

For cloud computing regulation to develop in a coherent manner to mature and bond along with other co-competent disciplines of regulation and provide persuasive answers a mid-solution needs to be found, one that will permit adopting the innovative attitude that IT law should be defined by but, at the same time, will not make the resulting principles look unrealistic or out of touch with the reality they aim at regulating. The path towards achieving this precarious balance goes through the field of global administrative law, its methods and tools.

421 Christopher T. Marsden (note 411).; M. Gillen (note 415).

The term 'global administrative law' indicates an emerging field of law development that is founded on a twofold principle: on the one side, that a great deal of what has been recently termed in law and international studies as "global governance" essentially constitutes, one way or another, administrative action; and, on the other side, that it is more and more typical of such action to be regulated by administrative law-kind principles, rules and mechanisms – particularly, those putting am emphasis on participation, transparency, accountability and review[422]. Consequently, global administrative law is a concept and set of methods for developing regulatory frameworks regarding cross-border phenomena of modern life which does not seek to turn a blind eye on existing legal norms and structures but rather aims to co-ordinate all suitable structures, procedures and normative standards for regulatory decision-making including transparency, participation, and review, and the rule-governed mechanisms for implementing these standards[423]. However, what it does differently compared to conventional sub-disciplines of international or public law is that, instead of limiting itself to the means available within each sub-discipline alone, it gathers all of the previously named resources that may be applicable to formal intergovernmental regulatory bodies but also to informal intergovernmental regulatory networks, to regulatory decisions of national governments where these are part of or constrained by an international intergovernmental regime, even to hybrid public-private or private transnational bodies[424]. To put it plainly, the main focus of global administrative law is not the specific content of substantive rules, but rather the coordination on the operation of existing or possible principles, procedural rules and reviewing and other mechanisms relating to accountability, transparency, participation, and assurance of legality[425] from different jurisdictions or legal orders with a view to achieving an as sound as possible global governance in the field under discussion, i.e., in this case, in IT and, specifically, in cloud computing regulation.

---

422 http://www.iilj.org/GAL/.

423 Benedict Kingsbury, Nico Krisch & Richard Stewart, *The Emergence of Global Administrative Law*, 68 Law and Contemporary Problems 15–62 (2005.)

424 Sabino Cassese, *Administrative Law without the State – The Challenge of Global Regulation*, 37 N.Y.U. J. Int 663–694 (2005.)

425 Alexander Somek, *The Concept of 'Law' in Global Administrative Law: A Reply to Benedict Kingsbury*, 20 Eur J Int Law 985–995 (2009.)

ii. The general theory on global administrative law and its principles

Pursuant to the definition above, the theory backing global administrative law instead of viewing clearly divided levels of regulation (private, local, national, intergovernmental etc.), affirms the existence of numerous overlaps among different actors and layers forming the wider pool of 'global administrative space'[426]. These overlaps can occur between international institutions and transnational networks, but also domestic administrative bodies when these form part of international regimes or when their acts can provoke transboundary regulatory effects[427] or even when the subject matter for which they are responsible extends by nature beyond the geographical borders of their competence, just as it happens with cloud computing.

Global administrative law and its principal device the 'global administrative space' were devised precisely due to the pressing need for the law, with relation to several regulatory issues, to get detached from the conventional understandings of international law by virtue of which there is a sharp separation between the domestic and international element[428]. However, in an ever increasing range of regulatory affairs this global administrative space is nowadays taken up by actors such as transnational private regulators, hybrid entities such as public-private partnerships involving states or inter-state organizations, national public regulators whose regulatory call has external effects but may not be controlled by the central executive authority, informal inter-state bodies with no treaty basis or formal interstate institutions (such as the United Nations system of organizations) affecting third parties through administrative type actions[429]. As it can be easily inferred, a great deal of the administration of global governance has become highly decentralized and not very systematic. This arrangement affects not only the executive but also the judiciary practice with national courts finding themselves in a position where they need to review the acts of international, transnational, even national bodies that are essentially administering decentralized global governance systems; in this manner, na-

426 Benedict Kingsbury, *The Concept of 'Law' in Global Administrative Law*, 20 Eur J Int Law 23–57 (2009.)

427 N. Krisch, *The Pluralism of Global Administrative Law*, 17 European Journal of International Law 247–278 (2006.)

428 Benedict Kingsbury (note 426).

429 Sabino Cassese (note 424).

tional courts also form part not only of the review but of the actual administration of a global governance regime[430], given that they are called to interpret laws developed by bodies on the regulatory level of global administrative law or ones that they address cross-border phenomena.

Equally confluent as the actors making it are also the sources of global administrative law; due to the fact that it is practiced at multiple fora, its norms may come to be the result of convergence among different sources of obligation applicable to a matter, ranging from national laws to regulations of law-applying institutions, to contracts establishing private rights based on those laws, to rules of international law on the same issues.

iii. Theoretical foundations of global administrative law based on US and EU administrative law

Scholarship in the US has been pondering on the legitimizing elements of global administrative law for several years since the term came to the forefront of academic discourse. Lately and after extensive debate, it has been proposed that for global administrative law the same fundamental principles that define US administrative law should apply as well[431]. These are:

- Transparency: in US public administrative legal discourse the call for transparency is fulfilled by means of a series of practices, namely, publication of agency rules, decisions, procedures and policies, as well as public access to agency records.
- Fair and equitable decision making procedures: the main means of guaranteeing fairness and equal treatment in public administrative procedures under US law are notice of proposed agency decisions and opportunity of affected or interested persons to submit evidence and argument to the decision maker.
- Decision requirements: decisions made up following procedures prescribed by US administrative law should be accompanied by agency statements of factual findings and reasons for decisions, based on an administrative record that includes relevant agency records and submissions by affected or interested persons.
- Availability of judicial review of final agency decisions.

430 Alexander Somek (note 425).

431 Richard B. Stewart, *The Global Regulatory Challenge to U.S. Administrative Law*, 37 N.Y.U. J. Int 695–762 (2006.)

- Legality: the term refers to the need for reassurance regarding any decision made by public administrative agencies that it was made in conformity with binding legal norms, including those established by the Constitution, statutes, Executive Orders (if reviewable), and agency regulations and adjudicatory decisions.
- Reasoned and responsive exercise of discretion: this principle refers to the need for assuring that the deciding agency has considered relevant alternatives and their implications and provided a reasoned justification for its choice among the alternatives, giving due account and responding to the material evidence and arguments in the submissions of affected or interested persons.

At the same time, the doctrine of global administrative law has received considerable attention within EU legal scholarship as well. Besides, as Hans-Heinrich Trute is noting, the European Union, with all its administrative authorities that are competent for regulating on numerous issues along with national counterparts from the EU's Member States, is possibly one of the prominent venues where essential administrative law and practice with acute cross-border characteristics is made[432]. Consequently, it is only reasonable that there has been discourse on the theoretical foundations of global administrative law in Europe as well the outcome of which finds democracy and the rule of law as the principles at the core of global administrative praxis. In particular, for European legal thinking 'the legitimating principles of any Western administrative law system are found in the twin ideals of democracy and the rule of law'[433]. To a certain extent, as the European Union has demonstrated through its enlargement or cooperation procedures with third countries[434], it holds these two ideals as the cradle of every system of administrative law. Within the EU itself, democracy and the rule of law have matured into constitutional principles, firmly embedded in the political arrangements and institutional texts of the Union[435]. As a result, these dual values have come to be regarded sine qua non conditions for any Western system of government and political theory. Expectedly, this also applies for global and transnational systems of gover-

432 Hans-Heinrich Trute, *Law and Knowledge – Remarks on a Debate in German Legal Science*, 32 Ewha Journal of Social Sciences 34 (2016.)

433 Carol Harlow, *Global Administrative Law: The Quest for Principles and Values*, 17 Eur J Int Law 187–214 (2006.)

434 P. P. Craig & G. de Búrca (note 287).

435 *Id.*

nance, such as the ones developed under the auspices of global administrative law.

i. Legal pluralism in global administrative law

i. The proposal

The juridical concept of 'legal pluralism' has been part of the discourse about how laws are made, how their applicability is determined and how supremacy is recognized for several decades. Naturally, at the beginning, legal pluralism could be perceived only through the lens of sovereign jurisdictions, which were largely concurrent with national legal systems. Until about mid-1980s scarce were the scholars that had come forward to suggest an idea of synthesis and co-existence under rules of hierarchy of laws and norms from varying legal orders, on a regional or even global scale[436].

Equal was the evolution of the meaning of legal pluralism which is defined as 'the existence of multiple legal systems within one (human) population and/or geographic area'[437]. At the early steps of legal pluralism as an arrangement among co-existing laws 'one human population' was generally understood to mean the populace of a country or the people of the same tribal origins who, even though they might have been living across different, but as a rule neighboring, countries, were allowed to uphold at least one additional legal system apart from that of the state where they resided. Similarly, the notion of 'geographic area' usually meant the territory of a sovereign state or, at best, a region extending across more but still neighboring countries. This remains the case also today, as plural legal systems are particularly prevalent in former colonies, where the law of a former colonial authority may exist alongside more traditional legal systems (i.e. customary law)[438]. However, as the mechanics of coexistence and cooperation among different laws are evolving, today legal pluralism is not understood only through the stricto sensu interpretation discussed

436 John Griffiths, *What is Legal Pluralism?*, 18 The Journal of Legal Pluralism and Unofficial Law 1–55 (1986.)

437 *Id.*

438 *Id.*

above but there is a lato sensu dimension of legal pluralism as well[439]. Through that perspective, the vital space for legal pluralism can be much broader than the borders of a sovereign state; it can extend to entire geographical regions, continents or even the world. It goes without saying that the population bound by the rules of a system constructed under the rules of legal pluralism can be much greater; it can actually even include the global population[440].

Indeed, legal pluralism can be met today as a tool in almost all sectors of law, and definitely in administrative law[441], which is the focus point of this dissertation. What is more, in topics such as the internet the very concept of legal pluralism in global administrative law is suggested as the tool with which to come up with a system of governing rules that will offer pragmatic governance to such a particular phenomenon as the web. As this study will propose legal pluralism as one of the most important tools in constructing the principles of a universally oriented regulatory framework for cloud computing, it is essential to discuss in advance the main characteristics of this approach:

The fact that legal pluralism has spread across different sectors of law over the years means that it has been enriched as legal method with numerous constituencies[442]. Several of them compete for primacy, with different patterns emerging in different institutional settings. Although the entire cadre resulting thereof is highly varied and inconsistent, one can identify three dominant approaches:

- the nationalist approach[443]; it is considered as the classical and probably still the dominant among constituencies of legal pluralism. Its main claim is that final control over regulatory decisions should lie at the national level.
- the internationalist approach[444]; contrary to the former, this approach views the international community of states as the main constituency. In this context, on such issues as human rights or the environment, in-

---

439 Brian Z. Tamanaha, *Understanding Legal Pluralism: Past to Present, Local to Global*, 30 Sydney L. Rev. 375–411 (2008.)

440 Benedict Kingsbury, Nico Krisch & Richard Stewart (note 423).

441 Paul Schiff Berman, *The New Legal Pluralism*, 5 Annual Review of Law and Social Science 225–242 (2009.)

442 Paul Schiff Berman, *Global Legal Pluralism*, 80 S. Cal. L. Rev. 1155–1238 (2006.)

443 Sally Engle Merry, *Legal Pluralism*, 22 Law & Society Review 869–896 (1988.)

444 Baudouin. Dupret (note 370).

ternational law is regarded as having already moved beyond the narrow confines of the state perspective. The internationalist approach deems that nowadays law is increasingly shaped by concerns common to all states[445].

- the cosmopolitan approach[446]; it goes even further in proposing a genuinely global constituency for issues of global governance. The cosmopolitan shares with the international approach the view that accountability to national constituencies is insufficient. It is firmly founded on a theoretical framework of liberal individualism according to which the role of modern states is not to act as vessels of fundamental diversity but only as organizational tools to ensure division of labor and harness the dangers of a world state[447]. For cosmopolitans, the basic constituency in law nowadays would not be based on the community of states, but on the global community of individuals, on a truly global public. However, there is still great ambiguity as to how accountability should be institutionalized in the cosmopolitan perspective. The proposals voiced so far range from representative options such as a world parliament to more liberal proposals[448].

Bearing in mind the nature of cloud computing, this study will primarily use elements from the nationalist and internationalist approach in its effort to construct a dedicated regulatory framework for the cloud. It is true that, from a very bold perspective, the cosmopolitan element could be also utilized; nevertheless, a realistic analysis of where things stand right now can reveal that the general legal and political mindset, at a global scale, is not ready for the adoption of a purely universal legal system. Therefore, this dissertation will primarily focus on constructing a governance spectrum for cloud computing which will serve the global nature of the cloud, as its subject matter, but, at the same time, will pay respect to the divergence and the clear dividing lines that remain strong and are expected to stay so among various state or regional jurisdictions. After all, legal history has repeatedly proven that law matures much better when the next step is taken upon what is already in place as prevalent legal culture than by trying

445 Earl M. Maltz, *Statutory Interpretation and Legislative Power: The Case for a Modified Intentionalist Approach*, 63 Tul. L. Rev. 1–28 (1988.)

446 Ralf Michaels (note 382).

447 Richard Jones, *Legal Pluralism and the Adjudication of Internet Disputes*, 13 International Review of Law, Computers & Technology 49–68 (1999.)

448 Paul Schiff Berman (note 442).

to take strides from the current status quo to profoundly different constructions. In the first instance, the rate of adoption of the newly proposed legal framework is by far greater both by law subjects and law makers or controllers while, in the second case, the theoretical frameworks brought forward face great difficulty in gaining acceptance and recognition.

ii. The problems of legal pluralism

Understandably, legal pluralism is far from flawless as an approach to the challenge of constructing efficiently working legal frameworks[449]. Going over its main weaknesses will allow to identify what are the main gaps we will need to fill up in constructing a governing framework for cloud technologies and will permit well in advance to look elsewhere for regulatory solutions on certain challenges associated to the cloud for which legal pluralism does not provide persuasive answers.

One problem is the lack of certainty: as legal pluralism suggests a balancing act among various legal orders, the disappearance of a clearly competent authority and the resulting fluidity of decisions, the clarity and stabilization that we usually expect from the law can be compromised[450]. On most issues, however, a pluralist order will operate much more smoothly exactly because it is suggested as a way to adjudicate on issues that necessitate fluidity in handling by nature. And, of course, if it appears necessary to provide for greater clarity and stability in some contexts, one might decide to establish institutions along jurisdictional lines, or even on a federal model by sacrificing a certain amount of procedural fairness for the sake of substantive goals. In the end, legal pluralism offers significant tradeoffs, and it is highly debatable whether the added uncertainty of a pluralist order is indeed as problematic as the risk of blockade and the lack of inclusiveness of conventional models.

A yet more serious problem is power disparities[451]. Pluralist approaches (even those of a less radical level) have long had to face the objection that some groups, societal, regional or even of global proportions, possess superior organizational capabilities and, in general, more power than others, so that relying on free interplay between them will merely favor the

449 Baudouin. Dupret (note 370).
450 Ralf Michaels (note 382).
451 N. Krisch (note 427).

powerful at the expense of the weak. Yet it is absolutely questionable whether a pluralist landscape would be much different in this respect from a classical, hierarchically ordered structure. This will ultimately have to be assessed in specific contexts of global regulation, but as we know from domestic contexts, differences in organizational capacities are extremely important also in procedural models with clearly defined participation rights for affected interest groups; the power relations outside an institution are always to some extent reflected inside it, despite provisions for formal equality[452]. Therefore, reluctance to adopt elements of legal pluralism only because of fear that they might put affected parties on disadvantageous positions, while this inequality is a feature already inherent to the current arrangements of public administration law is not enough reason to dismiss the pluralistic perspective altogether[453].

A pluralist global administrative law may not correspond to anybody's ideal; its design is far too open-ended and leaves too much room for political struggle. Yet this is precisely its virtue. Being nobody's ideal, legal pluralism refrains from taking sides in the fundamental contests that define the global order[454]. Bracketing its current deficiencies, and finding ways to work around them pragmatically, may after all not only be prudent but also morally preferable. What is more, it might also be politically advantageous: rather than stabilizing a particular institutional setting, a pluralist order is poised to open up space for the political transformation of a structure of global governance whose legitimacy is far from settled[455]. In parallel to that, putting legal pluralism to work for constructing regulatory arrangements for naturally global phenomena such as cloud computing, will not only help us achieve fruitful answers to the pressing need for efficient regulation of such phenomena but it will also contribute to the maturing process of the new generation of administrative law and governance that today's multilayered global agenda calls for[456].

452 Baudouin. Dupret (note 370).
453 N. Krisch (note 427).
454 *Id.*
455 Brian Z. Tamanaha (note 439).
456 A. Froomkin (note 322).

j. Can effective cloud computing regulation be achieved through international law? Not really.

Having extensively talked about the nature of cloud computing, the technologies it is based on and the applications it facilitates, one would reasonably bring forward the idea of regulating the cloud with recourse to the tools offered by international law, i.e. an international convention, an international body inspecting its application etc. Alas, the differences in perceiving the key legal issues associated with the cloud, such as privacy, secure communications and online anonymity, to name a few, make this option invalid or, at least, insufficient[457]. What is more, it would be highly problematic to try to regulate the cloud only via recourse to international law given, first of all, the way the primary world jurisdictions understand their own relationship to it[458].

Case law of the EU's and US' top courts are the ultimate pool of evidence for anyone who would like to understand how these two jurisdictions understand the hierarchical structure binding them to the international legal order. Over the years, this perception has been clarified, enriched and evolved for each of the two legal orders on the occasion of various cases with greatly diversified subject matters. We will examine here the latest instances where the CJEU and the US Supreme Court touched upon the issue of the relationship between the EU and the US legal order, respectively, and international law.

As far as Europe is concerned, the CJEU had the chance to elaborate on how the EU views its relative position against the international legal order most recently in the context of cases C-402/05P and C-415/05P, Kadi and Al Barakaat[459], the judgments on which were published by the Grand Chamber of the Court on 3 September 2008[460]. The cases dealt with certain UN Security Council resolutions which named the two plaintiffs as suspects for terrorist activities and called for the imposition of certain restrictive measures on them, mostly affecting their financial liquidity and

457 Y. Benkler (note 362).

458 Paul M. Schwartz (note 157).

459 Yassin Abdullah Kadi and Al Barakaat International Foundation v Council of the European Union and Commission of the European Communities. Joined cases C-402/05 P and C-415/05 P. ECLI:EU:C:2008:461.

460 P. Takis Tridimas & Jose A. Gutierrez-Fons, EU Law, International Law and Economic Sanctions Against Terrorism: The Judiciary in Distress?

assets in an attempt to prevent them from indeed perpetrating or supporting terrorist acts. The plaintiffs received a judgment in their favor and the CJEU decided to freeze the execution of the measures prescribed by the UN Security Council resolutions on the grounds that they would profoundly violate undisputable values firmly held within the EU legal order regarding fundamental human rights.

Despite the praise which Kadi has drawn from various quarters[461], the reasoning of the Court in this case reaffirms once more "the uncomfortable image the EU has traditionally held for itself as a virtuous international actor in extrapolation to the exceptionalism of the US"[462]. It also reinstates a long-standing political ambition of the European Union to carve out a distinctive international role for itself as a 'normative power' committed to effective multilateralism under international law[463]. What is also paradoxical, yet at the same time demonstrative of where the European Union currently poses itself in relation to international law, is the fact that such a cornerstone judgment about the role, relationship and authority of international law in connection to the EU is versed in some of its most important parts in rather chauvinist and parochial tones. Additionally, it should be pointed out that this decision was delivered not by a court of a powerful nation-state but by the top court of an international organization, which is itself a creature of international law. Nonetheless, the CJEU in Kadi chose to keep a certain distance from the international legal order and place itself and the EU at a distinct, not directly hierarchical position, in relation to the international legal structure.

An equally striking case, this time affirming the privileged role the USA reserves for itself in relation to the international law is Medellin v Texas 552 U.S. (2008)[464]. This case dealt not with Security Council resolutions but with a judgment of the International Court of Justice, which the US Supreme Court found not enforceable in the US without prior congressional action.

---

461 H.S.P.L.C.E.L.P. Eeckhout & P.L.T. Tridimas, Yearbook of European Law 2009, v. 28 (2010.)

462 Grainne de Burca, *The EU, the European Court of Justice and the International Legal Order after Kadi. Harvard International Law Journal*, 1 Fordham Law Legal Studies Research 1–51 (2009.)

463 Annalisa Ciampi, *The Potentially Competing Jurisdiction of the European Court of Human Rights and the European Court of Justice*, 28 Yearbook of European Law 601–609 (2009.)

464 Jose Ernesto Medellin v. State of Texas, 552 US 491 (2008.)

Although starting off from totally different context, the striking similarity between the reasoning and interpretative approaches of the US Supreme Court in Medellin and that of the CJEU in Kadi are clear evidence of a very important truth: the relationship EU and US reserve for themselves and the international legal order is at the very least standing at the opposite end from their professed embrace of international law and institutions[465]. Without defying international law, it is clear that both these jurisdictions – which, it should not be failed, are the two most important ones on a global scale – prefer to keep certain reservations and room for flexibility regarding their treatment towards international laws. Even if, in the meantime since 2008, Europe's political institutions have asserted time and again the EU's distinctive role as a global actor committed to multilateralism under international law, and even if the Lisbon Treaty nowadays enshrines the 'strict' commitment to international law in EU's foundational texts, the European Court chose to use that much-anticipated Kadi ruling as the occasion to proclaim the internal and external autonomy and separateness of the EU's legal order from the international domain, and the primacy of its internal constitutional values over the norms of international law[466]. Similarly, the US has kept a comparatively preferential approach for itself against bodies of law or treaties of the international domain; in fact, it could be argued that from the US side this special self-positioning has been even firmer than from the European side.

In light of the above observations, it becomes almost self-evident that, since Europe and the US view their relative connection to the international jurisdiction in such a precarious manner, international law and its instruments per se cannot be viable means for achieving universal and harmonized cloud computing regulation. Since both these jurisdictions keep their distances from such high-ranking instruments of international law as resolutions of the UN Security Council or rulings of the International Criminal Court, it is highly unlikely that they will unreservedly comply with a supposed treaty that would venture to impose a universal way of handling cloud computing related matters. Having demonstrated the importance of the cloud as a facilitator for a wide range of economic activities with undeniable profitability, it is only reasonable to expect that the chances of an

465 Grainne de Burca (note 462).

466 Daniel Halberstam, *Constitutionalism and Pluralism in Marbury and Van Gend*, in: U of Michigan Public Law Working Paper (2008.)

international convention on cloud computing to be abided by and applied unreservedly are rather dim.

k. A comparatist approach and synthesis is the only way; moving forward to regulate cloud computing through legal pluralism

Having exhaustively discussed all options or arbitrary proposals currently on the table regarding ways in which the cloud could be effectively regulated, it becomes evident that none of the conventional routes or methods for leveling the field over how a specific subject matter is regulated is enough. Cloud computing cannot be governed solely by governmental authorities, nor can it be directed by the free market alone. Similarly, it cannot be governed globally with norms and rules inspired by one and only jurisdiction, be it the European, the US one or any other, nor can its handling become harmonious via a typical international convention.

However, it should be made clear that regulating the cloud will not be an easy venture. At first, cloud computing is one of the most contemporary subject matters that world jurisdictions have to find a way to effectively govern nowadays. This means that caution is necessary in order for law makers to have clear and thorough knowledge of what cloud computing actually is before sitting down to write any law about it. Simultaneously, its novel nature in comparison to other phenomena calling for governance, even to those very close in nature and characteristics to it, means that it will not be easy to make affected parties be bound by laws that will be based on norms different from the traditional ones. It will not be possible to build up these laws or the foundations they should be built upon, based on the views and appraisals of only one school of law. Consequently, this study will follow the middle way in its effort not to build up a universally applicable law about cloud computing but, pragmatically thinking, in formulating the set of principles every law and jurisdiction should take account of when working on a cloud computing law. This path is that of legal pluralism, upon which the following chapters will walk after analyzing, in a comparative manner, and synthesizing the best practices held about the cloud in EU and US law.

Embarking on a legal discourse that needs to be genuinely creative and strongly persuasive at the same time, we will largely rely on the Nico

Krisch's version of 'legal pluralism in a regional context'[467]. In this configuration of legal pluralism, Krisch departs from the traditional norms limiting legal pluralism to one or neighboring legal orders and proposes tools that advocate harmonization on a broader, regional scale (for instance, within Europe, between the EU and the ECHR countries). The aim of this approach is to recognize the common principles within a region that could serve as a basis for better coordinated laws but without aiming to subordinate one jurisdiction to the other but, instead, to promote their reproach through mutual persuasion, while emphasizing the autonomy and authority of each unit[468]. Then, once the connecting links between the EU and US regulatory views over the different aspects of the cloud are accumulated, this dissertation will conclude by demonstrating how these findings can be applied to the European, the US and the rest of the world's jurisdictions paving the way for a system of laws governing cloud computing which will easily interconnect with each other.

After all, much as it is already technically feasible to perceive the cloud as one, purely boundless and global space, totally defiant of geographical or borders of any other nature, in real life terms it would be unrealistic and, possibly, of little use at the moment, to directly propose the adoption of a 'globally applicable law on cloud computing' of any nature. Therefore, instead of dealing with the challenge of regulating such unique phenomena as the cloud in highly experimental ways, it is much wiser to focus on more pragmatic solutions; schemes that strike an accord between originality necessitated by the nature of the cloud and balancing of interests and long-held perceptions of rivaling legal orders are the way to go. One such scheme will be constructed hereafter.

467 N. Krisch (note 427).
468 Daniel Halberstam (note 466).

CHAPTER 6. Jurisdiction and accountability in the cloud

a. Introduction – scope of this chapter

Having defined the research methodologies that will be utilized in the context of this analysis, the following chapters will be dedicated in presenting findings and putting forward proposals with regard to regulation of legal issues arising from on involving cloud computing as the standard technology for facilitating the vast majority of uses and processes it today's IT landscape. For starters, one needs to examine the main issues that any regulatory scheme applying to the cloud should deal with. Therefore, in the following two chapters we will consider the questions that any kind of legislative text meant specifically for cloud computing and its applications should provide answers for before, ultimately, moving on to bringing together proposals and best practices from either the EU or the US school of thought regarding the cloud and arguing on how these could be better coordinated between the two jurisdictions. At first, in the present chapter the issues of who is accountable for incidents occurring in a cloud-based environment and how authorities or courts claim jurisdiction to adjudicate on these incidents will be examined.

PART I: Jurisdiction in the era of cloud computing

a. The currently prevailing legal norms in EU law for claiming jurisdiction over cases involving data transfer and processing

Given the lack of a body of legislation specifically dealing with cloud computing, one needs to look into neighboring fields of legislation in order to describe the current status quo about how laws dealing with issues involving digital data claim jurisdiction among each other.

As it has been explained already[469], EU laws are the ones with the most articulated reasoning in matters related to the Internet and its implement-

469 See Chapter 3.

ing technologies[470]. The most representative piece of law among all IT-related EU legislation is the General Data Protection Regulation. Since we currently are at the crossroads between the GDPR and its long-lived predecessor, the Data Protection Directive (DPD), it is worth analyzing how both these laws settled the issue of territorial and material scope for their provisions. In this way, it will be possible to draw conclusions with regard to the trend EU laws follow on this matter, which, it can already be briefly stated that it is expansive.

Firstly, then, in the DPD three main grounds were described as the ones that suffice to justify jurisdiction on an IT-related case. In particular, the GDPR's forerunner generally recognized three different grounds for determining its applicability on personal data processing affairs. These were:

- establishment of the data processor under examination[471],
- public international law[472] and
- use of equipment within the jurisdiction[473].

In a cloud computing context, the above grounds determined the extent to which a user or provider of cloud computing services, even if not incorporated, residing or headquartered in an EEA Member State, could become subject to obligations under EU data protection law as a result of:

- having a subsidiary, branch or agent, or a mere data centre, in the EEA; or
- making use of a data centre located in the EEA, or other equipment located in the EEA.

i. Establishment – Art. 4 para. 1(a) DPD

The DPD stipulated that each EEA Member State had to apply the Directive's provisions as this was implemented in that Member State if 'the processing is carried out in the context of the activities of an establishment of the controller on the territory of the Member State'. In other words, the controller had to have an establishment on the ground of that Member

470 See also Chapter 2.
471 Art. 4 para. 1(a) Directive 95/46/EC (DPD) (note 143.)
472 Art. 4 para. 1(b) Directive 95/46/EC (DPD) (note 143.)
473 Art. 4 para. 1(c) Directive 95/46/EC (DPD) (note 143.)

State and should process personal data 'in the context of the activities of that establishment'.

In fact, what is described above is, one could say, a two-step test as it was examined whether

- the data controller has an 'establishment' on the territory of an EU Member State, and
- whether the controller processes personal data in the context of the activities of that establishment.

If the answer to both questions was yes, then the Member State which hosts the data controller on its soil had to implement the DPD to personal data processing activities carried out by that controller, regardless of where in the world they took place – outside or inside the EEA.

It is worth briefly mentioning that the criterion of 'the context of the activities of an establishment of a controller', which was among the main ones in EU law under the Data Protection Directive had, over the years and with the evolution of technology, come to cause a great deal of friction as to its precise interpretation[474]. In the latest years when the DPD was still in force, Art. 29 Working Party had stated three factors which should be taken into account when assessing this criterion[475]:

- the degree of involvement of the establishment(s) in the activities in the context of which personal data are processed;
- the nature of the activities as a secondary consideration and
- the goal of ensuring effective data protection.

Art. 29 WP went on to suggest that a 'who is doing what' test should be applied in the sense that the test required a determination of:

- who carries out the relevant activities and
- whether there is data processing in the context of these activities.

The involvement of the establishment in the activities is the most important of these factors.

The wide interpretation of 'in the context of the activities of an establishment' that was put forward meant that a cloud provider with one or

---

474 Joel Reidenberg, *Technology and Internet Jurisdiction*, 153 University of Pennsylvania law review 1951–1974 (2005.)

475 Article 29 Working Party, Opinion 3/2009 on the Draft Commission Decision on standard contractual clauses for the transfer of personal data to processors established in third countries, under Directive 95/46/EC (data controller to data processor), available at: http://ec.europa.eu/justice/data-protection/article-29/documentation/opinion-recommendation/index_en.htm.

more establishments in the EEA was also subject to this provision. This had two important consequences[476]:

- EU data protection law could be applicable even if no processing of personal data was carried out at the establishment of the cloud provider, and
- because of the nature of cloud services and the geographical dispersion of their facilities, more than one establishment of the same cloud provider in the EEA may be involved in activities, so that the controller is subject to two different national implementations of the DPD.

One contemporary case, sparked by the use of technological resources heavily based on cloud computing technology that is demonstrative of how loosely Europe has been interpreting until now the criteria it upholds for determining jurisdiction on a cloud computing related case was the so called 'Google Italy'[477] one.

The case referred to a video which was posted on September 8, 2006 in Google Videos showing a disabled student being bullied and insulted by three of his colleagues (while another student was recording with her mobile phone, and ten more were watching the scene without intervening). The video, with a duration of about 3 minutes, was viewed by a significant number of people, counting more than 5000 downloads. Eventually it had made it to being the most popular one in the category of "video divertenti" (funny videos). Users of Google posted various messages in the comments section of the video; apparently, some flagged it as being inappropriate and some e-mailed Google requesting for it to be removed. On 7 November 2006, the Italian Postal Police, after a communication from a citizen, requested Google to remove the video, which was deleted on the same day. As a result, the video had been available in total for about two months after it was initially posted. On the aftermath of the incident, three lawsuits were filed against

- the students molesting the victim of the bullying attack on the video
- the teacher and school authorities of the facility where the incident took place for failing to prevent the incident
- Google Italia and its executives for criminal defamation and violation of data protection rules. With regard to data protection, the accusation

---

476 *Id.*

477 Raul Mendez, *Google case in Italy*, 1 International Data Privacy Law 137–139 (2011.)

was that Google Italy was processing personal data, and in particular health data, illicitly, for the purpose of making a profit[478].

Leaving aside all other aspects of the case, it is worth summarizing the main findings related to the issue of responsibility of the internet service provider (in this case, Google and its cloud based service Google Videos), which was found to exist by application of the very broad in scope EU legislation[479] in force at the time. A major part of commentary has found the decision of the Italian judge in this case defective in various regards. Most importantly, the decision was slammed because it failed to conceptualize the role of platform providers in the context of the web 2.0[480], and their enabling function with regard to user-driven generation of contents; in other words, it failed to understand the edgy difference of cloud empowered platforms. In any case, this was just one example of several similar cases that arose during the years of the DPD which, especially as cloud technologies were taking more and more over older conventional IT solutions, made clear that the cloud era brought with it the need for a profound shift in the ways in which jurisdiction was recognized in relevant affairs.

ii. International law – Art. 4 para. 1(b) DPD

The second criterion through which EU law in the years of the DPD determined jurisdiction in data processing and handling matters is that of international law. Precisely, European data protection laws applied where the controller was not established on a Member State's territory, but the law of at least one Member State applies by virtue of international law[481]. Such would be, for instance, the case of a ship or aircraft under a particular Member State's flag. In the context of cloud computing, this may be rele-

478 Sentenza n. 1972/2010. Tribunale Ordinario di Milano in composizione monocratica. Sezione 4 Penale. Available at http://speciali.espresso.repubblica.it//pdf/Motivazioni_sentenza_Google.pdf (16.02.2016). P. 102/103.

479 G. Sartor & Viola de Azevedo Cunha, M., *The Italian Google-Case. Privacy, Freedom of Speech and Responsibility of Providers for User-Generated Contents*, 18 International Journal of Law and Information Technology 356–378 (2010.)

480 Tim O'Reilly & John Battelle, Web Squared: Web 2.0 Five Years On.

481 W. Kuan Hon, Julia Hörnle & Christopher Millard, *Data Protection Jurisdiction and Cloud Computing. When are Cloud Users and Providers Subject to EU Data Protection Law? The Cloud of Unknowing, Part 3*, 26 International Review of Law, Computers & Technology (2012.)

vant for cloud facilities, e.g. data centers, which may be set up on vessels or platforms floating outside the territorial waters of any Member State[482].

iii. Equipment – Art. 4 para. 1(c) DPD

The final grounds on which the DPD had been traditionally basing jurisdiction to apply its data protection law in cases relevant to the provision or use of cloud computing services was the 'equipment' criterion[483]. Under this, even if the data controller 'is not established on Community territory', the application of a Member State's data protection law may nevertheless be valid if this controller 'makes use of equipment, automated or otherwise, situated on the territory' of that State for the purposes of processing personal data, unless the equipment is only used 'for transit through' Community territory. We should also not fail to point out that there is no requirement that the personal data processed had to relate to EEA individuals.

iv. Changes to current status quo by the upcoming GDPR

Under the newly arriving regime of the GDPR, the issue of material and territorial scope of European legislation on data processing and transfers (still the piece of law closest to the nature of the data related activities executed via cloud computing) will become even broader. In particular, the GDPR will apply to organizations which have EU "establishments", where personal data are processed "in the context of the activities" of such an establishment[484]. As long as this test is met, the GDPR applies irrespective of whether the actual data processing takes place in the EU or not. The term "establishment" was analyzed by the Court of Justice of the European Union in the 2015 Weltimmo vs. NAIH case[485]. In there the

482 While this may sound futuristic, Google has obtained a patent in the United States for such data centers built on ships. So in future there may well be data centers on ships moored outside territorial waters, with the possibility of flags of convenience being used for data protection law purposes.

483 W. Kuan Hon, Julia Hörnle & Christopher Millard (note 472.)

484 Art. 3 para. 1 Regulation (EU) 2016/679 (GDPR) (note 25.)

485 Weltimmo s.r.o. v Nemzeti Adatvédelmi és Információszabadság Hatóság, Case C-230/14, (OJ) ECLI:EU:C:2015:639.

CJEU confirmed that establishment is a "broad" and "flexible" phrase that should not hinge on any particular legal form. An organization may be "established" where it exercises "any real and effective activity – even a minimal one" – through "stable arrangements" in the EU. The presence of a single representative may be sufficient. In that case, Weltimmo was considered to be established in Hungary as a result of the use of a website in Hungarian which advertised Hungarian properties (which meant, according to the Court's interpretation that it was "mainly or entirely directed at that Member State"), use of a local agent (who was responsible for local debt collection and acted as a representative in administrative and judicial proceedings), and use of a Hungarian postal address and bank account for business purposes – even though Weltimmo was incorporated in Slovakia. Organizations maintaining EU sales offices, which promote or sell advertising or marketing targeting EU residents, are therefore expected to be subject to the GDPR as well – since the associated processing of personal data is considered to be "inextricably linked" to and thus carried out "in the context of the activities of" those EU establishments[486].

Non-EU established legal entities will be subject to the GDPR as well whenever they process personal data about EU data subjects in connection with:

– the "offering of goods or services" (payment is not required);
– "monitoring" of their behavior within the EU[487].

For the criterion of "offering of goods and services" (but not monitoring) to be fulfilled, mere accessibility of a site from within the EU is not sufficient. It must be apparent that the organization envisages that activities will be directed to EU data subjects. Contact addresses accessible from the EU and the use of a language used in the controller's own country are also not sufficient. However, the use of an EU language or currency, the ability to place orders in that other language and references to EU users or customers will be relevant indications that will be taken into account and assessed. The CJEU has examined when an activity (such as offering goods and services) will be considered "directed to" EU Member States, even though in a different context unrelated to data processing (i.e. under the "Brussels 1" Regulation (44/2001/EC) governing jurisdiction in civil and

486 Google Spain SL, Google Inc. v AEPD, Mario Costeja González, Case C-131/12, (OJ) ECLI:EU:C:2014:317.

487 Art. 3 para. 2 Regulation (EU) 2016/679 (GDPR) (note 25.)

commercial matters[488]). Its comments are one of the few leads we have so far in our effort to interpret the same aspect of the GDPR. In addition to the considerations mentioned above, the CJEU notes that an intention to target EU customers may be illustrated by:

- "patent" evidence, such as the payment of money to a search engine to facilitate access by those within a Member State or where targeted Member States are designated by name; and
- other factors – possibly in combination with each other – including the "international nature" of the relevant activity (e.g. certain tourist activities), mentions of telephone numbers with an international code, use of a top-level domain name other than that of the state in which the trader is established (such as.de or.eu), the description of "itineraries from Member States to the place where the service is provided" and mentions of an "international clientele composed of customers domiciled in various Member States"[489].

It should be noted though that this list is not exhaustive and the question should be determined on a case-by-case basis, especially until a certain amount of time has passed by after the GDPR officially enters into force and enough experience from its actual implementation is accumulated.

It is not clear at this transitional point between the DPD and GDPR eras whether non-EU organizations offering goods and services to EU businesses (as opposed to individuals) will fall within the scope of the "offering goods and services" test in Article 3(2)(a) GDPR. "Monitoring" specifically includes the tracking of individuals online with the intention of creating profiles, including where this is used to take decisions to predict personal preferences, behaviors and attitudes[490].

Organizations subject to the GDPR's long-arm jurisdictional reach must appoint an EU-based representative. As analyzed immediately above, under the Data Protection Directive, organizations targeting EU data subjects only had to comply with EU rules if they also made use of "equipment" in the EU to process personal data. However, this led national supervisory

---

488 Council Regulation (EC) No 44/2001 on jurisdiction and the recognition and enforcement
of judgments in civil and commercial matters, (OJ) L 012, 16/01/2001 P. 0001 – 0023.

489 Pammer v Reederei Karl Schlüter GmbH & Co and Hotel Alpenhof v Heller; Joined cases (C-585/08) and (C-144/09), ECLI:EU:C:2010:740.

490 For more on profiling and automated decision making, refer also to Chapter 4.

authorities, who were seeking to assert jurisdiction, to develop arguments that the placing of cookies, or requesting users to fill in forms, would amount to the use of "equipment" in the EU. It is hoped that the GDPR provisions will make easier to demonstrate that EU law applies; although, whenever organizations have no EU presence, enforcement may be just as difficult as before.

From the above, it becomes apparent that EU data protection law creates for itself an ever-wider space of material and territorial scope. The same can generally be said for any jurisdiction, in principle: every legal order is inherently striving to impose itself as much as possible over others wishing to secure for its subjects an as extended as possible (physical as well as material) vital space of legal security. This, however, respectively increases the chances for conflicts among jurisdictions. Therefore, the need for coordination among different legal orders grows even more important so that frictions and jurisdictional uncertainty are avoided, as much as possible. Shifting the focus from data processing as a particular activity to cloud enabled processes involving data in general and developing cloud computing regulation rules through this generic perspective will offer a much more suitable ground for common understanding among different legal orders.

b. Technology and internet jurisdiction: a process of parallel 'give and take'

The rise and evolution of technology, especially in the field of IT, has decisively defined many different aspects of people's lives over the latest decades. Reasonably, this technological omnipresence has also spurred new legal disputes and cases that called for adjudication. As a result, this new genre of legal cases has affected all different aspects of judicial procedure including the one of determination of jurisdiction. Initially, cases that were born out of technological evolution were mostly seeking to deny jurisdiction, choice of law, and enforcement to states where users and victims were located[491]. Those cases have been described by a certain num-

491 Joel Reidenberg (note 474).

ber of scholars as a type of "denial-of-service" attack[492] against the legal system, in particular to the jurisdictions of users and victims.

However, after this initial type of technology-spurred cases that threatened to stir an imbalance between jurisdictions of countries that were home to IT providers over those of users or victims of malicious practices involving IT innovations, the trend was reversed[493]. The continued surge in IT has already tamed and will further undermine the initial technological assault on state jurisdiction. This reverse of the tide was made possible thanks to the fact that as computing gets more sophisticated, so it enhances the processing capabilities and power of users' computers[494]. These technologically advanced machines are gradually giving to the victim's state a wider nexus of tools for dealing with offending acts, while it greatly facilitates the establishment of a direct relationship with the offender for purposes of personal jurisdiction and choice of law[495]. Even more, some of these innovations additionally enable states to enforce their decisions electronically and, consequently, bypass the problems of foreign recognition and enforcement of judgments[496].

This peculiar 'war' between exercises of state power through assertions of jurisdiction and technologically spurred legal issues has proven to be beneficial for technology itself[497]. In fact, out of this friction came considerable momentum that helped the advancement of pioneering granular technologies[498] and the consolidation of new service markets for legal compliance[499].

In conclusion, the assertion of sovereign jurisdiction to protect citizens might indeed be a tricky thing that is far from being settled and, actually, it urgently needs to be revisited. Additionally, another aspect of the matter is that the phenomenon is likely to advance the fundamental public policy premise that the rule of law should be supreme to technological determin-

---

492 Sean P. Kanuck, *Information Warefare: New Challenges for Public International Law*, 37 Harv. Int'l LJ 272–568 (1996.)

493 Joel Reidenberg (note 474).

494 Joel Reidenberg (note 173).

495 Reidenberg, J. R., Schwartz, P. M. (note 174).

496 Joel Reidenberg (note 175).

497 Joel Reidenberg (note 474).

498 *Id.*

499 Lawrence Lessig & Paul Resnick, *Zoning speech on the Internet: A legal and technical model*, 98 Michigan Law Review 395–431 (1999.)

ism[500]. Nevertheless, the multiplicity of states with jurisdiction over Internet activities is also likely to stimulate creativity towards new Internet services such as more accurate and selective filtering technologies, stronger security zones and more robust, customized compliance capabilities via sophisticated applications. In that sense, and taking for granted that the variety of choice on the jurisdictional front is not going to cease from existing any time soon, an attempt to build a minimum threshold of understanding between competing jurisdictions about what they view and understand as 'cloud computing' or by other terms related to IT advancements and applications could even serve as one extra catalyst that would accelerate innovation. 'Playing' with known rules but, at the same time, having to come up with arrangements that will work with all different interpretations of these rules is a condition favorable to technological evolution[501].

These observations are also backed by two of the most prominent academics in the field of IT law and regulation[502]. From one side, Paul Schwartz has formulated the thesis that "different parties in the cloud can contribute inputs, outputs, analytics, and execute different kinds of actions. The result of this distributed computing environment is to permit dramatic flexibility in processing decisions – on a global basis."[503]

On the other side, Lawrence Lessig has portrayed this unconventional relation between legal rules and technological capacities with an emphatic dictum: "code is the law of cyberspace."[504] Indeed, the architecture of the internet – its code, network protocols and enabling technologies – is what determines what can or cannot be done on the network[505]. Lessig went so far to actually suggest that "as the underlying code of the network ultimately dictates the rules to which users are compelled to obey (whether or not these rules are actually endorsed by the law), it becomes a de facto law"[506].

---

500 *Id.*

501 Joel Reidenberg (note 474).

502 E. Kosta, Consent in European Data Protection Law (2013); Steffen Kroschwald ed. (note 317).

503 Reidenberg, J. R., Schwartz, P. M. (note 174).

504 L. Lessig, Code and other laws of cyberspace (1999.)

505 Lawrence Lessig, *Law Regulating Code Regulating Law*, 35 Loyola University Chicago Law Journal 1–14 (2003.)

506 Joel Reidenberg (note 474).

c. From data protection law to international jurisdiction on the internet; adapting laws to modern needs and reality

As defined under public international law 'jurisdiction is a State's right to regulate conduct in matters not exclusively of domestic concern'[507]. It needs to be made clear that the notion of 'jurisdiction' must not be confused with neighboring terms as choice of law, 'conflict of laws', or 'applicable law', which deal with the question of which law or laws shall be applied in a given case. However, as the complexity of matters seeking judicial remedy increases, jurisdiction and choice of law as concepts become closely related, and the distinction between them has become increasingly vague[508].

In an effort to trace the updated meaning of 'jurisdiction' when it comes to issues stemming from cloud computing technologies, one may depart from neighboring legal fields which are already sufficiently regulated. Probably the closest field from which useful information could be extracted to serve as the basis for a theoretical discourse about the question of jurisdiction in cloud computing matters is that of data protection. Data protection law should not be regarded as falling entirely within either private or public law. In fact, the body of law known today as data protection derives from a wide variety of legal sources, namely consumer protection law, human rights law, internal market law, and others[509].

As Jon Bing has stated: 'Data protection legislation will typically contain provisions of a public law nature, relating to an authority and its duties and decisions. But the law will also often include civil law provisions, typically on liability for data protection violations. The provisions of data protection legislation may therefore have to be qualified as belonging to different areas of law, to which different relevant connection criteria are assigned. Following the traditional method, different aspects of one case may then have to be decided by different lex causae, which easily may lead to distortions as the legislation is conceived as an organic whole

507 C. Kuner, *Data Protection Law and International Jurisdiction on the Internet (Part 2)*, 18 International Journal of Law and Information Technology 227–247 (2010.)

508 *Id.*

509 C. Kuner, *Data Protection Law and International Jurisdiction on the Internet (Part 1)*, 18 International Journal of Law and Information Technology 176–193 (2010.)

where the different provisions support an appropriate solution'[510]. One should not forget that the origins of data protection law in consumer protection and human rights law may also indicate that courts and data protection authorities could regard some of its rules as ordre publique, i.e. directly and unconditionally enforceable regardless of the applicable law[511].

While, as it is known, public international law only applies directly to relations between States, it also serves another purpose as the basic limiting standard of the international legal order and the testing ground for jurisdictional rules affecting private parties in different States as well[512]. In fact, even for the specific field of IT, the Article 29 Working Party has recognized that "jurisdiction under data protection law should be evaluated under public international law"[513]. Besides, the legality of jurisdictional rules under international law is important because of the global nature of the Internet. Since both major legal systems that are under focus in this study, i.e. those of the EU and the US, at least attempt to interpret domestic law in harmony with international law, the main assumptions of international law on jurisdiction can be vital in the quest for a harmonized approach on cloud related matters.

Although there is a certain degree of overlap between them, jurisdiction in international law is generally divided up into three different categories[514]:

- **Legislative or prescriptive jurisdiction**, which is 'the power of a State to apply its laws to cases involving a foreign element'[515]. Legislative jurisdiction is, at most times, concurrent rather than exclusive[516]. A very typical example of legislative jurisdiction in the area of data

510 J. Bing, *Data Protection, jurisdiction and the choice of law* Privacy Laws & Policy Reporter 92–98 (1999.)

511 Christopher Kuner, *Internet Jurisdiction and Data Protection Law: An International Legal Analysis (Part 2)*, 18 International Journal of Law and Information Technology 227–257 (2010.)

512 *Id.*

513 Article 29 Working Party, Working document on determining the international application of EU data protection law to personal data processing on the Internet by non-EU based websites, available at: http://ec.europa.eu/justice/data-protection/article-29/documentation/opinion-recommendation/index_en.htm.

514 C. Kuner (note 507).

515 Uta Kohl, Jurisdiction and the Internet. A study of regulatory competence over online activity (2010.)

516 Svantesson, Dan Jerker B, Private international law and the internet (2012.)

protection law is the application of EU data protection law to a webpage located outside the EU that deploys cookies to process personal data of individuals residing within the EU area. In the field of cloud computing, one case where prescriptive jurisdiction would apply is when the servers of a cloud provider with whose resources personal data of individuals from within the EU area are processed are located outside the EU.

- **Adjudicative jurisdiction**, which means 'the power of a State's courts to try cases involving a foreign element'[517]. An example of this type of jurisdiction occurs when a European data protection authority that decides on a complaint submitted by an individual residing in the EU with regard to the processing of their personal data by an entity outside the EU. If, in addition, we consider data protection law as 'public law', adjudicative jurisdiction becomes identical to legislative jurisdiction[518]. Mutatis mutandis, an example of adjudicative jurisdiction in the realm of cloud computing occurs when a DPA investigates the practices of a cloud resources provider outside the EU, which are utilized for processing data belonging to EU law subjects.
- **Enforcement jurisdiction**, which refers to 'the power of one State to perform acts in the territory of another State'[519]. One such instance is when a European data protection authority moves to conduct an audit of an entity headquartered outside the EU. Similarly, in the case of cloud computing, enforcement jurisdiction occurs when a European DPA moves to carry out an audit on the facilities of a cloud provider headquartered outside the EU area.

It shouldn't be overlooked that the legality of any of these types of jurisdiction is closely connected with that of the other types, while any limitations on one type of jurisdiction may also have effects the scope of the others[520].

Logically, each of the different types of jurisdiction described above need a conceptual basis to be founded on[521]. The following are the juris-

517 Michael Akehurst, *Jurisdiction in International Law*, 46 Brit. Y. B. Int'l L. 145–258 (1972.)
518 Uta Kohl (note 515).
519 Michael Akehurst (note 517).
520 P. P. Craig & G. de Búrca (note 287).
521 C. Kuner (note 507).

dictional bases that have become most widely accepted, and that are most relevant to data protection law:

- **Territoriality**: Following the principle of territoriality, jurisdiction is determined based on the acts that have been committed within the territory of the judging state[522]. A variation of it is the 'objective territoriality principle', according to which the act under judgement was initiated outside but completed within the territory of the state, or a constituting element of the conduct under examination occurred within the territory of the state claiming jurisdiction[523]. Much as the territoriality principle is probably the most fundamental one for concretizing jurisdiction, the Internet greatly complicates application of it; as it has been already explained, it can be nearly impossible or resources-wise non-viable to localize an online action down to the territory of a particular State.
- **Personality:** Under the principle of personality, jurisdiction is asserted by the state of nationality of the perpetrator (active personality principle) or of the victim (passive personality principle)[524]. This jurisdictional principle is prevalent in criminal law; however, there are instances when it is applied also in civil law[525]. When it comes to cloud computing, a lot of details merit clarification before the personality principle can be applied; such as, how is the perpetrator among all those actors making a cloud-based processing possible, whether the cloud services user, who may also be the person that finally bears the burden of a cloud-based processing, can be billed as the victim of an act if he/she was also the one that had triggered off the processing etc.
- **Effects doctrine:** The 'effects doctrine' has traditionally been regarded as the most controversial of all jurisdictional bases[526]. According to it, jurisdiction is claimed based on the fact that a certain conduct outside a state has effects within the state[527]. Despite the relentless critique it has attracted, the effects doctrine seems to have become widespread, particularly with regard to assertions of jurisdiction over conduct on the

522 Svantesson, Dan Jerker B (note 516).
523 *Id.*
524 *Id.*
525 *Id.*
526 *Id.*
527 C. Kuner (note 509).

Internet[528]. The basic argument of opponents of the effects doctrine is that it is open-ended, since 'in a globalized economy, everything has an effect on everything'[529]. An additional point of friction is that 'the widening of the reach of effect based jurisdictional rules results in a widening of the gap between reasonable grounds for jurisdictional, and application of law, claims on the one hand and reasonable grounds for recognition and enforcement of foreign judgments on the other'[530].

- **Protective principle:** The protective principle has been conceptualized with the aim of protecting a state from acts committed outside its territory but which jeopardize its sovereignty[531]. Jurisdiction founded on this basis is usually limited exclusively to criminal law or serious violations that endanger the security of a country[532]; such instances would normally not include data protection violations. Besides, the focus of the protective principle is on protection of the state, not of individuals (who are the main subject of protection of data protection law)[533]. However, at least in the EU, Member States have been lately interpreting the protective principle under a much wider scope than security issues, so that it resembles an application of the objective territoriality or the effects doctrine and, of course, from that perspective many internet or cloud related issues are also included[534] (e.g. the calls for investigations on the wire-tapping of communications of civilians by foreign intelligence agencies as an anti-terrorist protective measure).

d. What is the problem with asserting jurisdiction over cloud-related cases under current EU laws?

Goldsmith and Wu, two of the most prominent figures of the wider area of IT law, have expressed the view that jurisdictional uncertainties related to

528 C. Kuner (note 507).
529 T. Schultz, *Carving up the Internet. Jurisdiction, Legal Orders, and the Private/Public International Law Interface*, 19 European Journal of International Law 799–839 (2008.)
530 Svantesson, Dan Jerker B (note 516).
531 *Id.*
532 C. Kuner (note 509).
533 *Id.*
534 *Id.*

Internet matters have been exaggerated[535]. In fact, they try to support this estimate by putting forward the following considerations:

- unilateral assertions of jurisdiction by States on the web are no different than those they make in other areas;
- technological fixes (like geolocation) offer ways in which entities can minimize their legal exposure against overlapping and exorbitant jurisdictional claims;
- there is no need to worry about all kinds of jurisdictions, just because you are doing business online. Instead, the parties need only take into consideration the relevant laws of states that are capable of taking enforcement action in relation to their case; for instance, the states which can initiate liquidation proceedings against assets of the defendant inside their territory;
- finally, it is argued that awareness is increasing that dealing with jurisdictional issues is part of the cost of doing business on the internet. However, these 'jurisdictional threats' are not always substantial; for instance, jurisdiction under EU law against a data controller without assets in the EU but has been using cookies on its website to process the data of Europeans should be of little concern to the controller, since there is no plausible chance of enforcement.

Even if these approaches are fair, by and large, the problems caused by online jurisdictional uncertainties in the context of data protection and cloud computing appear to be more serious than these[536]. As it has been already demonstrated 'cloud computing', as a term, is not synonymous to 'data processing' but it refers to a much wider range of technologies, which serve as facilitators of many different IT applications[537]. Consequently, if we continue to resort to laws that regulate the cloud without being specifically customized for the cloud, we will continue resorting to legislation that will cover a wide variety of online data-related tasks while lacking the necessary degree of specialization, thus increasing the odds for jurisdictional conflicts.

---

535 Jack L. Goldsmith & Tim Wu, Who controls the Internet? Illusions of a borderless world (2008.)

536 Christopher Kuner, *Internet Jurisdiction and Data Protection Law: An International Legal Analysis (Part 1)*, 18 International Journal of Law and Information Technology 176–202 (2010.)

537 See also Chapter 3.

Moreover, when the rules resolving jurisdictional matters with regard to a law are versed in such a broad and open to interpretation manner, while the chances that this law will indeed be enforced are not equally broad, there is an inherent risk that respect for this law from its subjects will eventually be diminished[538]. Statistics and experience prove that the gap between compliance and enforcement of European data protection law up to date has been certainly large, even within the EU[539]. At the current standpoint, which coincides with the end of the DPD era, relevant figures that can be retrieved for that piece of law speak volumes: for example[540], the Spanish DPA had stated that in 2007 it had received 8,463 notifications from data controllers about international data transfers. However, it has to be pointed out that all telephone calls, e-mails, faxes, Internet browsing activities, etc. executed between end users in Spain and countries outside the EU are also to be considered 'international data transfers' in the sense of data protection law. As a result, all these occurrences might also be subject to a duty of notification, which means that out of these 8,463 reports several can be essentially insignificant, while there may be millions or even billion others which may go on completely unreported[541].

Therefore, a balancing exercise is necessary in order for the EU body of law to acquire cloud-specific laws that will be more concrete and will primarily apply on actual instances where personal privacy and similar rights are at stake and not merely when a process fulfils the technical criteria for being defined as data processing.

e. Steps to reduce jurisdictional disputes from the perspective of EU law

Achieving greater jurisdictional clarity in conflicts related to cases caused by cloud-based applications or their uses is not possible solely by changes

538 *Id.*

539 European Parliament, Report on the First Report on the implementation of the Data Protection Directive (95/46/EC) (COM(2003) 265 – C5-0375/2003 – 2003/2153(INI)) (2004.)

540 C. Kuner (note 507).

541 For the full report that served as the basis for this case study: Agencia Española de Protección de Datos, Informe sobre transferencias internacionales de datos, Julio 2007, 5 (available at: https://www.agpd.es/portalweb/jornadas/transferencias_internacionales_datos/common/pdfs/report_Inter_data_transfers_colombia_en.pdf; last accessed: 19/2/2016.)

to jurisdictional rules. It can a priori be said that, given the fragmented landscape put together by different jurisdictions, there is not one such rule, or set of rules that could both envisage all cases where jurisdiction under cloud computing law would be justified, and at the same time, avoid unjustifiably extending jurisdiction in other cases. Notwithstanding, other measures compatible with the European legal thinking and practice so far could be taken that could help jurisdictional rules become more relevant and to the point while producing a more balanced framework for protection especially in cross-border cases. Such measures could include, primarily[542]:

- greater harmonization of the law: As demonstrated already, application of a state's data protection law and assertions of jurisdiction by that state seem to go hand in hand. Consequently, greater harmonization of data protection or cloud computing laws would contribute to reducing the number and the scope of jurisdictional conflicts ignited by them. Despite the primary role EU law has played so far in personal data[543], IT and alike legislations, the respective laws around the world are inspired by divergent cultural and legal values[544]. Harmonization of data protection and similar nature laws in a comprehensive, or universal, manner is unlikely to be achieved. However, as this project maintains as its primary thesis, a lot more could be done to achieve a quasi- or even a genuinely global understanding of key notions of cloud computing technologies and their most common implementations, prime among which is, undoubtedly, data protection law (for instance, terms like 'personal data', 'data controller' or 'data processor').
- cooperation between regulatory authorities: Cooperation among national or regional regulators can greatly contribute to the concretization of the scope and impact of jurisdictional conflicts[545]. A culture of rapprochement and coordination of enforcement actions, along with the adoption of common positions on important substantive legal issues are areas of cooperation where the world's DPAs could achieve real progress in the foreseeable future.
- technical solutions: Technical means such as geolocation, which are becoming more widely available, though not a solution per se, can help

542 *Id.*
543 Refer also to Chapters 4 and 5.
544 L. A. Bygrave (note 137).
545 C. Kuner (note 509).

reduce jurisdictional conflicts by helping to 'map' the Internet, thus making it easier to limit jurisdictional uncertainty[546].

- development of a theory of reasonableness[547]: As Lowenfeld suggests, any theory developed with the aim of providing answers to the broad issue of jurisdiction, at the end of the day, attempts to strike a compromise between legal certainty and flexibility. The rules that may, at any time, be adopted "need to be clear and definite enough to lead to an acceptable degree of legal certainty, but also flexible enough to cover unforeseen and complex situations, which suggests the need for a 'safety valve' that allows jurisdiction not to be asserted even when technically it could be"[548]. This concept, code-named as the 'concept of reasonableness', is intended to help resolve particular situations, typical among which are those when there is a jurisdictional conflict between regulators in two sovereign states[549].
- The use of the reasonableness doctrine to limit jurisdictional assertions was met, primarily, with strong criticism, as it seemed too vague a criterion to be useful in practice[550]. Mann also famously argued that jurisdiction should be based on a 'link' as an objective tie to the forum that is distinct from 'mere political, economic, commercial or social interests'[551]. However, as IT evolves and its main implementing technologies become more and more defiant of conventional boundaries, such as geographical or jurisdictional borders, we need to revisit suggestions like the reasonableness test and assess how they could offer answers to modern challenges.

---

546 Jack L. Goldsmith & Tim Wu (note 535); Zachary NJ Peterson, Mark Gondree, Robert Beverly, *A position paper on data sovereignty: the importance of geolocating data in the cloud* Proceedings of the 3rd USENIX conference on Hot topics in cloud computing (2011.)

547 Andreas F. Lowenfeld, International litigation and the quest for reasonableness. Essays in private international law (1996.)

548 Dan Svantesson, *Protecting Privacy on the 'Borderless' Internet – Some Thoughts on Extraterritoriality and Transborder Data Flow*, 19 Bond Law Review 168–187 (2007.)

549 C. Kuner (note 507).

550 Svantesson, Dan Jerker B., *Privacy, the Internet and Transborder Data Flows – An Australian Perspective*, 4 Masaryk University journal of law and technology 1 (2010.)

551 F. A. Mann & Académie de droit international de La Haye., *The doctrine of international jurisdiction revisited after twenty years*, 186 Recueil des cours = Collected courses 9–116 (1984.)

- greater interdisciplinary collaboration between the jurisdiction and data protection world and the IT world: Up to this point, there has been only limited interaction between scholars, international organizations, regulators, and others working on international jurisdiction or on data protection and the members of the IT industry, who are the minds that actually make possible all the applications that have ignited the problems which are discussed in this study. However, this one-sighted approach has to change and bodies dealing with international jurisdictional issues (such as The Hague Conference on Private International Law, UNCITRAL, and others) have to turn their interest also in IT, cloud computing and data protection law[552]. At the same time, they need to invite and closely collaborate with representatives from the IT industry, who can offer the input and ideas of someone with hands-on experience on the matter.

f. The internet jurisdiction risk of cloud computing under US law

After a thorough presentation of the jurisdictional risks associated to IT law and, in particular, cloud computing given the current thinking on determining jurisdiction in Europe, it is now time to turn to the US legal system and assess how American legal thinking deals with these questions.

i. The basics about determining jurisdiction under US law

US courts have struggled over jurisdictional issues related to the internet in cases of both domestic and international nature since many years[553]. The main legal instruments through which US justice has claimed and exercised jurisdiction over this type of cases are:

- Personal jurisdiction

Generally, according to US laws, courts exert personal jurisdiction over individuals or businesses that are residents of, or that are physically located within, a political jurisdiction, i.e., county, state, or country[554]. For an

552 C. Kuner (note 507).

553 Burke T. Ward & Janice C. Sipior, *The Internet Jurisdiction Risk of Cloud Computing*, 27 Information Systems Management 334–339 (2010.)

554 *Id.*

assertion of personal jurisdiction to be valid, it must satisfy the requirements of the 'due process clause'[555] prescribed in the Fifth and Fourteenth Amendments of the US Constitution. Under certain circumstances, a court can exercise personal jurisdiction over non-resident individuals and businesses under the authority of a state long arm statute[556]. Such statutes serve as a "long arm" to reach defendants outside of the geographical jurisdictional boundaries of the court. One such example of long arm jurisdiction would be a Missouri resident being served with a legal process by a California court.

– Sufficient minimum contacts and long arm jurisdiction

Beginning with International Shoe Company v. State of Washington (1945)[557], the US Supreme Court has held that due process requires that it be established that the non-resident defendant has sufficient minimum contacts with the state attempting to exercise jurisdiction[558]. The nature of the contacts has to be such that the exercise of jurisdiction did not offend traditional notions of fair play and substantial justice[559].

---

555 The Fifth and Fourteenth Amendments to the United States Constitution contain a due process clause. Due process refers to the administration of justice, acting as a safeguard from arbitrary denials of life, liberty, or property by the Government. The Supreme Court of the United States has adopted even broader interpretations of the clauses, which, as it is has found, provide four protections: procedural due process (in civil and criminal proceedings), substantive due process, a prohibition against vague laws, and, lastly, act as the vehicle for the incorporation of the Bill of Rights. Due process, in other words, ensures the rights and equality of all citizens.

556 Long-arm statute is one that allows for a state court to obtain personal jurisdiction over an out-of-state defendant on the basis of certain acts committed by an out-of-state defendant, provided that the defendant has a sufficient connection with the state.

557 International Shoe Co. v. Washington, 326 U.S. 310, 66 S. Ct. 154, 90 L. Ed. 95 (1945.)

558 Burke T. Ward & Janice C. Sipior (note 553.)

559 'Fair play and substantial justice' notion: a requirement or standard of fairness that must be made by a court's assertion of personal jurisdiction over a nonresident defendant in order to sufficiently deter a violation of the defendant's right to due process.
In International Shoe Co. v. Washington, the Supreme Court held that 'in order for a state court to exercise jurisdiction over a defendant whose residence is elsewhere, the court must establish that the defendant has such minimum contacts with the state that the exercise of jurisdiction over the defendant does not offend traditional notions of fair play and substantial justice'. The main factors used to make this determination are:

The minimum contacts standard[560] necessitates at least some physical presence prior to determining jurisdiction. In commercial transactions, the minimum contacts standard has been found to be met, in general, by the presence of a store, warehouse, salesperson, agent, or physical presence[561]. An example of a transaction is the execution of a sales contract; an example of an occurrence is an automobile accident. Overall, a long arm statute gives jurisdictional statutory authority to a local court to hear a case and make a judgment against an out-of-state defendant.

– Long arm statutes to assert internet jurisdiction

The development of the internet has spurred a series of US States to enact long arm statutes enabling them to assert jurisdiction over defendants who take part in e-commerce or other internet activities[562]. One of the oldest such instances, nearly a decade ago, is Georgia's Computer Systems Protection Act, which contains rules for authorizing jurisdiction over computer related crimes[563]. The act stipulates that Georgia will have jurisdiction over an out-of-state defendant 'in any county for which, to which or through which any use of a computer or a computer network was made, whether by wires, electromagnetic waves, microwaves or any other means of communication'[564]. The said statute had been met with certain reservations by its opponents; the most important among the arguments[565] was that the act was viewed as an attempt to regulate interstate commerce and violate the dormant commerce clause[566]. The dormant commerce clause prohibits states from unduly burdening interstate commerce. Their argu-

---

i. the difficulty for the defendant of appearing in the court
ii. the state's interest in deciding the case
iii. the plaintiff's interest in the convenience of the court
iv. the effectiveness of the relief to be obtained there.

560 'Minimum contacts' is a term used in the United States law of civil procedure to determine when it is appropriate for a court in one state to assert personal jurisdiction over a defendant from another state.

561 *Id.*

562 *Id.*

563 Georgia Computer Systems Protection Act, H. B. No. 822 (available under http://www.oit.gatech.edu/georgia-computer-systems-protection-act; date of last access: 19/2/2016.)

564 Id.

565 *Id.*

566 The "dormant commerce clause", also known as the "negative commerce clause", is a legal doctrine that courts in the United States have formulated out of the commerce clause in Article I of the United States Constitution. The commerce

ment is based on prior Supreme Court decisions where the Court invalidated statutes that attempted to regulate interstate commerce or violated the dormant commerce clause[567]. Since then, a lot more statutes of similar nature have been set up by US states in their effort to claim jurisdiction and exert power over the complex issues instigated by the online world and its facilitating technologies.

ii. Jurisdiction under the influence of technological evolution; practices for alleviating jurisdiction risks in the US and internationally over IT-related cases

As technology changes and evolutions in IT, in particular, impact society, laws are forced to live up to the demands of these changes. These adjustments of laws to the new reality are accomplished through amended legislation, judicial decisions, or both. Similarly, US law has moved to respond to these challenges and the new questions they raise over the issue of jurisdiction not only via enactment of new laws that have moved their focus from physical presence to the economics and effects of the commercial activity[568]. In part, this evolution was also brought about by a series of cases involving mail order vendors; yet, it did not result in an absolute jurisdictional standard for e-commerce[569]. These precedent cases are used in courts for bolstering a still fervent argumentation regarding jurisdiction.

---

clause expressly grants to the US Congress the power to regulate commerce "among the several states." Conversely, the dormant commerce clause expresses the idea that this grant of power implies the opposite power — i.e., a restriction deterring a state from passing laws that would improperly burden or introduce discrimination practices against interstate commerce. This restriction is self-executing and immediately applicable even in the absence of a conflict between state and federal statutes, but Congress may allow states to pass legislation that would otherwise be forbidden by the dormant commerce clause.

567 *Id.*

568 *Id.*

569 An indicative list of such cases brought out by US courts would include:
i. Bensusan Restaurant Corp. v. King, 1996; Federal District Court for the Southern District of New York denied jurisdiction by focusing on the local nature of the alleged infringing activity (Bensusan Restaurant Corp. v. King, 1996; Manolopoulos, 2003)
ii. Zippo Mfg. Co. v. Zippo DotCom, Inc., 1997; Federal District Court for the Western District of Pennsylvania determined jurisdiction on a "passive vs. ac-

In the end, no conclusive answer exists yet as to how to address the jurisdiction risk posed by the most up-to-date IT tools, cloud computing in particular. On the contrary, US laws are far from offering a tried and settled test as to determine how to exert jurisdiction on the internet in the US or internationally[570]. The majority of US scholarly opinion maintains the position that the cloud is inherently global, calling for a cross-jurisdictional solution[571]. On the other hand, cloud computing providers systematically seek to reduce liability by proposing cloud service agreements with "as is" provisions[572] and no warranty[573]. This means that most cloud services are provided without any assurance or promise of a specific level of performance. In response, businesses, for the moment and until the issue of jurisdictional rules regarding the cloud is settled, prior to adopting cloud computing need to consider internet jurisdiction risk, as well as other legal issues[574], before deploying a cloud service. The most important criteria against which a cloud service needs to be evaluated before it is adopted or rejected by a business, and which ideally should be assessed both in their virtual and physical dimensions are currently regarded to be[575]:

---

tive" or "sliding scale" test, cited as precedent in many subsequent cases (Geist, 2001; Hestermeyer, 2006; Manolopoulos, 2003; Minnesota v. Granite Gate Resorts, Inc., 1997; Rosenthal, 2003; Rustad & Koenig, 2006; Waldmeir, 2003; Ware, 2006; Zippo Mfg. Co. v. Zippo Dot Com, Inc., 1997)
iii. People Solutions, Inc. v. People Solutions, Inc., 2000; Federal District Court for the Northern District of Texas held that personal jurisdiction should not be based on the mere possibility that it is possible to do business (People Solutions, Inc. v. People Solutions, Inc., 2000).

570 Joel Reidenberg (note 474).

571 Michael R. Nelson, *The Cloud, the Crowd, and Public Policy*, 25 Issues in science and technology 71–76 (2009.)

572 "As is" is a term used in contract law to disclaim some implied warranties for an item being sold. "As is" denotes that the seller is selling, and the buyer is buying an item or server in whatever condition it is at the time the buy is effected, while the buyer is accepting the item "with all faults", whether or not immediately apparent. An "as is" contract puts the buyer in a situation described as the "buyer beware" status, in which buyer is advised to take the time to examine the item or service before accepting it or to ask expert advice for this assessment.

573 McAlpine C., Weigh Legal Risks of Cloud Computing, available at: http://www.baselinemag.com/c/a/Legal/Weigh-Legal-Risks-of-Cloud-Computing-869422 (19 February 2016.)

574 See also Chapter 7.

575 Burke T. Ward & Janice C. Sipior (note 553).

- considering how serious the jurisdiction risk is when compared to a company's corporate strategy;
- establishing a governance structure tackling cloud computing particularities across the enterprise;
- determining the appropriate cloud computing model before selecting a service, i.e. picking a service which complies with the company's adopted cloud protocols;
- partnering with the cloud provider instead of simply subscribing to its services in order to secure an, as much as possible, customized service; and
- securing adequate liability insurance that will keep them immune, to a certain degree, against the financial exposure of internet liability.

g. Corporate strategy as a pre-emptive measure for facing the long arm of cloud jurisdiction

As a rule, businesses maintain that they should comply with the laws of all countries in which they conduct business and avoid violating laws in countries in which they do not do business[576] but in which their facilities, applications or the data they handle physically reside. Consequently, this global legal environment which, however, is contradicted by the fragmented landscape of different legal orders, demands that modern businesses' corporate strategies directly address jurisdiction risk both on its virtual and physical dimensions[577]. In the end, proper evaluation of jurisdictional implications has become a de facto and constant managerial activity, at least until the jurisdictional hurdles the cloud poses are effectively tackled by law.

i. Virtual and physical environments

The overall behavior of businesses towards cloud computing need also take into account the double nature, which is almost inherent to all kinds of cloud-related business making[578]. That is to imply that businesses uti-

576 *Id.*
577 Reidenberg, J. R., Schwartz, P. M. (note 174); Reinhard Posch (note 240).
578 Burke T. Ward & Janice C. Sipior (note 553).

lizing the cloud almost unanimously operate in two environments, the virtual, and the physical ones[579]. These two may be regarded as separate and distinct; however, corporate strategy must comprehensively address legal issues raised by both of them[580].

ii. Accepting the inherent nature of cloud jurisdiction risk

In conclusion, it is evident from the examination that has been carried out that, under the present status quo of US laws, the jurisdiction risk associated with cloud computing is continuous and inherent. Therefore, businesses are advised to maintain corporate strategies that steadily look for ways to reduce this risk. The practical way to achieve this is by conducting a detailed legal analysis and assessment of those risks across different countries and multiple jurisdictions, certainly in those which are relevant for each undertaking (i.e. the legal order where the company resides, where it has its data storage facilities or where its services are accessible etc.).

Based on this constant monitoring mechanisms, the governing body of a business is expected to make conscious and deliberate decisions or adaptations thereof as to where and how cloud computing processes of the enterprise are conducted. These strategic decisions are made and reviewed based on criteria such as a company's capabilities and resources, knowledge base, applicable domestic and foreign laws and perceptions of risk in conducting business activities[581].

h. Where are cloud data centers located? How jurisdiction plays a major part in deciding on geographic location, economic and environmental parameters in cloud computing

Having examined how Europe and the US treat the issue of determining jurisdiction over cloud computing, it is worth briefly summarizing how the above practices bear real effect on the actual cloud computing business. Essentially, what makes cloud computing possible is the data centers

579 Robert Ware, *The strategic use of American cyberlaw and cyberspace jurisprudence*, 48 Managerial Law 303–321 (2006.)

580 Burke T. Ward & Janice C. Sipior (note 553).

581 Robert Ware (note 579).

where data of the users of various services are hosted and which provide the resources necessary for the execution of any processing tasks involving that data. Anyone who is interested in setting up a data center that will offer services based on cloud computing technologies and protocols evaluates the following four primary considerations of where in order to choose where their data center will be constructed[582]:

- Suitable physical space in which the warehouse–sized buildings that will host the data center's hardware will be located
- Proximity to high–capacity Internet connections
- The availability of affordable electricity or other energy resources
- The laws, policies, and regulations of the local jurisdiction

Interestingly but not surprisingly, one of the major factors weighing decisively on the decision regarding the location of cloud computing data centers is the jurisdictional issues that the chosen location will give rise to. As it has already been sufficiently demonstrated, the laws, policies, and regulations of a particular jurisdiction can have a significant impact both on the cloud provider and the cloud user. Governments and legislators can either stifle or promote the development of cloud computing within a particular jurisdiction with the decisions they are empowered to make and the laws they can enact on the topic.

We have already examined the main challenges the issue of jurisdiction raises with regard to doing business in the field of cloud computing. Similarly, numerous and equally gravitational law and policy concerns exist also for cloud users as a result of the jurisdiction risk associated to the cloud[583]. For users, the most crucial of these issues and expectations include[584]:

- Access: users expect to be able to access and use the cloud where and when they wish without any hindrance from the cloud provider or third parties.
- Reliability: users expect the cloud to be a reliable resource, especially if they assign to their cloud provider tasks that are of a critical nature to their business or online presence, in general.

582 Paul T. Jaeger, Jimmy Lin, Justin M. Grimes & Shannon N. Simmons (note 208).

583 Paul T. Jaeger, Jimmy Lin & Justin M. Grimes, *Cloud Computing and Information Policy: Computing in a Policy Cloud?*, 5 Journal of Information Technology & Politics 269–283 (2008.)

584 Paul T. Jaeger, Jimmy Lin, Justin M. Grimes & Shannon N. Simmons (note 208).

- Security: users expect that the cloud provider will not allow unauthorized access to both data and code, and that these will remain secure at all times.
- Data confidentiality and privacy: users expect that their cloud provider, other third parties, and governments will not monitor their activities, with the exception of cloud providers selectively monitoring usage for quality control purposes.
- Liability: users expect clear delineation of liability if serious problems occur.
- Intellectual property: users and third party content providers expect that their intellectual property rights will be upheld.
- Ownership of data: users expect to be able regulate and control the information that is created and modified using the cloud services they have chosen.
- Portability: users expect that data and resources stored in one cloud facility can be easily moved or transferred to another facility or service with little or no effort.
- Auditability: users, particularly corporate, expect that providers will comply with regulations or at least be able to provide them the option to have them audited per regulation requirements.

PART II: Accountability on the cloud

a. Accountability: the essentials from data protection to cloud computing

Having discussed the issue of how to claim jurisdiction over cases seeking judicial resolution in the field of cloud computing and the broader area of IT law, it is now time to look on the other side of the coin. Besides establishing rules that answer the question what court or jurisdiction is competent to adjudicate on a case, immediately afterwards comes the question of who is to be held responsible about that case.

In the most up-to-date fields of human activity, the term used to refer to this responsibility about an act or incident is 'accountability'[585]. The term

585 Siani Pearson & Andrew Charlesworth, *Accountability as a Way Forward for Privacy Protection in the Cloud*, in Cloud computing. First international conference, CloudCom 2009, Beijing, China, December 1-4, 2009 : proceedings, 131–144 (Martin Gilje Jaatun, Gansen Zhao & Chunming Rong eds., 2009.)

is anything but new but recently it has been coined with several meanings: from an ethics and governance point of view (stricto sensu accountability), accountability is implied as answerability, liability, and, of course, as the respective expectation of account-giving[586]. Viewed as a sub-sector of governance (lato sensu accountability, accountability has been associated with issues in public, nonprofit as well as private (corporate) sector, even within individual contexts[587].

In recent governance theories, accountability has expanded beyond the basic concept of "being called to account for one's actions"[588]. Several researchers have brought forward a description of accountability as a relationship, an at least two-party structure with account-giving between its constituents at its core[589]. In an illustrative manner, accountability is the bond between actor A and actor B when "A is accountable to B when A is obliged to inform B about A's (past or future) actions and decisions, to justify them, and to suffer punishment in the case of eventual misconduct"[590].

It goes without saying that, as a tracking and reporting mechanism, accountability cannot function without proper accounting practices and mechanisms; in other words, an absence of an accounting workflow automatically means an absence of accountability[591]. On a generic level, the essential elements for a solid accountability policy are[592]:

- commitment of the organization adopting accountability to the main principles of it and adoption of internal policies consistent with external criteria.
- mechanisms that will put privacy policies into effect, such as relevant tools, training and education.

586 Clarence A. Dykstra, *The Quest for Responsibility*, 33 The American Political Science Review 1–25 (1939.)

587 M. Bovens, The Quest for Responsibility: Accountability and Citizenship in Complex Organisations (1998.)

588 Richard Mulgan, *'Accountability'. An Ever-Expanding Concept?*, 78 Public Administration 555–573 (2000.)

589 Andrew Charlesworth (note 185).

590 Andreas Schedler, Larry Jay Diamond & Marc F. Plattner, The self-restraining state. Power and accountability in new democracies (1999.)

591 Siani Pearson & Andrew Charlesworth (note 585).

592 Centre for Information Policy Leadership, Data Protection Accountability: The Essential Elements A Document for Discussion, available at: http://www.huntonfiles.com/files/webupload/CIPL_Galway_Accountability_Paper.pdf (19 March 2015.)

- systems enabling constant oversight internally, towards collecting the data necessary for regular assurance reviews and, eventually, external verification.
- transparency and mechanisms facilitating individual participation in the accountability process.
- means for remediation and external enforcement.

Accountability in the broad field of data management and protection is designed with a view to make some strong protection processes for data possible[593]. Where implemented, accountability allows the said organization much more extensive flexibility to adapt its data practices[594]. Of course, in order for it to function properly and efficiently, it requires that the organization commit to and actively demonstrate its upholding of responsible policies and of systems necessary to ensure those policies are carried out in a manner that protects information and the individuals to which it belongs or refers[595]. In other words, accountability as a governance practice, requires that an organization remains accountable no matter where the information it handles is processed. Functioning under the prism of accountability, a data-related organization is less interested in the rules that exist where the data is processed and more in those applicable where the obligation is first established[596]. That said, it becomes evident that data management accountability is purpose oriented and constructed based on a teleological perspective, putting emphasis not on when and where a breach occurred but rather on who had the obligation to take every measure possible to prevent the breach from happening based on their position and role in the data cycle.

b. Accountability is not self-regulation; clearing the picture between two comparable but critically different concepts

Having described the nature and content of the term 'accountability' (stricto and lato sensu), it is vital to clear an ambiguity as to what account-

593 *Id.*

594 David R. Johnson, Susan P. Crawford & John G. Palfrey, *The accountable net: Peer production of internet governance*, 9 Berkman Center for Internet & Society at Harvard Law School Virginia Journal of Law and Technology 1–32 (2004.)

595 *Id.*

596 Siani Pearson & Andrew Charlesworth (note 585).

ability in the cloud would be in essence. There has been a considerable share of scholars and industry experts who have been equating accountability in cloud computing with the self-regulation structure the industry and policy actors devised in order to regulate internet names and numbers in the second half of the 1990s[597]. The model of ICANN[598] was a response to the need for effective internet governance and involved creating an entirely new institutional and property rights framework[599]. At its core lied the problem of who owned probably the most important, valuable assets of the internet, i.e. the name and address spaces[600]. Under the ICANN scheme, control of these assets was voluntarily transferred from an informal set of competent agencies loosely belonging to the US government and its private contractors to a formal, internationally representative, legally incorporated entity[601]. As a result of this 'migration' a whole range of sophisticated property rights issues came up[602]. ICANN, as an organization and as a structure, had to cope with as challenging issues as how to reconcile domain name registration with trademark protection, what rules or procedures governing access to the root of the domain name space would be, how much control a domain name registry would have over the zone files containing the authoritative list of second-level names and many more[603]. These questions, purely legal in nature, were even further complicated by the global, trans-jurisdictional scope of the system. Ultimately, the US Department of Commerce gave answer to these issues by basically devolving global state power to ICANN[604].

597 Milton Mueller, *ICANN and Internet governance: sorting through the debris of "self-regulation"*, 1 info 497–520 (1999.)

598 ICANN (Internet Corporation for Assigned Names and Numbers) is a nonprofit organization, organized from the Secretary of State of the State of California in the U.S. that is responsible for coordinating the maintenance and methodologies of several databases, with unique identifiers, related to the namespaces of the Internet – and thereby, ensuring the network's stable and secure operation. ("ICANN Bylaws", 30 July 2014. Retrieved 30 June 2017.)

599 *Id.*

600 Jonathan G. S. Koppell, *Pathologies of Accountability. ICANN and the Challenge of "Multiple Accountabilities Disorder"*, 65 Public Administration Review 94–108 (2005.)

601 Milton Mueller (note 597).

602 *Id.*

603 Jonathan G. S. Koppell (note 600).

604 Milton Mueller (note 597).

This enormous venture of self-regulation seems comparable but is definitely not identical to the concept of accountability[605] that has been previously discussed and is put forward as a way to achieve pragmatic cloud computing regulation. The harmonization reached via ICANN was based on the strong motives given to the market to seize control of the process and the property rights issues that stemmed from it and, more or less, to try and win in a struggle for power[606]. Accountability, on the other hand, is not about deciding who among market factors will retain more power over the others but, rather, about putting in place a governing scheme that will clearly delineate roles for the actors of the cloud computing sphere, describe their rights and duties, what function(s) they are expected to fulfil across the cloud computing cycle and what kind of responsibility they carry as a result of only partially or wrongly fulfilling those functions. In other words, accountability is not an initiative left entirely to the good will of private sector[607]. It is a two-level process whereby, on the one hand, the legislator and the empowered inspecting authorities make sure a set of rules and regulations is upheld and, on the other hand, private actors – stakeholders of the cloud market – self-adhere to those rules a priori and not only when a breach is found to have been committed from them[608]. In other words, for accountability to bear fruit, a pre-emptive rather than a punitive logic is necessary.

c. Accountability in the cloud cannot be sufficiently settled with existing EU laws

The way relevant EU legislation has been constructed until today, does not offer an adequate scheme that would effectively govern cloud computing from the perspective of accountability and not merely culpability, as it has been happening so far. There are primarily two main proposals that merit serious consideration in order for the EU regulatory thinking to be in a position to offer realistic solutions in the challenges posed by cloud tech-

605 Marcel Machill, Thomas Hart & Bettina Kaltenhäuser, *Structural development of Internet self-regulation*, 4 INFO 39–55 (2002.)

606 Milton Mueller (note 597).

607 Marcel Machill, Thomas Hart & Bettina Kaltenhäuser (note 605).

608 *Id.*

nologies[609]. Firstly, the binary distinction between controllers and processors, sitting right now at the heart of the regulatory scheme utilized to decide on cloud-related issues, is unsuitable for a cloud computing environment and should be abolished[610]. Alternatively, a wholly new principle of end to end accountability needs to be introduced, one that would run through the cloud business chain and will at all times hold the different actors accountable for their share of duties in the broader task of making sure the cloud cycle runs smoothly. Secondly, in order to strike a finer balance between protection of privacy and the fostering and further growth of the cloud sector and business, it is suggested to introduce in the cloud industry a logic already present in other pieces of EU legislation about similar matter, for instance, in the Privacy and Electronic Communications Directive[611]: in particular, it is high time to start thinking whether it makes sense for pure infrastructure cloud providers to be treated as neutral intermediaries, unless and until they have the requisite knowledge and control over a specific bunch of data (in the form of access to it, at least for more than incidental purposes). In this way, the industry will benefit, on the one hand, from not having to bear the burden of a constant suspicion in case a breach occurs at some point over the cloud computing cycle. At the same time, by setting aside infrastructure as a prima facie reason for breaches of the cloud cycle, we profit from not sticking to a convenient and obvious answer but focusing instead on the actual actors of the cloud computing business that could, due to their role and the processes they execute, cause a harmful incident involving certain volumes of data and their owners or subjects.

In detail, after doing away with the simplistic binary controller/processor distinction, it is suggested that the cloud industry be reorganized based on an end to end accountability approach[612]. This approach will lead the greater sector to be arranged over a continuum or spectrum of parties, of whom only those that indeed process data at some point through the data life cycle will be considered as potentially culpable. Additionally, this ac-

---

609 Siani Pearson & Andrew Charlesworth (note 585).

610 J. Domingue, D. Fensel & J. A. Hendler, Handbook of Semantic Web Technologies (2011.)

611 Martin Gilje Jaatun, Gansen Zhao & Chunming Rong eds., Cloud computing. First international conference, CloudCom 2009, Beijing, China, December 1-4, 2009 : proceedings, vol. 5931 (2009.)

612 David R. Johnson, Susan P. Crawford & John G. Palfrey (note 594).

countability will not be vague nor will it only be affirmed when a wrongdoing occurs[613]. It will, instead, have varying degrees of obligations and liabilities, directly analogous to the position of the party in the cloud cycle, the scope it is supposed to be serving and the processes for which it is fair to be held responsible[614]. This approach would not only bring the actual responsible parties to the forefront of culpability but it would also contribute to the quest for achieving a more appropriate balance between commercial and privacy considerations in light of the complex and dynamic nature of today's cloud computing industry.

d. Providing answers to the privacy challenges of cloud computing under US law; the importance of the Fourth Amendment principles

In general, we are used to be regarding the US as a legal culture with not as much preoccupation about privacy as Europe. While that might have been true until recently, things have rapidly been changing especially under the effect of events of considerable magnitude, such as the Snowden scandal and other threats or direct intrusions to citizens' privacy that have come to light as of late. The origins of the quest for protection of privacy in the American legal culture are found in a landmark decision of the US Supreme Court, Katz v. United States[615]. The case was a chance for the US Supreme Court to revisit its stance on the basic principles of the Fourth Amendment of the US Constitution[616]. In the same decision, the

613 *Id.*

614 Andrew Charlesworth (note 185).

615 Katz v. United States, 389 U.S. 347 (1967): in this United States Supreme Court case the nature of the "right to privacy" and the legal definition of a "search" were extensively discussed and profoundly updated to mirror modern challenges. The Court in its ruling refined previous interpretations of the unreasonable search and seizure clause of the Fourth Amendment to also include immaterial intrusion with technology as a search, overruling previous decisions, i.e. Olmstead v. United States and Goldman v. United States, that had adopted more restrictive views on the matter. In Katz, the US Supreme Court also extended Fourth Amendment protection to all areas where a person has a "reasonable expectation of privacy".

616 The Fourth Amendment of the U.S. Constitution reads, "[t]he right of the people to be secure in their persons, houses, papers, and effects, against unreasonable searches and seizures, shall not be violated, and no Warrants shall issue, but upon

US Court put also forward the 'reasonable expectation of privacy test'[617]; with regards to it, one of the concurring judges, Justice Harlan, outlined a two-fold requirement for the call for protection to be justified; that the person demonstrated a subjective expectation of privacy over the object and that the expectation was reasonable[618].

The focus of the analysis regarding the reasonable expectation of privacy in Katz was on how courts generally define searches of containers under the Fourth Amendment[619]. Nevertheless, the same decision also stood for another important principle of Fourth Amendment jurisprudence: that "the Fourth Amendment protects people, not places."[620] As a result, this decision marked for the first time a shift of focus in US legal thinking from "persons, houses, papers, and effects,[621]" which are the spaces or areas where the Fourth Amendment principles directly apply to, towards a broader view which extended protection to privacy interests in intangible communications[622].

This novel approach to protection of privacy has to be once more updated today to give meaningful responses to the issue of intangible digital data, their handling and the main tools for processing them, such as cloud computing[623]. Although computers and the devices or technologies prevailing in today's IT sector are more technologically complex than brief-

probable cause, supported by Oath or affirmation, and particularly describing the place to be searched, and the persons or things to be seized."
The ultimate goal of this provision is to protect people's right to privacy and freedom from arbitrary governmental interventions. Private intrusions not acting in the color of governmental authority were exempted from the Fourth Amendment at the time of its adoption.

617 The reasonable expectation of privacy is a legal test essential in defining the scope of the applicability of the privacy protections of the Fourth Amendment to the United States Constitution. The test is essentially related but not the identical to the 'right to privacy', which is a much broader concept central to EU law and many other legal systems that have developed under EU law influence.

618 Katz v. United States (note 615.)

619 DAvid Couillard, *Defogging the Cloud: Applying Fourth Amendment Principles to Evolving Privacy Expectations in Cloud Computing*, 93 Minnesota Law Review 2205–2239 (2009.)

620 Katz v. United States (note 615.)

621 U.S. Constitution, amend. IV.

622 *Id.*

623 D. Scott Blake, *Let's Be Reasonable: Fourth Amendment Principles in the Digital Age*, 5 SEVENTH CIRCUIT REV. 491–531 (2010.)

cases or even perhaps telephone calls, US courts have already held that computer searches are limited by the Fourth Amendment[624].

There have already been instances where courts have extended the protective legal structure which has its origins in the Katz case into the cloud computing world[625]. In particular, the district court in D'Andrea case[626] recognized that virtual containers do exist in the cloud, hence protection of privacy is a legitimate request also in the realm of cloud computing. However, legal scholars still believe that the US justice needs to take further steps in order not just to recognize the legitimacy of the call for privacy protection on the cloud but also to legitimize certain types of tools that will facilitate the fulfilment of this call[627]. Consequently, there have been voices calling upon US justice to also acknowledge the legitimacy of virtual concealment efforts, namely, encryption, password protection, and the practical obscurity of unlisted links, as means of opacity in the cloud context[628]. It is suggested that if these steps were taken, courts would then be in a position to make a case-by-case determination as to whether a user's behavior online or his recourse to tools such as passwords, encryption, or obscurity techniques were reasonable in a given situation or went beyond legitimate[629]. On the other hand, this delineation of what is permissible and what is not in the cloud environment, will also boost the previously discussed call for accountability over culpability in the cloud. Consequently, while maintaining its distinct position from other jurisdictions, the US

---

624 For example, in Maes v. Folberg, 504 F. Supp. 2d 339, 347 (N.D. Ill. 2007), an Illinois federal district court found that the plaintiff, a state employee, had a reasonable expectation of privacy in her government-issued laptop computer because there was no evidence that the plaintiff was on notice that her laptop was subject to search. The court relied upon O'Connor v. Ortega, which held that government employees are protected from unreasonable searches by their government employers. Maes, 504 F. Supp. 2d at 347–48 [citing O'Connor v. Ortega, 480 U.S. 709, 715–16, 725–26 (1987)]; cf. Muick v. Glenayre Elecs., 280 F.3d 741, 743 (7th Cir. 2002) (holding that plaintiff's privacy expectation was destroyed because his government employer "announced that it could inspect the laptops that it furnished for the use of its employees").

625 David Couillard (note 619).

626 United States v. D'Andrea, 648 F.3d 1 (1st Cir. 2011.)

627 D. Scott Blake (note 623).

628 S. S. Smith, Web-based Instruction: A Guide for Libraries (2006); David W. Opderbeck, *Encryption Policy and Law Enforcement in the Cloud*, 49 Connecticut Law Review (2017.)

629 Jack L. Goldsmith & Tim Wu (note 535).

legal system can also take steps towards harmonization of the universal legal landscape regarding cloud computing regulation.

e. Achieving effective regulation of the cyberspace: discussing particularities of the web and how these should be mirrored in modern laws about aspects of the digital world

In every matter calling for regulation, the ultimate aim of policymakers has always been to strike a balance between protecting the rights of the parties affected by the legislation, on the one hand, and the constraints that need to be introduced for the enjoyment of these rights not to create conflicts between different law subjects, on the other[630]. For example, in the field of intellectual property law, the aim of policymakers is to strike a balance between securing some protection for creators for their work while ensuring that that protection does not reach so far as to pose conflicting situations.

The same challenging balance has to be struck in the field of privacy. Every free society believes that there is some realm of individual life that should be free of surveillance or invasion[631]. Among societal factors, there are those who are strong promoters of this privacy realm, which they believe that sits beyond government regulation. There are, of course, other more moderate voices who assert that this realm at least should be presumptively free from state control. Opposite all these sit the policymakers who need to fine tune all tendencies into an efficient regulatory scheme[632].

The question that comes naturally to mind is how policymakers achieve this balance and what factors they need to take into account when designing laws. The traditional school of thought in legal science supports that in designing a law only those factors directly tied to the subject matter that is

630 Lawrence Lessig (note 505).

631 This view is documented, for example, in Lawrence v. Texas, 123 S. Ct. 2472, 2475 (2003). Justice Kennedy wrote: Liberty protects the person from unwarranted government intrusions into a dwelling or other private places. In our tradition, the State is not omnipresent in the home. And there are other spheres of our lives and existence, outside the home, where the State should not be a dominant presence. Freedom extends beyond spatial bounds. Liberty presumes an autonomy of self that includes freedom of thought, belief, expression, and certain intimate conduct.

632 *Id.*

to be regulated need to be considered[633]. Consequently, in long-established fields of law, such as intellectual property, the balance is achieved by considering the sum of statutory and common law protections. Similarly, a fair statutory scheme for privacy protection takes into account the same kind of protections, as well as the constitutional perspective[634]. In other words, from the traditionalists' perspective policymaking is simply the process of tuning legal code[635]. Any changes in policy, from this point of view, simply map changes in legal code[636].

Nonetheless, as it has become clear already, when it comes to regulating aspects of the cyber world and its enabling technologies, policy making cannot be done solely based on legal code[637]. Instead, it is essential to maintain a continuous interaction between the legal code and the architecture or technology within which this code will be called to function on every occasion, i.e. in every different phase of technological status quo[638]. This applies to virtually all aspects of the internet, such as privacy and, of course, now cloud computing. In its early days, the Internet, its architecture and its technologies produced relative anonymity for users[639]. The very first internet protocols were neither designed for nor based on recognizing who people were, where they came from, or what use they were making of the Internet[640]. That information, back in the time, was not embedded in the basic Internet protocol, which meant that the basic protocols protected users from inadvertent releases of such information. Consequently, the balance between privacy and respect for the user's fundamental rights and, on the other hand, the interests of those doing business on or for the internet was much easier to strike. However, things have rapidly changed today, with a great deal of internet services and applications being based on the personalization of the work environment or the tying of the service to each and every individual user[641]. In view of these, the bal-

633 *Id.*
634 Paul Schiff Berman, *Cyberspace and the State Action Debate: The Cultural Value of Applying Constitutional Norms to 'Private' Regulation*, 71 University of Colorado Law Review 1263–1310 (2000.)
635 L. Lessig (note 504).
636 *Id.*
637 *Id.*
638 Joel Reidenberg (note 474).
639 L. Lessig (note 504).
640 *Id.*
641 See Chapter 2.

ance policymakers have to achieve between conflicting tendencies and interests of the internet sphere actors has become all the more precarious.

As of late, there have been increasingly louder voices arguing that the best way to make the internet and its surrounding ecosystem, including cloud computing, flourish is to limit or refrain from regulation of it, giving it the chance to self-regulate itself[642]. Much as it is supposed to support a liberal take on cyberspace, this unwillingness to regulate eventually defeats the very values that is supposed to be defending[643]. It should not be overlooked that, all the more so after the recent developments regarding internet security around the world, citizens and a big share of the internet stakeholders in general, voice stronger and stronger calls for a more efficiently regulated virtual world[644]. In other words, the answer to the particular nature of the internet, which decisively affects its regulatory needs, is not to go from the extreme of overregulation to that of non-regulation.

It is not the first time that the law will need to work hand in hand with other sectors in order to provide efficient answers to novel challenges[645]. A spirit of openness is necessary. As many are beginning to recognize, probably the most salient feature of cyberspace is its ability to embed controls that resist or reinforce values that we bring to it[646]. This capacity is a unique asset in designing and implementing effective laws for the cyber world and its constituting parts, i.e. also for cloud computing. Understanding the manner in which these values are resisted or reinforced will allow us to design a regulatory scheme that will promote accountability while, at the same time, will make cloud computing and all the areas where it is used more user-friendly and less of a mystery, boosting its prospects as a business sector as well.

---

642 Chris Reed (note 363).
643 Lawrence Lessig (note 505).
644 See also Chapter 3.
645 Siani Pearson & Nick Wainwright, *An interdisciplinary approach to accountability for future internet service provision*, 1 IJTMCC 52–72 (2013.)
646 Lawrence Lessig (note 505).

f. Tackling the issue of perspective in internet law; an essential step towards a pragmatic accountability regime

Law, in doctrine and in practice, can be understood from either an internal or external perspective[647]. The internal perspective is the one adopted by judges and lawyers who work within the legal system. In their official function, these actors of the law cycle are required to view the law as a set of rules with legitimacy and moral authority[648]. On the contrary, the external perspective is predominant among sociologists, economists, and historians, i.e. experts who approach law and legal conduct as epiphenomenal, as a reflection of deeper forces unrecognized by the players within the law cycle[649]. Simply put, the internal perspective approximates a first-person view or insider's view of the legal system, whereas the external perspective is a third-person view or observer's view of the law[650].

The problem of perspective is also present in Internet law and how this is resolved will largely determine the nature and shape of regulation that will be set in place to regulate the internet and, consequently, cloud computing. Experience proves that in a surprising number of situations, the outcome reached when applying law to one case from an internal or an external perspective is profoundly different[651]. The cyber space and its subdomains or enabling technologies are a prime example of such fields where major regulatory challenges essentially boil down to clashes between the internal and external perspective[652]. To further complicate matters, neither perspective is a priori right or wrong, nor is any of the two more or less legitimate. Both perspectives can prove to be perfectly viable depending on the circumstances; therefore, courts and commentators switch between them frequently without even recognizing the change[653].

The essential task of a regulator is to apply legal rules to facts and reach meaningful solutions to outstanding conflicts between them[654]. In the case

647 E. Douglas Litowitz, *Internal versus external perspectives in law: toward mediation*, 26 Florida State University Law Review 127–150 (1998.)
648 Orin S. Kerr (note 230).
649 E. Douglas Litowitz (note 647); Philip Leith, *The socio-legal context of privacy*, 2 IJC 105–136 (2006.)
650 E. Douglas Litowitz (note 647).
651 Orin S. Kerr (note 230).
652 Paul Schiff Berman (note 634).
653 Orin S. Kerr (note 230).
654 E. Douglas Litowitz (note 647).

of the internet and cloud computing, however, there are two strongly competing understandings of reality. On one side, there is a virtual reality, which is the one we come to view through the internal perspective and, on the other side, there is a physical reality, which we perceive when viewing cloud computing from the external perspective[655]. This brings the regulators (and all other actors involved in cloud governance) before a dilemma as to which perspective should be adopted when attempting to regulate the cloud. By choosing the perspective, we choose the reality; by choosing the reality, we choose the facts; and by choosing the facts, we choose the law[656].

From the internal perspective of cloud users, cloud computing is the work environments of the cloud-based services they are using, and they understand regulating the cloud as the task of projecting real world situations to the virtual world of cyberspace, spotting the analogies between the two and trying to match the rules between them[657]. To external observers, in contrast, cloud computing is the physical infrastructure and the constituting parts of the cloud environment; for them, applying law to the internet means applying the law to the constituting parts that made feasible the operation of the cloud network[658].

A direct 'product' of this ongoing divide between the internal and external perspective in internet law has been the increasingly popular concept of 'internet governance' which has already been discussed[659]. Internet governance can be defined as the study of how law, legal institutions, and computer code collectively regulate and define the virtual world of cyberspace[660]. Internet governance, as a normative structure, has been nourishing from this sharp division along internal and external perceptions of the internet, and this should come as no surprise[661]. In essence, internet governance seeks to expose the analogies between the process of creation

---

655 Renzo Marchini, Cloud computing. A practical introduction to the legal issues (2010.)

656 Lawrence Lessig (note 505).

657 Sean Marston, Zhi Li, Subhajyoti Bandyopadhyay, Juheng Zhang & Anand Ghalsasi (note 116).

658 *Id.*

659 See Chapter 5.

660 Francesca Musiani & Internet Policy Review, Decentralised internet governance: the case of a 'peer-to-peer cloud' (2014.)

661 David S. Wall, *Digital Realism and the Governance of Spam as Cybercrime*, 10 Eur J Crim Policy Res 309–335 (2004.)

of rules in the physical world (traditional questions of governance) and the creation of rules in cyberspace (internet governance)[662]. Similarly, extended to the issue of cloud computing, a sound governance scheme, which will in turn permit a sound accountability mechanism, strives to identify connectors between the challenges and points of concern of the cloud ecosystem users and actors and the external perceptions held about the cloud by the regulators.

In social sciences, the terms "internal" and "external" are normally used to compare different ways of analyzing a phenomenon such as religion and law. The internal perspective is the view of a participant in the system, who feels bound by its rules; the external perspective is the view of a third-party observer who does not consider himself bound[663].

As far as law is concerned, this bipolar internal vs. external view was famously applied by H.L.A. Hart in The Concept of Law[664]. According to Hart, viewed from the internal perspective, the law as a system holds that we are bound by its rule, and indicates faith in the power and authority of legal reasoning and doctrine. In contrast, when perceiving law externally, legal rules are understood merely as dressing for other forces that generate observable regularities of behavior but have little additional significance[665].

Nevertheless, when it comes to the internet and cloud computing, the two perspectives mirror two different representations of reality[666]. In a nutshell, the external perspective brings to surface physical reality, and the internal perspective exposes virtual reality. For instance, accessing a website on a browser can be interpreted as either sending a request to a remote server that sends back text and pictures (physical reality), or getting access to a place where certain information is hosted (virtual reality). An internal and an external viewer form two strikingly different understandings of the same thing[667]. Of course, there can be users who have an understanding of both realities simultaneously[668]; technically savvy users, with a certain

662 Orin S. Kerr (note 230).

663 Gustavo Ribeiro, *No Need to Toss a Coin: Conflicting Scientific Expert Testimonies and Intellectual Due Process*, 12 Law, Probability and Risk 1–44 (2013.)

664 H. L. A. Hart, The concept of law (1998.)

665 John T. Noonan, *THE CONCEPT OF LAW. By H. L. A. Hart. Oxford: Oxford University Press, 1961. Pp. viii, 263. 21s*, 7 Am. J. Juris. 169–177 (1962.)

666 Orin S. Kerr (note 230).

667 E. Douglas Litowitz (note 647).

668 Orin S. Kerr (note 230).

level of awareness about technology can very efficiently follow the external view along with the internal. Nonetheless, the internet and cloud computing as its main facilitator necessitate a choice between these two representations of reality. A user may be aware of both realities at the same time, but will have to choose to accept only one at a time when trying to understand online experiences. On the contrary, while regulators, alone or with the assistance of specialized advisors, may well be able to distinguish between the two versions of the cloud reality, they cannot act so in extremis as plain users: they need to come up with a set of rules of law which will serve the interests, respond to challenges and, ultimately, strike a balance between both perceptions of the cloud computing phenomenon in order for this law to provide thorough and not partial answers. This is the only way in which the accountability mechanism that will be put in place can work all the way through different stages of the cloud cycle, be objective and essentially universal, even if it will have of course to respect jurisdictional particularities.

g. The road to an accountable cloud computing goes through the road to an accountable internet: how to achieve a sound internet governance

Cloud computing is, without doubt, the main and major facilitator of the internet. And just as we have seen that there is only one internet, there is also only one basic concept of cloud computing. Particular arrangements may change from one facility to the other, specific technical features may be added or blocked or be only partially available from one cloud environment to the other but the general idea of the cloud, the technologies it is based on, the fundamental principles it has been built upon and the functions it is supposed to fulfil are universal and the same regardless of where a cloud facility is located, from where it is accessed or where it gives access to. However, although there is only one internet and only one core concept of cloud computing, there is neither a global system operator nor a global regulator. And even if there were such an operator, it would be in such an advantageous and powerful position that, in the end, it would not be accountable to anyone, let alone the system it ruled over[669]. Even in the extreme case when an election of an online government was possible, the

669 David R. Johnson, Susan P. Crawford & John G. Palfrey (note 594).

only way for it to produce truly uniform laws would be by systematically discriminating against the interests of minorities in a heterogeneous world[670]. However, the key to a genuinely global internet and cloud computing administration is not to cede power over either of these to a central authority. What we need, instead, is to painstakingly describe and commonly agree on the elements that make up the internet and the cloud, as concepts, the actors taking part in the cloud computing network, the role each on them holds in the course of the cloud chain and the responsibilities they carry, or else, the duties they are expected to fulfil. As long as we create this common ground of understanding, each of the regional governing systems or authorities responsible for ruling over the internet or cloud computing across the globe will have a starting point from which to produce laws that will preserve the autonomous character of the jurisdiction from which they originate but, at the same time, will very efficiently interact with each other and produce viable and borderless solutions. As the internet and cloud technologies continue to evolve, new tools that make this interconnectivity even easier and more effective will become available[671]. Along with laws based on a minimum common understanding, technological tools with better and better functionalities will enable us to single out actors on the cloud that uphold or banish others that abuse trust, good will and ethics. In this way, accountability of the internet as a whole will be continuously augmented and, simultaneously, accountability of cloud computing, as the main technology that makes the web possible, will also be continuously improving.

h. Effective accountability for cloud computing

A cornerstone characteristic of the way cloud computing services are organized nowadays is the outsourcing from cloud service providers of non-core aspects of their business to third parties[672]. That, along with the effec-

670 *Id.*

671 Julia Black, *Constructing and contesting legitimacy and accountability in polycentric regulatory regimes*, 2 Regulation & Governance 137–164 (2008.)

672 Siani Pearson & Andrew Charlesworth (note 585).

tively boundless nature of the cloud from a geographical perspective[673] renders the complexity of the service provision ecosystem even greater, even though many times that may not be visible to an individual or business end user[674]. Nevertheless, it is imperative to device a way for each of these links in the cloud cycle to be held accountable, among themselves and to the regulator for how each of them manages, uses, and passes on data and other related information (e.g. metadata)[675].

This chain of accountability, which will be illustrated in detail later on, will allow the members of a cloud ecosystem to ensure that the obligations and specific duties each one undertakes to protect data while they are within the reach of their responsibility are duly observed at all times and uninterruptedly; in this manner, data remain continuously protected by all who process them at any point of the cloud cycle, irrespective of where that processing occurs at each time. Of course, this will not only apply when a data subject will directly use cloud services, but also when such services will be provided in an enterprise cloud setting.

The legal essence behind this concept of a chain of accountability is discussed in Chapter 7 of this study. However, an overview of how and on what principles this cycle will be built can already be described[676]: service providers, implementing accountability mechanisms, will provide users with control and transparency over data in the cloud. The links between them as elements of the chain of accountability should not understood as simply technical linkages; they will be genuine accountability relationships between supplier and customer, embodied in contracts, addressing regulatory obligations, ensuring each partner will use interoperable policies and functioning efficiently and effectively for the supplier and the

673 Mark Gondree & Zachary N.J. Peterson, *Geolocation of data in the cloud*, in the third ACM conference, 25 (Elisa Bertino, Ravi Sandhu, Lujo Bauer & Jaehong Park eds.)

674 Paul T. Jaeger, Jimmy Lin, Justin M. Grimes & Shannon N. Simmons (note 208).

675 Mark Gondree & Zachary N.J. Peterson (note 673).

676 Siani Pearson, Vasilis Tountopoulos, Daniele Catteddu, Mario Sudholt, Refik Molva, Christoph Reich, Simone Fischer-Hubner, Christopher Millard, Volkmar Lotz, Martin Gilje Jaatun, Ronald Leenes, Chunming Rong & Javier Lopez, *Accountability for cloud and other future Internet services*, in 2012 IEEE 4th International Conference on Cloud Computing Technology and Science (CloudCom), 629–632.

service user[677]. Additionally, apart from the overall chain of accountability extending from end to end over the supply chain, shorter, mole localized accountability bonds will also be possible as a result of deployment of accountability-enhancing mechanisms throughout the service network[678].

All the above linking and controlling mechanisms will be made possible also thanks to trusted third-party services, which will offer monitoring, certification, trust modelling and other functionalities that support any accountability structure[679]. All these inherent and third-party accountability tools will, on the one side, enable providers to implement accountability, on the other side will support users in assessing the trustworthiness of each service and, will also offer to governance actors effective ways to check and monitor the use of data in the cloud[680].

i. Accountability as a way to further reinforce privacy in the cloud

Following the discourse we have presented so far, accountability in the cloud can, in the end, be defined as the management of the availability, usability, integrity and security of the data used, stored, or processed on the cloud, and, as a term, it encompasses all processes by which a particular goal – the prevention of harm to the subjects of the data in question – can be achieved[681]. Towards this end, a combination of public law (legislation, regulation), private law (contract), self-regulation and privacy technology uses (system architectures, access controls, machine readable policies) is deployed[682].

Traditional national and international privacy protection approaches, which had been constructed under the heavy influence of public law are characterized today by declining effectiveness as technological develop-

677 Rolf H. Weber, *Accountability in the Internet of Things*, 27 Computer Law & Security Review 133–138 (2011.)

678 *Id.*

679 Centre for Information Policy Leadership (note 592).

680 Siani Pearson, Vasilis Tountopoulos, Daniele Catteddu, Mario Sudholt, Refik Molva, Christoph Reich, Simone Fischer-Hubner, Christopher Millard, Volkmar Lotz, Martin Gilje Jaatun, Ronald Leenes, Chunming Rong & Javier Lopez (note 676).

681 IEEE ed., An audit logic for accountability (2005.)

682 Siani Pearson & Andrew Charlesworth (note 585).

ments render the underlying regulatory techniques obsolete[683]. In view of the above, the solution towards achieving a viably regulated cloud computing and, in general, IT technologies landscape is that of accountability. What is particularly suggested is a holistic approach combining private and public accountability[684]. Public accountability is made possible thanks to an active interaction between subjects of PII[685], regulatory bodies, such as data Commissioners and data controllers and it is dependent upon highly transparent processes[686]. Private accountability, on the other hand, is made possible thanks to the interaction between data controllers and data processors, and is founded on contract law, technological processes, and practical internal compliance requirements[687]. Along with the change from traditional legal structures to the regime of accountability comes also a shift of focus regarding the way in which the integrity of a cloud network and of the data hosted therein is meant to be achieved. In fact, accountability is not based on setting up extensive procedural or bureaucratic requirements for processing activities but rather on reducing the risk of (disproportionate in context) harm to the subjects of PII and, consequently, on reducing the amount of negative consequences for the data controller[688]. The decisive differentiating point between the previous and the newly proposed status quo is the acceptance that absolute avoidance of harm is an impossible goal in a disaggregated environment, such as a cloud service[689]. Therefore, focusing on enhancing the ability to respond flexibly and efficiently to harm that occasionally arise will provide a more efficient form of privacy protection than the enforcement of blunt compliance criteria.

---

683 L. A. Bygrave (note 137).

684 Siani Pearson & Andrew Charlesworth (note 585).

685 Personally identifiable information (PII) is any data that could potentially identify a specific individual. Any information that can be used to distinguish one person from another and can be used for de-anonymizing anonymous data can be considered PII.

686 Daniel J. Weitzner, Harold Abelson, Tim Berners-Lee, Chris Hanson, James Hendler, Lalana Kagal, Deborah L. McGuinness, Gerald Jay Sussman & K. Krasnow Waterman (note 21).

687 *Id.*

688 Siani Pearson & Andrew Charlesworth (note 585).

689 Fa-Chang Cheng & Wen-Hsing Lai, *The Impact of Cloud Computing Technology on Legal Infrastructure within Internet—Focusing on the Protection of Information Privacy*, 29 2012 International Workshop on Information and Electronics Engineering 241–251 (2012.)

In the way cloud computing has been regulated till today, i.e. from the legal and regulatory approach, geographic location is of prime importance to enforcement[690]. Under the accountability regime, location becomes less relevant because of assurances that data will be treated as described regardless of jurisdiction[691]. Accountability can also contribute towards the enforceability of laws that apply to cloud computing either via the imposition of criminal penalties for misuse or with the assistance of technology[692].

Last but not least, the current regulatory structure places too much emphasis on recovering tools and procedures, if things go wrong, and not so much on trying to get cloud computing actors to 'do the right thing' for privacy in the first place[693]. On the contrary, a hybrid accountability mechanism built up via a combination of legal, regulatory and technological resources extending across public and private accountability domains is a practical way of securing effective cloud regulation[694]. Constructed in this manner, the accountability based regulatory framework for cloud computing can offer appropriate answers to the questions stemming from the privacy issues that arise and are rooted in cloud computing. In chapters 8 to 10 of this study, the legal principles of this accountability mechanism are described and analyzed.

690 Mark Gondree & Zachary N.J. Peterson (note 673).
691 Siani Pearson & Nick Wainwright (note 645).
692 Rolf H. Weber (note 677).
693 *Id.*
694 Siani Pearson & Nick Wainwright (note 645).

CHAPTER 7. Risks and compliance in cloud computing environments – views from Europe and the USA

a. Introduction – scope of this chapter

The aim of this chapter is to continue the analysis on the fundamental issues that any piece of regulation aiming to regulate legal issues arising out of the use of cloud computing should provide answers for. After having gone over the issues of accountability and jurisdiction, we will now look into defining what are the main risks posed by the cloud as a technology, to the extent that it is possible to make such an assessment being based on the current state-of-the-art of cloud computing technology. Additionally, the main compliance policies are discussed, in order to be assessed for sufficiency and compatibility with the main legal norms and values prevailing in the discussion for the construction of a working regulatory framework for the cloud.

PART I: THE RISKS ASSOCIATED WITH CLOUD COMPUTING

a. Privacy issues raised on the cloud: existent for all kinds of data across all types of cloud networks

Cloud architecture poses by nature implications for the privacy of all different kinds of information hosted on cloud networks[695]. Be it personal, business or governmental information, in order to capitalize on efficiency and maximize the economies of scale, cloud ecosystems usually adopt technological concepts that stand on the axis between security and privacy[696]. And although piling up on security safeguards is one way to deal with the insecurities that come along with the cloud, privacy issues cannot

---

695 Refer also to Chapter 2.

696 Robert Gellman, Privacy in the Clouds: Risks to Privacy and Confidentiality from Cloud Computing, available at: https://www.worldprivacyforum.org/2011/11/resource-page-cloud-privacy/ (20 April 2015.)

and should not be disregarded when trying to grasp the bigger picture and construct an all-inclusive regulatory scheme for cloud computing[697].

A crucial factor determining the privacy and confidentiality risks a cloud computing user faces are the terms of service and privacy policy established by the cloud provider in the predesigned service agreement that the customer is required to sign. Several efforts have been made to present in a collective manner the different versions of service agreements proposed by various cloud computing service providers. Nevertheless, it is true that we are far from achieving an adequate level of awareness among users about the varying versions of contractual clauses available on the market for the kind of cloud service they are looking for[698]. Nor would it of course be legally sound to force the market to adapt to one specific prototype for conditions for offering cloud services[699]; that would be an undesirable market intervention, only paving the way to illegal disruption. As a result, this diversification of terms of service is here to stay and from a market point of view, it will not go away any time soon. Consequently, the challenges to privacy of users' data depending on the cloud provider they engage with are a challenge that needs to be adequately tackled with, in the context of a regulatory regime for the cloud.

For certain types of information and specific categories of cloud computing users, privacy and confidentiality rights, obligations, and status may change when a user discloses information to a cloud provider[700]. This is, for example, the case when a government authority switches to cloud computing in order to cover its data storage needs or when the same type of body deserts, mostly for reasons of economies of scale, its privately owned and maintained storage facilities over hosting and storage services from one of the private suppliers on the market (differentiation of privacy status within the same jurisdiction). Similarly, a change in the privacy status emerges in the example of data referring to health records when such archives migrate from cloud computing facilities located in one specific jurisdiction to different servers somewhere else in the world (differentiation of privacy status as a result of changing jurisdiction).

697 Paul Schwartz, *Information Privacy in the Cloud*, 161 University of Pennsylvania law review 1623–1662 (2013.)

698 Robert Gellman (note 696).

699 *Id.*

700 *Id.*

Disclosure and remote storage may have adverse consequences for the legal status or protection of personal or business information[701]. For instance, there are clear differences between the handling of data referring to tax and income information of citizens or businesses in Europe and the US. Similarly, business-owned data are under clearly varying protection between EU and US law[702].

As it has already been demonstrated[703], the location of information in the cloud may also have significant effects on the privacy and confidentiality protections of information and on the privacy obligations of those who process or store the information as well as on how the upholding of these obligations is legally evaluated. Additionally, co-existing jurisdiction laws may result in information in the cloud having more than one legal location at the same time, with differing legal consequences[704]. Privacy of data on the cloud can also be put in question due to different laws that may oblige a cloud provider to examine user records for evidence of criminal activity and other matters. And these are just very few examples of the differences in treatment data on the cloud may receive depending on which laws a certain cloud facility, network controller, cloud service provider or data processor is subject to.

In summary, legal uncertainties make it difficult in various ways to assess the status of information in the cloud as well as the privacy and confidentiality protections available to users.

The above risks to privacy are generally more likely to occur in the context of the US legal system[705]. The following are some characteristic instances of US laws which set fertile ground for undermined privacy of data stored on or transferred via cloud computing networks, certainly when compared to the prevailing legal thinking in Europe:

701 Robert Gellman (note 696); Clare Sullivan, *Protecting digital identity in the cloud: Regulating cross border data disclosure*, 30 Computer Law & Security Review 137–152 (2014.)

702 See Chapter 3.

703 See Chapter 6.

704 Id.

705 Robert Gellman (note 696).

i. United States v. Miller

In this cornerstone case brought before the US Supreme Court in 1976, Mitch Miller[706] was charged with carrying alcohol distilling equipment and whiskey on which liquor tax had not been paid. The Bureau of Alcohol, Tobacco, and Firearms (ATF) issued subpoenas to two of Mr. Miller's banks, The Citizens & Southern National Bank of Warner Robins and the Bank of Byron requesting records of Miller's accounts. The banks complied with the subpoenas, and the evidence was used during Miller's trial in the United States District Court for the Middle District of Georgia. Miller was convicted and appealed his conviction alleging that his Fourth Amendment rights were violated. The United States Court of Appeals for the Fifth Circuit ruled in his favor. The case was then brought before the US Supreme Court with the question whether Miller's bank records had been illegally seized in violation of the Fourth Amendment. The Court answered negatively; in a 6-3 opinion, it reversed the Fifth Circuit and held that Miller had no right to privacy in his bank records. Writing for the majority, Justice Lewis F. Powell asserted that the "documents subpoenaed are not [Miller's] 'private papers',"[707] but instead, part of the bank's business records. Consistent with Hoffa v. United States[708], the Court found that Miller's rights were not violated when a third party – his bank – transmitted information that he had entrusted them with to the government.

While the prevailing aspects of the specific case are arguably unique to banking, the decision brought out by the US Supreme Court in Miller stands generally for the proposition that an individual's personal record held by a third party does not have the same constitutional privacy protection as the one that applies to the same record when this is held by the individual. From a privacy perspective, this proposition and the doctrine it has fostered are unsettling because of the volume of personal information necessarily held by third parties today[709]. In the cloud context, cloud service providers could very likely be regarded as third parties in the meaning of United States v. Miller.

706 United States v. Miller, 425 US 435 (1976).
707 Id.
708 Hoffa v. United States, 385 US 293 (1966).
709 *Id.*

ii. The Electronic Communications Privacy Act (ECPA) – a step ahead but obscurity lingers

The Electronic Communications Privacy Act (ECPA)[710] is legislation dating back to 1986 and was enacted by the United States Congress with the aim of extending government restrictions on wire taps from telephone calls to the field of transmissions of electronic data by computer as well as adding new provisions prohibiting access to stored electronic communications.

In an electronic environment, the ECPA provides certain protections against government access to electronic mail and other types of computer records held by third parties (e.g., Internet service providers or cloud service providers). ECPA was an attempt to bring the constitutional and statutory protections against the wiretapping of telephonic communications into the computer age. Since its enactment and all the more so nowadays, ECPA is generally regarded as a difficult law to understand and apply[711]; on the one hand, it is an old law that relies and was inspired by a model of electronic mail and Internet activity that is generations behind current practice and technology. It is commonly agreed that ECPA is significantly out-of-date, at least in certain aspects[712]. Nevertheless, it reflects a legislative recognition that some Internet activities do merit protection from the Miller doctrine that there is no reasonable expectation of privacy in records maintained by third parties. The difficulty with ECPA, however, is figuring out what those protections apply to and when.

710 ECPA (Pub. L. No. 99-508, 100 Stat. 1848 (Oct. 21, 1986), codified at 18 U.S.C. §§ 2510-22, 2701-11, 3121-26) was an amendment to Title III of the Omnibus Crime Control and Safe Streets Act of 1968 (the Wiretap Statute), which was primarily designed to prevent unauthorized government access to private electronic communications. Since its enactment, the ECPA has been amended by the Communications Assistance for Law Enforcement Act (CALEA) of 1994, the USA PATRIOT Act (2001), the USA PATRIOT reauthorization acts (2006), and the FISA Amendments Act (2008).

711 *Id.*

712 *Id.*

iii. The USA PATRIOT Act

The USA PATRIOT Act[713] includes provisions allowing the FBI to access virtually any business record. Although a court order is required, the FBI's authority under the USA PATRIOT Act is sufficient to extend also to a record maintained by a cloud provider. The authorities granted by the USA PATRIOT Act weaken certain privacy protections from the ECPA, and they generally allowed for an expansion of the government's ability to compel disclosure[714]. What is more, anyone who receives an order to disclose information under a provision of this Act is highly limited in their ability to disclose that they have received such an order[715]. Consequently, a user who provided records to a cloud provider for storage or processing is highly unlikely to know that the government obtained those records if this has been effected under a provision of the USA PATRIOT Act.

iv. The HIPAA and compelled disclosures

Potential threats to privacy currently exist for cloud services and the use of them under US law not only in relation to demands from the central government or other government agencies, but also with regard to demands that are permissible by law from private parties. One typical such example

713 The USA PATRIOT Act (note 215) was signed into law by President George W. Bush on October 26, 2001. Its title is in fact a ten-letter acronym (U.S.A. P.A.T.R.I.O.T.) that stands for "Uniting and Strengthening America by Providing Appropriate Tools Required to Intercept and Obstruct Terrorism Act of 2001". On May 26, 2011, President Barack Obama signed the PATRIOT Sunsets Extension Act of 2011, a four-year extension of three key provisions in the USA PATRIOT Act: roving wiretaps, searches of business records, and conducting surveillance of "lone wolves"—individuals suspected of terrorist-related activities not linked to terrorist groups. Resulting from a lack of Congressional approval, parts of the Patriot Act expired on June 1, 2015. However, with the enactment of the USA Freedom Act on June 2, 2015 the expired parts were restored and renewed through 2019. Nevertheless, Section 215 of the law was amended to stop the National Security Agency (NSA) from continuing its mass phone data collection program. Instead, phone companies are nowadays obliged to retain the relevant data and the NSA can obtain information about targeted individuals with permission from a federal court.

714 *Id.*

715 *Id.*

is the HIPAA[716] Privacy Rule, part of the respective HIPAA Act, which imposes some limits on compelled disclosures of health data that are provided for by this law. In detail, a legal demand by a private party to a cloud provider for disclosure of protected health information has to follow the procedures set out in the rule governing judicial and administrative proceedings. In general, the rule stipulates that anyone seeking access to information constituting part of a patient's health record via a court order, subpoena, discovery request, or the like must notify the patient, who has an opportunity to object to the disclosure. The said necessity under HIPAA means that a cloud provider should duly notify prospective customers that it maintains patient records to which specific procedures apply if the provider receives an order for disclosure of a record that is held (stored or processed) on behalf of an entity making use of the provider's services[717]. While the burden of those procedures falls on the person seeking the records, problems of control and compliance have never ceased to exist also on the part of providers.

While HIPAA provides for such a process of notification as a safeguard to users' privacy, other personal information shared by a business with a cloud provider will most likely receive less detailed treatment with regard to an obligation for disclosure by the provider. It goes without saying that when a cloud provider allows anyone to use its resources without any contractual or other prearrangement, the provider may have little or no knowledge about the information that a user puts on the cloud. If a cloud provider is not legally obliged to consult with the user, is not motivated to consult with the user, or is actively prevented from notifying the user, any subsequent disclosure by means of a court order or subpoena may have undesirable consequences for the user or for the ultimate data subject.

716 HIPAA (Health Insurance Portability and Accountability Act), Pub.L. 104–191, 110 Stat. 1936, was passed by Congress in 1996. It is the federal law that establishes standards for the privacy and security of health information, as well as standards for electronic data interchange (EDI) of health information.

717 *Id.*

v. The Fair Credit Reporting Act

The Fair Credit Reporting Act[718] (FCRA) is one more example of US legislation that nurtures potential undermining for users' privacy on the cloud. The Act imposes limits on the use of credit reports specifically to what is defined as a 'permissible purpose' by it[719]. If a creditor stores a credit report with a cloud provider and a third party obtains the report from the cloud provider, the legal limit on use of it could be violated.

A violation of the FCRA may also occur if the cloud provider uses the stored credit report for an improper purpose. Despite imposing a restriction on uses of credit reports, the FCRA does not have a mandatory procedure comparable to the one articulated by HIPAA that would require informing a cloud provider that it has information subject to disclosure limits. As a result, a crediting institution that stores records with a cloud provider may unexpectedly confront legal problems due to this vagueness in law.

The above examples are demonstrative of how privacy can be put under question and should not be taken for granted in today's cloud cased environments under the laws that currently regulate them. In previous parts of this research, we have already explored similar pathologies for privacy under the current EU legislation[720]. In conclusion, it should be admitted that differences in legal culture and traditions do not result in 'right or wrong' situations, i.e. conditions where one legal order is right and the other wrong about privacy. On the contrary, conditions undermining privacy may be traced in both cases. Therefore, convergence and the promotion of a minimum common ground of understanding becomes necessary for a sound governance of cloud computing technology and its uses.

---

718 The Fair Credit Reporting Act (FCRA), title VI of Pub.L. 91–508, 84 Stat. 1114, is a piece of U.S. Federal Government legislation enacted to promote the accuracy, fairness, and privacy of consumer information contained in the files of consumer reporting agencies. It was originally passed in 1970 and is enforced by the US Federal Trade Commission, the Consumer Financial Protection Bureau and private litigants.

719 *Id.*

720 See Chapter 4.

b. Threats to privacy means threats to security: the two prominent issues that go hand in hand in cloud computing environments

Threats to privacy in cloud environments are usually followed or set fertile ground for subsequent threats to security as well. In fact, the best angle from which privacy and security concerns that can arise when moving to the cloud are best observed and, thus, profoundly understood is from a risk–based perspective[721]. On further articulation, privacy and security risks on the cloud can be divided into operational, regulatory and compliance risks[722].

As it has already been extensively argued[723] many of the privacy and security concerns raised in the context of cloud computing are a direct consequence of the nature of the cloud; particularly in the early years of cloud adoption, its benefits had been invariably presented in terms of cost reduction, thus overlooking some of the inherent risks the new technology was bringing along, which have been left until now insufficiently addressed from a regulatory and, at times, also from a technological point of view. According to this angle, the cloud achieves its renowned economies of scale, that have actually enabled it to rise so quickly as a ruling technological standard in the field of IT services, thanks to a transformation of the nature of IT provision from specific, internally hosted and managed IT resources to commodity hardware and software platforms hosted outside the organizational boundary[724]. As it is known, in order to achieve this low-cost offering, cloud providers may switch customers' data and processes from one hardware facility to another; it is precisely this switching that nourishes some of the most common privacy and security issues with regard to the cloud.

The risks posed to privacy and security are relevant not only to cloud customers but also to cloud service providers. And this is not merely due to marketing or customer satisfaction reasons. As it has already become evident and will further be demonstrated on the course of this study, any loophole left in the overall structure of cloud computing environments and

721 A. E. Whitley, P. L. Willcocks & W. Venters (note 119).

722 Webster, J., & Watson, R. T., *Analyzing the past to prepare for the future: Writing a literature review.*, 26 MIS quarterly 13–23 (2002.)

723 See also Chapters 2 and 3.

724 Willcocks, Leslie P., Venters, Will and Whitley, Edgar A. (note 111).

the regulation thereof poses serious legal questions as well, apart from liabilities of any other nature.

Consequently, from a cloud computing customer's point of view, be it an average private customer or a big enterprise user or even an entity belonging to the wider administrative and government sector, the first set of questions relating to concerns that the use of the cloud is bringing forward are:

- Users wish to receive guarantees that their data and processes are not accessible to staff working for the cloud service provider or to other users running their processes on the same hardware environment as them[725].
- Users wish to have reassurances that, when the use of the hardware by them comes to an end (either because the specific service can no longer meet their demands, because the cloud hardware is decommissioned or because the cloud provider relocates the customer's services to other, cheaper computing resources) any data stored on that hardware is irreversibly removed. In the event the cloud provider is bound by any legal provision to retain data, users wish to have guarantees that their data will remain accessible to them during the retention period[726].
- Specifically in the case of cloud providers hosting mission critical services, users demand reassurances regarding the effectiveness of the cloud provider's disaster recovery plans[727].
- One of the greatest issues for cloud users, as it usually happens with every market growing in an accelerated manner, is the risk of attempts, on behalf of service providers, to lock–in the customer by methods, such as the use of non–standard hardware configurations or by making it impractical for them to transfer their data and processes to another provider[728].
- It is very typical for cloud facilities to host in their resources multiple service providers' data and processes. Sharing a storage facility with multiple other service providers can have unintended consequences that cannot be easily measured in advance. For example, one unpre-

725 A. E. Whitley, P. L. Willcocks & W. Venters (note 119).

726 Willcocks, Leslie P., Venters, Will and Whitley, Edgar A. (note 111).

727 DER HESSISCHE DATENSCHUTZBEAUFTRAGTE, Key data protection points for the trilogue on the General Data Protection Regulation (2015.)

728 Siani Pearson, Taking account of privacy when designing cloud computing services (2009.)

dictable consequence of Amazon and DynDNS hosting WikiLeaks was that these services were targeted by hackers with consequent adverse effects on other users of their services[729].

From a cloud provider's point of view, some of the major privacy and security concerns raised by cloud computing and the way it is technically built are:

- In an effort to respond to their users' worries, cloud providers apply different levels of staff accreditation to demonstrate to their customers that their staff will not misuse the data held on their cloud hardware. The number of different levels of staff accreditation and the distinctive features of each one of them has constantly been a matter of concern among cloud service providers[730].
- In response to the demand for safeguard mechanisms that permit unequivocal deletion of data hosted on a cloud facility after a user's quitting of the use of that facility, cloud providers look into the possibilities for developing such tools for data–wiping processes. In the context of such plans, cloud providers have to deal also with the issue of the cost, in capital and resources, for making these tools available to their customers, as well as whether it makes sense to give these options as standard tools to all users or offer them on a premium basis[731].
- A major challenge for cloud providers is also to put in place recovery mechanisms that will help contain the damage caused as a result of a major outage of service[732].
- Last but not least, cloud providers face the challenge to balance between offering commodity products on the basis of price and service quality and offering distinctive capabilities which might raise customer concerns about lock-in[733].

The privacy and security concerns described above are obviously common to users and suppliers of cloud computing services in both the EU and the US. However, the fundamentally different approaches the two jurisdictions take on privacy result in fragmented responses to common issues. While in the EU privacy is regarded as a fundamental human right, in the US it is viewed as a demand that businesses need to meet in order to pre-

---

729 A. E. Whitley, P. L. Willcocks & W. Venters (note 119).

730 Siani Pearson (note 728).

731 Francesca Musiani & Internet Policy Review (note 660).

732 Siani Pearson (note 728).

733 *Id.*

vent specific, serious risks of economic harm that may result from misuses of sensitive personal data[734]. These divergent approaches, however, work on the opposite direction of the tendency for more and more universal cloud services. Therefore, since cloud ecosystems and facilities are growing more and more unaffected of any kind of regional boundaries, an equally convergent mindset needs to be adopted towards setting up rules that will be based on shared principles and will create a minimum common understanding for tackling the risks rising out of the use of cloud computing.

c. Privacy risks posed by the cloud put into question cornerstone elements of information privacy laws

The architectural foundations of cloud computing technologies, along with the questions it raises regarding privacy and security of data and processes hosted in cloud ecosystems, have all contributed in basic definitions of information privacy law being challenged. Legislation developed in Europe before cloud computing, which became so widely used in the field of IT and data processing, understood information privacy law as a body of legislation concerning the processing of personal data[735]. Yet, with the arrival of cloud questions have been raised as to the meaning of both "personal data" and the "processing" of that data"[736].

The decisive criterion for the application of privacy law in the European Union is the assessment of whether personal data are involved. As it has been already demonstrated[737], personal data under EU law is any information that refers to "identified or identifiable" persons[738]. More explicitly, the EU Data Protection Directive would define that "an identifiable person is one who can be identified, directly or indirectly, in particular by reference to an identification number or to one or more factors specific to his physical, physiological, mental, economic, cultural or social

734 Nancy J. King & V. T. Raja (note 245).

735 Gerrit Hornung, *Regulating privacy enhancing technologies: seizing the opportunity of the future European Data Protection Framework*, 26 Innovation: The European Journal of Social Science Research 181–196 (2013.)

736 Paul Schwartz (note 697).

737 See Chapter 4.

738 Directive 95/46/EC, art. 2(a) (note 143).

identity"[739]. As long as the information at hand refers to identified or identifiable persons, information privacy law applies. This approach has been transposed to the newly introduced Data Protection Regulation[740] as well.

Following this track, the GDPR goes one step further to offer more details in an overall effort of greater specificity, wherever possible, compared with the Directive. Under the Regulation, the definition of persons as "identified" or "who can be identified" (i.e. identifiable) brings to the forefront the critical concept of direct or indirect identification by "means reasonably likely to be used"[741]. In this matter, EU law has been heavily influenced by German law, which has since long held the "means reasonably likely to be used" as the key criterion in defining whether or not a piece of information is identifiable[742]. The Regulation also sets out some additional typology criteria that help to make the relevant analysis more concrete: in that sense, it is specified that identification may be effected "by reference to an identification number, location data, online identifier or to one or more factors specific to the physical, physiological, genetic, mental, economic, cultural or social identity of that person"[743]. These additional details provide useful guidelines for the successful execution of the required assessment of whether some information refers to a specific person or not.

Looking into the United States and how the same issue is viewed under the American legal thinking, the decisive element there is whether a piece of information relates to an identified person[744]. Unlike the EU's proposed Regulation, which offers a central point of reference regarding how to reach this determination over specific data, in the US there is no universal test but rather a variety of them scattered around federal and state statutes and regulations for deciding when information relates to an identified person[745]. Overall, it can be noted that US law does not extend as far as identifiability in order to grant to specific information the quality of falling under information privacy law; as a general rule, the U.S. threshold approach

739 Id.

740 Regulation (EU) 2016/679, Art. 4(1) (note 25).

741 Regulation (EU) 2016/679, Preamb. 26 (note 25).

742 Anne Arendt, Ulrich Dammann & Spiros Simitis, Bundesdatenschutzgesetz (2011.)

743 Regulation (EU) 2016/679, Art. 4(1) (note 25).

744 Paul M. Schwartz & Daniel J. Solove (note 16).

745 Paul Schwartz (note 697).

for defining information as personal is reductionist when compared with the European Union's expansionist approach[746]. Under US law, personal information is typically found to be at stake only when the data under examination refers to a currently identified person[747]. Except for the points of difference, there are also similarities in the EU and U.S. legal approaches to determining the moment when information falls within the scope of information privacy law. Rather than drawing a fixed line between personal information and non-personal information, both legal systems establish a determination mechanism that depends on a number of factors, such as technology and corporate practices[748].

It is crucial to point out, however, that whether information becomes personal information in a networked environment depends on decisions made throughout the world, sometimes in real time. Consequently, it is getting increasingly difficult to decide a priori if certain kinds of cloud data processing have to be determined by privacy information law provisions or not[749]. This difficulty is all the more intensified with the ever-greater adoption of the cloud, which has managed to profoundly destabilize the regulatory approaches to personal information in the European Union and United States alike.

From the perspective of EU law, the cloud has increasingly been accepted as a "means reasonably likely to be used", thus being considered as responsible for making more information "identifiable" and, consequently, more extensively, if not entirely, falling under information privacy law. Yet, it should not be overlooked that identifiable information is not synonymous to identified information, while there are indeed instances of identifiable information which may never elevate into the status of identified information[750]. Furthermore, different risks are associated with the possible identification of data compared to information already related to an identified person[751]. Therefore, EU legislation needs to fine-tune itself in order to strike a balance between its expansionist protection approach regarding privacy and the necessary vital space cloud computing necessitates in order to flourish as a technology. At the same time, the US ap-

746 Paul M. Schwartz & Daniel J. Solove (note 16).
747 *Id.*
748 *Id.*
749 Paul M. Schwartz (note 157).
750 Paul Schwartz (note 697).
751 Ulrich Dammann & Spiros Simitis (note 169).

proach appears too narrow: certain information may only be identifiable and not identified, but even so it might bring with it a substantial risk of identification[752]. As a result, certain rearrangements are necessary for US law, as well, in order to live up to the elevated privacy risks posed for information in such a dynamic environment, as today's cloud-based internet.

d. The other side of the coin: how cloud computing's architectural advantages can turn into threats for privacy

Privacy is a key business risk and compliance issue and even more so in the field of IT. Given that it sits at the intersection among social norms, human rights and legal mandates, privacy has been a key comparative criterion for all kinds of IT providers and this also applies for those active in the field of cloud computing. Conforming to legal privacy requirements or meeting client privacy expectations with regard to personal identifiable information, requires from businesses offering cloud related services to demonstrate a firm level of supervision over such processes at all stages of the cloud computing cycle, from collection to destruction[753]. On the other hand, the cloud has been traditionally praised for its competitive advantages over its predecessors, namely its abilities to scale rapidly, in-house or through subcontractors, to store data remotely and to share services in a dynamic environment. However, these very advantages can also become disadvantages in the effort to maintain a level of privacy assurance sufficient to sustain confidence in users. In particular, the main insecurities raised by the cloud's sui generis architecture are:

– Due to outsourcing: The widely-used practice of outsourcing of data processing by nature raises governance and accountability questions[754]. In detail, the use of outsourcing makes it imperative to develop rules and processes which will permit to clarify at all times which party is responsible (statutorily or contractually) for upholding legal require-

752 Paul Schwartz (note 697).

753 Neil Robinson, Lorenzo Valeri, Jonathan Cave, Tony Starkey, Hans Graux, Sadie Creese & Paul P. Hopkins (note 119).

754 ACM ed., Controlling data in the cloud: outsourcing computation without outsourcing control (2009); Heinz-Dieter Schmelling, *Motivation. Wie verhält sich die IT-Sicherheit zum IT-Outsourcing?*, 40 Datenschutz und Datensicherheit – DuD 635–639 (2016.)

ments regarding privacy, or to verify that appropriate data handling standards are set and followed[755]. In an effort to further uphold privacy, effective methods for auditing third-party compliance with privacy laws and standards are also needed. Such methods will help determine to what extent it is safe to further sub-contract processing, and to confirm the identities and bona fides of sub-contractors[756]. Extensive use of outsourcing also necessitates rules that will permit to allocate rights in the data that are transferred between data processors and their subcontractors or that they will even settle other instances, such as whether and how such data are transferable to other third parties upon bankruptcy, takeover or merger of the entity that initially undertook the outsourcing[757].

- Due to offshoring[758]: Offshoring is another practice widely used by cloud service providers in their effort to maximize their competitive advantages and secure an even wider client base. At the same time, though, outsourcing of data processing increases risk factors and legal complexity. An indicative list of the complex issues that a cloud computing service which relies on outsourcing and offshoring can raise includes issues of jurisdiction, choice of law and enforcement[759]. A comprehensive cloud computing regulatory framework must include rules that will help settle these issues.
- Due to relying on virtualization: Cloud computing has been made possible largely thanks to the extensive use of virtualization[760]. However, sharing hardware, which is basically what virtualization is all about, carries along multiple security risks; among others, loss of control over data location or who has access to it at any given time. In fact, these insecurities will be even graver for certain types of data as a result of their nature[761]. For example, transactional data is a typical example of a byproduct with unclear ownership; when transferred or processed on

755 Neil Robinson, Lorenzo Valeri, Jonathan Cave, Tony Starkey, Hans Graux, Sadie Creese & Paul P. Hopkins (note 119).

756 *Id.*

757 ACM ed. (note 754).

758 Neil Robinson, Lorenzo Valeri, Jonathan Cave, Tony Starkey, Hans Graux, Sadie Creese & Paul P. Hopkins (note 119).

759 Neil Robinson, Lorenzo Valeri, Jonathan Cave, Tony Starkey, Hans Graux, Sadie Creese & Paul P. Hopkins (note 119); Heinz-Dieter Schmelling (note 754).

760 For more see Chapters 2 and 8.

761 A. van Cleeff, W. Pieters & R. J. Wieringa (note 119).

virtualization based networks, it can be hard to define whose duty is at any given time during the data life cycle to protect it[762].

- Due to the autonomic elements of cloud computing technology: Given that technological processes on a cloud environment have been granted a degree of autonomy in decision making (as they, for example, have the possibility to automatically adapt service resources to meet continuously varying needs of customers and service providers) it becomes more and more challenging for enterprises to maintain consistent security standards or to provide appropriate business continuity and back-up[763]. This is a natural consequence of the fact that it may not be continuously possible to determine in real time and with specificity where data processing will take or is taking place within the cloud.

All these risks make it clear that in a regulatory framework specifically developed for the cloud, rules will need to take into account the cloud's architectural specialties and offer constructive answers regarding them. Some proposals about how this could be achieved on the management and governance of the cloud level have already been presented in the introduction of accountability as a suitable managing framework for the cloud[764].

e. The affluence of consumer data on cloud computing and particular threats to them because of the cloud's specificities

Cloud computing is a high-end technology which has rapidly grown to be utilized for managing a wide range of commonplace information. One could persuasively argue that the cloud today is basically the internet, although, as it has been already explained, these two notions are not identical[765]. A logical outcome of this widespread deployment of cloud computing has been that the cloud is the vessel that hosts a staggering affluence of data and information from billions of common users[766]. A lot of this data may seem rudimentary from a wider perspective yet for individual users they constitute their very personal and sensitive information.

762 Neil Robinson, Lorenzo Valeri, Jonathan Cave, Tony Starkey, Hans Graux, Sadie Creese & Paul P. Hopkins (note 119).

763 *Id.*

764 See Chapter 6.

765 See Chapter 2.

766 Paul Schwartz (note 697).

The need to host or process this exponentially growing data has fueled the creation and use of massive cloud data centers, and cloud service providers such as Amazon have already invested enormous amounts in building and operating large data centers that provide a seemingly "infinite capacity" of computing resources to their clients[767]. All these facilities and the countless different types of information that is hosted on them pose certain risks apart from the ones we have already discussed in relation to how the life cycle of data evolves on the cloud computing network. Firstly, energy grids that power these data centers may be subject to attacks, which could be lengthy. Such power outages or other data center hardware-related disasters could have a significant impact on the business continuity of service providers[768]. If a provider's disaster recovery procedures for its data centers are inadequate, this sensitive data described beforehand run the risk of being lost or irreparably damaged. Secondly, current laws do not necessitate from cloud service providers to disclose sufficient information about the security policies and disaster recovery procedures they have designed in relation to their data center operations[769].

From a data architectural point of view, cloud service providers use certain data management practices which also raise concerns regarding the integrity and safety of consumer data and call for concrete regulatory rules that will moderate such risks in the context of a specific set of cloud computing laws[770]. Data commingling[771] is the first important such risk and it occurs when different items or kinds of data are stored in such a manner that they become commonly accessible while they are supposed to remain separated. In a cloud environment, this can very easily occur where different customer data sits on the same server presenting a continuous security vulnerability. The reason why cloud service providers choose to store data from different clients in the same data files is, as expected, the wish for optimal utilization of resources, especially if different cloud users concur-

767 Neil Robinson, Lorenzo Valeri, Jonathan Cave, Tony Starkey, Hans Graux, Sadie Creese & Paul P. Hopkins (note 119).

768 *Id.*

769 W. Kuan Hon, Christopher Millard & Ian Walden, *The Problem of 'Personal Data' in Cloud Computing – What Information is Regulated? The Cloud of Unknowing, Part 1*, 1 International Data Privacy Law 211–228 (2011.)

770 Neil Robinson, Lorenzo Valeri, Jonathan Cave, Tony Starkey, Hans Graux, Sadie Creese & Paul P. Hopkins (note 119).

771 M. Zhou, R. Zhang, W. Xie, W. Qian & A. Zhou (note 119).

rently use the same applications on the same cloud server[772]. It needs to be made clear that commingling in data is not only a matter of digital data colocation but it also refers to physical commingling.

The other data practice that poses risks on consumer data hosted on the cloud is data aggregation[773]. Aggregation practices raise significant challenges for protecting sensitive consumer data in cloud computing environments[774]. Public clouds, i.e. those where the great majority of cloud services nest, typically aggregate numerous clients' data into single files, and the latter actually share applications, processing power, and data storage space all at the same time[775]. A single instance of an unauthorized penetration into one cloud server facility that houses large volumes of data may provoke a massive compromise of sensitive data of multiple cloud users at the same time[776]. In a way to put in place countermeasures for this risk, it has been suggested that cloud users, primarily businesses, should be in a position to screen the cloud computing users with whom they share the same servers, applications, and data files to verify whether those other users have good reputations[777]. Also, in an effort to reduce the risk of data espionage, it is suggested that cloud users should be able to opt out of the commingling of their data with those from competitors[778]. However, these are only business choices or tools and are offered mainly as market incentives, hence, they cannot be held as standard practice neither can they be enforced by law.

Currently, on a statutory level, actors of the cloud market try to deal with these insecurities posed to consumer data with ad-hoc cloud service agreements. However, just as it has been proved that these are not an adequate answer to the problem of jurisdiction determination on the cloud[779],

772 *Id.*

773 Data aggregation is the process of transforming scattered data from numerous sources into a single new one. The objective of data aggregation is to combine sources together as such that the output is smaller than the input. This helps processing massive amounts of data in batch jobs and in real time.

774 Dawn Song, Elaine Shi, Ian Fischer & Umesh Shankar, *Cloud Data Protection for the Masses* Computer 39–45 (2012.)

775 *Id.*

776 Neil Robinson, Lorenzo Valeri, Jonathan Cave, Tony Starkey, Hans Graux, Sadie Creese & Paul P. Hopkins (note 119).

777 Dawn Song, Elaine Shi, Ian Fischer & Umesh Shankar (note 774).

778 *Id.*

779 See also Chapter 6.

they cannot deal inclusively with the issue of risks to data integrity either. In fact, it is more often so that individual cloud users do not have enough gravitational significance to negotiate the terms of cloud service agreements, particularly when they use the services of large public cloud service providers such as Amazon, Microsoft, Dropbox or Google[780]; in all these cases, there is a wide disparity in bargaining power between the parties which makes the chances to achieve a negotiated service agreement highly unrealistic due to lack of adequate bargaining power in this context[781].

In conclusion, the cloud as an industry is mainly footed by billions of plain private users who entrust with cloud service providers a great variety of their personal consumer data under pre-negotiated terms and conditions. All these clients lack the negotiating capacity to force the companies from which they are supplied with their computational needs to offer them contractual agreements with all the reassurances and safeguards that would allow them to feel secure about their data. Therefore, it is imperative need that a comprehensive cloud computing regulatory regime is put in place, which will set a level playing field for cloud users and service providers alike.

f. Reviewing security, privacy and trust issues on the cloud from an EU perspective

Having systematically examined the main points of concern regarding security, privacy and trust issues in cloud computing environments from a technical viewpoint and also through the angle of US law, this part of this study concludes with some observations regarding these issues from a European perspective. For starters, it is worth clarifying how EU legal thinking defines the main threats raised by cloud environments:

- Under the EU doctrine, security in the cloud concerns the confidentiality, availability and integrity of data or information[782]. Security as a

780 Neil Robinson, Lorenzo Valeri, Jonathan Cave, Tony Starkey, Hans Graux, Sadie Creese & Paul P. Hopkins (note 119).

781 Jack L. Goldsmith & Tim Wu (note 535).

782 Neil Robinson, Hans Graux, Maarten Botterman & Lorenzo Valeri (note 275). Kirstin Brennscheidt (note 119).

cloud necessity, may also include authentication and non-repudiation[783].

- Privacy refers to the expression of or adherence to various legal and non-legal norms regarding the right to private life. In the European context, ensuring privacy in the cloud has until today been understood as compliance with the European Data protection Directive[784] and since May 2018 with the respective Regulation. The main traits the concept of privacy in the cloud bears under the relevant tradition in EU law can be summarized down to these principles: consent, purpose restriction, legitimacy, transparency, data security and data subject participation[785].
- Trust is the concept encompassing the assurance and confidence that people, data, entities, information or processes will function or behave in expected ways[786]. The way trust in the cloud is interpreted as an idea under EU law is broken down to several different genres, i.e. trust from human to human, machine to machine (for example, handshake protocols negotiated within certain protocols[787]), human to machine (e.g., when a consumer reviews a digital signature advisory notice on a website[788]) or machine to human (e.g., when a system relies on user input and instructions without further verification to execute a process[789]). From a more thorough perspective, trust should be regarded as the logical consequence of progress towards achieving the broader security or privacy objectives the cloud industry has imposed on itself as essential.

Given the way these terms are interpreted in European legal thinking and the generally stricter protection that EU law grants to cloud related matters than US law, cloud computing raises serious challenges also for EU legislators. In fact, a new EU law aimed at regulating the cloud has to deal not only with the task of providing updated answers to commonly known IT problems as these are now readapted in light of cloud technologies but also to ensure that these answers will be fit for the market and technologi-

783 Neil Robinson, Lorenzo Valeri, Jonathan Cave, Tony Starkey, Hans Graux, Sadie Creese & Paul P. Hopkins (note 119).

784 Neil Robinson, Hans Graux, Maarten Botterman & Lorenzo Valeri (note 275).

785 See also Chapter 4.

786 Siani Pearson & Nick Wainwright (note 645).

787 Neil Robinson, Lorenzo Valeri, Jonathan Cave, Tony Starkey, Hans Graux, Sadie Creese & Paul P. Hopkins (note 119).

788 *Id.*

789 *Id.*

cal standards set out by cloud computing. Indeed, a great share of experts on the EU cloud services market have expressed the opinion that certain aspects of European data protection law (notably the rigid controller-processor model and the reliance on geographic location of data processing as an important factor in determining applicable rules) lead to substantial difficulties in practice[790]. Given that these understandings on which existing EU laws with which the cloud is attempted to be regulated have largely been rendered obsolete or unimportant by cloud technologies, a profoundly different approach is urgently needed.

What is also important to point out is the fact that, despite the strict rules regarding data protection, in practice there appears to be a substantial degree of poor compliance with them, especially in relation to transfers to third countries or data subject rights[791]. Both these topics merit careful analysis and consistent and clear responses in the context of a body of regulation dedicated to efficient governance of the cloud. Even in areas of data where more restrictive regulatory frameworks are in force, such as sensitive data mainly from health and financial industries, just adding extra impediments to data migrations or requiring that such data be processed only locally are not adequate measures to alleviate risks related to them[792].

Given the prevailing legal doctrine regarding IT technologies and the data tasks effectuated through them, the essential elements of an effective regulatory regime for the cloud should be transparency, availability and accountability. Transparency is an important element in the struggle to meet security, privacy or trust obligations, since it brings to the forefront the (contractual) will of all cloud actors (be them users, service providers, inspecting authorities etc.) to fulfil the globally accepted privacy principles that will make up for a sound and secure cloud environment[793]. Availability arises as a prerequisite since in a sound governance framework for the cloud availability for reporting and inspection of cloud actors is of

790 Neil Robinson, Hans Graux, Maarten Botterman & Lorenzo Valeri (note 275).

791 W. Kuan Hon & Christopher Millard, *Data Export in Cloud Computing. How Can Personal Data Be Transferred Outside the EEA? The Cloud of Unknowing, Part 4*, 9 SCRIPT-ed (2011.)

792 *Id.*

793 Daniel J. Weitzner, Harold Abelson, Tim Berners-Lee, Chris Hanson, James Hendler, Lalana Kagal, Deborah L. McGuinness, Gerald Jay Sussman & K. Krasnow Waterman (note 21).

prime importance as an assurance for application of the commonly accepted privacy and security requirements[794]. Finally, accountability, as it has already been demonstrated[795], is an important factor arising directly from one of the main legal challenges with regard to cloud computing: namely that commitments from parties to the cloud life cycle must be clear and enforceable in practice[796]. This, in consequence, stimulates trust throughout the cloud cycle and further intensifies the bonds between providers and users of cloud services[797].

In summary, it has become evident from the discourse into the issue of risks related to cloud computing that the legal and, hitherto, the contractual framework for the cloud needs to become sufficiently stable and comprehensive to promote the trustworthiness of the legal relationships that are created among actors of the cloud life cycle[798]. At the same time, this requirement for trust and continuous accountability needs to be reconciled with the inherent flexibility of the cloud computing architecture[799]. In practice, this can only be achieved by ensuring that the rights, responsibilities and liabilities of each actor are clearly outlined, and that the expectations from each link in the cloud chain are at all times transparent and adequately ensured. If these conditions are met, then compliance (and accountability) become more realistic and lead to a viable and, simultaneously, trustworthy governing scheme for cloud computing.

PART II: CLOUD COMPLIANCE

a. Introductory remarks on the concept of 'cloud compliance'

Cloud compliance is the general principle that cloud-delivered systems must be compliant with standards that the cloud users face[800]. In other words, a cloud network and the providers of it or the services that are

794 Neil Robinson, Lorenzo Valeri, Jonathan Cave, Tony Starkey, Hans Graux, Sadie Creese & Paul P. Hopkins (note 119).
795 IEEE ed. (note 681).
796 Centre for Information Policy Leadership (note 592).
797 Neil Robinson, Lorenzo Valeri, Jonathan Cave, Tony Starkey, Hans Graux, Sadie Creese & Paul P. Hopkins (note 119).
798 *Id.*
799 Liang-Jie Zhang & Qun Zhou (note 96).
800 Siani Pearson (note 728).

made possible thanks to it, need to live up to a series of expectations that the users of this network have in order to regard the network as a secure, safe and trustworthy one. Having gone through the overview of the perils that cloud computing might entail for the data users entrust it with, it has been made clear that effectively dealing with these risks is not just a regulatory matter but also an issue of credibility. Consequently, cloud compliance is for owners, controllers and service providers of a cloud network the litmus test in their relationship with cloud users as is accountability in their relation to regulatory authorities inspecting the overall cloud industry. Just as a cloud ecosystem has to meet specific standards set by its supervising public authorities to get the green light and be lawfully commercialized, it also needs to meet the same approval in the eyes of its actual users. After all, the risks that an effective body of law governing the cloud will try to keep under control or even resolve are the worries that users of cloud computing need to be reassured about. In conclusion, analyzing what cloud compliance constitutes of and discussing how these necessities will be pursued by an effective regulatory framework for the cloud is as important as highlighting how public authorities need and should inspect such a heavily customer-oriented industry.

b. Effective regulation of technology: the need to define policy tools and policy actors

Lawrence Lessig[801] had already since the 1990s put forward the regulation of privacy as 'an example of law taming code' in order to uphold expectations of users of IT technologies: in Lessig's doctrine, the state as an actor has the discretionary power to impose changes on code in order to increase the ability of the individual to exercise privacy choices[802]. This regulatory approach, involving the Platform for Privacy Preferences (P3P)[803], is fabricated upon the conception of privacy as a property

801 L. Lessig (note 504).

802 *Id.*

803 The Platform for Privacy Preferences Project (P3P) is a protocol permitting to websites to declare their intended use of information they collect from web browser users. It was developed with the aim of giving users more control of their personal information when browsing. It was officially launched in 2002 but there had been only limited implementations of it mainly due to its difficulty and lack of value.

right[804], in which the giving (or withholding) of consent is the cornerstone for protecting privacy. According to this predicament, the need for collective action by the state in order to enable individuals to control their own privacy by ensuring the availability of respective tools that will allow them to do so, is of prime significance for a well-functioning and soundly-regulated IT environment. It also constitutes an exemplary pattern of interaction among different constituents playing a role in the IT market.

Generally, a doctrine like this, which makes provision for specific policies and tools that enable private parties to have an actual say in how their right to privacy is handled, fits more comfortably in regulatory environments such as that of the USA, where political and business environments have shown a considerable resistance to more direct legislative solutions, such as non-consumerist, human rights-based conceptions of privacy, and, as a result, the range of alternative regulatory solutions has traditionally been restricted. However, at least as the prevailing legal thinking has been until now, such a doctrine mostly contrasts with the approach of European countries and the European Union. As it has been previously explained in detail[805], in the EU legal doctrine so far has been promoting more active roles for collective rather than individual actors, such as regulatory agencies. These have been the entities to play – in principle, at least – the key parts in the regulatory mechanisms for governing IT technologies and the markets dependent on them by executing the powers entrusted to them to implement legislation. Consequently, so far European law vests the main protective initiatives for privacy to state actors rather than individual citizens or consumers, or technological mechanisms.

In mid-2000s, when the revolution of cloud computing was still very nascent but indications about the cloud's potential were already growing, Murray's[806] doctrine of 'cyberspace regulation' was introduced in academic discourse putting emphasis on the need to identify distinct actors active within multi-level regulatory regimes[807]. Presenting his doctrine on an abstract level, Murray put forward an illustrative matrix to conceptualize multi-dimensional regulatory fields, i.e. fields of regulation with multi-

804 Charles D. Raab & Paul de Hert, *The Regulation of Technology: Policy Tools and Policy Actors* TILT Law & Technology Working Paper Series (2007.)

805 See Chpaters 2 and 3.

806 Andrew Murray, The regulation of cyberspace. Control in the online environment (2007.)

807 *Id.*

ple actors carrying some type of regulatory capacity for specific actions[808]. This conception was then tested against actual regulatory case-studies and led Murray to argue against static 'command and control' regulatory models in fields with actors spread through various levels. In the end, Murray concluded that in such multi-layered regulatory fields, regulation attempted exclusively via external interventions, typically manifested through law, is likely to be rather disruptive than effective. This is mainly so due to the fact that regulation produced entirely by actors on the superior levels of the system is grounded in insufficient understanding of the processes and interactions that are meant to be regulated. Instead, he argues in favor of a more dynamic, complementary and symbiotic approach, which acknowledges that regulators and regulates are not separate, and which relies on hybrid rule-making processes rather than instruments produced out of single-direction flows[809].

c. Incorporating users' privacy concerns into the rules governing design and deployment of cloud environments

Maintaining adequate levels of protection of data and privacy is not only a matter of legal importance but also crucial for responding to users' expectations in relation to the cloud. This challenge becomes even more complicated when the restrictions on cross-border data transfers are also to be upheld. This is not just an accountability issue, in the sense of self-disciplinary measures. As cloud services process users' data on machines that users do not own or operate themselves, serious privacy issues are raised which can undermine users' control and privacy options. However, privacy is a fundamental human right, enshrined in the United Nations Universal Declaration of Human Rights[810] and the European Convention on Human Rights[811]. Out of this basic privacy provisions come various special forms of privacy, including 'the right to be left alone'[812], the 'control of

808 *Id.*
809 *Id.*
810 The Universal Declaration of Human Rights, General Assembly resolution 217 A (1948), Art. 12.
811 The European Convention on Human Rights (ECHR) (note 343), Art. 8.
812 Siani Pearson (note 728).

information about ourselves'[813] or the newest concept of 'the right to be forgotten'[814]. These are all privacy manifestations which have been inspired by the way individuals have been interpreting their right to privacy over the years and they all play a crucial role in the way cloud technologies are or should be applied.

Apart from the concerns raised for privacy because of the very technological architecture of the cloud, another source of potential undermining effects for privacy on the cloud is that it is a dynamic environment, which facilitates, for instance, service interactions that can be created in a more dynamic way than traditional e-commerce scenarios[815]. In cloud enabled data paths, personal and sensitive data can move through an organization or cross organizational boundaries in various simultaneous trajectories. However, data remains at all times attributable to its original subjects, adequate protection of the information of which is as important as maintaining other aspects of legal compliance.

Apart from the multiple routes made available to data in their constant flow from one terminal point to another, cloud computing also makes possible for new services to be made available in the cloud, which come out of combining two or more individual services[816]: for instance, a cost-efficient 'pictures on demand' service could be made commercially available by combining a printing service with a cloud storage service. As this procedure of service combination grows into more layers, it typically leads to less and less control over aspects, such as the privacy of the data carried out for and due to the use of these services[817]. Additionally, while before the introduction of cloud computing such on-demand services involving data were made possible via traditional multi-party enterprise schemes, nowadays convergence happens on the services level, with the owner of provider of each service not even being necessarily aware of the combinations[818]. What is more, there might also be varying degrees of security, diverse privacy practices and controls in each of the component services. And given that, as every cloud service, they almost necessarily involve collection, storage or disclosure of personal and sensitive user data, poten-

813 *Id.*

814 Gerrit Hornung (note 735).

815 Siani Pearson (note 728).

816 *Id.*

817 Siani Pearson & George Yee (note 280).

818 Siani Pearson (note 728).

tial users need to receive adequate and persuasive reassurances before actually deciding to use them. It is precisely at this point, where cloud compliance comes to act as the catalyst that turns users' expectations into cloud service providers' self-discipline processes.

In light of the above observations on privacy expectations users have from cloud computing systems, the privacy concepts and principles that have prevailed may be summarized as follows[819]:

- Notice, openness and transparency: it is increasingly becoming a standard user expectation that cloud services which need to collect users' information duly inform them about the kind of information they collect, the ways in which they intend to use it, the amount of time that they intend to keep it, if it will be shared with any third parties, and the by-products of the further uses they intend to make of it. It is also expected that cloud service providers notify users before making any changes as to how the information is or will be used.
- Choice, consent and control: cloud services users expect to be given the freedom of choice whether they allow this information to be collected or not. Data subjects are also entitled to giving their consent to the collection, use and disclosure of their personally identifiable information.
- Scope/minimization: only information essential to fulfil the stated purpose should be collected or shared. The collection of data should be minimized to what is necessary for the service purpose.
- Access and accuracy: cloud services users expect at all times to be able to access the personal information service providers collect about them, to review what is being held about them, and to verify its accuracy.
- Security safeguards: users expect that safeguards are in place to prevent unauthorized access, disclosure, copying, use or modification of personally identifiable information
- Means to challenge compliance: users must have the possibility to challenge, ideally via official procedures, a provider's privacy processes.
- Limitation of purpose: users expect that their data will only be used for the purpose for which it was collected. This purpose is expected to be a clearly specified one. Data subjects are to be informed about the rea-

819 Refer also to Chapters 8, 9 and 10.

sons why their data is being collected and shared in advance or, at the latest, at the time of collection.

- Limited use – disclosure and retention: users expect that data will only be used or disclosed for the purpose for which it was collected and should only be disclosed to parties authorized to receive it. Additionally, personal data are expected to be aggregated or anonymized with suitable methods. Personal information should only be kept strictly for as long as necessary.
- Accountability: users expect that a provider has in place inspecting personnel that ensures that privacy policies and practices are followed at all times. Audit functions also play a crucial role towards monitoring data accesses and modifications.

As it easily becomes evident, the main expectations of users, which are the actual content of the concept of cloud compliance, are identical with respective elements of the suggested accountability scheme for the cloud[820]. This comes as no surprise given that, as it has been previously demonstrated, cloud compliance is the other side on the coin of sound cloud governance[821]. Much as providers try or should even be made to incorporate the above expectations already since the phase of preliminary design of their services, it may prove challenging to know exactly how their service will evolve. In conclusion, the flexible nature of cloud computing as technology necessitates respectively more adaptable design specifications. Consequently, the development of a regulatory framework for it comes also to challenge traditional thinking about legislation production[822]. In particular, as user requirements change, taking full advantage of the multiple possibilities offered by the cloud, so may functionality and privacy requirements[823]. On a regulatory level, this means that laws governing the cloud need to be produced via processes that will allow for more frequent and effective reassessment or that will aim at more generically formulated norms so that the gap between the legal and technological, as well as the service state-of-the-art can be shortened.

820 Siani Pearson & Andrew Charlesworth (note 585).
821 Refer to Chapter 5.
822 L. Lessig (note 504).
823 Siani Pearson & George Yee (note 280).

d. Pragmatic answers regarding the deployment of secure and privacy-proof cloud networks

The rate at which cloud computing is expanding across sub-domains of the IT sector proves its lasting nature as a technology. It has also been adequately demonstrated that trying to put geographical or other kinds of boundaries to the cloud is ineffective and out of touch with how cloud computing is being used in real life. Neither users nor cloud service providers will voluntarily quit from taking advantage of the full potential of cloud applications, which is decisively shaped by the universal nature of this technology. Therefore, also from the perspective of regulating how service providers should set up their services to make them compatible with cloud users' expectations, the focus should primarily be on restricting unauthorized access to intelligible data, rather than restricting data export[824] or other kinds of data processing that can be executed on the cloud. The current restrictions, via which data processing in the cloud is attempted to be regulated, should be replaced by requirements regarding accountability, transparency and security, i.e. with measures that will boost cloud compliance.

In fact, the preoccupation about setting boundaries is rather unnecessary if close attention is paid to how resources allocation in a cloud network actually works. While the popular view seems to be that in cloud computing data moves around the network continuously and almost randomly, making it virtually impossible to know where a specific bunch of data are located at any time, in practice this is often not so. In most cases, data are copied or replicated to different data centers, for business continuity/back-up purposes[825], rather than being constantly circulated through the networks storage facilities by being deleted from one data centre and re-created in another. Additionally, the primary copy of a set of data (e.g. data of a specific user inserted on a particular SaaS application) is at most times stored in the same data centre[826]. This typically is the one geographically closest to the user in question, for latency reasons (i.e. for achieving the optimum speed of access and response for the user[827]), even if it is also likely that they are stored in fragments distributed amongst different stor-

824 W. Kuan Hon & Christopher Millard (note 791).
825 *Id.*
826 *Id.*
827 *Id.*

age hardware within that data centre[828]. Consequently, regulating the cloud with a view to improving data allocation capabilities on cloud networks is not a real priority. If need be, the provider will most likely know where a user's data fragments are stored, on a data centre if not on equipment level.

Overall, it becomes evident that the regulatory focus regarding cloud computing needs to shift from where the data is or can be saved or processed to the intention (i.e. the purpose) for which it is saved or processed at any time by a specific actor of a cloud network. This approach towards cloud computing regulation through the teleological perspective will be thoroughly presented as the final outcome of this study[829].

e. Incentivizing privacy and security by encouraging the adoption of privacy enhancing technologies

In order to achieve a regime of effective data protection on the cloud, under the present and projected status quo of cloud technologies, legal instruments are not enough by themselves. A crucial tool in that direction will also be the availability of privacy enhancing technologies (PETs)[830]. It is beyond the scope of a legal research project to describe in detail the nature of PETs. Nevertheless, it should not fail our attention how PETs can assist in achieving optimum levels of privacy and security and why it is, therefore, important that their adoption be prescribed or, at least, encouraged by law[831].

The intrinsic and, largely, legitimate aim of service providers and users of cloud computing is the maximization of profit[832]. In this context, data protection could remain relevant as long as there is demand for it on the market. On the other hand, if such demand ceases or becomes minimal,

---

828 *Id.*

829 See Chapter 10.

830 Privacy enhancing technologies (PETs) is a generic term referring to a set of computer tools, applications and mechanisms which, integrated in online services or applications, or used in conjunction with such services or applications, enable online users to protect the privacy of their personally identifiable information (PII) which they have handed over to and is handled by such services or applications.

831 W. K. Hon, C. Millard & I. Walden (note 119).

832 See also Chapter 2.

privacy and the technologies making it possible may quickly become a mere cost driver or even end up being irrelevant in the design process because it neither causes nor reduces costs.

Therefore, in the context of an effective regulatory scheme for the cloud, it is crucial to emphasize the idea of service responsibility for service providers[833]. Rules can assist in that direction and have a relevant impact in several manners:

- by providing external incentives, such as binding requirements and restrictions or liability regulations[834].
- by exerting influence on intrinsic goals of service providers; in other words, by stimulating the market for PETs using data protection audits or quality certifications as means of pressure for providers to embrace these technologies[835].
- even by going as far as establishing guidelines for the participation of scholars and practitioners in interdisciplinary research that will be aimed at devising methods for privacy enhancing design of cloud-based services. The multi-faceted nature of the cloud means that, apart from legal experts, interdisciplinary research into the ever-enhanced privacy and security standards of cloud computing should also bring together experts from a wide range of areas, such as computer science, organization and management science, economics and political science.

In following parts of this study[836], it will be argued that PETs are no one-way solution, as far as regulatory handling of the cloud is concerned. Rather, they are just a tool that could offer greater assurance to consumers about the security of cloud systems. However, the philosophy behind PETs can already offer invaluable insight towards a thorough set of regulatory principles for the cloud which, coupled the expertise available from the technical front can ultimately lead to robust and efficient cloud regulation rules.

---

833 *Id.*
834 See also Chapter 6.
835 *Id.*
836 See Chapter 10.

CHAPTER 8. Principles for regulating the cloud (1); conclusions from the ontology of cloud computing networks

a. Introduction – scope of this chapter

Having gone through the norms, prevailing schools of thought and currently applicable regulatory approaches regarding cloud computing or the IT applications more closely related to it in Europe and the US, it is now time to look into the principles and best practices that could be derived from each of the two jurisdictions and could serve as guidelines for regulating the cloud, as a unique technology and the backbone of the IT environment of today and tomorrow.

The following parts of this study will be organized in a manner that will have a twofold aim:

- To explain why we need rules specifically for cloud computing besides those already governing the numerous applications based on it
- To formulate these rules not in the strict form of a draft law but as generic regulatory concepts that each jurisdiction can then adopt and adapt to the particularities of its own legal conventions being sure, however, that, if the laws developed have these concepts at heart, the overall governance of the cloud will be more efficient on a cross-border scale.

The proposed principles will be grouped in three chapters, in particular:

- Those stemming from the architecture of the cloud computing network itself and respond to issues related to the way cloud infrastructure is compiled together (Chapter 8)
- Those stemming from the different actors participating across the cloud cycle, i.e. across the workflows developed and facilitated by cloud computing networks, and respond to the way cloud services, businesses and applications are organized and executed (Chapter 9)
- Those responding to the need to build a governance scheme for cloud computing that will differentiate between regulatory challenges on the local and the global level allowing for the concretization of minimum shared standards among different regulations that will permit a more

unified tackling of regulatory issues related to the cloud on a cross-jurisdictional basis (Chapter 10).

In comprehensively presenting the regulatory proposals organized into these three groupings, the following methodological tools will primarily be applied:

- Interdisciplinarity, primarily with regard to the principles falling under Chapters 8 and 9
- Legal pluralism, primarily for the principles falling under Chapters 9 and 10
- Harmonization of norms, primarily for the principles under Chapter 10.

b. Constructing the ontology of the cloud; is the cloud one and only thing after all?

One of the most common misconceptions regarding cloud computing is that, in laymen as well as in the regulator's eyes, it is usually seen as a concept with just one meaning, that of the means or the medium for the transfer, storage or processing of personal data. Actually, the term 'cloud computing' is much more multi-layered and complex than that and, before getting down to talk about it as a term signifying a whole range of applications serving the above purposes, it is crucial to realize that the cloud has various different facets on a hardware/architectural level[837]. Particularities in the nature of these facets already lead to the first regulatory principles necessary for an efficient governance of cloud computing.

In computer science, describing and documenting all variations of a technology or the hardware implementations that make it possible is a process called (IT) ontology[838]. In detail, in computer science and information science, an ontology is an official, analytical naming and mapping of the types, properties, and interrelations of the entities that exist for a particular domain of discourse, i.e. a particular domain of the overall sec-

837 Deepak Puthal, B.P.S. Sahoo, Sambit Mishra & Satyabrata Swain, *Cloud Computing Features, Issues, and Challenges: A Big Picture*, in 2015 International Conference on Computational Intelligence & Networks (CINE), 116–123 (KIIT University ed.)

838 Lamia Youseff, Maria Butrico & Dilma Da Silva, *Toward a Unified Ontology of Cloud Computing*, in 2008 Grid Computing Environments Workshop, 1–10.

tor[839]. In other words, ontology in IT is a practical application of philosophical ontology, with a taxonomy[840]. An ontology task, in essence, compartmentalizes the variables needed for specific types of computations and, additionally, establishes the relationships between them[841].

Ontology as a tool and practice is increasingly common in several fields of the wider IT sector[842]. To name a few, the fields of artificial intelligence, the Semantic Web, systems engineering, software engineering, biomedical informatics, library science, enterprise bookmarking, and information architecture all resort to ontologies to limit complexity and organize information about and within them[843]. These ontologies can then be applied to problem solving[844]. The same practice is suggested as a key tool in our effort to analytically comprehend, systematize and, ultimately, regulate cloud computing.

There are several methodologies with which it is possible to map down the ontology of an IT field[845]. The one mostly proposed in relevant literature as the most suitable to grasp and successfully organize all relevant

---

839 John F. Sowa, *Top-level ontological categories*, 43 International Journal of Human-Computer Studies 669–685 (1995.)

840 *Id.*

841 Lamia Youseff, Maria Butrico & Dilma Da Silva (note 838).

842 Ling Liu & M. Tamer Özsu, Encyclopedia of database systems (2009.)

843 *Id.*

844 Xiaolong Jin & Jiming Liu, *From Individual Based Modeling to Autonomy Oriented Computation*, in International Workshop on Computational Autonomy, 151–169 (2003.)

845 The two fundamental genres of ontology are domain and upper ontology. Domain ontologies (or domain-specific ontologies) represent concepts which belong to part of the world. Particular meanings of terms applied to that domain (i.e. the world) are provided by domain ontology. For instance, the word card has several meanings. An ontology about the domain of poker would model the "playing card" meaning of the word, while an ontology about the domain of computer hardware would model the "sound card" and "video card" meanings. A main feature of domain ontologies is that they represent concepts in very specific, even eclectic ways, becoming often incompatible. As systems that rely on domain ontologies expand, they often need to merge domain ontologies into a more general representation. At the same time, different ontologies in the same domain arise due to different languages, different intended use of the ontologies, and different perceptions of the domain (based on cultural background, education, ideology, etc.).

Another major type is upper ontology (or foundation ontology), i.e. a model of common objects that are generally applicable across a wide range of domain on-knowledge regarding the cloud is composability[846]. Composability, as an ontology typification method, is inspired by composability as a system design principle[847]; the latter heavily deals with the inter-relationships of components of a system; in this case, of the cloud, as a field of IT[848].

For reasons of clarity and simplicity, the ontology of the cloud that is endeavored here should be conventionally pictured as a stack of layers. Then, each layer shall encompass one or more cloud services. In addition, cloud services sharing comparable levels of abstraction will be classified as belonging to the same layer, while abstraction will be measured as per which type of users each service is targeted at[849]. For instance, all cloud software environments (i.e. cloud platforms) target programmers, while cloud applications target end users. Therefore, cloud software environments would be all classified in the same but in a different layer than cloud applications, which would, however, also fall all under the same layer.

Under composability, one cloud layer is classified as being higher in the cloud stack, when its services can be composed from the services of the underlying layer[850]. For example, when it comes to the cloud application layer, since cloud applications are made possible, i.e. are developed, using cloud software environments, it can be said that cloud applications are composable from cloud software environments, and, consequently, the cloud application layer is higher in the cloud stack[851]. Following this logic, the cloud stack is composed from bottom up of the following layers:

- The Firmware/hardware layer (HaaS)
- The Software Kernel layer
- The Cloud Software Infrastructure layer, which is further broken down to Computational Resources (IaaS), Storage (DaaS), and Communications (CaaS)

tologies. It usually employs a core glossary that contains the terms and associated object descriptions as they are used in various relevant domain sets.
Lastly, a hybrid is an ontology incorporating elements from both the domain and upper model.

846 Lamia Youseff, Maria Butrico & Dilma Da Silva (note 838).
847 John F. Sowa (note 839).
848 Lamia Youseff, Maria Butrico & Dilma Da Silva (note 838).
849 *Id.*
850 John F. Sowa (note 839).
851 Lamia Youseff, Maria Butrico & Dilma Da Silva (note 838).

- The Cloud Software Environment layer and,
- The Cloud Application layer (SaaS)[852].

An analytical presentation of these layers will permit us, afterwards to pinpoint some essential regulatory guidelines for the cloud.

i. The Firmware/Hardware layer

By application of the tools described above, the ontology scheme of the cloud has the firmware/hardware layer at its foundations. It comprises the actual physical hardware and infrastructure that form the backbone of the cloud, as technology and as network[853]. On this layer, the main users are big enterprises with voluminous IT requirements which, most commonly, are in need of a service constituting of subleasing hardware which they will then use for their own computational needs or purposes (HaaS)[854]. As a rule, the entities acting as HaaS providers at this level have the tasks of operating, managing and upgrading the said hardware on behalf of their consumers, for as long as the sub-lease contracts they have entered into with customers remain in force. One of the classic examples of HaaS are the contracts banking service providers enter into with big data storage providers in order to cover their computational needs[855]. At this layer, users have predefined workloads with characteristics that impose strict performance requirements.

ii. The Software Kernel layer

On this cloud layer are to be allocated all pieces of basic software management for the physical servers composing the cloud. Software kernels[856] at

852 IEEE INFOCOM 2010 – IEEE Conference on Computer Communications.

853 Mike P. Papazoglou & Willem-Jan van den Heuvel, *Service oriented architectures. Approaches, technologies and research issues*, 16 The VLDB Journal 389–415 (2007.)

854 *Id.*

855 Morgan Stanley's sublease contract with IBM in 2004.

856 In computer science, the kernel (also named the nucleus) is a computer program that constitutes the core of a computer's (or computer network's) operating system. The kernel has complete control over everything that occurs in the system. As such, it is the first program loaded on system startup, and it then manages the

this level are implemented as an OS kernel[857], hypervisor[858], virtual machine monitor[859] and/or clustering middleware[860]. Traditionally, grid computing applications were deployed to run on this layer on several interconnected clusters of machines[861]. However, due to the absence of the virtualization element in grid computing, those tasks were closely tied to the actual hardware infrastructure; consequently, providing migration, checkpointing and load balancing to the applications at this level used to be a complicated task[862]. In the meantime, a considerable body of research in grid computing has led to several grid-developed concepts being realized today in cloud computing[863].

---

remainder of the startup process, as well as input/output requests from software, by translating them into data processing instructions for the central processing unit. It is also responsible for managing memory, and for communicating with computing peripherals, like printers, speakers, etc. The kernel is a fundamental part of a modern computer's operating system. Mutatis mutandis, in the context of a cloud computing network the kernel is its most basic software, the one managing its most fundamental and elementary functions and processes, which are basically dedicated in making sure that the network itself will run properly.

857 The OS kernel as a term essentially is synonymous to the term 'software kernel'.

858 A hypervisor or virtual machine monitor (VMM) is a piece of computer software (there are firmware or hardware typifications of hypervisors but they call outside the scope of this study) that creates and runs virtual machines. The hypervisor presents the guest operating systems with a virtual operating platform and manages the execution of the guest operating systems. The term hypervisor is a variant of supervisor, a traditional term for the kernel of an operating system: the hypervisor is the supervisor of the supervisor, with hyper- used as a stronger variant of super-.

859 A virtual machine is a software computer that, like a physical computer, runs an operating system and applications. The virtual machine is comprised of a set of specification and configuration files and is backed by the physical resources of a host.

860 In the context of a computing cluster, the activities of computing nodes are orchestrated by "clustering middleware", a software layer that sits atop the nodes and allows the users to treat the cluster as by and large one cohesive computing unit, e.g. via a single system image concept.

861 Stephanos Androutsellis-Theotokis & Diomidis Spinellis, *A survey of peer-to-peer content distribution technologies*, 36 ACM Comput. Surv. 335–371 (2004.)

862 2008 Grid Computing Environments Workshop.

863 Ian Foster, Yong Zhao, Ioan Raicu & Shiyong Lu (note 92).

iii. The Cloud Software Infrastructure layer

The cloud software infrastructure layer hosts fundamental resources which are essential so that other higher-level layers can be used to construct new cloud software environments or cloud applications. The main reason why resources allocated on this layer are set apart from the two highest levels in the cloud stack is that the latter can bypass the cloud infrastructure layer in directly building their system[864]. Often this bypass can enhance the efficiency of the system, yet it comes at the cost of simplicity and minimum development efforts necessary[865]. The services allocated on this layer are further divided into: computational resources, data storage, and communications.

- computational resources: Virtual machines (VMs) are the most common form for providing computational resources to cloud users at this layer which they can subsequently use to customize the software stack for performance and efficiency[866]. Conventionally, such services are dubbed Infrastructure as a Service (IaaS)[867]. Virtualization is the enabling technology which offers unprecedented flexibility to users in configuring their settings while protecting the physical infrastructure of the provider's data center[868]. However, since VMs can by nature co-exist on the same data storage hardware facility, the lack of a strict performance isolation between them while sharing the same physical node can at any time result in the inability of cloud providers to give strong guarantees for performance to their clients[869]. Such weak guarantees, unfortunately, can inject themselves up the layers of the cloud stack[870].
- data storage: The second infrastructure resource is data storage, which constitutes what cloud computing is probably most widely known for: allowing users to store their data at remote storage facilities and access them anytime from anywhere[871]. This service is commonly quoted as Data-Storage as a Service (DaaS), and it permits cloud applications to

864 Deepak Puthal, B.P.S. Sahoo, Sambit Mishra & Satyabrata Swain (note 837).
865 Mike P. Papazoglou & Willem-Jan van den Heuvel (note 853).
866 Refer also to Chapter 2.
867 Refer also to Chapter 2.
868 Refer also to Chapters 2 and 6.
869 Dimitrios Zissis & Dimitrios Lekkas, *Addressing cloud computing security issues*, 28 Future Generation Computer Systems 583–592 (2012.)
870 Lamia Youseff, Maria Butrico & Dilma Da Silva (note 838).
871 See Chapter 2.

scale beyond their limited servers. Data storage systems are as a standard expected to meet several rigorous requirements for maintaining users' data and information, including high availability, reliability, performance, replication and data consistency[872]; however, precisely because of the conflicting nature of all these requirements, no system can implement all of them together[873]. For instance, availability, scalability and data consistency are regarded as three conflicting goals from a technical point of view. Given that those features are hard to be simultaneously achieved with general data storage systems, DaaS-providers implement their system to favor one feature over the others, while indicating their choice through their SLA. However, there is no legal warranty at the moment regarding the minimum that needs to be achieved for any one of the most common performance requirements causing considerable irregularities and, thus, insecurities throughout the cloud market.

- communication: As cloud systems evolve and become more and more popular and the means for developing a wide range of IT services for the general public, so does the need for guaranteed quality of service for network communication, with communication becoming a vital component of the cloud infrastructure. As a result of this demand, cloud systems have focused on developing features enhancing communication capability in a service-oriented, configurable, schedulable, predictable, and reliable manner[874]. Towards this end, the concept of Communication as a Service (CaaS) emerged. Although at the beginning this model was the least discussed and adopted in commercial cloud systems, it is gaining more and more in popularity over the last years[875]. Inter alia, systems that belong to CaaS are VoIP telephone systems, audio and video conferencing as well as instant messaging apps are cloud applications that are already or are expected to be based on CaaS[876].

---

872 See Chapter 2.

873 *Id.*

874 Ozalp Babaoglu, M. Jelasity, Anne Marie Kermarrec, Alberto Montresor & Maarten van Steen, Operating Systems Review (ACM), available at: http://dl.acm.org/citation.cfm?doid=1151374.1151379.

875 Mike P. Papazoglou & Willem-Jan van den Heuvel (note 853).

876 Lamia Youseff, Maria Butrico & Dilma Da Silva (note 838).

The three sublayers composing the infrastructure layer also share common challenges besides the ones particular to each of them. Among others, security of the services, availability and quality are the most commonly addressed concerns for all cloud infrastructure components[877].

iv. The Cloud Software Environment layer

The following layer in cloud ontology is the cloud software environment layer (or, simply, the software platform layer). Users of this layer are cloud applications' developers, who implement their applications for and deploy them on the cloud[878]. Providers of this layer, on the other hand, supply developers with a programming-language-level environment aimed at facilitating interaction between programming environments and cloud applications, as well as at accelerating deployment and supporting scalability necessary for those cloud applications[879]. Services provided by cloud systems in this layer are commonly referred to as Platform as a Service (PaaS)[880]. A classic example of systems in this layer is Google's App Engine, which provides a python runtime environment and APIs for applications to interact with Google's cloud runtime environment or SalesForce's Apex language permitting developers of cloud applications to design the page layout, workflow or customer reports according to the logic of their applications[881]. In a nutshell, cloud software environments facilitate the process of the development of cloud applications[882].

v. The Cloud Application layer (SaaS)

The cloud application layer is the one closest to the end-users of the cloud. It basically corresponds to the very cloud-based applications we all know and use in daily life, from our email service, to Dropbox or similar file storage and management services etc. This model has exponentially

---

877 Deepak Puthal, B.P.S. Sahoo, Sambit Mishra & Satyabrata Swain (note 837).
878 Lamia Youseff, Maria Butrico & Dilma Da Silva (note 838).
879 *Id.*
880 See Chapter 2.
881 Xiaolong Jin & Jiming Liu (note 844).
882 Lamia Youseff, Maria Butrico & Dilma Da Silva (note 838).

gained popularity for all the reasons explained in earlier parts of this study[883].

c. Different uses but the same ontology: what does this mean for cloud computing regulatory principles?

From the analysis in the previous section in combination with the technical overview of cloud computing in Chapter 2 of this study we can draw the conclusion that there is a clear dichotomy between cloud computing as a technical arrangement, as a technology and infrastructure, on the one side, and the cloud as the applications through which we have the possibility to use in various forms the capacity of this infrastructure, on the other.

Viewing the above observation through the basic reasoning proposed by the doctrine of law and knowledge[884], which is rapidly gaining popularity particularly in public law, it can be argued that this dichotomy has caused a fussy picture, at least on the front of end-consumers and on the regulatory front, due to the fact that the infrastructural nature of the cloud is not, at most times, immediately visible and, therefore, comprehensible to non-technically-savvy actors. It is of course, undeniable that there are lots of different ways to deploy the same kind of infrastructure and this means that the (regulatory) challenges coming with one type of cloud environment will not necessarily be the same with those of another. For instance, a great deal of issues regarding privacy raised by public clouds are non-existent or they are satisfactorily tackled when the same resources are utilized to set up a private cloud computing network[885]. However, the technical expertise, the mechanical skills and the very materials (i.e. pieces of

883 See Chapter 2.

884 Hans-Heinrich Trute (note 432). For further details on the doctrine of law and knowledge and the broader issue of how knowledge converts into or affects the law, refer to: Hans Christian Röhl, Wissen, zur kognitiven Dimension des Rechts, vol. 9 (2010); Gunnar Folke Schuppert & Andreas Vosskuhle, Governance von und durch Wissen, Bd. 12 (2008); Mariana Valverde, Law's Dream of a Common Knowledge (2009); Brett M. Frischmann, Michael J. Madison & Katherine Jo Strandburg, Governing knowledge commons (2014); Friedrich A. von Hayek, *The Use of Knowledge in Society*, 35 The American Economic Review 519–530 (1945); Adrian Vermeule ed., Local and Global Knowledge in the Administrative State (2013.)

885 See Chapter 2 for the difference between public and private cloud networks.

hardware) that are necessary in order to build up either a public (with just the standard protection features) or a private (with as advanced protection features as possible) cloud ecosystem are, in essence, the same. In both cases, and in every other in between, one will need pieces of the same kind of infrastructure, the same kind of information science and IT engineering knowledge that will permit one to put those pieces of hardware into meaningful working arrangements and, of course, even the features that will differentiate them and make them stand apart from each other will be based on the same technical principles and scientific intel that makes the overall concept of cloud computing technology possible. Consequently, it becomes evident that, despite the great variety in which cloud services and networks appear on the market and the substantial differences which might exist between all these variations of cloud environments, there is a common underlying connecting tissue that binds them all, and that is the knowledge (of informatics, computing engineering and other disciplines) related to them which is one and the same.

To put it more illustratively, let's take the example of two data hosting and sharing facilities, such as Dropbox, one public and commercially available and the other private and customized to be accessible by a specific circle of users only, probably also cut out in a manner that will provide answers to their very particular needs. It is true that a great deal of elements of the two applications might look totally different from each other, from the interfaces to the layers and tools each of them uses to ensure privacy and security for its users. But no matter how different the two applications may look, the basic principles and knowledge behind them are the same; as a result, from each of these two manifestations of the cloud there are minimum common expectations which call for minimum shared regulatory principles that would settle them in a unanimous manner. This unanimity could and should be not just within the boundaries of one jurisdiction but on a cross-jurisdictional basis. This does not in any case necessitate some kind of unification of different jurisdictions into one or the introduction of one extra supranational legal order just for the sake of IT regulation. Jurisdictional particularities and traditions of every legal order could very well be upheld and respected in the field of IT law as it is done in any other legal sector. What we need to make sure is that these commonly shared principles will advance the achievement of the same goals from every jurisdiction on each and every matter of cloud computing regulation.

In other words, the challenge is not to homogenize IT laws or pulverize jurisdictional particularities. It rather is to set common goals and establish rules that will contribute to their achievement. The path towards achieving these goals can and will expectedly be different, both because cloud computing manifests itself through various different arrangements and because two or more identical cloud networks in different environments will naturally be treated in differentiated manners according to the legal culture in each environment. However, as long as the same purposes are pursued and, ultimately, materialize, the path and the means need not be identical.

With this in mind, the ontology of the cloud as it was previously analyzed allows us to define a first set of regulatory principles for cloud computing based on the knowledge that makes the cloud possible.

d. Mapping the life cycle of data on cloud computing networks: risks, security and privacy issues as indicators for the nature of cloud computing regulation rules

Having analyzed what cloud computing as technology and technological arrangement actually consists of via the tool of ontology, it is worth also mapping down the life cycle data follows while circulating through the various layers presented above. Presenting the blueprint of the path of data through the cloud will also allow us to pinpoint the risks they are exposed to from a technical perspective. This knowledge, which, as it has been argued in the case of cloud ontology already, is universal and applies to all different kinds of cloud networks no matter whether they host public services or others available only to a limited circle of users, can then lead us to the concretization of the regulatory principles stemming from the ontology of the cloud.

For starters, in the context of the analysis following below, the term 'data life cycle' should be interpreted as referring to the entire process from generation to destruction of any kind of digital data[886]. This path consists of seven distinct stages, the essence, features and main risks of which are summarized as follows. It needs to be noted that, in keeping with the dynamic relations between the different layers of the cloud ontol-

886 Deyan Chen & Hong Zhao, *Data Security and Privacy Protection Issues in Cloud Computing*, in 2012 International Conference on Computer Science and Electronics Engineering, 647–651 (2012.)

ogy as they were previously analyzed, the stages of the data life cycle on the cloud can occur equally dynamic. It is only for descriptive easiness that they are hereunder separately analyzed and their sequence of presence does not imply at all that each stage is immune to or sealed from the others.

i. Data generation

Data generation describes the moment when data is actually created for the first time, regardless of whether it is original or data resulting from processing of preexisting data sets[887]. At this stage of data generation, the ownership status of data is also determined[888]. In pre-cloud IT environments users of whichever size, i.e. from individual users to large scale organizations, used to own and manage the data they were the creators of[889]. However, in an IT environment where data increasingly, if not by default, migrate to the cloud immediately after their creation or they are even created directly there, the issue of ownership cannot be answered so self-evidently. In other words, regulatory principles are need which will either allow the question of data ownership to be answered at all times during the circulation of data on a cloud network or, if so preferred, will provide enough safeguards to data owners regarding what extend of their personal private information is being collected by other actors on the cloud network. Last but not least, principles that will determine under which conditions data owners may put a stop to collection and use of personal information regardless of the layer within the cloud network where such practice occurs are also necessary. However, it needs to be made sure, at the same time, that these rules need be realistic and promise realistic levels of protection to data owners, unlike what seems to happen with the respective provisions of the GDPR[890].

---

887 Michael Backes & Peng Ning eds., Computer security – ESORICS 2009. 14th European Symposium on Research in Computer Security, Saint-Malo, France, September 21-23, 2009 : proceedings, vol. 5789 (2009.)

888 Elen Stokes, *Regulating Technologies: Legal Futures, Regulatory Frames and Technological Fixes by Roger Brownsword and Karen Yeung (eds)*, 73 The Modern Law Review 682–689 (2010.)

889 Xiaolong Jin & Jiming Liu (note 844).

890 See Chapter 4.

ii. Transfer

Another fundamental block of the overall life cycle of data on the cloud is the transfer of them. As a rule, in the pre-cloud enterprise status quo data transmission did not require encryption or, at the most, only simple data encryption measures would suffice[891]. However, in the new enterprise environment facilitated by cloud computing, where it is far from given that the network of one enterprise does not overlap with that of another, transfers of data are commonplace and both data confidentiality and integrity should be ensured in order to prevent tapping and tampering by unauthorized users[892]. From a technical point of view, this cannot be guaranteed by data encryption alone nor with technical measures only[893]. For optimal data integrity in the cloud confidentiality is also crucial[894] and it can only be achieved if trustworthy transfer protocols are legally necessitated. In fact, these should be maintained not only throughout the length of a single cloud network but also during circulations of data from one network to the other. In other words, the relevant rules providing for integral transfer mechanisms should be developed having in mind both the horizontal and the vertical data transfers which are possible in cloud environments.

iii. Use

While being used on the resources of a network digital static data appear in either of the following formats: as static data being used on a simple storage service (such as most of storage services addressed to end-users, like Amazon S3 or Dropbox) where data encryption is already feasible[895]. However, static data on the cloud can also be used by cloud-based applications on the PaaS or SaaS layer and, in those cases, data encryption is not always feasible[896]. In fact, on layers prior to the end-applications level data encryption is very likely to lead to problems of indexing and query, ab-

891 S. Subashini & V. Kavitha (note 119).

892 Nir Kshetri, *Privacy and security issues in cloud computing. The role of institutions and institutional evolution*, 37 Telecommunications Policy 372–386 (2013.)

893 Deyan Chen & Hong Zhao (note 886).

894 Deyan Chen & Hong Zhao (note 886); David W. Opderbeck (note 628).

895 Ozalp Babaoglu, M. Jelasity, Anne Marie Kermarrec, Alberto Montresor & Maarten van Steen (note 874).

896 *Id.*

normalities which would undermine the smooth functioning of the overall cloud network[897]. It turns out that, contrary to what may be commonly perceived as a result of the perception simple end cloud services try to cultivate on customers[898], in cloud just as in traditional IT environments, the data being treated is almost not encrypted for any program that deals with it on a layer prior to the end applications level[899]. Moreover, due to the multi-tenancy feature[900] of cloud computing models, the data being processed by cloud based applications is in many instances stored together with the data of other users at least when they are used by applications and actors other than the end users. Given that this technical arrangement is technically utopic that it will cease to exist, it becomes evident that regulatory principles defining codes of conduct for any actor using data at any point during their life cycle and on any layer of a cloud network are necessary.

iv. Sharing

Data sharing, which is a function continuously performed by data owners and several different types of actors that have access to data stored on a cloud network, is an action expanding the use range of the data thus rendering data permissions more complex[901]. This is of course a very known issue about cloud computing, which existing legislation is already striving to cope with, at least with regard to the specific cloud-enabled applications for which there is regulation in place. However, given that data owners

897 Deyan Chen & Hong Zhao (note 886).

898 Huaiqing Wang, Matthew K. O. Lee & Chen Wang (note 12).

899 Deyan Chen & Hong Zhao (note 886).

900 "Software multitenancy", which is largely considered as one of the cornerstone features of cloud computing, refers to a software architecture in which a single instance of software runs on a server and serves multiple tenants. The term "tenant" denotes a group of users who share common access with specific privileges to the software instance. Under multitenant architecture, a software application is designed to provide every tenant a dedicated share of the instance – including its data, configuration, user management, tenant individual functionality and non-functional properties. Multitenancy contrasts with multi-instance architectures, where separate software instances operate on behalf of different tenants. For more, refer to: Krebs, R., Momm, C., & Kounev, S. (2012). Architectural Concerns in Multi-tenant SaaS Applications. Closer, 12, 426-431.

901 (note 852).

can authorize data access for one party, which can further share the data with another party without the consent of the original data owner and taking into account that this chain of sharing occurrences can go on and on extending to users that are far from the jurisdiction of the data owner, we can never realistically expect that simply by devising new methods for extending law applicability universal legal safety cannot be achieved. Therefore, only the endorsement of common regulatory principles on the cloud and the use as foundations of cloud governing laws by as many jurisdictions as possible can be expected to provide trustworthy answers to the issues discussed.

v. Storage

Possibly the most common activity with regard to data on the cloud is storage. In fact, data is stored on cloud networks in two distinct contexts, i.e. in IaaS environments, such as those of any standard cloud storage service, and in PaaS or SaaS environment, where data related to the core code of cloud based applications are stored[902].

In computer science, data stored in cloud storages is treated in the same manner as data stored in any other kind of facility, pre-existing or concurrent to cloud computing[903]. With that in mind, computer science literature applied to data stored on the cloud the classic three criteria in order to assess how securely they are stored[904]: confidentiality, integrity and availability.

As far as data confidentiality is concerned, the solution advanced so far from a technical perspective is data encryption[905]. The particularities of cloud environments, involving large amounts of data transmission, storage and handling, as well as processing speed and computational efficiency of encrypting large amounts of data, make the use of symmetric encryption

902 Deyan Chen & Hong Zhao (note 886).

903 Ozalp Babaoglu, M. Jelasity, Anne Marie Kermarrec, Alberto Montresor & Maarten van Steen (note 874).

904 Nir Kshetri (note 892).

905 Robert Gellman (note 696).

algorithms[906] more suitable than asymmetric ones. Moreover, another key question coming immediately after the choice of the most suitable encryption pattern is key management[907] and who is responsible for it. An ideal answer would be that it is the data owners but, for the time being and in the foreseeable future, average users do not possess enough expertise to manage these keys and, as a standard, they entrust key management with the cloud providers. Consequently, the enormous range of tasks for the latter means their key management responsibilities are way more complex and difficult to cope with but, in any case, imperative. Switching focus to data integrity[908], the essential question is how users, who put several gigabytes or more of data into the cloud, can check the integrity of it. This turns out to be not an easy question to answer given that rapid elasticity as an elementary feature of cloud computing resources makes it impossible for the average end user to know where their data is being stored at all times[909]. As data is dynamic in cloud storage environments, traditional technologies to ensure data integrity may not be effective[910]. Last but not least, in a traditional IT environment the main threat to data availability comes from external attacks[911]. In the cloud, however, in addition to external attacks, there are several other factors that may put data availability under threat[912], namely the availability of cloud computing services; whether cloud providers have committed themselves to continue to operate in the future or what safeguards they have undertaken in case their op-

906 Symmetric-key algorithms (applied in symmetric encryption) are algorithms for cryptography that use the same cryptographic keys for both encryption of plaintext and decryption of ciphertext. The keys may be identical or there may be a simple transformation to go between them. In the actual practice of data cryptography, the keys represent a shared secret between two or more parties that can be used to maintain a private information link. This requirement that both parties have access to the secret key is one of the main drawbacks of symmetric key encryption, in comparison to public-key encryption (which is what is known as asymmetric key encryption). For more details, refer to: Hans Delfs & Helmut Knebl, Introduction to cryptography. Principles and applications, 2007: 1 (2007); Christof Paar & Jan Pelzl, Understanding cryptography. A textbook for students and practitioners (2010.)

907 Hans Delfs & Helmut Knebl (note 906).

908 Deepak Puthal, B.P.S. Sahoo, Sambit Mishra & Satyabrata Swain (note 837).

909 See also Chapter 2.

910 Deyan Chen & Hong Zhao (note 886).

911 S. Subashini & V. Kavitha (note 119).

912 Michael Backes & Peng Ning eds. (note 887).

eration is suspended; or whether the cloud storage services provide trustworthy backup functionalities.

As it becomes evident from the analysis above, there is not a single nor an obvious answer as to which actor throughout the layers of a cloud network is responsible for making sure storage of data standards live up to the expectations that have been described as essential. In other words, having in place rules that put the burden of such issues to specific entities relevant to specific types of cloud-enabled business will never be a regulatory strategy generic enough to provide us with answers to these challenges in every instance, even in situations which may not be market applicable at this point but are technically feasible in any case. As a result, the need for general cloud computing regulatory principles emerges once more.

vi. Archival

The key criteria for evaluating archiving of data from a technical perspective[913] are the storage media on which archival is done, whether off-site storage is provided or not and, last but not least, how long archival storage lasts. If the media chosen for archival are portable and, at some point, they get out of control, the archived data are exposed to the risk of leakage. On the other hand, if cloud service providers do not provide off-site archiving, availability of data is put under question. In addition, archival services are not adequate if they are not made to last over a certain minimum amount of time; otherwise, they may result in availability or privacy threats. These issues occurring with reference to archiving as a fundamental function of cloud services should also be answered in the framework of a set of generic regulatory principles for the cloud.

vii. Destruction

When a given set of data is no longer required, it needs to be destroyed[914]. The physical dimension of cloud computing storage facilities as well as

---

913 Deyan Chen & Hong Zhao (note 886).; Dimitrios Zissis & Dimitrios Lekkas (note 869).

914 Deyan Chen & Hong Zhao (note 886).

the archiving capabilities cloud services are supposed to offer in order to increase integrity and availability of data pose questions as to after what point data can be regarded to have been effectively deleted without any possibility of being restored[915]. Given the different variations of data and the different instances throughout the cloud ontology when they might be created or be rendered useless, it becomes again evident that generic principles for governing the cloud are highly advisable.

e. Regulatory principles derived from the ontology of cloud computing

Bearing into account the ontology of the cloud as it was analytically described above we can recognize on each layer certain functions and/or actors that primarily aim at the same goals with their functions no matter whether the cloud network they are part of is a public or private one. Therefore, making use of the teleological perspective, it can be argued that, despite the particularities of each network and its specific features, which may neutralize some challenges or, anyway, make them easier to be tackled by respective actors, we can agree on minimum rules that will need to be observed by the network and its constituent entities so that the ultimate goal of the entire workflow is fulfilled[916]:

i. On the hardware/firmware layer

As we have seen, this constitutes the backbone of the cloud network, primary gravity is placed on the issue of security, integrity and (constant) availability of resources[917]. Given that, regardless of whether a cloud network's infrastructure is utilized by the network owners themselves or whether it is outsourced to third parties, it has to maintain at all times high levels of security and integrity in order for the data stored or the processes executed on it to be available and run smoothly at all times[918], rules contributing to the achievement of these prerequisites are of vital importance. This trend can already be observed across various examples of resource

915 Dimitrios Zissis & Dimitrios Lekkas (note 869).
916 See also Chapter 5.
917 Stephanos Androutsellis-Theotokis & Diomidis Spinellis (note 861).
918 See also Chapter 5.

outsourcing on this layer, with service level agreements (SLAs) imposing strict rules and obligations to cloud network owners/managers who lease, in whole or in part, their resources to third parties[919]. Given that these requirements of integrity and constant availability are already considered as sine qua non by all affected actors[920], it is high time for them to be incorporated into laws. All the more so if we take into account the fact that the current regime of SLAs, which are the subject matter of negotiation between contracting parties, regularly leads to situations of imbalances where, even within the same market, greatly variable degrees of integrity and trustworthiness are required or expected from cloud infrastructure owners, even though their resources will be utilized for the provision of cloud-based services or the execution of equally sensitive computational tasks[921]. It goes without saying that the relevant rules should legislate on the minimum standards necessary leaving of course room for even more elevated commitments at the discretion of the parties in each and every case. Regulating on the minimum standards and leaving room for more elevated commitments at the discretion of the parties will also contribute to the rules that will be adopted being more harmonized on a cross-jurisdictional level since law subjects of a particular jurisdiction will be able to expand their activities to others simply by adapting the standards on all or part of their infrastructure to those prescribed by the jurisdiction(s) they wish to enter. As it has been demonstrated[922], mechanics of the cloud perfectly permit the infrastructure of a cloud network to be treated either unanimously or in a compartmentalized manner. Consequently, if the law states the minimum standards a cloud network needs to uphold at all times, it is then always possible to divide part of the overall resources and adjust it to further elevated standards in order to satisfy requirements of more than one jurisdictions at the same time. The only requirement would be, of course, to have a basic principle of non-confluence between resources utilized for processing tasks falling under rules dictating different standards. This does not imply at all that the principle of ultimate utilization of resources (which it should never be forgotten that it is one of the core features of the cloud[923]) should be compromised. On this issue, we

919 Xiaolong Jin & Jiming Liu (note 844).
920 See also Chapter 5.
921 Lamia Youseff, Maria Butrico & Dilma Da Silva (note 838).
922 See Chapter 2.
923 Refer also to Chapter 2.

should once again resort to the engineering flexibilities that characterize cloud technologies and can ensure that resources of a network dedicated to processing tasks falling under the rules of a specific jurisdiction will abide by the minimum standards set by the rules of that jurisdiction and will adapt themselves when switched to tasks governed by different laws.

Regarding the security challenges at this level, from a technical point of view at HaaS a developer has better control over security[924]; nevertheless, the length of this grip should not provoke any security gap in the virtualization element of the cloud network. Similarly, on the other side of the coin, virtual machines have in principle the capacity to address these integrity of virtualization issues, yet in practice there are a lot of security questions that remain unsettled[925]. The other security element that keeps calling urgently for resolution is the unwavering quality of the information that is put on the cloud supplier's infrastructure. The powerful presence of virtualization across all types of cloud processing and the proximity in which it brings data from different users make both holding a definitive control over information and paying respect to the physical area/resources that hosts it primary responsibilities of the information owner/cloud resources user[926]. It becomes clear that, in order to achieve most extreme trust and security on the HaaS layer, a few procedures starting from both sides of the provider and user need to be coordinated. Currently, security obligations of both supplier and client incredibly vary from one cloud network to the other due to different cloud administration models which, at the lack of minimum requirements prescribed by laws, are arbitrarily developed by the market[927]. Undoubtedly, a private cloud is better protected against security threats on the infrastructure level compared to a public cloud. Nonetheless, regardless of the deployment model every single cloud facility has one elementary yet extremely crucial challenge to live up to: protecting the physical infrastructure of data centers[928]. Relevant basic rules should reflect on damage done by any natural disaster but also any damage done to the facility deliberately. It should not fail our attention that in every case the infrastructure that needs to be protected is not only the hardware where data is processed and stored but also that where it is

924 S. Subashini & V. Kavitha (note 119).
925 *Id.*
926 Lamia Youseff, Maria Butrico & Dilma Da Silva (note 838).
927 *Id.*
928 *Id.*

getting transmitted[929]. In the cloud reality data transmitted from the source to destination typically may pass through the resources of a large number of third parties[930]. Consequently, rules need to be established that will also prescribe for the minimum security benchmarks that these third parties will need to guarantee at all times, in a generic manner and without reference only to particular types of data processing. Regardless of the fact that heavy security measures are normally set up in the cloud, still information is transmitted through ordinary internet routes[931]. It goes without saying, then, that there is also the need to establish rules that will necessitate from cloud infrastructure providers to seal their facilities against threats that may intrude to them from the world wide web. There are already several technical options that can help secure transmission of information inside the cloud[932]. Encryption techniques tackle those needs to a certain degree yet they are not connection oriented[933]. Concerns with respect to interruption of the flow of information or even interception of it by outer non-clients of the network through the web need to additionally be considered. In a nutshell, security on the HaaS layer has both an internal and an external dimension and the principles regulating it need to make sure that every cloud environment will be not only internally secure and integral but also sealed and isolated towards the internet to also deter external security threats, such as cyber-criminal attacks.

ii. On the software/kernel layer

As it has already been described, on this layer we find the basic software tools needed for the management of the physical servers that compose the cloud network. The roles and duties appearing on this level are almost identical to those of the hardware layer, only focusing on the software as-

---

929 Mike P. Papazoglou & Willem-Jan van den Heuvel (note 853).

930 Ling Liu & M. Tamer Özsu (note 842).

931 Lamia Youseff, Maria Butrico & Dilma Da Silva (note 838).

932 Cong Wang, Qian Wang, Kui Ren & Wenjing Lou, *Privacy-Preserving Public Auditing for Data Storage Security in Cloud Computing*, in IEEE INFOCOM 2010 – IEEE Conference on Computer Communications, 1–9; Niels Fallenbeck & Claudia Eckert, *IT-Sicherheit und Cloud Computing*, in Handbuch Industrie 4.0 Bd.4, 137–171 (Birgit Vogel-Heuser, Thomas Bauernhansl & Michael ten Hompel eds., 2017.)

933 Ling Liu & M. Tamer Özsu (note 842).

pect and processes for keeping the cloud at its foundations sealed and integral from external threats[934]. Therefore, with regard to any regulatory principles stemming from this stack, reference is made to the recommendations analyzed in the previous section, i.e. the hardware layer.

iii. On the cloud software infrastructure layer

As it was analytically presented, fundamental resources to other higher-level layers are provided through this layer, which are then used to construct new cloud software environments or cloud applications. This is the first instance across the cloud network where we observe that the roles of provider and user of the resources of the network are so closely intertwined and enter each other's territory[935]. To put it more descriptively, a software infrastructure provider is at the same time a user of the network's resources, as he uses part of the network's hardware resources to host his processing activities that make the services it offers to entities of the above layers possible. In addition, a user of the software infrastructure providers' services is, at the same time, a provider of other cloud-based services addressed to end users of the network. This intertwining of roles brings to the forefront the need for cloud computing rules to be based on the teleological principle and follow, as much as possible, generic formulation patterns and depart from the case-based logic[936]. The blurred lines between roles and functions of actors on the cloud software infrastructure layer reveal the need to establish rules that will delineate duties, rights and obligations for entities across the cloud network without personalizing them or referring to specific arrangements/applications made possible thanks to the uses of the resources of that network.

---

934 S. Subashini & V. Kavitha (note 119).

935 Ozalp Babaoglu, M. Jelasity, Anne Marie Kermarrec, Alberto Montresor & Maarten van Steen (note 874).

936 William N. Eskridge & Philip P. Frickey, *Statutory Interpretation as Practical Reasoning*, 42 Stanford Law Review 321–384 (1990); Henry Prakken, *An exercise in formalising teleological case-based reasoning. Artificial Intelligence and Law*, 10 Artificial Intelligence and Law 113–133 (2002.)

iv. On the PaaS and SaaS layers

The last two layers of the ontology, corresponding to the cloud software environment and the cloud application layer, are the ones commonly referred to as PaaS[937] and SaaS[938]. With regard to them, some observations regarding security issues and, respectively, rules that should be established to regulate them merit to be raised. On the PaaS layer, what actually happens on a technical level is that the administration supplier gives partial control to the customer in order for the latter to be able to manufacture applications on top of that layer[939]. However, for these applications to function properly and without interruptions, it is imperative that no insecurities beneath the software environment level occur. The cloud software environment layer is meant to empower cloud application designers to assemble their own particular applications on top of the platform[940]. Therefore, system durability and trustworthiness in relation to the underlying layers is of primary significance. Until now, this has been reflected on the affirmations suppliers bring on the table when negotiating contract services with potential customers[941]. Till now, these clauses have been observed to be of great variety extending even to questionable security gimmicks in an effort, on behalf of suppliers, to enter into a kind of assurances fight towards potential customers, which have been found to extend to technical safeguards of doubtful trustworthiness[942]. Therefore, rules establishing the minimum that should be achieved regarding these standards of safety are necessary. In fact, these rules are technically possible to be based even on objective technical measurements that will survey the viability of each cloud network's application security features at this level[943]. Some of those measurements with immediate application are defenselessness scores[944] and patch scope[945]. These indices can show the quality of application coding based on the security features and the way the resources of each cloud network are brought together. One additional reason why secu-

937 See Chapter 2.
938 See Chapter 2.
939 Deepak Puthal, B.P.S. Sahoo, Sambit Mishra & Satyabrata Swain (note 837).
940 Dimitrios Zissis & Dimitrios Lekkas (note 869).
941 Lamia Youseff, Maria Butrico & Dilma Da Silva (note 838).
942 Nicholas Platten (note 42).
943 S. Subashini & V. Kavitha (note 119).
944 Stephanos Androutsellis-Theotokis & Diomidis Spinellis (note 861).
945 *Id.*

rity standards on the cloud software environment layer need to be reaffirmed via clear rules is that, especially when it comes to software-related vulnerabilities, such weaknesses or malicious elements of a cloud network can easily extend as far as the web applications that will be made available to users via the said cloud network, thus endangering or undermining the integrity of the wider web. Therefore, clear precautionary rules that will aim at containing them already on the PaaS layer are strongly advisable and urgently needed.

v. On the SaaS layer in particular

On the upper level of the cloud ontology, the cloud application layer or SaaS, lie the end cloud-based applications that are made available to end users with the only prerequisite that they have access to the internet, even partially, or that they can in any other technically feasible way access the cloud network where the service they make use of is hosted. The quintessence of affairs on this layer is that the client needs to be able to rely on the supplier to feel safety, in a whole range of different aspects[946]. Initially, it is elementary from the part of the supplier that he must actively prove that he can keep his clients from seeing or accessing without authorization one another's information. Simultaneously, it is imperative that the provider guarantees and makes sure that the application will be always accessible, not just because the other way around would put the client's confidence in the application in danger but also because, from a legal point of view, making sure that the application is always on and users can access it anytime they wish is a strong determinant towards the fact that the provider made sure users had unwavering and continuous possibility to exercise the expected functions through the application environment, among which also precautionary safety controls about their data. Thanks to SaaS, it is becoming increasingly possible (and popular) to switch to net program or software applications over 'old-fashioned', (usually) offline ones[947]. Consequently, primary focus is not so much on portability of uses, given that, after all, the new cloud-based apps usually do offer simpler and friendlier interfaces to users to do things. Rather, the focus lies nowadays

946 (note 852).
947 Xiaolong Jin & Jiming Liu (note 844).

on safeguarding or upgrading the security element in comparison to the standards offered in this front by the older applications and achieving effective information relocation and resource management while maintaining the elevated security standards as well[948]. What this model and its set targets practically mean is that in SaaS programming the service provider may host the application on its own private server farm or on a cloud computing facility administering it through a framework provided by an outsider supplier (e.g. Amazon, Google, etc.)[949]. This arrangement, where the involved actors and what each one of them is expected to carry out are so open, in terms of multitude, is one more pointer to the need of stablishing rules on cloud regulation that will focus on the teleological principle, i.e. on who is expected to achieve what only 'who' should be understood in a generic sense (as a number of actors and not specific entities) and 'what' should be understood in the sense of functionality or body of functionalities within all those comprising the network and not as specific manifestations that come out when these functionalities are put to work. The cornerstone of the SaaS model, is that data is stored at the SaaS provider's data center, along with the data of other users[950]. Even more, if the SaaS provider is depending on a public cloud computing service, users' data might be stored on the same facilities along with the data of other unrelated SaaS applications. It is also quite a standard practice that the cloud supplier imitates the information at numerous locations across borders for reasons of keeping up the high accessibility prerequisite[951]. Consequently, there are several security issues raised such as data security, network security, data locality, data integrity, data segregation, data access, authentication and authorization[952]. Apart from any specialized rules that may establish specific standards or security policies as the necessary minimum, it is essential to take the leap and move from the specific to the broad context: technology and the constant evolution of science related to the cloud will make available more and more tools that will add up to the security levels of cloud networks[953]. As a result, it is not so imperative to legislate on which specific measures cloud networks should adopt to stand above the

948 S. Subashini & V. Kavitha (note 119).
949 John F. Sowa (note 839).
950 See Chapter 2.
951 See Chapter 2.
952 S. Subashini & V. Kavitha (note 119).
953 Dimitrios Zissis & Dimitrios Lekkas (note 869).

benchmark for network security but, rather, on what should be achieved in terms of security-related milestones. In other words, the SaaS layer of the cloud ontology and the way it is constructed exposes the need to develop a cloud regulation framework that will have at its core, not the ephemeral features of such a rapidly evolving phenomenon. Now that we have decomposed and exhaustively analyzed what the cloud actually is about, it is evident that cloud computing regulation should not be regarded as a new body of law that will replace existing legislation on particular manifestations of cloud computing, because of the latter being insufficient or dysfunctional. On the contrary, the proposed laws will come to serve as the currently missing cohesion element from the field of IT law, the one that will boost the integrity of this corpus of legislation as it will take advantage of its inherent features and will focus on its inherent flaws, at the same time, trying to correct them or, at least, seal cloud networks, as much as possible, against them.

CHAPTER 9. Principles for regulating the cloud (2); based on the roles and functions across the cloud workflow

a. Introduction – scope of this chapter

Having examined the cloud down to its detail as technology and after proposing the regulatory principles that should be put in place to efficiently respond to the challenges posed by the technical particularities of it, it is now time to direct our attention to the way the cloud is perceived from the outside as an autonomous concept and an entity or environment which is defined by organic and functional self-sufficiency. In other words, our focus will now shift to the fact that, when a cloud computing network is understood as a workflow chart, it should be at any time possible to point down the entry and exit point in it, to define the distinct functions performed in order for the entire workflow to produce the expected end-product and, respectively, to recognize the duties, obligations and expectations anchored to every such function and, consequently, to the actor (or actors) performing it.

Reference has already been made, in earlier parts of this study[954], to the issue of the internal vs. external perspective in law and how this is all the more crucial when it comes to internet law and cloud computing, in particular. In light of this theorem, and having already explored the cloud in an analytical manner with regard to its 'inner nature' as a technology and technical arrangement – an aspect of it that could be described as its internal dimension with regard to laws governing it – it is now time to research into the question of what constitutes the external aspect of cloud computing and whether we can pinpoint further regulatory principles for it stemming from that perspective of looking into cloud computing.

But first and foremost, it is necessary to look into the question of whether the cloud does have an external, apart from an internal aspect and what it constitutes of.

954 See Chapters 4 and 5.

b. Viewing cloud computing from the outside; what else is the cloud apart from its infrastructure and the science behind it?

One of the most discussed legal notions in recent years is that of the internal versus the external perspective of law[955]. The concept has become of particular importance and is gaining more and more in prominence as legal subject matters become of a continuously more complex nature, with multiple levels of reference and substance that does not stem only from themselves but also through extrapolation to other notions or phenomena that interact with them, one way or another[956]. Simultaneously, this internal vs. external structure refers to the two distinct ways in which a regulatory subject matter can be observed and, consequently, analyzed and regulated[957]. Actually, this aspect of the topic applies to even more legal phenomena, not only modern but also more traditional ones. It refers to rules that are developed to regulate a phenomenon just by observing the phenomenon itself as opposed to rules which are developed in order to settle regulatory issues arising from the interaction of the said phenomenon with other subject matters or actors external to it[958].

Focusing on the realm of the internet, and bearing in mind that a regulator's main challenge is to create rules that will be clear enough to allow the lawyer and law subjects, in general, to simply apply legal provisions to facts, a difficult question pops up: "what are the 'facts' when it comes to the world of the internet and IT?"[959]

The facts of anything related to the Internet depend on whether you look for them focusing on physical or virtual reality[960]. From the angle of virtual reality, we view the Internet from the perspective of a user who understands the virtual world of cyberspace and the actions and processes happening there as an analogy to the equivalent instances in the offline, physical world. Alternatively, we can perceive internet facts based on the physical reality of how the network operates. From this angle, Internet

955 Orin S. Kerr (note 230).

956 Trevor Bench-Capon & Giovanni Sartor, *A model of legal reasoning with cases incorporating theories and values. AI and Law*, 150 Artificial Intelligence 97–143 (2003.)

957 Orin S. Kerr (note 230).

958 *Id.*

959 Urs Gasser, Cloud Innovation and the Law: Issues, Approaches, and Interplay (2014.)

960 L. Lessig (note 504).

transactions are interpreted based on how the network actually works "behind the scenes" and on the inside, irrespective of the perceptions of a user[961]. When it comes to cloud computing, so far, we have been producing laws which primarily focus on the external perspective and are developed to provide answers to the regulatory challenges we perceive when observing the cloud through the applications that are made possible thanks to it. However, as it has already been demonstrated in the previous chapter[962], we still miss critical aspects of the cloud which remain unregulated and which we can only understand if we observe the cloud from the inside, i.e. from the perspective of an entity that is participating itself to a cloud network's workflow or from the angle of an observer who focuses on each of these distinct entities and the role(s) they play across the life cycle of a cloud network regardless of what the external manifestation of their function(s) may be. We have already executed this internal observation in the previous chapter, where the cloud was analyzed as far as its infrastructural element is concerned. However, in order to have the complete picture of the cloud's internal world, it is imperative to examine it also from the aspect of how the life cycle developed around this infrastructure looks like, how it works, what processes it is made of and which actors and with which roles take part in those processes. After all, we should not forget that the final manifestations of the cloud, i.e. the end cloud based applications that reach end users, need a facilitating background to be hosted in, which should not escape our attention as to the regulatory issues that may arise within it. Last but not least, this enabling background corresponds to the internal aspect of a work line which aims at making available the various cloud based applications to the market, i.e. to their pool of intended users, regardless of whether they pay a fee to make use of them (as it is usually the case) or not.

There have already been scholars who have attempted to view the realm of the Internet from this internal perspective[963]. Actually, Lawrence Lessig[964] has gone as far as attributing to code makers, such as Microsoft and AOL, qualities of 'virtual governments that exercise real control over the virtual world of cyberspace' suggesting that we should consider subjecting their decisions not just to plain legal but to constitutional scrutiny.

961 *Id.*
962 See Chapter 8.
963 Bibliographical index (or internal reference.)
964 Lawrence Lessig (note 505).

It is quite revealing to examine the famous theory of Lessig arguing that "code is law"[965] through this internal vs. external perspective lens. In fact, the very phrase "code is law" reveals a relationship between the internal and external perspectives. In detail, on the software front "code is law" extrapolated through the internal vs. external perspective prism means that what is perceived as code from the external perspective has the gravitas of law from the internal one. A software program's code stipulates the architecture of the virtual world that a user encounters while making use of that program. Consequently, as external code is internal law, we need to regulate not just the manifestations of this program in the external world but also its functioning from an internal perspective. Mutatis mutandis, in the case of cloud networks, for a complete regulatory framework to be put together we need to regulate not just what users are confronted with as the external manifestation of the cloud processing done for them to receive the end applications they have asked for but also the processing itself as it happens on the inside of the network, as well as the different stages through which the processing passes and the agents that push it forward at each one of these stages.

Viewing Lessig's theory through this internal vs. external perspective prism helps us also understand how he went as far as proposing the application of constitutional norms in cyberspace[966]. Lessig has probably been the most tenacious scholar to date suggesting that the Internet should be directly subject to constitutional norms from an internal perspective. He has actually found it is high time to apply rules of constitutional gravity to the world the Internet user perceives, just as we do to the offline world. In order to determine who is subject to which constitutional norm in the Internet realm, Lessig proposed the paradigm of state actor as our guide. We can determine who is a state actor online, according to Lessig[967], by looking at the online world from an Internet user's perspective and determining who has powers that resemble those of the government. In this way, Lessig suggests, we will be able to transpose constitutional values to cyberspace just by recognizing the user's perception of the online world as the functional equivalent of the physical world. With regard to cloud computing, it is not necessary to go as far as constructing such an exhaustive hierarchical order for laws applicable to everything related to the cloud.

965 L. Lessig (note 504).
966 Lawrence Lessig (note 505).
967 *Id.*

As a first step, it would already make a substantial difference to recognize the difference between the external manifestations of the cloud and its internal aspects and deal with the need to concretize rules that will regulate the latter. **The relationship between these two pools of laws (i.e. the already existing and abundant one of laws regulating cloud-based applications and the currently nascent or almost non-existent but needed one of rules regulating the cloud per se) is not hierarchical but rather complimentary: enriching the latter will further boost the efficiency of the former.**

The prism of perspective for dealing with and regulating the cloud proves that rules specifically constructed for cloud computing do add up something new to the broader sector of internet law — not so much with respect to how we approach the law, but more in the way that we approach the facts surrounding the cloud. Modeling the reality of cloud computing reveals that this is not as simplified as we have been thinking so far, and that we need to look into both dimensions of the cloud, the internal and the external one, in order to get the whole picture.

The dual perspective through which it is either possible or necessary to view all sorts of systems that make information and data exchange possible is not anything new[968]. Actually, the first instance in which the internal and external perspectives competed with each other demonstrating that they both exist and that they are both essential in understanding and regulating communication enabling systems is the famous telephone wiretapping case of Olmstead v. United States of 1928[969]. In summary, that case dealt with government agents who had wiretapped the telephone lines of a former police officer who operated a bootlegging operation in violation of the Alcohol Prohibition laws. The authorities tapped the phone lines from a city street without entering the plaintiff's private property. At first and second degree, Olmstead argued that the wiretapping had violated his Fourth Amendment rights. The Justices' opinions are demonstrative of how decisive the adoption of either the external or the internal perspective was already since that time for adjudicating (and regulating) on issues and phenomena of the wider data and communications realm. Writing for a 5-4

968 Kenneth A. Bamberger & Deirdre K. Mulligan, *Privacy on the Books and on the Ground*, 63 Stanford Law Review 247–316 (2011.)

969 Olmstead et al. v. United States; Green et al. v. United States; McInnis v. United States, 277 U.S. 438, 43 S. Ct. 394; 67 L. Ed. 785; 1923 U.S. LEXIS 2588; 24 A.L.R. 1238.

majority, Chief Justice Taft rejected Olmstead's argument following a reasoning tantamount to an external comprehension of the telephone network. According to Taft, "the telephone network consisted of electrical lines that permitted its users to send communications out into the world. By using a telephone Olmstead and his co-conspirators had opted to send their communications out from the protected spaces of their houses and into the unprotected space of the public city street"[970].

In contrast, Justice Brandeis's dissenting opinion portrayed an internally comprehended account of the same event. In Brandeis' opinion[971], it was "immaterial where the physical connection with the telephone wires leading into the defendants' premises was made." Rather, "the proper question was whether from a telephone user's perspective, the wiretapping appeared as the equivalent of a search and seizure". Brandeis thought that it appeared so: "Whenever a telephone line is tapped, the privacy of the persons at both ends of the line is invaded, and all conversations between them upon any subject, and although proper, confidential, and privileged, may be overheard."

Of course, what Justice Brandeis described does not entirely amount to Lessig's internal perspective of cyberspace or the herewith suggested internal aspect of cloud computing; however, it is interesting to note how close he came: Brandeis, in a pioneering manner, understood telephony not just as a service but, in addition to it, as infrastructure; in fact, he conceived the telephone network as the technological means of creating a private space for its users. Already almost a century before, the divide between Taft and Brandeis was not so much a contest between dogmatic and dynamic interpretation of laws, as it was a clash of perspectives for interpreting the facts of the case. Taft applied an external perspective of the telephone network, while Brandeis used an internal one.

Needless to say, this case was only a primary forerunner to the whole issue of the internal vs. external perspective and the great importance these two have today with regard to regulation of the internet, as a whole, or cloud computing, more precisely. Given that the telephone simply transmits sound from one place to another, its ability to generate a virtual reality is very limited. Consequently, telephone cases with an internal-external dynamic have been rare through all previous decades since the in-

970 Id.
971 Id.

vention of telephony, and considered as a whole, they cannot account for a recurring problem of perspective. Things are fundamentally different though, when we focus on the most modern technologies facilitating communication today through the transmission and exchange of all kinds of data and not just sounds[972]. The advanced technology of the Internet has elevated to a universal level a problem that remained largely marginal in the early steps of the telephone network. Some could use the opportunity to cast in doubt whether the problem of perspective is truly "new". This is, however, of little importance. What truly matters is that, one way or another, the problem recurs more and more in Internet law, challenging us to confront it across a wide range of substantive areas[973]. What is more, while in some sub-sectors of IT law effective regulation is achievable only by choosing to focus on one of the two perspectives, when it comes to regulating cloud computing, it is not a matter of choice anymore; rather, it is of vital importance to look into the issues raised by both perspectives and come up with rules that will deal with all of them in order to end up with an all-inclusive range of regulations that will manage to persuasively answer to all challenges posed by the cloud.

c. Completing the picture of the inner side of the cloud; regulatory challenges stemming from the cloud network's business workflow

It has by now been established that, in order to end up having a complete set of rules that will be dealing with cloud regulation in a holistic manner, it is imperative to look into all aspects of the internal side of cloud computing. According to extensive literature[974], the internal perspective of the cloud also includes, apart from what pertains to its infrastructure and raw

972 M. Armbrust, A. Fox, R. Griffith, A. Joseph D., R. Katz H., A. Konwinski, G. Lee, D. Patterson A., A. Rabkin, A. Stoica & M. Zaharia, Above the Clouds: A Berkeley View of Cloud Computing, available at: http://www.eecs.berkeley.edu/Pubs/TechRpts/2009/EECS-2009-28.html (2 March 2015.)

973 Colin J. Bennett & Charles D. Raab, The governance of privacy. Policy instruments in global perspective (2006.)

974 For a comprehensive review of what the cloud and cloud networks actually consist of as technical arrangements, refer to: Ines Houidi, Marouen Mechtri, Wajdi Louati & Djamal Zeghlache, *Cloud Service Delivery across Multiple Cloud Platforms*, in 2011 IEEE International Conference on Services Computing, 741–742 (IEEE Staff ed., 2011); Hoang T. Dinh, Chonho Lee, Dusit Niyato & Ping Wang,

machinery, all structures, workflows and the organizational scheme under which the entire cloud network is set in motion and operates. These workflows could be more easily understood as the organigram of the cloud network, consisting of the actors taking part in it and the functions each of them is performing. What is more, our attention will now move on the service composition methods[975], namely aggregation[976], customization[977] or

---

A survey of mobile cloud computing. Architecture, applications, and approaches, 13 Wirel. Commun. Mob. Comput. 1587–1611 (2013); Thomas Erl, Richardo Puttini & Zaigham Mahmood (note 46); Liang-Jie Zhang & Qun Zhou (note 96); Won Kim, *Cloud computing architecture*, 9 IJWGS 287–303 (2013); Wei-Tek Tsai, Xin Sun & Janaka Balasooriya, *Service-Oriented Cloud Computing Architecture*, in ITNG 2010. Information Technology New Generations : proceedings of the Seventh International Conference on Information Technology :12-14, April 2009, Las Vegas, Nevada, USA, 684–689 (Jameela Al-Jaroodi & Shahram Latifi eds., 2010); Yashpalsinh Jadeja & Kirit Modi, *Cloud computing – concepts, architecture and challenges*, in 2012 International Conference on Computing, Electronics and Electrical Technologies (ICCEET), 877–880 (2012); Bu-Qing Cao, Bing Li & Qi-Ming Xia, *A Service-Oriented Qos-Assured and Multi-Agent Cloud Computing Architecture*, in Cloud computing. First international conference, CloudCom 2009, Beijing, China, December 1-4, 2009 : proceedings, 644–649 (Martin Gilje Jaatun, Gansen Zhao & Chunming Rong eds., 2009); Liang-Jie Zhang & Qun Zhou (note 96); Christian Baun, Marcel Kunze, Jens Nimis & Stefan Tai, Cloud Computing (2011); Vijay Sarathy, Purnendu Narayan & Rao Mikkilineni, *Next Generation Cloud Computing Architecture: Enabling Real-Time Dynamism for Shared Distributed Physical Infrastructure*, in 2010 19th IEEE International Workshop on Enabling Technologies. Infrastructures for Collaborative Enterprises, 48–53 (IEEE ed., 2010.)

975 Stefanie Leimeister, Markus Böhm, Christoph Riedl & Helmut Krcmar, *The Business Perspective of Cloud Computing: Actors, Roles and Value Networks* ECIS 2010 Proceedings (2010). For more on service composition in cloud computing, refer to: Amin Jula, Elankovan Sundararajan & Zalinda Othman, *Cloud computing service composition. A systematic literature review*, 41 Expert Systems with Applications 3809–3824 (2014); Cheng Zeng, Xiao Guo, Weijie Ou & Dong Han, *Cloud Computing Service Composition and Search Based on Semantic*, in Cloud computing. First international conference, CloudCom 2009, Beijing, China, December 1-4, 2009 : proceedings, 290–300 (Martin Gilje Jaatun, Gansen Zhao & Chunming Rong eds., 2009.)

976 See also Chapter 7.

977 For further details on the margins for customization on cloud computing networks refer to: Rajkumar Buyya, Chee Shin Yeo, Srikumar Venugopal, James Broberg & Ivona Brandic, *Cloud computing and emerging IT platforms. Vision, hype, and reality for delivering computing as the 5th utility*, 25 Future Generation Computer Systems 599–616 (2009); Tharam Dillon, Chen Wu & Elizabeth

service distribution channels[978], and what kind of dynamics and interrelations these processes develop, which may lead consequently to corresponding regulatory challenges that need to be dealt with. It needs to be pointed out right from the beginning that, although the following arguments will primarily be presented in light of the way cloud networks aimed at facilitating commercial applications of the cloud are built, the observations and recommendations made here largely fit also with those cloud networks deployed for the provision of hybrid or private services[979].

It is a very well-established practice in the industry[980] to classify cloud services along different layers; and we have already seen a most detailed and representative such listing[981]. Various cloud services fall all in one of the five layers of this ontology, which represent a level of abstraction, permitting the user to set aside all underlying or higher-ranking components and thus providing simplified focus to the resources or functionality that correspond to each one of them. However, the actors and entities making all these services possible can be spotted in more than one layers of the overall ontology[982]. At the same time, one entity that can occupy the position of one specific (and with particular tasks) actor on one layer can simultaneously occupy the position and responsibilities of a different actor on another layer[983].

Chang, *Cloud Computing: Issues and Challenges*, in 24th IEEE International Conference on Advanced Information Networking and Applications (AINA), 2010. 20 – 23 April 2010, Perth, Australia; proceedings, 27–33 (Elizabeth Chang ed., 2010); Lamia Youseff, Maria Butrico & Dilma Da Silva (note 838); Wei-Tek Tsai, Xin Sun & Janaka Balasooriya (note 974).

978 For a broader review on the issue of service distribution channels on cloud networks refer to: Kaiqi Xiong & Harry Perros, *Service Performance and Analysis in Cloud Computing*, in World Conference on Services-I, 2009, 693–700 (Liang-Jie Zhang ed., 2009); Thomas Erl, Richardo Puttini & Zaigham Mahmood (note 46); M. Armbrust, A. Fox, R. Griffith, A. Joseph D., R. Katz H., A. Konwinski, G. Lee, D. Patterson A., A. Rabkin, A. Stoica & M. Zaharia (note 972); Hoang T. Dinh, Chonho Lee, Dusit Niyato & Ping Wang (note 974).

979 Kristina Irion (note 220).

980 Cong Wang, Qian Wang, Kui Ren & Wenjing Lou (note 932).; Lamia Youseff, Maria Butrico & Dilma Da Silva (note 838).; Benoit Dupont (note 111).

981 See Chapter 2.

982 Sean Marston, Zhi Li, Subhajyoti Bandyopadhyay, Juheng Zhang & Anand Ghalsasi (note 116).

983 *Id.*

With these in mind, it becomes clear that in order to single out the regulatory challenges posed by the workflow on which cloud networks typically run today a detailed review of the actors present throughout these networks and their typical roles is required. It needs to be made clear that the actors that will be analyzed hereunder can be present and found on many different layers of the cloud network ontology. Therefore, their order of presentation is random and does not imply any hierarchical or significance sequencing among them:

i. The customer[984] (or user) of cloud computing services

It is the actor who, through various distribution channels buys and makes use of the different cloud services commercialized by the provider[985]. The channels through which the customer can finally receive the services of his choice can be various, namely directly from the service provider or through a platform provider or through a reseller[986]. It needs to be stressed out that a customer of a cloud service can be found on all layers of the cloud ontology. One of the most characteristic elements of customers of cloud services is the ways in which they interact with the service itself, with only rare exceptions to the rule given that, even those that may also have physical access to the infrastructure facilitating the service they use some kind of tool or intermediary facility to interact with the resources of that infrastructure[987]. In particular, users access cloud computing to enjoy the services of their choice using networked client devices, such as desktop computers, laptops, tablets and smartphones, but also practically any Ethernet enabled device. As time goes by, several of these devices turn into actual cloud clients, as they rely more and more exclusively on cloud computing in order to execute all or the majority of their applications being rendered essentially useless without it[988]. As it becomes evident, it

984 Stefanie Leimeister, Markus Böhm, Christoph Riedl & Helmut Krcmar (note 975).

985 *Id.*

986 Stephanos Androutsellis-Theotokis & Diomidis Spinellis (note 861).; Lothar Determann, *What Happens in the Cloud: Software as a Service and Copyrights*, 29 Berkeley Technology Law Journal 1096–1129 (2015.)

987 Mike P. Papazoglou & Willem-Jan van den Heuvel (note 853).

988 *Id.*; J. Hoover, *Compliance in the Ether: Cloud Computing, Data Security and Business Regulation*, 8 Journal of Business & Technology Law 255–273 (2013.)

would be unrealistic to go as far as standardizing these devices with which users get access to the cloud; that would be a totally unfounded intervention to the market of these products[989]. Therefore, the need for defining minimum requirements that these devices should satisfy emerges so that cloud customers can expect and actually get a minimum quality of access to the network no matter what medium they choose to enter it with. Some would argue that the solution to this need would be for regulators to define the minimum specifications of the pieces of hardware used to facilitate access to the cloud. However, it makes much more sense to define the minimum conditions (in terms of security etc.) that access to the cloud should have than trying to homogenize the range of devices suitable for it. This approach makes even more sense if we bear in mind that many cloud applications do not require some sort of specific software on the client from which they are accessed[990]; instead, a web browser to interact with the cloud application would suffice. Apart from this main path for users to access the cloud, there is a smaller group of customers who make use of highly niche services[991] which necessitate the use of specific client software dedicated to them (for instance, virtual desktop clients and most email clients). At last, there is a pool of customers[992] who use a number of legacy cloud applications (mostly from the front of business applications) that are delivered via a screen-sharing technology. All of the above strengthen the argument that we need rules that will mandate the minimum conditions under which customers will have access to cloud networks and the services they wish to use through them, since regulating how the means of access should look like would be too complicated and an unnecessarily interventionist route. If customers are assured, thanks to clear and established rules, that any of the lawfully commercialized cloud services on the market meets the minimum requirements guaranteeing safe and unequivocal access to it, then it is only logical that customer safety and trust will increase, opening up simultaneously the way for providers to freely antagonize for anything superior to those minimum standards maintaining

989 Benoit Dupont (note 111).

990 Christof Weinhardt, Arun Anandasivam, Benjamin Blau, Nikolay Borissov, Thomas Meinl, Wibke Michalk & Jochen Stößer (note 65).

991 Stefanie Leimeister, Markus Böhm, Christoph Riedl & Helmut Krcmar (note 975).

992 *Id.*

a level of market competition that can only prove further beneficial to customers.

ii. The service provider[993]

It often also called IT vendor, is the actor within a cloud network typically executing development and operation of services that offer value to either the customer or the aggregate services provider. Service providers, within the range of their functions, develop applications that are offered and deployed on the cloud computing platform and, to this end, access hardware and infrastructure contributed to the network by the infrastructure providers[994]. Bearing in mind the above definition, we can now analyze the specificities of the role of service provider and the respective regulatory challenges that come along with them;

- Firstly, it is essential to point out that, despite the fact that a service provider can also function as a customer within the flow of a cloud network, this happens only in relation to hardware resources which are necessary for the deployment of the services addressed to cloud customers or aggregators[995]; this kind of buys (i.e. referring exclusively to hardware) are already sufficiently and effectively regulated by existing commercial transactions laws and they should not be equated to the observations made above regarding the functions of the cloud computing customer.
- One of the most important tools in the hands of service providers on the cloud is monitoring performance[996] of their services and the network's resources in order to do any tweaking or other interventions necessary for the performance index to remain or reach optimal levels. In conducting these performance measurements service providers need to be forced by law not to compromise core features that their services are supposed to offer to cloud customers, namely privacy of users' data, protection of their identity etc.

---

993 Siani Pearson & Nick Wainwright (note 645).

994 M. Armbrust, A. Fox, R. Griffith, A. Joseph D., R. Katz H., A. Konwinski, G. Lee, D. Patterson A., A. Rabkin, A. Stoica & M. Zaharia (note 972).

995 Sean Marston, Zhi Li, Subhajyoti Bandyopadhyay, Juheng Zhang & Anand Ghalsasi (note 116).

996 Lothar Determann (note 986).

- Security is one of the competitive advantages that boosted cloud computing to the absolute standard technology of today's internet and data networks[997]. As it has already been analyzed, security on the cloud is improved in comparison to older technologies due to a number of factors, such as centralization of data, increased security-focused resources, etc[998]. Nevertheless, there are still unsettled issues concerning the security of core cloud services such as the ones made available by service providers. The main points of concern over security on the cloud on the service providers level are uncertainty over the possibility of loss of control over certain types of sensitive data, or the lack of security for stored kernels[999]. What improves security on the cloud over older, traditional systems is its capacity to devote resources to solving security issues (on a proactive or a posteriori basis) in a magnitude and volume that many customers cannot afford to by themselves or which they do not possess the technical skills to address[1000]. Rules are, therefore, necessary that will force service providers to deploy these security optimization techniques on a standard basis and not just as a competitive advantage. At the same time, security on the cloud becomes an all the more complex idea when data is distributed over a wider area or over a greater number of devices, as well as in multi-tenant systems shared by unrelated users[1001]. Additionally, user access to security audit logs may be difficult or impossible as the expanse and complexity of the cloud network increases. Therefore, regulators need to strike a balance between the conflicting interests of security and optimization of the cloud networks economies of scale (which is the main drive behind the increasing vastness and confluence of totally estranged streams of data over the same network[1002].
- The above points of concern exist in the cases of public and hybrid clouds. In private clouds, most of these issues are not applicable given that the infrastructure owner and the service provider are, as a rule, one and the same entity. However, it is not reasonable to claim that the an-

---

997 Siani Pearson & George Yee (note 280).
998 See Chapter 2.
999 See Chapter 8.
1000 Benoit Dupont (note 111).
1001 Kenneth A. Bamberger & Deirdre K. Mulligan (note 968).
1002 Private cloud installations are in part motivated by users' desire to retain control over the infrastructure and avoid losing control of information security.

swer to these security concerns would be the replacement of all public and hybrid cloud facilities by private ones given that this would financially unrealistic and would automatically compromise the cloud's most cherished element, i.e. the dynamics achieved due to virtualization. Between hybrid and public clouds, the former offer, in general better answers to the security concerns outlined above; however, at present and, likely, in general they cannot be the rule. Therefore, any rules established with a view to defining the minimum standards cloud networks should respect in light of the issues discussed with regard to service providers need to be designed with the case study of public clouds in mind.

- A key issue in relation to service providers in the cloud is the problem of legal ownership of the data[1003], which essentially translates to the question of whether the service provider can profit from users' data stored in the cloud. This issue will grow more and more in significance as the cloud penetrates the neighboring fields of big data and IoT, at the heart of which lie vast amounts of data originating from thousands of different users or entities[1004]. At the moment, most Terms of Service agreements remain silent on the question of ownership. The ideal answer would be, similarly to what has been argued before, the choice of network equipment upon which cloud customers would have immediate physical control over the computer equipment (private cloud); however, this is only rarely a choice. The present unregulated landscape with relation to legal ownership of data stored in the cloud creates great incentives to public cloud computing service providers to prioritize building and maintaining strong management of secure services. However, things will get all the more complicated as the big data and IoT applications multiply, given that in those cases the consent of data subjects regarding collection of data attributable to them is not always explicit nor can it be taken for granted[1005]. Moreover, as it widely the case, plain end users do not pay the necessary attention to service contracts, which is largely the case with regard to service agreements of most popular cloud services. The fact that for the time being the issue

1003 Hassan Takabi, James B. D. Joshi & Gail-Joon Ahn (note 119).; see also Chapter 6.

1004 Hunton Privacy Blog (note 269).; Viktor Mayer-Schönberger & Kenneth Cukier (note 321).

1005 *Id.*

of legal ownership of data remains unanswered does not necessarily mean that this will always be the case. As economic incentives will grow with the push from big data and IoT applications, service providers may very expectedly decide to deal with this question deliberately and in a manner not entirely balanced between theirs and the interests of their customers. Therefore, a clear answer to the issue on behalf of the law will only work to the benefit of customers, who are generally the inferior side in this equation. What is more, the sooner the issue is settled on behalf of cloud regulators the more balanced and fair the final settlement can be between the need of customers for non-exploitation of their data and the drive of service providers to maximize the profits they can derive from the data they host on their systems. Last but not least, looking at this issue now that big data and IoT have not yet reached their full capacity (although it is, of course, undeniable that they are on a steep rise) will permit cloud regulators to regulate on the matter of legal ownership with a clearer head and not under the pressure the whole topic may have in the near future, calling for immediate over proactive measures.

iii. Infrastructure providers[1006]

As actors of the cloud workflow, infrastructure providers are tasked with supplying the network with the computing and storage services needed in order for all subsequent software applications to run within the cloud. In other words, as we have already seen[1007], the infrastructure provider serves as the actor maintaining the technical backbone of the network. The resources offered by this actor are essentially scalable hardware for the services[1008] upon which the service providers offer their services. Infrastructure providers are alternatively called IT vendors. Typically, the consumer of what an infrastructure provider offers does not manage or control the underlying cloud infrastructure but retains control over operating systems, storage, and deployed applications, possibly even limited control of

---

1006 Stefanie Leimeister, Markus Böhm, Christoph Riedl & Helmut Krcmar (note 975).

1007 See Chapter 2.

1008 Ozalp Babaoglu, M. Jelasity, Anne Marie Kermarrec, Alberto Montresor & Maarten van Steen (note 874).

select networking components (e.g., host firewalls). It becomes evident then, once again, at this point, that rules describing attribution and extend of responsibility and culpability between infrastructure providers and service providers (who are the customers of the former but providers to cloud applications customers) towards end users of the applications/services developed on a cloud network are crucial. In detail, the most basic cloud-service model[1009] is that where providers offer computing infrastructure – virtual machines and other resources – as a service to subscribers. It needs to be stressed out that Infrastructure as a service (IaaS), by today's state-of-the-art in the cloud business, refers to online services that set the user free from the details of infrastructure like physical computing resources, location, data partitioning, scaling, security, backup etc. Those virtual machines, which are the vessels of most IaaS, are run by hypervisors[1010], i.e. companies that sit between the actual owners of the cloud network's infrastructure and the customers buying the right to use part of that infrastructure in the form of IaaS. This arrangement is yet one more argument in support of the need for developing rules that will clearly define how obligations and culpability are distributed among actors of the cloud workflow, particularly at this rudimentary level. In addition, it is common practice that hypervisors arrange themselves in pools within the cloud operational system in order to be able to support large numbers of virtual machines and to scale services up and down according to customers' varying requirements[1011]. The connection to the network's actual physical resources is then made possible via Linux containers[1012] running in isolated partitions of a single Linux kernel[1013] which connects them directly to the

1009 Xiaolong Jin & Jiming Liu (note 844).

1010 Stefanie Leimeister, Markus Böhm, Christoph Riedl & Helmut Krcmar (note 975).

1011 M. Armbrust, A. Fox, R. Griffith, A. Joseph D., R. Katz H., A. Konwinski, G. Lee, D. Patterson A., A. Rabkin, A. Stoica & M. Zaharia (note 972).

1012 LXC (Linux Containers) are an operating system-level virtualization method for running multiple isolated Linux systems (containers) on a control host using a single Linux kernel. The Linux kernel provides the functionality that allows limitation and prioritization of resources (CPU, memory, block I/O, network, etc.) without the need for starting any virtual machines, and also namespace isolation functionality that allows complete isolation of an applications' view of the operating environment, including process trees, networking, user IDs and mounted file systems. (Definition cited as formulated under: https://linuxcontainers.org/lxc/introduction/; last accessed on 7/11/2016.)

1013 See also Chapter 8.

physical hardware. Containerization[1014] offers at this level better performance than virtualization, because there is no hypervisor overhead. Also, container capacity auto-scales dynamically with computing load, which eliminates the problem of over-provisioning and enables usage-based billing.

iv. Aggregate services providers (aggregators)

This is a niche sub-type of service provider that offers new services or solutions 'by combining pre-existing services or parts of services to form new services and offer them to customers'[1015]. As a result, aggregators are by nature a customer (from the perspective of the service provider) and a service provider (from the perspective of the customer). They can be further sub-divided into aggregators that focus on the integration of data and others that mostly offer aggregation of services with the former being quoted as data integrators[1016]. The main function of those is making sure that already existing data is prepared and is usable by different cloud services and can be regarded as a sub-role of aggregators with a primary focus on technical data integration. Similar types of cloud network actors are the "system integrator" or "business process integrator" or the "service mediator"[1017]. These terms describe, in general, aggregators that focus more on the technical aspects necessary for data and system integration while '(service) aggregators', as a generic term, also includes the business aspects of merging services to come up with new service bundles. The quasi-binary nature of aggregators stresses even more the need for cloud regulation rules that will permit allocation of responsibilities and culpability on each instance of cloud business workflow regardless of whether it

1014 Containerization is a lightweight alternative to full machine virtualization that involves encapsulating an application in a container with its own operating environment. This provides many of the benefits of loading an application onto a virtual machine, as the application can be run on any suitable physical machine without any worries about dependencies. (Definition cited under: http://www.webopedia.com/TERM/C/containerization.html; last accessed on 7/11/2016.)

1015 Stefanie Leimeister, Markus Böhm, Christoph Riedl & Helmut Krcmar (note 975).

1016 Sean Marston, Zhi Li, Subhajyoti Bandyopadhyay, Juheng Zhang & Anand Ghalsasi (note 116).

1017 *Id.*

corresponds to an already known type of cloud service or a novel, still insufficiently charted one.

v. The platform provider[1018]

This is the actor that functions as the provider of an environment within which cloud applications can be deployed. We could place this actor on the same level as the kernel software that we have already seen in the context of the ontology of the cloud[1019]. Platform providers act as a kind of catalogue of reception in which different service providers offer services. Platform providers offer the technical basis for the marketplace where cloud services aimed at the end user are offered. It is very important to point out that platform providers can be hosted on the same development level and cloud space with the subsequent services they facilitate. However, it is also possible to have them located on totally different facilities as well. This raises serious issues of integrity of the data they handle as well as of the connections that bind them with the services nested in them, which points again towards the need for clear regulations referring to the inner side of cloud networks and the business cycles that are in full motion within them.

vi. The cloud services consultant

Lastly, the ever more complex structure of the cloud business has provided fertile ground to one more type of actor within the cloud business cycle, i.e. the **cloud services consultant**[1020]. Entities performing consulting for the customers on a cloud network serve as support for the selection and implementation by the latter of relevant services in order to create value for their business model[1021]. One might argue that the cloud consultant does not entirely fall within what we have described as the cloud network business workflow; nevertheless, those actors, in the context of assessing cloud customers' needs and coming up with the most suitable services for

1018 J. Hoover (note 988).
1019 See also Chapter 8.
1020 *Id.*
1021 J. Hoover (note 988); Norman Pelzl (note 65).

their needs, have often access to or an overview of customers' data. Therefore, they should also be considered as actors of the cloud business cycle and have their selves and their functions subjected to any rules put together for managing the internal aspect of cloud networks.

d. The innovative nature of cloud computing business and the legal challenges raised as a result thereof

The revolutionary elements cloud computing has by nature as a technology have also had their effect on the way business is done in the cloud market. We have already gone through novel roles and actors appearing in the business cycle of cloud computing and have also seen into what they do new or differently compared to the past[1022]. These innovations, in roles and tasks, have already ignited demand for original rules that will resolve issues unique to them. Apart from the points that have already been raised though, it is important to take a step back and look at the broader picture of the cloud market and business. Defined and clearly affected by the pioneering elements cloud computing inherently possesses, the way the relevant market sector works also offers interesting hints pointing to the way and characteristics that rules governing the cloud should have.

For starters, it is important to emphasize that the broader cloud computing business is characterized by several different types of varieties[1023] which are also characteristic of the cloud per se and are, therefore, becoming more and more prevalent in numerous areas of the IT economy that rely on cloud computing:

- Variety in norms: The cloud's standard order of business is defined by a plurality of state actors, greatly varying in size, magnitude and authority, ranging from national government agencies to supranational institutions[1024]. All these, equipped with a certain degree of formal rule making capacity have engaged in enacting a diverse set of (partly overlapping or otherwise interacting) norms aimed at regulating certain manifestations of the cloud computing phenomenon. Up to now though, their regulatory compass has left mostly untouched the essence of cloud computing per se, i.e. the cloud as a technology made possible

1022 See Chapter 2.

1023 Willcocks, Leslie P., Venters, Will and Whitley, Edgar A. (note 111).

1024 See Chapter 5.

thanks to a certain technological arrangement and as a workflow/ a lifecycle for any kind of digital or digitized data with several actors taking part or contributing to it and several exits from the cycle, each one marking one of those manifestations of the cloud towards its end users or recipients of the end-products of this workflow.

- Variety in control mechanisms: Due to the novelties it brought with, cloud computing has nurtured a great deal of new approaches to the issue of its regulation as a phenomenon. To a certain extent also because of the lack of concrete rules and laws governing the cloud per se, and further driven by the speed at which phenomena (i.e. applications, systems, products, services etc.) facilitated by cloud computing appear, there has been a plethora of alternative regulatory approaches to cloud computing[1025], besides traditional, hierarchical mechanism of control. Until now legal and regulatory approaches to cloud computing include alternative modes of control, such as market regulation, the shaping of social norms, and design requirements. All of these tools have resulted in the conception and establishment of a wide range of legal dicta regarding the cloud, which it is high time to be systematized and codified into a code of rules that will not necessarily replace of body of law we already have regarding manifestations of cloud computing but will work as the foundations for the entire construction of IT law.
- Variety in controllers: In the race to effectively regulate all manifestations of cloud computing and the applications it has given life to, traditional state regulatory bodies, namely government agencies or courts, continue to play a key role. However, the speedy and innovative evolution of the broader IT sector the cloud has made possible, also served as fertile ground so that important control functions be attributed to alternative governance institutions[1026], for instance standard setting bodies and trade associations. Of course, the regulatory competence of the latter is not on a par with that of full-capacity lawmakers. However, it should not fail our attention that many of them experience the cloud and the practices developed around and through it from much closer than conventional legislators. Without suggesting that they should fully and officially be made part of the law-making process with regard to rules on cloud computing (after all, law production as such is not yet

1025 See Chapters 3 and 4.
1026 See Chapter 6.

mature enough to undergo such a major makeover), it is definitely advisable to take what these actors have to say about how to effectively regulate the cloud seriously into account. As it has been demonstrated several times throughout this study, these alternative governance institutions are much closer to the inner, most fundamental aspects of the cloud computing phenomenon and already possess much more advanced ways of interpreting the cloud through interdisciplinary and, thus, more analytical lenses. To fully comprehend cloud computing, regulators need to profoundly grasp not just what computing results in for the real world but also what it actually is, how it actually works and on how many different dimensions (geographic, technical and jurisdictional ones) it is moving in parallel. Working hand in hand with such entities that can assist this quest for deeper Interdisciplinarity is key to successful and efficient cloud regulation.

- Variety in controllees[1027]: so far in the cloud computing related ecosystem of laws, businesses that provide cloud services to consumers have been the key regulatory subjects. However, as it has been extensively demonstrated[1028], a broader range of actors is relevant if we are to build up a holistic range of regulatory tools for the cloud. From those entities putting the cloud together, as infrastructure, to those setting the stage for cloud service providers to market their offerings to consumers, to actors facilitating access of the users to the APIs of cloud services, there is a long path with multiple players whose roles and functions have been so far insufficiently mapped and remain in a state of regulatory limbo. Even governments themselves play their part in governance efforts for the cloud, in the sense that, possibly for the first time in history to such an advanced degree, they need to outdo themselves and, without going as far as succumbing part of their sovereignty to some form of abstract supranational IT-dedicated legal order, they nevertheless need to develop cloud computing laws that will be able to plug into each other.

1027 Urs Gasser (note 959).
1028 See Chapter 8.

e. Summarizing the issues raised by the new modus operandi established in IT market by cloud computing; where is there a need for new cloud computing rules and what precisely should their content be?

The cloud market and the way it functions, as they have been extensively described and analyzed so far, have expectedly given rise to a heated debate about a series of key issues related to the cloud computing phenomenon. In previous parts of this study, we have already presented the main fronts on which the cloud computing reality has stirred debate and concern. Many of these issues are the product and result of the very architecture of the whole cloud market structure and of four basic risk factors on which it is founded[1029]: Outsourcing, centralization, internationalization and, as a result of the previous three, systemic complexity. Now that we have examined in such an analytical manner not only what issues the establishment of the cloud as standard IT technology has raised but also how it works and how the market created around it is functioning, it is worth summarizing those issues and arguing on which of them could be the subject matter of rules dedicated to regulating the cloud or which they are already dealt with by other pieces of legislation:

i. Data protection

Undoubtedly, data protection has been brought forward as the main issue to be closely watched and monitored as to the effects that can be brought upon it by cloud computing. There are several reasons behind this, namely the fact that since by definition cloud as a technology is almost always interrelated one way or another to data or that data protection has come, to a certain extent, to be regarded almost as synonym to 'risks posed by cloud computing' in public debate[1030]. We have already seen that, indeed, the architecture of cloud computing and the sensitive nature of data stored in cloud-based environments do raise concerns regarding individual rights and related safeguards, such as data quality, processing transparency, and international data transfers with good reason. It would be unfair to claim that legislators have failed to comprehend the urgency of the matter and work on legal tools that allow us to deal with this issue. However, just as

1029 Benoit Dupont (note 111).
1030 See Chapter 7.

the GDPR is on the countdown before coming into force in Europe and other such initiatives are also underway in the US, there has been rightful warnings voiced that, in our haste to safeguard our data as efficiently as possible, we are moving in the wrong direction. EU law is dealing with data as if these continue to be under the effective control of their owners[1031] in today's data technology landscape, while this is not entirely true nor is it the most efficient way to go after data protection. On the other hand, US law insists on the path of granting preferential treatment to government and state agencies regarding their possibility to get access to any of their subjects' data, while recent experience has proved that this is no longer safe (the technical lacunae that permit the state to get access to citizens' data could as well be exploited by others for malicious purposes) and it is growing less and less bearable by data owners[1032]. Our discourse so far and the exposure of what cloud computing is really about has only highlighted that, while it is absolutely essential to work on the front of data protection and maintain relevant rules updated at all times, it is high time to closely examine and regulate the actual medium and field where the whole game with data is played, i.e. the cloud networks themselves and cloud computing itself as the actual vessel for practically any computational process imaginable nowadays.

ii. Data Security

It is regarded by many that security issues are the second biggest risk the cloud has given rise to with regard to the countless amounts of data hosted on cloud network facilities[1033]. Consequently, issues such as data security standards, contractual rules, and legal obligations have risen among top preoccupations[1034]. Already, several specific problems have been brought to the forefront with equally numerous solutions that have been put to discussion. These include, for instance, digital signature legislation, breach notification laws, rules regulating how data can be stored in the cloud, se-

---

1031 See Chapters 6 and 7.
1032 See Chapter 3.
1033 Nicholas Platten (note 42).
1034 See also Chapters 5, 6 and 7.

curity audit requirements etc.[1035]. While on these topics there are already several legal options on the table, we are still missing the most crucial element, i.e. rules that will allow us to determine who is to bear the blame in case such security breaches occur and, most importantly, who is truly responsible at any given time to prevent such breaches from happening. The analysis of the inner architecture of cloud networks and the mapping of actors playing their roles across the cloud workflow only bring to surface the need for such dedicated cloud computing legislation, which will not cripple or render obsolete but it will rather help already existing IT laws become more focused and effective upon application.

iii. Data retention

One of the practices that thrived thanks to cloud computing but also because of modern challenges and policies such as economic regulation or national security obligations is retention of data with the use of cloud computing[1036]. Consequently, we are increasingly facing the challenge of balancing between the development, implementation, and operation of retention practices against civil liberties and other fundamental rights[1037]. For the time being, regulatory approaches trying to uphold these fundamental liberties against such practices are largely based on the theory of consent of the data subjects with regard to collection of data attributable to them. This is the default point adopted in the GDPR as well[1038] and it is, in generally, regarded as the next big frontier in the quest for empowering data subjects in their struggle to preserve their data. However, important as these steps may be, they fail to recognize one elementary fact about data in the era of cloud computing: from the moment when data enter the cloud, they are by default out of the data subject's control[1039]. Therefore, the burden of preserving the integrity of users' data, of determining when and under what conditions they could be handed over to third parties or

1035 Kenneth A. Bamberger & Deirdre K. Mulligan (note 968).; Urs Gasser (note 959).

1036 Eoghan Casey, Handbook of digital forensics and investigation (2010); Reilly, D., Wren, C., & Berry, T., Cloud computing: Forensic challenges for law enforcement. In Internet Technology and Secured Transactions (ICITST.)

1037 Paul Schwartz (note 155).

1038 See Chapter 4.

1039 Hassan Takabi, James B. D. Joshi & Gail-Joon Ahn (note 119).

state authorities or to what extent they should make it permissible for third parties to have access to users' data needs to transferred to the actors facilitating the cloud computing business workflow. Of course, it is certainly no harm for data subjects to maintain the prerogative of consent; however, without rules that will define who among the various actors handling users' data on the course of a cloud-based computational procedure is tasked with respecting users' choice in terms of that consent, the front of data retention will remain only partially regulated.

iv. Consumer protection

The rate at which cloud computing services are becoming the mainstream choice for virtually all groups of IT services consumers, from individuals to big-scale enterprise users, has subsequently given rise to a series of consumer protection issues in the cloud market[1040]. These concerns are mainly fueled in light of the fact that users of cloud services have to agree to prefabricated terms and conditions that apply to the services they wish to use. Additionally, it is common truth that communication between cloud providers and consumers or the feasibility of existing consumer protection laws to regulate these relationships are all characterized by information and power asymmetries[1041]. Improvements on that front are also to be expected; to a certain extent they are bound to happen as consumers will be pushing forward for their interests and will seek protection for them in more concentrated manners. However, the asymmetry between service providers and users of cloud services is most unlikely to cease to exist any time soon, if it can, at all. Therefore, it is again on the front of regulation of cloud computing per se where it is possible, via rules that will clarify which cloud actor is responsible for which specific tasks and duties at each time within the cloud business workflow, to partly outdo the difference of power observed between consumers and cloud computing service providers. Yet again, the proposed cloud-specific rules are not meant to substitute but, rather, to complement consumer laws with the aim of achieving the best possible balance between the two ends of the cloud market equilibrium.

1040 Kenneth A. Bamberger & Deirdre K. Mulligan (note 968).
1041 Paul M. Schwartz (note 157).

v. Intellectual Property

IP rights are of paramount importance on the cloud given that a great deal of all digital content available on the cloud is subject to intellectual property rules and can be of great financial value to right holders[1042]. From social media to the publication industry, the cloud hosts numerous activities, either digital since conception or converted into digital formats in order to adapt to modern demand, which involve materials subject to IP laws. The exploitation of intellectual property in the cloud environment is often fervently contested. For instance, low entry barriers for large-scale distribution of copyright protected content raises concerns about possible piracy on the side of rightholders. Strengthening IP rights and putting in place better enforcement mechanisms are among issues mentioned in most cloud policy debates[1043]. While it is true that modernizing and reinforcing IP laws can decisively contribute to better protection of relevant rights in the times of cloud economy, protection will not be complete before establishing rules that will define which of the cloud network actors are, at each time, charged with upholding those rights. In fact, cloud computing regulation should not stipulate just on cloud computing actors being deterred from offending the rights of their users (among which IP rights as well) but it should oblige them to actively take action towards better protection of them.

vi. Competition

Given the size and value of commerce and economic activity done on the cloud, it goes without saying that competition law and affairs would be stirred due to cloud technologies. In particular, the centralized nature of cloud computing infrastructures, questions of ownership, antitrust and, perhaps most importantly, interoperability issues have emerged[1044]. The thorniest problems are thought to be contractual concerns (e.g., adhesion forms of contracts), the lack of portability and conflicts between open and closed standards. Needless to say, competition issues raised as a result of

1042 Stefanie Leimeister, Markus Böhm, Christoph Riedl & Helmut Krcmar (note 975).

1043 Paul M. Schwartz (note 157).

1044 Urs Gasser (note 959).

the introduction of cloud computing are too vast a field to be discussed on the sidelines of this study. However, it could be briefly argued that at the heart of the quest for a better functioning and with fairer competition conditions cloud market lies one predominant tool: interoperability. Given that the cloud economy is, to a great extent, founded on the flexibility with which users can go up or down on the amount of computational resources they use at any given time depending on their needs, it only makes sense that they should enjoy this flexibility not only within the resources of a specific service provider but also when transiting from one to the other. Cloud computing specific rules should definitely incorporate regulations regarding the minimum interoperability standards cloud providers should guarantee to their customers at all times and throughout the cloud business workflow. In addition, interoperability will be even further advanced if cloud computing laws are founded on similar principles on a cross-jurisdictional basis contributing to the advancement of fair competition, for the benefit of both service providers and customers, on a universal basis or, in any case, on such an extensive level as possible[1045].

vii. Trade

Although steps are constantly made towards bringing down such measures restricting free economic activity in the field of cloud computing worldwide, there are still several such procedures or requirements that hinder cloud business. For instance, there are several types of registrations cloud companies have to go through in a given country before they can provide services there (for instance, the EU-US Privacy Shield agreement that replaced the Safe Harbor agreement[1046]) that create trade barriers for cloud providers or the harmonization of government procurement rules. It would certainly be too optimistic or even unnecessarily bold to claim that merely

1045 Also refer to Chapter 11.

1046 The EU-US Privacy Shield is a framework agreement for transatlantic exchanges of personal data for commercial purposes between the European Union and the United States. One of its purposes is to permit US companies to more easily receive personal data from EU entities under EU privacy laws meant to protect European Union citizens. The EU-US Privacy Shield is a replacement for the International Safe Harbor Privacy Principles which were declared invalid by the European Court of Justice in October 2015 by virtue of judgment in Case C-362/14 Maximillian Schrems v Data Protection Commissioner.

by introducing fundamental cloud computing laws such trade barriers could be totally abolished[1047]. However, in so far as the rules governing the functioning of the very cloud networks and their actors applicable in each jurisdiction are based on common core principles, obstacles to cloud computing business can be expected to be minimized.

viii. Jurisdiction, applicable law, enforcement[1048]

In order to make the most out of economies of scale, cloud computing heavily resorts to the flow of data across jurisdictional boundaries, be it at the local, national, or regional level[1049]. As it has already been analyzed, this potentially global flow of data naturally triggers questions of jurisdiction, applicable law, and enforcement. It has also been argued that, bold as that may be, it does not appear to be very realistic at this moment to move any time soon towards a regime of global regulation of cross-jurisdictional data flows[1050]. Even more, it is even questionable whether such a big leap from the existing jurisdictional status quo for the cloud to a substantially different, universalized one would make sense or whether it would be met with positive feelings from all affected parties, even if we suppose that it was achieved somehow. However, it is certain that jurisdictional frictions would be significantly softened if rules that dealt with the cloud market and the characteristics it and the entities active within it truly have are put in force. As these rules are proposed to be primarily founded on the teleological perspective[1051], they will definitely help to track down which actor of a cloud business workflow was responsible for what function at any given instance of the cloud workflow; once the entity upon which responsibility or culpability is attributable is identified, answering the question of jurisdiction and other neighboring topics will become an easier task.

1047 Margot Kaminski, *Why trade is not the place for the EU to negotiate privacy* Internet Policy Review (2015.)

1048 See also Chapters 6 and 7.

1049 See Chapter 6.

1050 See Chapters 5 and 6.

1051 See Chapter 5.

ix. Compliance[1052]

Cloud computing providers need not only to abide by general laws, but also to comply with an ever-growing body of very detailed sector-specific regulations (e.g., regarding financial, educational, or health data) and master the interplay among them, especially in instances of cross-jurisdictional nature. Similar to what has been argued before with relation to jurisdiction, rules regulating all that is happening on the internal aspect of cloud networks will help determine at each time which is responsible for what function during the computational process, thus making it easier to determine the entity responsible for upholding compliance requirements as well.

x. Transparency

This is the challenge with which a regulation specialized in the cloud could make a difference. Transparency and clarity are central concerns in the wider cloud environment touching upon a wide range of issues from contractual arrangements to regulatory approaches over a wide range of applications and manifestations related to the cloud as a technological, organizational, and economical phenomenon[1053]. The proposed rules, which are meant to primarily shed light and regulate what is actually happening in the day-to-day function of cloud networks and the business workflow that is made possible thanks to them, will decisively contribute to making the broad picture around cloud computing clearer and more transparent. By adopting rules that will help at each time to clear out who among a cloud network's actors is responsible for which of the events taking place within the cloud workflow, not according to a standard description of duties and tasks for each actor but as a result of an ad hoc analysis of processes that are underway, actors that are taking part in them and what role they are precisely carrying in any given time, chances augment that handling and regulation of affairs on any given instance will be conducted in a transparent and just manner.

1052 See Chapters 6 and 7.

1053 Nicholas Platten (note 42).

xi. Responsibility and liability[1054]

The proposed rules governing the internal aspect of cloud networks and the cloud business cycle will help, in a very similar manner to the one related to transparency, the need for fairer and more pragmatic allocation of responsibility and liability on the cloud. The great variety of instruments currently available in determining and allocating responsibility and liability over any harmful incident involving cloud technologies will be decisively better applied if reinforced by a set of rules on cloud computing with the nature and principles proposed hereby. Instruments for determining wrongdoing[1055] and liability in IT and, hence, in the cloud are numerous, ranging from traditional approaches (criminal law, civil liability, and risk insurance) to concepts such as corporate social responsibility. If coupled with a set of governance principles on the very functioning of cloud networks, their efficiency can do not worse than improve.

xii. Infrastructure

As it has been earlier discussed[1056] infrastructure of cloud networks, which is naturally the raw material for building the entire cloud phenomenon altogether, is needed in abundance as the use of the cloud spreads. Therefore, cloud computing providers heavily invest in more and more facilities of this kind across various geographical locations trying to optimize as much as they can, at the same time, any relevant economies of scale, i.e. by choosing locations for their server hubs which take advantage of favorable energy and climate conditions or which are within jurisdictions that offer attractive investment benefits for IT infrastructure providers to lay out their facilities within their limits. These jurisdictions do not necessarily belong to countries with generally well-developed and robust IT laws. Therefore, establishing rules which will permit us to track down responsibility all the way down to the infrastructure level can contribute, via the teleological and the principle of extra-territoriality, to legal safety overall in relation to using cloud technologies.

1054 Refer also to Chapter 7.
1055 Benoit Dupont (note 111).
1056 See Chapters 2 and 8.

f. What challenges lie ahead in designing cloud computing regulation rules?

In designing the proposed cloud computing regulations, lawmakers will have to make many choices in response to several questions regarding the cloud computing phenomenon and how several of its parameters should be regulated. As per every law-making procedure[1057], designing the bouquet of cloud computing rules is a process with three distinct phases, namely conceptualization, implementation and assessment[1058]. The challenges and optimal ways to tackle them are discussed hereunder in light of the analysis on the internal perspective of cloud computing.

i. Challenges in conceptualizing cloud computing regulation

Challenges during the conceptualization phase of cloud computing laws are basic "horizontal" challenges law makers are confronted with when considering the regulation of any technological innovation[1059]. In the case of cloud computing, three appear to be the main challenges based on the analysis so far: justification of law and regulation, trade-offs between policy objectives, and conflicts among the different roles held by governments in relation to the cloud phenomenon.

– Justification

In every law-making process governments or, in general, legislative authorities, have a certain range of mechanisms available to detect legal and regulatory issues related the subject matter of the laws they are about to design. As it is commonly admitted, what issues do finally make it onto the legal and regulatory agenda greatly depends on the prevailing political economy in which an issue, in this case cloud computing, emerges and diffuses; accordingly, these conditions may vary across countries. As far as the cloud is concerned, analysis[1060] so far has demonstrated that, although the two jurisdictions under examination in this study (i.e. EU and

1057 For an in-depth analysis of what risks building any system of laws inherently carries as a process refer to: Alden Heintz, *The Dangers of Regulation*, 29 J Communication 129–134 (1979.)

1058 Trevor Bench-Capon & Giovanni Sartor (note 956).

1059 John G. Palfrey & Urs Gasser (note 235).

1060 See Chapter 3.

the US) may be following distinctly separate routes in the way they handle IT and, in particular, data-related issues, in both of them there is a strong momentum in civil society for taking decisive measures and adopting laws that will clear out the current blurry picture when it comes to regulating cloud technologies. This unanimous call for action should be heard by regulators and, apart from being a call for them to act, it can also serve as a perfect tool in working on producing rules for the cloud that will be based on common principles and will, therefore, be possible to be presented to both jurisdictions with an increased likelihood of being met favorably and embraced by all affected actors.

Moreover, on the outset of every law-making process, identification of legal and regulatory issues through mechanisms such as horizon scanning typically includes an assessment of the need for intervention, for instance in case a market failure is looming or has already occurred. When it comes to the cloud though, justification of law and regulation especially targeted at it becomes more complicated due to the fact that there is plenty of anecdotal evidence but not much empirical data available yet on its precise impact in a given area of concern[1061]. However, as analysis has shown already[1062], while there are truly numerous regulatory tools touching upon different manifestations or applications of cloud technologies, there still remains a lot of insecurity and friction both among these various tools and among different jurisdictions. The reason for that is that we are still missing the connecting substance among all these rules, i.e. we have yet to put in place rules regulating the cloud itself. Once such rules come to exist, and especially if a certain degree of universality is achieved in relation to their founding principles, all pre-existing rules will blend better with each other.

– Trade-offs

The wider field of IT regulation has been an area where, in the process of designing laws, there is traditionally heated debate regarding tensions and, not rarely, trade-offs among values that are attempted to be promoted and

1061 Primavera De Filippi, Primavera De Filippi & Luca Belli, *Law of the Cloud v Law of the Land: Challenges and Opportunities for Innovation*, 3 European Journal of Law and Technology 156–173 (2012); Deepak Puthal, B.P.S. Sahoo, Sambit Mishra & Satyabrata Swain (note 837).; Neil Robinson, Lorenzo Valeri, Jonathan Cave, Tony Starkey, Hans Graux, Sadie Creese & Paul P. Hopkins (note 119).

1062 See Chapter 4.

underlying policy objectives[1063]. In the case of cloud computing, such friction is clearly visible whenever lawmakers seek to establish or strengthen frameworks aimed at enhancing consumer trust in cloud computing technology. For example, whenever an update process on privacy legislation is underway, in Europe or in the USA, it always goes hand in hand with the concerns that respective massive surveillance programs on behalf of states pose on that privacy. This had been particularly true, for instance, during the recently terminated negotiation process regarding the EU's GDPR, which faced a lot of turbulence in light of other legislative initiatives of the European Commission focusing on the issues of health research or banking to name a few[1064]. Actually, those parallel policies contradicting the values of privacy and confidentiality of electronic communications, among others, are usually targeting cloud computing services and providers of them 'incriminating' them in the eyes of users for the harmful events which they may have to eventually undergo. However, this often leads to a blurry picture as to who is responsible for preserving safety and security of data in the cloud, who is tasked with balancing between the objectives pursued by different laws which, however, aim to regulate the same subject matter (e.g. data transfers). The proposed regulatory scheme for cloud networks, which will put emphasis on clearing out which cloud actor is tasked with what specific duties at each time throughout the cloud workflow, will help to shed light also on the issues of responsibility for abiding with the plethora of laws regulating individual manifestations or uses of cloud computing. Moreover, the proposed set of principles for regulating the cloud should also touch upon the issue of superiority between conflicting rules affecting the same areas of cloud-related activity[1065] putting an end to the insecurities that still so manifestly exist despite an

---

1063 J. Hoover (note 988).

1064 For further analysis on the points of conflict between the GDPR and other regulatory initiatives of EU law refer to: Paul de Hert & Vagelis Papakonstantinou, *The new General Data Protection Regulation. Still a sound system for the protection of individuals?*, 32 Computer Law & Security Review 179–194 (2016); Dias, Renata Dalle Molle Araujo, *The Potential Impact of the EU General Data Protection Regulation on Pharmacogenomics Research*, 36 Med. & L. 43–58 (2017); John Mark Michael Rumbold & Barbara Pierscionek, *The Effect of the General Data Protection Regulation on Medical Research*, 19 Journal of medical Internet research e47 (2017); Alexander Roßnagel ed. (note 285).

1065 See also Chapter 11.

already wide range of legal tools attempting to deal with all outstanding issues in the wider field of IT.

– Role conflicts

The third most important challenge that will expectedly come up when designing laws regulating the cloud is, as it has become evident of the analysis in this and the previous chapter, the conflict of roles that the same actors are tasked with at different instances of the cloud computing workflow. In fact, role conflicts occur not only with regard to actors of the network but also on behalf of governments, in the sense of legislative, regulatory or executive bodies[1066]. An extensive review of broad cloud computing strategies implemented by governments around the world indicates that governmental bodies typically play more than one role in relation to the cloud[1067]. In fact, on most occasions, governmental organizations are simultaneously users, regulators, coordinators, promoters, researchers, even service providers within the context of cloud computing. This double pool of conflicts from the part of cloud actors and governmental authorities alike, calls for immediate settlement in the context of a regulatory framework for the cloud. As it has been argued earlier, putting in place rules that will answer the question of who is responsible for what within a cloud network not based on specific applications of the cloud, as case studies, but in a generic, role-description based manner, will decisively help in clearing out conflicting situations as these. To the extent that this is achieved, it will be beneficial not only for reinforcing the sentiment of trust to the law from users of cloud computing but it will also further encourage adoption of the cloud from stakeholders both domestically and internationally.

ii. Challenges in implementing cloud computing regulation

Beyond the conceptualization phase, drafting rules for the cloud is a process which is also possible to stumble upon a series of challenges most relevant to the implementation of these rules. Bearing in mind the analysis so far, three such challenges seem particularly noteworthy: problems with re-

1066 Stefanie Leimeister, Markus Böhm, Christoph Riedl & Helmut Krcmar (note 975).

1067 A. Froomkin (note 322).

gard to definitions, timing issues, and the challenge of appropriate tool selection.

– Metaphors and definitions

In any case of drafting rules for an innovative or unprecedented phenomenon, lawmakers and regulators typically resort to analogies or metaphors to understand and describe it[1068]. However, metaphors have the capacity to dictate regulatory thinking at the conceptual level and then influence approaches to the law at the implementation level. Similarly, the definitions used to describe this new phenomenon that is to be regulated or certain aspects of it can affect the way we approach these laws. So far, regulators wishing to define cloud computing in the context of any laws relevant to manifestations of it, confronted with the high degree of technicality and the fluidity in the cloud computing environment, have chosen not to develop their own technical definitions, but instead resort to definitions set forth by standard setting organizations. One such definition, which has been already discussed earlier in this study[1069], is the NIST cloud computing definition that was the proposed in the US Cloud Computing Act of 2012[1070], which sought to establish a new type of violation involving unauthorized access to computer systems in the Computer Fraud and Abuse Act[1071]. The proposal was met with criticism from legal scholars for its definitional vagueness[1072]. And this, despite the fact that the NIST definition of cloud computing is generally regarded as one of the most technically accurate regarding the cloud to date[1073]. Following the analysis presented so far, it is strongly recommended that a future regulatory framework for cloud computing should be based on a definition that will not only describe what cloud computing does, from a technical perspective, but also explain its dual nature as a concept, i.e. that it is not just about the external manifestations we see of it but also about the way the

---

1068 Trevor Bench-Capon & Giovanni Sartor (note 956).

1069 See Chapter 4.

1070 "S. 3569 — 112th Congress: Cloud Computing Act of 2012." www.GovTrack.us. 2012. November 8, 2016 https://www.govtrack.us/congress/bills/112/s3569.

1071 Refer also to Chapter 6.

1072 Goldman E., The Proposed "Cloud Computing Act of 2012," and How Internet Regulation Can Go Awry, available at http://www.forbes.com/sites/ericgoldman/2012/10/02/the-proposed-cloud-computing-act-of-2012-and-how-internet-regulation-can-go-awry/#7b0b6424113a; lastly accessed on 11/8/2016.

1073 See Chapter 4.

underlying technology and hardware are organized around certain actors to construct, all together, a dynamic and continuously changing business workflow. In this way, the subsequent rules will not only reflect on the external but also on the internal aspect of cloud computing dealing with the whole range of cloud-related issues calling for regulatory arrangement.

– Timing

Another critical question inherent with every law under development is the timing in which designated rules will intervene to settle the issues they refer to. In particular, when it comes to laws referring to rapidly changing areas of technology, determining the right timing when the negotiated provisions will apply is a critical factor for the effectiveness of them[1074]. As a result, lawmakers and regulators need to carefully consider timing issues when attempting to strike a balance between the creation of a friendly environment for cloud service providers on the one hand and safeguarding users on the other. Ideally, the relevant actors use a broad range of analytical tools in this process, including an assessment of the maturity of the technology, standards, and markets with strong network effects[1075], to name the most crucial ones. Throughout this study, it has been repeatedly argued that, while laws on the applications made possible thanks to cloud computing technologies usually adopt a punitive or repressive approach trying to describe in what way could harmful effects from malpractice with these applications could be limited, cloud computing regulation should adopt a primarily proactive approach focusing on who is charged with what functions and duties in that context throughout the cloud network. In this manner, it is expected that affected entities will be better aware of their duties and the preparations required to live up to depending on the role(s) they are playing within a cloud network, thus increasing the chances for smooth and transparent function of the cloud market and minimizing the odds for harmful events or spillovers thereof.

– Tool Selection

Last but not least, one key implementation challenge regulators invariably face when designing a law is to select the appropriate tool that is best suited to solve the regulatory issues or legal problems that had been pinpoint-

1074 Paul M. Schwartz (note 157).

1075 Gabriela Zanfir ed., What Happens in the Cloud Stays in the Cloud, or Why the Cloud's Architecture Should Be Transformed in 'Virtual Territorial Scope' (2013.)

ed and led to the formulation of a said piece of legislation[1076]. Truth be told, the fact that so far law making in the field of IT has been focusing on particular manifestations of IT technologies has resulted, for the moment, in lack of data which does not permit to immediately understand the contours of the problem of regulating the cloud itself in detail[1077]. Conversely, on the side of remedies, matching problems with tools repeatedly turns to be complicated by the fact that data about the performance of a given remedy in a specific context rarely exist in advance. In any case, given that we are talking about a sector with so many overlapping and interconnected phenomena, the use of a remedy tool with regard to each of them should align with the mix of policy instruments chosen by regulators for neighboring phenomena. Necessarily, putting in place and selecting the right tools requires considering a number of factors including political, technical or market contexts, to name a few. In response to this challenge, the proposed regulatory framework on the cloud should be constructed not with a view to replacing existing tools and remedies but with the aim of supplementing them, helping, particularly, to clear out the picture as to which remedy is more suitable and at whom among the different cloud actors it is addressable at any given time.

iii. Projecting challenges in the assessment phase of a regulation on the cloud

In the context of every law drafting process the latest step of work is to make a projection of the negotiated rules being applied and assess what will be the actual status quo in the field they aim to regulate after they enter into force. With relation to a potential law regulating the cloud the following are the main challenges regulators need to make an estimate about for the post-application period.

– Measures of success

The most common front where assessment challenges arise in law-making is that of establishing criteria with which it is possible to measure whether a law has been successful and at what extent[1078]. It is a fact that among different jurisdictions there is no generally accepted and stable set of crite-

1076 Urs Gasser (note 959).
1077 Benoit Dupont (note 111).
1078 Urs Gasser (note 959).

ria to evaluate the performance of various tools lawmakers and regulators have at their disposal across different regulatory contexts. In some cases, such criteria might focus on parameters such as coerciveness, directness, automaticity, and visibility[1079]. In others, criteria such as effectiveness, efficiency, and flexibility might rather be used[1080]. What is more, while at the moment a law is adopted everyone agrees that there should be constant evaluation of its effectiveness and, after a relative period of time since its introduction there should be an assessment as to the necessity of any modifications to it, more often than not these priorities atone or do not get much attention at all. Beyond instruments, it is often not clear what success means for a piece of legislation, in particular with respect to the outcomes of technology regulation. As it has been analyzed[1081], for instance, in one jurisdiction success for a law regulating data transfers can mean making it as conditional as possible to let any such transfer happen, while in another it can mean having corrective tools available for anyone that may suffer any kind of damage from one such transfer to amend it once it occurs. Moreover, the complexity of such normative questions regarding the result of regulatory interventions and whether it can be evaluated positively or negatively only increases where multiple tools regarding distinct but definitely adjacent manifestations of a wider phenomenon are at work simultaneously, or where a variety of instruments are used to pursue different and, at times, even conflicting policy objectives, as discussed before[1082]. It is possibly still too premature to know how regulating the very core of the cloud computing phenomenon will affect the overall functioning of the IT field. Nevertheless, bearing in mind the analysis so far and the fact that the proposed rules regarding the cloud from its internal perspective are not meant to replace but to supplement and fortify already existing legislation on the most important cloud-based phenomena and applications, two indexes could already serve as measurements regarding the success of cloud laws: on the one hand, the extent at which frictions over which jurisdiction takes prerogative over the others are alleviated. On the

1079 Coglianese, C., Measuring Regulatory Performance: EVALUATING THE IMPACT OF REGULATION AND REGULATORY POLICY, OECD, Expert Paper No. 1, August 2012, available at https://www.oecd.org/gov/regulatory-policy/1_coglianese%20web.pdf (lastly accessed: 11/8/2016.)

1080 Id.

1081 See Chapter 6.

1082 See Chapter 5.

other hand, given that the proposed principles on cloud regulation are meant to harmonize the effects of laws of different jurisdictions by respecting, at the same time, the different approaches each of these take on the same issues, a measurement of success for the proposed regulatory principles can be the degree at which the protective effect achieved within one jurisdiction is also deemed to be satisfactory under the standards of the other. If these two measurements do not reach adequate values, then even further refinement will be in order.

– Collateral effects

Regulation in general and all the more so regulation of such innovative phenomena as IT technologies can lead to collateral effects[1083]. A distinctive example of this type of challenge are the side-effects of the Digital Millennium Copyright Act in the US[1084], which was enacted aiming – among others – to put in place additional layers of protection of copyrighted works, but has been arguably used in ways totally unintended by the legislator. In the case of rules regulating the cloud from the internal perspective, the most likely collateral effect is the one most common with reference to any piece of IT legislation, i.e. the possibility that it may fail to comprehend the way technology will evolve and become soon ineffective or create legal voids that could be exploitable in unintended manners[1085]. However, this is a possibility that can never be totally taken off the table; the soundest advice IT regulators should always bear in mind is that rules referring to such dynamic phenomena as IT technologies require from them constant high alert and a keen eye to spot whenever the time has come for the next update. Besides, the fact that the proposed rules are not meant to extend to external manifestations of the cloud but touch only its internal aspects guarantees that, so long as cloud computing remains the standard facilitating IT technology, the rules on it can only work to the benefit of both technological progress and users' interests at the same

1083 Trevor Bench-Capon & Giovanni Sartor (note 956).

1084 The Digital Millennium Copyright Act (DMCA) is a US copyright law implementing two 1996 treaties of the World Intellectual Property Organization (WIPO). It criminalizes production and dissemination of technology, devices, or services intended to circumvent measures (commonly known as digital rights management or DRM) that control access to copyrighted works. It also criminalizes the act of circumventing an access control, whether or not there is actual infringement of copyright itself. In addition, it heightens the penalties for copyright infringement on the Internet. Pub. L. 105-304; 112 Stat. 2860 (1998.)

1085 Chris Reed (note 363).

time. The aim is to regulate the cloud not in order to disrupt it but in order to better streamline its capacities and channel them in ways that will maximize their positive while decreasing their negative potential.

– Ability to learn

Regulating such a state-of-the-art phenomenon like cloud computing, always calls for an assumption of uncertainty. The cloud computing legal and regulatory environment is characterized by high degrees of technical complexity and fast changing market conditions, to name only a few of its volatile aspects[1086]. These combined with the rest of the conceptual, implementation, and assessment phase challenges bring to the surface the need for regulatory systems to incorporate feedback channels, and mechanisms of self-assessment and correction[1087]. Putting in place such safeguards is anything but trivial for the longevity of cloud computing regulation. Options so far have included sunset clauses, periodic reviews, and consultation mechanisms[1088], but often these prove to be either relatively crude or not adequately flexible to live up to the speed of evolution of high-end technologies and corresponding market dynamics; the long-lasting review process of technology-relevant European Union legislation, only recently verified through the labyrinthine process of adoption of the GDPR is indicative thereof. Adopting rules on the cloud with the features and generic nature proposed in this study will not solve this challenge per se but will definitely set in motion a very crucial process towards the corroboration of IT law as an independent legal discipline. Rules focusing on the internal aspect of cloud networks could serve as the missing link that will ignite the chain of events that will offer to IT laws as a body of legislation the systematization and coherence they are currently missing, as it will be argued in the conclusions of this study.

1086 See also Chapters 2 and 8.

1087 J. Hoover (note 988).

1088 Coglianese op cit n 128 supra.

CHAPTER 10. Principles for regulating the cloud (3); the adoption of cloud computing regulation as the big leap forward from governing to governance in IT law

a. Introduction – scope of this chapter

Reference has already been made in earlier parts of this study[1089] to the need for cloud computing and the regulation of it to do the transition from a regime of governing to one of governance, more in touch with the real nature and features of the cloud phenomenon. In this chapter, following the analysis focusing on the technical and organizational/workflow aspects of the cloud, attention is paid to how this transition towards a new regulatory understanding regarding cloud computing can be set in motion and what are the fundamental concepts it should be based on. Moreover, concrete regulatory principles that will facilitate this transition are proposed for adoption by major jurisdictions with regard to the cloud phenomenon, again not with a view to homogenizing the way the cloud is legally dealt with but to making sure that, while respect will continue to be paid to the specificities and particularities of each jurisdiction and legal tradition, ultimately all major jurisdictions will work towards achieving comparable results/effects from the way cloud computing is regulated.

b. Doing laws based on the local and global experience: the differences in approach and the need to combine both perspectives in the case of cloud computing

State and all other regulators, of a lower or higher level, have to deal with an increasing number of policy matters that are defined by what is often described as a global, borderless nature. On the other hand, when called to produce laws that will be used for regulating these matters, those regulators have to work and formulate rules based on the experience and knowl-

1089 See Chapters 5 and 6.

edge they already have or to which they have access to and the objectives they wish to achieve through these regulations[1090], in terms of the results they hope to get back from applying these laws and the extent, geographic and material one, in which these laws will be applicable. This issue of being tasked with the production of laws applicable to a limited geographic area but having the potential to affect or touch upon issues that do affect the lives and activities of practically every law subject worldwide has been in the centre of attention of prominent scholars[1091], several of whom coming from the liberal movement. In particular, the tradeoff between regulating on the local and global level and the respective local or global knowledge upon which this rule making process is based has been at the centre of attention of Friedrich Hayek and his program[1092]. In Hayek's bipolar construction, on the one side lies 'the scope of the administrative state's regulatory jurisdiction; this is the large-scale question of government versus markets'[1093]. The second level is 'the internal organization of the regulatory bureaucracy, within the area committed to the administrative state's regulatory jurisdiction'[1094].

On each of the two sides of the equilibrium lie respective but substantially differing sources of knowledge, information, experience and expertise[1095]. In particular, on the one side there is the scope of the administrative state with its internal organization. On this side, Hayek puts emphasis on the benefits of local knowledge and adaptation to the contingencies of

1090 J. Goldring (note 258).

1091 This issue is continuously discussed in legal scholarship. For a thorough overview on it and its aspect which are of closer relation to this research, refer to: Martin Boodman, *The Myth of Harmonization of Laws*, 39 The American Journal of Comparative Law 699–724 (1991); Giandomenico Majone, *Policy Harmonization. Limits and Alternatives*, 16 Journal of Comparative Policy Analysis: Research and Practice 4–21 (2014); Antony Anghie & C.G Weeramantry, Legal visions of the 21st century: essays in honour of judge Christopher Weeramantry (op. 1998); M. J. Eger, *Emerging Restrictions on Transnational Data Flows: Privacy Protection or Non-Tariff Trade Barriers*, 10 Law & Pol 1055–1105 (1978); Alfred Aman, *A Global Perspective on Current Regulatory Reform: Rejection, Relocation, or Reinvention?*, 2 2 Indiana Journal of Global Legal Studies 429 (1995) 429–464 (1995).

1092 Friedrich A. von Hayek, The road to serfdom (2005); Friedrich A. von Hayek (note 884).

1093 Friedrich A. von Hayek (note 1092).

1094 *Id.*

1095 Adrian Vermeule ed. (note 884).

time and place, but fails to do justice or downplays a major tradeoff: that centralized inclusive regulation is indispensable for epistemic coordination[1096]. As classic liberal theory teaches[1097], 'spillovers, externalities, and lost opportunities for economic synergy may arise not only because of conflicts of interest and problems of collective action, but also for epistemic reasons': in the chain of a production process for laws on the cloud, this translates into actors (i.e. legislators) with thick localized information who, confined by this short perspective, may be myopic about what other actors of the chain (i.e. the actors actively comprising the cloud computing workflow) are doing. In the end, a major challenge for any kind of law, no matter how extensive is the range of its geographical validity, is not just effective command-and-control, but also epistemic coordination and the creation of common knowledge and measures that 'dispel the local myopia of market actors'[1098].

In view of this double challenge for any kind of law, the question rises how all the relevant but also ample knowledge could be collected and coordinated in order to serve as the raw material for efficient, pragmatic and to-the-point laws. According to Hayek, the administrative state itself, with its range of institutions can take up the task of 'aggregating thick local knowledge, including the tacit, practical knowledge from daily experience'[1099] which is so crucial for the production of efficient legislation. Taking the case of the European Union as an example, the EU Parliament itself stands as a body of representatives with local knowledge from real life experience from different parts of Europe, while the various administrative agencies carrying some degree of competence on a given subject matter often incorporate actors with industry-specific or area-specific skills and information. The administrative state, which largely coincides with what we perceive as the (conventional) regulator, possesses much more than abstract or statistical technocratic expertise; every state structure, be it a national, federal or intergovernmental, even an international

1096 Michèle Lamont, *Rethinking Expertise. By Harry Collins and Robert Evans. Chicago. University of Chicago Press, 2007. Pp. 153. $37.50*, 115 American Journal of Sociology 569–571 (2009.)

1097 Adrian Vermeule ed. (note 884).

1098 *Id.*

1099 Friedrich A. von Hayek (note 1092).

one, has developed a representative bureaucracy devoted to the gathering and exploitation of local knowledge[1100].

In issues so complex as information technology and the cloud, there is heated debate as to which regulator is better qualified to do laws for them. There have been scholars who have argued in favor of local regulators and others who favor national or federal ones[1101]. As it has been argued throughout the course of this study, there is no right or wrong choice with regard to this issue. Actually, regulating the cloud is not an issue of who is better qualified to do it but rather of how it will be done and what it will aim for. In fact, actual state practice from national or federal states, proves that, absent some constitutional restrictions, regulatory bodies from all levels can intervene and regulate on most matters so that the subjects involved in each regulatory affair (for example, the actors that were presented in earlier parts of this study when it comes to cloud computing[1102]) can be constrained by state regulation as well as federal, in the case of federal states, or intergovernmental, as it happens, for instance, with EU law[1103]. Actually, provided that there is efficient coordination, in a number of domains federal or intergovernmental regulation may serve for clearing the way for state regulation that will ultimately contribute to regulatory uniformity, in order to reduce legal uncertainty.

In light of these, it must be made clear that the existence of multiple levels of regulators and regulations in no way undermines the importance of the administrative state's function to operate through command-and-control regulation[1104]. It is just that, in complex matters, such as the ones with which the law has to deal with in today's post-modern reality, this coordinating function[1105] of regulation may often be pursued through predominantly informational and epistemic measures[1106] instead of classic command-and-control rules.

Consequently, while the Hayekian construction succeeds in recognizing the two sides of actors when it comes to regulation prepared by the admin-

---

1100 Adrian Vermeule ed. (note 884).

1101 M. Gillen (note 415).

1102 See Chapter 9.

1103 *Id.*

1104 Adrian Vermeule ed. (note 884).

1105 Robert B. Ahdieh, *The Visible Hand: Coordination Functions of the Regulatory State*, 09 Emory University School of Law, Public Law and Legal Theory Research Paper Series 578–649 (2009.)

1106 *Id.*

istrative state, it stopped before realizing the importance of local knowledge towards efficient regulation, most likely due to the fact that complicated regulatory phenomena such as cloud computing were largely not a reality until a couple of decades ago. However, IT and cloud computing are perfect case studies to start off from Hayek's position and, after combining it with the principles of the theory on knowledge and the law[1107], to arrive in a modern formula that will guarantee the production of equally or, even better, more efficient regulation in the future.

Nevertheless, at the same time, Hayek's bipolar structure serves to conceptualize the competing pools of actors in the field of regulation and law making, in order for us to have the complete picture of dynamics that should be taken into account and need to be compromised in order for laws to actually work and achieve real results in the end. In particular, any law for a phenomenon so dynamic as the cloud cannot only aim at taming the forces of the market in favor of local knowledge about the needs that should be entertained from a particular set of rules. Actually, the market is only one of the institutional mechanisms for generating and then aggregating local knowledge[1108]. But it would be reckless to stress, from the one side, the importance of local knowledge for concluding efficient laws, and, at the same time, argue that only market mechanisms are good enough for collecting and aggregating it[1109]. Instead, one must carry out a fair institutional comparison between, or among, all institutional possibilities for contributing to the creation and maintenance of efficient laws. Specifically, and contrary to the voices putting forward the irrelevance of obsolescence of it, the regulatory state itself can still be justified as one of the key mechanisms for aggregating local knowledge. Similarly, as it has been repeatedly argued throughout this study, in the field of cloud computing regulation achieving the optimal results is not a question of choosing who, among competent potential regulators, does better or the best laws. Rather, what it is really needed is to coordinate among all these competent regula-

1107 I. Augsberg, Informationsverwaltungsrecht: Zur kognitiven Dimension der rechtlichen Steuerung von Verwaltungsentscheidungen (2014.)

1108 D. Dyzenhaus & T. Poole, Law, Liberty and State: Oakeshott, Hayek and Schmitt on the Rule of Law (2015.)

1109 For additional considerations on the issue of how it is best to aggregate knowledge for regulating the cloud, refer also to the analysis on the theory of 'law and knowledge' and how it could be used as a valid method to construct a cloud regulatory framework as outlined in Chapter 7 of this study.

tors, to agree on elementary common principles that will define all the pieces of laws they may bring out and to make sure that, in the end, they will all work towards the same end result: a pragmatic and as timeless as possible regime of sound governance instead of an ever anxious to catch up with new standards regime of governing.

The next point of friction in the debate about how to build efficient laws for the cloud refers to the nature these laws should have, i.e. whether they should be designed with a broad and generic perspective in mind or whether they should be developed on an ad hoc basis, following actual developments within a regulator's area of competence the challenges and outstanding issues of which they would attempt to settle. In the theory of the administrative state as it has been promoted in the USA[1110], these two genres of law are described as synoptic and contextual laws, respectively[1111]. Although the terms are not unanimously adopted, they are the most illustrative ones in capturing the antithesis in thinking behind the style and philosophy of laws each of them represents. It also needs to be underlined that, of course, in reality there is no such clear-cut dividing line between the two types of laws; this dichotomy is more of a conventional scheme than a depiction of reality, in which there is expectedly a continuum between the two extremes[1112] and various degrees of synoptic or contextual elements in each piece of legislation. However, the scheme is useful in order for the possibilities that each path or type of law offers to be appreciated and comprehended.

If we would need to name one scholar as the leading proponent of synoptic laws, Justice Stephen Breyer of the US Supreme Court would probably be the most suitable choice. Throughout his scholarly path, Breyer has gone as far as expressing the idea that regulating risk via laws has become such a complicated challenge in modern societies that in effect it requires

1110 H. M. Collins, Tacit and explicit knowledge (2013.)

1111 Adrian Vermeule ed. (note 884).; D. Dyzenhaus & T. Poole (note 1108).. For further details on the antithesis between synoptic and contextual laws and the broader reasoning behind generic versus ad hoc approaches in scientific discourse, refer to: Ricardo Alonso, Wouter Dessein & Niko Matouschek, *When Does Coordination Require Centralization?*, 98 American Economic Review 145–179 (2008); Nicholas Bagley & Richard L. Revesz, *Centralized Oversight of the Regulatory State*, 106 Columbia Law Review 1260–1330 (2006).

1112 Stephen G. Breyer, Breaking the vicious circle. Toward effective risk regulation, vol. 1992 (1993.)

regulators who possess global knowledge[1113]. In his view, for any regulation to be a working one, 'it should achieve to reflect and take into account an overview of all socially or economically relevant risks for the subject matter it touches upon; it should attempt to present them in order of priority and it should regulate them just to the point at which the net social costs of regulation are equal to the benefits, but no more'[1114].

On the opposite side of synoptic regulation lies uncoordinated, socially wasteful regulation by a vast number of partially-informed and only to-a-certain-degree competent agencies and bodies. However, such a dispersed regulatory body is expected, and to an extent it has already been proved so, to suffer from three main drawbacks[1115]:

- tunnel vision[1116], a kind of obsessive focus in which regulatory agencies go as far as eliminating the entire amount of the particular risk within their jurisdiction, even if the costs of doing so far exceed the benefits;
- random agenda selection, which refers to the tendency of uncoordinated agencies to devote resources to regulating risks on different grounds than a ranking of expected social benefits; and
- Inconsistency, a condition in which uncoordinated agencies regulate similar risks differently or different risks similarly.

Such a picture could be observed overall currently with the myriad pieces of law regulating different aspects of cloud-facilitated IT applications and processes, due to the fact that there is still no common basis with regard to regulating their actual facilitator, i.e. the cloud. The problem occurs indeed not only within the same jurisdiction (i.e. in the case of federal states where both federal and regional or local bodies have concurrent competence) but also in the case of intergovernmental jurisdictions, such as the EU. As it has been observed, with the case of the American administrative state in mind: "decentralized organizations have a natural advantage in adapting decisions to local conditions, since the decisions are made by managers with the best information about those conditions. However, such organizations also have a natural disadvantage since the manager in charge of one division is uncertain about the decisions made by others."[1117]

1113 *Id.*

1114 *Id.*

1115 Michèle Lamont (note 1096).

1116 Adrian Vermeule ed. (note 884).

1117 *Id.*

However, as it has been explained, absolutely synoptic or contextual laws do not exist and all the more so, absolutely synoptically or contextually organized administrative structures do not exist either. Despite the assertions of both camps, neither can claim that they possess by privilege full rationality or absolute expertise; rather, bounded rationality affects both decentralized and centralized decision making[1118]. In a centralized orientation, bounded rationality manifests itself in a 'one size fits all' policy. In a decentralized arrangement, bounded rationality is traced as a lack of awareness of synergies across subdivisions. Instead, just as it was the case with the mechanisms for collecting and aggregating knowledge, lawmaking entities of all levels can be useful and have a role to play in efficiently regulating cloud computing. What is important in order for them to succeed in this aim is to coordinate among them so that they don't overlap with each other.

In summary, the distinction between local and global knowledge as well as the one between synoptic and contextual legislation is essential for understanding the issues of knowledge production, collection and aggregation as well as the topic of rule-making from all its aspects and extremes. As it has been demonstrated, the way regulatory bodies arrange how they collect and aggregate information as well as how they coordinate among themselves in order to define areas and subfields of competence ought to be a central agenda item in the debate and efforts for setting up a prescriptive and proactively oriented legal and political theory across a variety of topics and definitely with regard to cloud computing. Hayek's views, which served as the starting point for this discourse, may be directly relevant to these questions, but at the same time they have also turned out to be largely untenable. Regulation of complex issues such as the cloud cannot be left to just one type of actors relevant with the phenomenon, be them the market or regulators only. The market is definitely an important aggregator of information, including local knowledge but, at the same time, an imperfect one; on the other side of the administrative state construction lies another type of actors, equally essential but imperfect in themselves, i.e. all the different kinds of administrative authorities competent for the subject matter of a certain legislation, in our case all bodies that deal, one way or another, with cloud computing. All these entities do have and they will continue to have a meaningful role to play in the strive

1118 Stephen G. Breyer (note 1112).

to achieve efficient cloud regulation. Therefore, among the tasks of those that will be assigned to draft cloud computing laws should not be to try to prioritize the role and significance of certain bodies against others or, even more, to legislate that only certain among them are competent but some others are not. Instead, the task of a future body of cloud computing laws should be to coordinate the activities and regulatory priorities of all concurrent governing authorities of the field so that, in the end and while showing respect to the legal traditions and particularities of the environment within which each of them rules, the desirable effects of advanced legal certainty, coherence and market safety will be achieved for the cloud domain on an as universal level as possible.

c. The ability of law to learn and evolve; how to achieve law evolution in the case of cloud computing

Legal theory suggests in multiple ways that one of the cornerstone features of laws is their dynamic nature[1119]; their capability to change and evolve following respective social and political influences. As human societies progress or, anyway, develop economically, technologically and culturally, new challenges and disputes come to surface. As a rule, lower courts and other types of law applying bodies (e.g. arbitrators or independent authorities) decide on cases in light of existing legal rules[1120]; however, the results they achieve and the quality of the solutions proposed with their decisions eventually do not live up to changing political, social and cultural realities. It is precisely that moment when legislatures, rule-making agencies or higher courts are called to respond by modifying the legal rules or applying them differently, making sure that the results of their decisions will conform to the new realities[1121].

It is generally accepted that there are two ways in which the effect of a rule can be modified, specifically by

---

1119 John A. Ferejohn & Barry R. Weingast, *A positive theory of statutory interpretation*, 12 International Review of Law and Economics 263–279 (1992.)

1120 John T. Noonan (note 665).. For more scholarly analysis on the ways in which the effect of a rule can be modified as well as a succinct reply to L. A. Hart's approach refer to: Lon L. Fuller, *Positivism and Fidelity to Law. A Reply to Professor Hart*, 71 Harvard Law Review 630–672 (1958).

1121 John T. Noonan (note 665).

- changing the rule itself, for example, by making amendments to preconditions or modifying listed exceptions to the rule, or
- changing the meaning of the rule's constituent concepts[1122].

Most scholars refer to the first type of change as 'change in the rule's structure' and to the second type as 'change in the meaning of the rule's terms'[1123]. Change in legal rules and their concepts are essential elements for achieving the much-cherished dynamism of law, a feature that is becoming more and more crucial in today's continuously changing world[1124].

Nevertheless, despite the indispensability of change for both legal concepts and rules, the way in which each of the two progress and are modified is not identical. For starters, change in neither of them can be one-sided; it is rather organized in a manner that legal philosophers standardly call 'open textured'[1125], as it is not defined by necessary and sufficient conditions which are universally valid over their domain of application. Instead, according to Herbert Hart's theory of law, "legal concepts have a 'core of settled meaning' in which there is little debate over interpretation and a 'penumbra' in which interpretation is debatable. Legal rules derive their dynamic nature in part through the dynamic, open-textured nature of the terms used in the rules"[1126]. Of course, evolution does not affect only on the level of drafting (i.e. with regard to how regulators deal with them) but also on the level of interpretation of their meaning. Consequently, not only do "rules change when new prerequisites, exceptions, or conclusions arise, but also when new interpretations of terms used in the rule are made as cases are decided and rules are applied"[1127].

In light of the above, it becomes evident that in the field of cloud computing, as in many other fields, improving regulation is not only a matter of replacing existing laws with newer ones because older rules have been found to have become obsolete. Laws and overall legal certainty are also improved by putting in place basic regulation that will help us interpret and apply pre-existing legislation in a more coherent and in touch with

---

1122 *Id.*

1123 Robert B. Ahdieh (note 1105).

1124 Stephen G. Breyer (note 1112).

1125 Tomasz Zurek & Michał Araszkiewicz, Modeling teleological interpretation (2013.)

1126 H. L. A. Hart (note 664).

1127 John T. Noonan (note 665).

technological reality manner. In addition, improvement is also achieved by agreeing on the fundamental concepts and principles that should be at the core of all executive laws across different jurisdictions in order for law subjects to enjoy, as much as possible, comparable levels of protection with reference to an issue which is of a genuinely borderless nature.

The process of legislators and bodies applying the law is often paralleled to a learning system[1128]. In the end, it becomes clear that rules and their constituent terms change in light of the experience of deciding new cases or dealing with novel phenomena (when on the law-making level). However, there are fundamental differences in how legislatures, agencies and courts can effect, through their practice, this change in legal rules. Legislating bodies and agencies are the actors in a position to effect structural changes to laws[1129]. Courts process and evolve rules and definitions, too, thus they also effect structural changes, but beyond that, a court also has the capacity to change the meaning of a rule's constituent terms as it applies the rule in deciding a new problem[1130]. In several parts of this study we have seen several legal procedures before courts which have pointed out the need for IT laws to evolve and update themselves in view of developments in actual life and technology. Such occurrences of court decisions on cloud-related matters which point to a need for further refinement of cloud computing regulation have also existed in recent years[1131], further strengthening the call for adoption of shared fundamental principles on cloud computing regulation that will facilitate the transition from a regime of governing the cloud within each and every jurisdiction to one of cloud governance on a cross-jurisdictional and as geographically broad as possible basis.

These arguments regarding learning as an integral part of the process of law evolution and reform would not be complete without a few observations with regard to the inherent differences between a law learning process and one of some other discipline, such as physics or chemistry or of a

---

1128 Kevin D. Ashley & Edwina L. Rissland, *Law, learning and representation*, 150 Artificial Intelligence 17–58 (2003.)

1129 KIIT University ed., 2015 International Conference on Computational Intelligence & Networks (CINE.)

1130 *Id.*

1131 Namely, C-362/14 Maximillian Schrems v Data Protection Commissioner (note 417) as well as Case C-131/12 Google Spain SL, Google Inc. v Agencia Española de Protección de Datos (AEPD), Mario Costeja González, Case C-131/12 (note 486).

machine learning program[1132]. In fact, a law learning process is different from a machine learning program in the sense that the latter may discover a new law of physics, for example, out of instances of its application but does not and cannot create one. On the contrary, a learning process in the context of a law's application is not only limited to observing facts with a view to discovering the rules that explain them but it can also make use of the knowledge gained through these observations in order to create laws that will determine how the instances under observation could evolve. And actually, this evolution does not need to be identical to what has been observed so far; it can rather be essentially different.

While this observation could be the starting point of a philosophical discourse of considerable depth regarding how laws are evolving through and because of everyday practice and the knowledge accumulated out of it[1133], it does not suffice to explain the complex constraints on courts, and even on legislatures, in formulating and adjusting legal rules[1134]. Lawmakers are by definition and at an always accelerated pace challenged with accommodating developing ethical norms, economic and political principles, social policies, public expectations, past commitments and decisions, language-related conventions, and technological advances[1135]. These processes[1136] of discovering legal rules, subjecting them to rigorous scrutiny with regard to the above complex criteria, and evaluating the tradeoffs they effect can differentiate from one jurisdiction to the other and this is absolutely expected if differing legal traditions are taken into account. However, in essence, formulating legal rules is a process of discovering what will work in accommodating these criteria, not creating arbitrary norms out of nothing without consequences. Therefore, depending on the legal sector that is each time under focus, rule-making cannot be a laboratory process, 'sterilized' of any kind of influence from neighboring or generally important legal orders, let alone when their subject matter extends well

1132 International Workshop on Computational Autonomy (2003.)

1133 I. Augsberg (note 1107).

1134 Robert B. Ahdieh (note 1105).

1135 Kevin D. Ashley & Edwina L. Rissland (note 1128).

1136 For more extensive analysis on the types of process of law making and amendment, refer to: Edward H. Levi & Frederick F. Schauer, An introduction to legal reasoning (2013); Ronald Dworkin, Law's empire (1986); Cass R. Sunstein, *ON ANALOGICAL REASONING*, 106 Harvard Law Review 741–791 (1993); Scott Brewer, *Exemplary Reasoning. Semantics, Pragmatics, and the Rational Force of Legal Argument by Analogy*, 109 Harvard Law Review 923–1028 (1996.)

across the conventional margins among various jurisdictions. This interdependence is becoming all the more decisive in dynamic topics such as cloud computing. Insisting that the body of laws governing the cloud in one jurisdiction can be totally sealed against the expectations of its subjects falling under the competence of different legal orders but being potentially affected by the said body of rules as well, directly or indirectly, does more harm than good. Most importantly, it degrades the quality of the overall learning system through which constant law modification and update is possible. In the end, if IT laws are to remain relevant and improve their livability in view of the lightning speed at which the phenomena they address are changing, they need to prioritize towards a governance regime that will conserve legal cohesion in an as broader as possible area of application. And cloud computing regulation, as the body of rules that will govern the foundations of IT, is the ideal starting point for this change in perspective to be set in motion.

d. How proportionality and teleological reasoning can help cloud computing regulation make IT laws overall more efficient

Teleological reasoning is one of the oldest and most established norms in law making and interpretation[1137]. Proportionality is a relatively newer concept yet it has gained considerable relevance particularly in light of the ever more complex phenomena calling for regulation across conventional jurisdictional borders[1138]. These two norms combined can make an actual difference in both legislation and adjudication in the field of cloud com-

---

1137 Teleological reasoning is a term used by multiple disciplines to refer to a whole system of thinking which attempts to describe things in terms of their apparent purpose, directive principle, or goal. Its name stems from the word 'teleology' (from Greek telos, meaning end or purpose). For more details with regard to how teleology has been applied in law, refer to: Donald H. Berman & Carole D. Hafner, Representing teleological structure in case-based legal reasoning: the missing link (1993). For further insights into the teleological interpretation of laws refer to: Aharon Barak & Sari Bashi, Purposive Interpretation in Law (2011); Frank B. Cross, Theory and practice of statutory interpretation (2012.)

1138 Proportionality is a general principle in law which spans several special (although related) concepts. The concept of proportionality is used as a criterion of fairness and justice in statutory interpretation processes, especially in constitutional law, as a logical method intended to assist in discerning the correct balance between the restriction imposed by a corrective measure and the severity of

puting. The reasoning behind such an argument stems from the very essence of legislative action and the forces driving it. In details, according to an established argumentation of which Giovani Sartor is a champion, "legislative action can be guided not only by constitutional action-norms, but also by constitutional goal-norms, which are meant to govern the legislator's teleological reasoning (indicating what values should be ad-

---

the nature of the prohibited act. Within criminal law, it is used to convey the idea that the punishment of an offender should fit the crime. Under international humanitarian law governing the legal use of force in an armed conflict, proportionality and distinction are important factors in assessing military necessity. The proportionality test was first developed in the High State Administrative Courts (Oberlandesgericht) in Germany in the late 19th century, and was applied to review actions by the police. The concept has been greatly enriched within European Union law, in which there are generally four stages to a proportionality test, namely,
there must be a legitimate aim for a measure
the measure must be suitable to achieve the aim (potentially with a requirement of evidence to show it will have that effect)
the measure must be necessary to achieve the aim, that there cannot be any less onerous way of doing it
the measure must be reasonable, considering the competing interests of different groups at hand.
Definition derived from: https://en.wikipedia.org/wiki/Proportionality_(law) (lastly accessed on 11/29/2016).
For more background information on the concept of proportionality, refer to: P. P. Craig & G. de Búrca (note 287)..
Most recently, proportionality is a key consideration in the discovery process, and has been extensively applicable to the wider area of e-discovery, where it has been attributed with significant cost-savings. Already, it is considered that proportionality will be of particular significance to new and developing areas of law, such as the law of legal technology. With regard to this point, read more at: Klaus Schmidt & Alejandro Laje, *The Proportionality and Solidarity Principles and Their Impact on Privacy Laws in German Jurisprudence*, 5 Laws 27–38 (2016).
For further details on the concept of proportionality as fundamental principle of law, refer to: Tor-Inge Harbo, *The Function of the Proportionality Principle in EU Law*, 16 European Law Journal 158–185 (2010); Robert Alexy, *On the Structure of Legal Principles*, 13 Ratio Juris 294–304 (2000); Evelyn Ellis, The principle of proportionality in the laws of Europe (1999); E. Thomas Sullivan & Richard S. Frase, Proportionality principles in American law. Controlling excessive government actions (2009); Dieter Grimm, *Proportionality in Canadian and German Constitutional Jurisprudence*, 57 University of Toronto Law Journal 383–397 (2007).

vanced), rather than to limit the range of its admissible outcomes"[1139]. Adjusting this thesis in the field of IT law, one could claim that IT legislation and particularly any that focuses on fundamental elements of telecommunication technologies such as the proposed cloud computing regulatory principles, should not only care about settling unresolved issues at any given time that they arise but it should be constructed with the ultimate broader status quo that is hoped to be achieved in the field through it in mind. In addition, right-norms are increasingly proving to be of equal function as goal-norms with regard to legislators and public authorities[1140]. This is increasingly so in the IT sector, where, as it has been already demonstrated in earlier parts of this study[1141], there is increasing pressure on legislators on behalf of the public to modify existing or conceptualize new IT laws taking into account not just the need for fluent functioning of the market but also for upholding the general public's calls for better privacy, safety and security in their use of IT technologies.

As a result, any legislative review, especially if it refers to areas of law in which the rights of law subjects are so closely dependent with reference to their protection to the goals prioritized by legislators, must assess, design and implement any legislative and administrative action by "evaluating the proportionality (the teleological appropriateness) of legislative choices"[1142]. To this end, legislators nowadays and those that will deal with cloud computing regulation, in particular, should be directed in their work by the notion of reasonableness, an idea wishing to promote mutual institutional deference with the aim of ultimately achieving collaboration without overlapping: general legal theory suggests that "a margin of empirical and axiological appreciation should be left to legislators, even when constitutional values are at issue"[1143]. Similarly, cloud computing regulators need to work towards rules governing the cloud that will not only focus on settling the issues arising out of each particular application of cloud technologies only but rather they will aim to be of a long-lasting

1139 Giovanni Sartor, *Doing justice to rights and values: teleological reasoning and proportionality. Artificial Intelligence and Law*, 18 Artif Intell Law 175–215 (2010.)

1140 *Id.*

1141 See Chapter 3.

1142 *Id.*. For more on this notion refer to: Elen Stokes (note 888).

1143 Trevor Bench-Capon & Giovanni Sartor (note 956).. For more refer also to: Giorgio Bongiovanni, Giovanni Sartor & Chiara Valentini eds., Reasonableness and Law, vol. 86 (2009.)

and generic nature, as much as possible, so that the further-reaching goals of legal security and coherence of protection for all types of law subjects within the broader IT sector are achieved. This proposal for drafting cloud computing laws with a teleological mindset, if put forward across jurisdictions, helps us to further elaborate on the nature of cloud computing laws, which need to be inspired by a spirit of proportionality as well so that frictions and collisions among legal orders are softened as much as possible. Useful experience from other fields of law where cross-jurisdictional alignment has already been achieved to a substantial degree (for instance, from the field of trade law or the law of the sea) can also assist this process of integrating the teleological and proportionality methods deep into cloud computing law-making. Last but not least, given that the cloud terrain still is at this moment only loosely and case-based regulated, it is a unique opportunity to work on cloud regulation inspired by the teleological reasoning right from the beginning facilitating the establishment of a regime of governance over one of jurisdictionally fragmented governing in the sector.

e. How technology itself can help establishing a sound system of governance in the field of cloud computing

The idea of utilizing technology in order to protect data against the risks posed to them by technology itself has been discussed for years and it actually forms part of the whole cloud computing technological mindset[1144]: the cloud was put forward as a successor to previous technologies for handling data processes, among others, thanks to the fact that it left a lot of room for both technology gimmicks that would optimize data processing as well as others that would enhance the safety and security standards under which this would be conducted. Of course, the whole idea of making use of technology's powers against its malice has been put forward with varied tension and it has even reached the extreme of arguing that, "if threats to and violations of data protection are factually impossible, then there is no need to impose legal restrictions"[1145]. Needless to say, there is no need to choose between extremes; the alternative to too much regu-

1144 David S. Wall (note 661).
1145 Gerrit Hornung (note 735).

lation does not need to be no regulation at all. However, technology can indeed be a great asset in an effort to move from traditional restrictions encompassing obligations and prohibitions to a new regulatory approach focusing on proactivity and due diligence without the need for a breach that calls for punishment or repair, as it is currently the case. In fact, as Roßnagel put it back in 2001, "by adopting and executing normative requirements as to the use of personal data, law and technology complement each other and form an 'alliance' to protect personal rights"[1146], privacy and integrity of IT technology and cloud computing as a whole.

Collaboration between law and technology on the front of privacy, security and integrity of communications online is becoming increasingly important as traditional regulatory instruments are often unable to cope with the challenges of modern data processing[1147]. Many of those long-established IT rules, being tied to the conventional enforcement authorities of national states, lose a considerable amount of their effectiveness in the fluid social sphere of the internet[1148]. Under these circumstances, effective data protection in today's cloud-dominated IT landscape cannot be guaranteed by legal instruments alone. Instead, a mixture of up-to-date, proactively oriented and precautionary regulations along with suitable technological assets and the series of specialized laws already in place is the key to achieving the best possible level of integrity, safety and security in the vast amount of cloud-facilitated applications. As data processing becomes pervasive, privacy enhancing technologies are increasingly important and an indispensable tool in the effort towards establishing a sound system of governance with regard to cloud computing and the entire environment of applications around it. Actually, the idea that technological support is indispensable in sealing data against the risks they face from technology-assisted processing is so strongly supported that in certain areas of comput-

1146 Alexander Rossnagel, Allianz von Medienrecht und Informationstechnik? Ordnung in digitalen Medien durch Gestaltung der Technik am Beispiel von Urheberschutz, Datenschutz, Jugendschutz und Vielfaltschutz; Dokumentation der Stiftungstagung (zugleich EMR-Workshop), der Alcatel SEL Stiftung für Kommunikationsforschung, des Instituts für Medienrecht (EMR), der Landeszentrale für politische Bildung (LpB) Baden-Württemberg, am 10. Mai 2001 im Landtag Baden-Württemberg, Stuttgart, Bd. 24 (2001.)

1147 R. K. Lippert & K. Walby, *Governing Through Privacy. Authoritarian Liberalism, Law, and Privacy Knowledge*, 12 Law, Culture and the Humanities 329–352 (2016.)

1148 M. Friedewald & R. J. Pohoryles (note 119).; Alexander Rossnagel (note 1146).

ing it appears as a sine qua non. Specifically, in ubiquitous computing[1149], it appears[1150] to be "a misperception to believe that it is possible to secure personal privacy and informational self-determination without technologies that provide anonymity, pseudonymization and transparency in a user-controlled way without hampering the user in his or her everyday business"[1151]. Such technologies are already available and they could not only be used in reinforcing generic cloud computing laws of the nature and scope that have been analyzed in the previous chapters, but they could also make possible privacy-friendly settings in cloud-based systems and appli-

1149 Ubiquitous computing (or "ubicomp") is a concept in software engineering and computer science where computing is made to appear anytime and everywhere. In contrast to desktop computing, ubiquitous computing can be exercised using any device, in any location, and in any format. A user interacts with the computer, which can be in many different forms, including laptop computers, tablets and terminals in everyday objects such as a fridge or a pair of glasses. The underlying technologies supporting ubiquitous computing include Internet, advanced middleware, operating system, mobile code, sensors, microprocessors, new I/O and user interfaces, networks, mobile protocols, location and positioning and new materials. (https://en.wikipedia.org/wiki/Ubiquitous_computing; lastly accessed on 11/29/2016)
Ubiquitous computing is also described as pervasive computing, ambient intelligence, or "everyware". Each term emphasizes slightly different aspects. Several experts suggest that an evolution of the concept of ubiquitous computing is also the notion of Internet of Things, when primarily concerning the objects involved. Ubiquitous computing touches on a wide range of research topics, including distributed computing, mobile computing, location computing, mobile networking, context-aware computing, sensor networks, human-computer interaction, and artificial intelligence. For more information on ubiquitous computing, refer to: Eva Nieuwdorp, *The pervasive discourse*, 5 Comput. Entertain. 13 (2007); Adam Greenfield, Everyware. The dawning age of ubiquitous computing (2006); Stefan Poslad, Ubiquitous computing. Smart devices, environments and interactions (2009).

1150 Giovanni Sartor (note 1139).; For additional information refer also to: Elgar Fleisch & Friedemann Mattern, Das Internet der Dinge. Ubiquitous Computing und RFID in der Praxis : Visionen, Technologien, Anwendungen, Handlungsanleitungen (2005); Alexander Roßnagel, Tom Sommerlatte & Udo Winand, Digitale Visionen. Zur Gestaltung allgegenwärtiger Informationstechnologien (2008.)

1151 Gerrit Hornung (note 735).. In addition with reference to this point, read: Alexander Roßnagel, Datenschutz in einem informatisierten Alltag (2007); Mireille Hildebrandt, *Profiling and the rule of law*, 1 IDIS 55–70 (2008).

cations, facilitate the much promoted opt-in principle[1152], make possible the configuration of personalized user-settings for routine data processing, speed up and optimize automatic deleting processes, permit the deployment of personalized identity management or transmit systems, organize, aggregate and document declarations of consent that any data subject may have issued for certain types of data processes etc.

Moreover, it should not be overlooked that, if the precautionary perspective is supposed to be the one with most relevance to a governance regime with a character as generic as possible in the field of cloud computing, technology-based sealing and protective measures are an invaluable supplement to cloud computing regulation. Besides, it should not be forgotten that arranging a precaution-oriented regulatory landscape with regard to the cloud will, in the future, be increasingly relevant since the growing amount of data processed via cloud networks, in the form of big data collected amass via IoT systems, respectively increases the risk that huge amounts of data subjects become identifiable, even though until recently such identification was not possible[1153].

Last but not least, it must be stressed out that any concept for data protection and technology-assisted cloud computing regulation needs to be designed by having two target groups in mind: producers of the respective technologies, as they were analyzed above[1154], who need to be legally obliged to ensure actual availability of the said technology, and users, that is, the various actors within the cloud workflow as they have been previously analyzed[1155], with the aim of forcing them to actually put these measures in practice. Both target groups need to have clear guidelines from regulators for the development and application of privacy-friendly tech-

---

1152 The opt-in principle in privacy law is a concept appearing in several jurisdictions and pieces of laws regulating aspects of privacy and refers to the active and affirmative consent of user and data subject to submit itself to the terms and conditions under which the data-involving processing at hand takes place. For more on the principle and its essence, refer to: Siani Pearson (note 728); Omer Tene & Jules Polonetsky, *Privacy in the Age of Big Data: A Time for Big Decisions*, 64 Stan. L. Rev. Online 63–69 (2011); Eve M. Caudill & Patrick E. Murphy, *Consumer Online Privacy. Legal and Ethical Issues*, 19 Journal of Public Policy & Marketing 7–19 (2000); Alfred Kobsa, *Privacy-enhanced personalization*, 50 Commun. ACM 24–33 (2007.)

1153 Alexander Roßnagel (note 1151).

1154 See Chapters 8 and 9.

1155 See Chapters 8 and 9.

nologies. At the same time, making official the adoption of such technologies, as an indispensable asset towards the establishment of the new governance-oriented regime in the field of cloud computing, will encourage actors of these groups to actually invest resources and effort in developing and implementing such technologies. It is up to regulators' bravery to make the body of cloud computing laws as relevant as possible at this point, by going as far as concretizing future-oriented criteria for the design of technology that may be even directly derived from cloud computing regulation[1156]. What is more, cloud computing laws could even provide business and growth opportunities or even incentivize the use of such technologies.

In conclusion, it should be pointed out that, much as the cloud has been a liberalizing force for IT markets per se, market forces alone are not a sufficient force for the development and spreading of PETs and, in general, technological applications aimed at enhancing the integrity of cloud networks. There are several reasons for this and, as usually with everything regarding the cloud, economies of scale are a primary one. In other words, technology is as a rule designed with a view to responding to certain functional requirements. Contrary to what the average non-technically mind may think, enhancing privacy is not, from a technical point of view, a functional requirement in itself[1157]. The most important (and legitimate, as we are talking about actors of an economic activity) aim of actors throughout the cloud workflow is the maximization of profit. In view of that, optimum data protection, the integrity and maximum coherence of the network are as relevant as demand of the network's offerings on the market continues to exist. If this demand is lowered, this may quickly become a counterforce for the technology tweaks discussed here, which could end up being irrelevant in the design process because they may either increase or they may not reduce costs. Therefore, much as cloud regulation could be benefited from technology assets in its effort to make the passing from a regime of case-based governing to generically established governance, it should not take this collaboration between law and IT for granted; rather, it should take positive action and institutionalize it.

1156 Alexander Roßnagel, Tom Sommerlatte & Udo Winand (note 1150).

1157 Gerrit Hornung (note 735).; Patricia L. Bellia, *Federalization in Information Privacy Law*, 118 Yale Law Journal 868–890 (2009.)

f. The key to achieving a sound system of governance in cloud computing regulation: legal interoperability and its significance as a concept in transnational law

Interoperability is a fundamental element of the entire IT sector and cloud computing, in particular. Today's IT networks are so highly interconnected among them that there are devices which are not built at all to function properly on their own, but must interact with other elements of software or hardware[1158]. Actually, by today's IT standards, it is even possible that a device that cannot interoperate with other products with which consumers expect it to do so to be considered essentially worthless[1159].

Maintaining the position which has been at the core of this study from the beginning, that regulating the cloud is a fundamentally interdisciplinary issue, it is now time to see not only how law should adapt to technological standards in order to efficiently govern cloud computing but also how and if legislation could profit from technological state-of-the-art. With this approach in mind, it is proposed that the concept of interoperability should extend beyond its purely technical dimension and make an important contribution to the development of transnational IT law, in general, and cloud computing regulation per se. Departing from the technological context of interoperability, there have been scholars who have brought forward the concept of cultural interoperability[1160]; this idea is now time to be further transplanted in the legal discipline, in which there have been already some voices championing for legal interoperability, in the sector of IT law, in particular. Legal interoperability should be, in other words, one of the core elements in the nature of laws that will be designed for governing the cloud.

Looking to define what legal interoperability constitutes of one needs to go back to the original concept of technical interoperability. Although no universal or unequivocally accepted definition of technological interoper-

1158 KIIT University ed. (note 1129).

1159 Ian Watson, The universal machine. From the dawn of computing to digital consciousness (2012.)

1160 Amedeo Santosuosso & Alessandra Malerba, *Legal Interoperability as a Comprehensive Concept in Transnational Law*, 6 Law, Inn Tech 51–73 (2014.)

ability really exists, two distinct components have been largely recognized[1161]:

- syntactic interoperability, which refers to the ability of diverse systems to communicate with each other and exchange data;
- semantic interoperability, which denotes the ability to interpret and use those data and pieces of information in a significant way, useful to the end user.

Mutatis mutandis, in the field of IT law interoperability is as efficient as each of these two elements are entertained, which means that:

- syntactics become all the more coherent as the legal discipline learns to communicate better with other sciences and exchange know-how and knowledge with them;
- semantics improve as the legal discipline learns to interpret and use the knowledge and know-how it receives from other sciences in such a way that they can help it with its goal to produce better rules, more suitable for the actual challenges of the IT reality.

In the context of technology, there are several ways in which syntactics or semantics can be improved, both technical and legal ones. For instance, intellectual property (IP) licensing agreements (as an example of a legal tool) and the use of open standards (as an example of a technical tool) are just two of the various methods in which the above components can be intensified and become more apparent[1162]. Following this logic, legal interoperability in the context of cloud computing regulation does not need and should not be a one-direction process, i.e. the legal sector only learning from the technical one. Much as legal rules need to be adapted to the technological status quo of the cloud, once put into force, if they have been designed taking into account how technology is and where it is heading at the time of their inception, can also point the way of technological advancement by broadening the route for aspects of this advancement that are believed by tech experts to be beneficial for the industry and end users or setting limits to other types of future progress which are feared to have a potentially derailing or adversary effect.

Nonetheless, interoperability does not receive a carte blanche in its technical and nor should it be given unlimited freedom in its legal dimension. As much as it is true that IT systems interoperability is an essential

1161 eHealth Governance Initiative, DISCUSSION PAPER ON SEMANTIC AND TECHNICAL INTEROPERABILITY (2012.)

1162 Amedeo Santosuosso & Alessandra Malerba (note 1160).

step forward, and there are numerous advantages (such as innovation, competition, flexibility and openness) which have been greatly boosted thanks to it[1163], there are many drawbacks that have been pointed out as well. In fact, IT scholars have expressed their concerns in relation to issues of security and privacy, as well as about the risk of excessive homogeneity[1164] or the so-called 'lock-in problem'[1165]. These are only a few indicators that revolutionary or groundbreaking as technical interoperability may be, it cannot be left to go unabated and without limits. Similarly, legal interoperability should not be adopted unconditionally nor should it be left to function beyond control in the cloud computing law making process and any other IT law making process for that matter. As it has been argued before, the legal discipline should maintain the upper hand and this can be not only protective for the final degree of efficiency of cloud computing laws, it can even be beneficial to the pace at which these laws will gain in efficiency overall.

Far-fetched as it may seem, the idea of legal interoperability is not an unrealistic one and the field of cloud computing regulation may actually be one of the most suitable sectors for this concept to be put into practice first. As a matter of fact, the conception of law as technology, which has been already analyzed in the course of this study[1166], can serve as a feasible frame for legal interoperability. That is to say, if it taken for granted that "political power or jurists can (as the theory of law as technology does) easily handle law, it should also be true that they could make law interoperable (if they wanted it)"[1167]. It goes without saying that the question is more complex and extends far beyond the aims of this study. However, as it will be argued in the conclusions of this analysis, one of the benefits of legislators actually settling down to deal with the challenge of cloud computing regulation can be that this so unique task will actually constitute a first and bold step towards bringing to the center of attention

1163 John G. Palfrey & Urs Gasser, Interop. The promise and perils of highly interconnected systems (2012.)

1164 *Id.*

1165 John G. Palfrey & Urs Gasser (note 235).

1166 See Chapters 4, 5 and 8.

1167 Amedeo Santosuosso & Alessandra Malerba (note 1160).

not only the need for horizontal but also for vertical interoperability[1168]. As to why IT and cloud computing law, in particular, could be an ideal starting point for putting interoperability at the heart of the rule making process, for now it is enough to recall the teachings of Carl Schmitt who was one of the first legal theorists that expressed the view that "law in modernity is another technology"[1169].

Last but not least, interoperability should of course not be interpreted only in relation to other disciplines or sectors of law but it should also have an interjurisdictional meaning. Having in mind the current status quo with regard to jurisdiction in cloud computing issues and the questions that the current regime leaves unanswered, as these were analyzed earlier[1170], interjurisdictional interoperability in cloud computing regulation should be constructed with the aim of explaining and encompassing the following aspects:

- answer why currently the way the cloud is regulated is neither unified nor uniform, in space and time (fragmentation) and what it needs to be done to achieve at least minimum working uniformity without pushing for unrealistic (and unnecessary) unification.
- answer why relevant IT laws are currently not hierarchically organized in a coherent way and how cloud computing regulation could contribute to that direction.
- it should always save room for flexibility for itself and not develop in a necessarily directional manner, as a crucial role in the field of IT and the cloud will always be played by spontaneous developments, be them unforeseen technological advancements or applications of current technologies which do not fit any of the known technical models till that time.
- it should develop taking into account all the different actors taking part in the wider cloud computing cycle, either as integral actors of the

1168 The issue of vertical vs. horizontal interoperability of laws, in particular IT ones, is a vast one and extends beyond the scope of this analysis. However, for a brief introduction to the issue, refer to: Xenofon Kontargyris, From effective to efficient regulation of ICT (2): the big leap towards embracing vertical, apart from horizontal, interdisciplinarity, available at: http://www.juwiss.de/88-2016/ (13 September 2017) (lastly accessed on: 09/13/2017.)

1169 Jens Meierhenrich, Oliver Simons & Friedrich Balke, The Oxford Handbook of Carl Schmitt, vol. 1 (2015.)

1170 See Chapter 5.

cloud workflow[1171] or on a cross-border basis[1172]. The differences of them in nature and legitimacy need to be reflected in the wording and spirit of cloud computing laws.

- interjuridictionally oriented cloud computing laws need to be processed always having in mind that they will continuously form part of a highly technified global environment.

g. A brief summary of the trends on privacy regulation through time in a global context; the transit to a cloud computing regulation governance regime is not a free fall into the unknown

From the beginning and across several parts of this analysis we have extensively talked about the various regulatory approaches on privacy and which of them managed to surface as the prevailing ones in major jurisdictions through time. Although emphasis was mostly given to the most recent concepts of privacy, i.e. the ones that were influenced or even initiated by the arrival and gradual establishment of IT, the idea of privacy in relation to different types of communication among people has been on the table since much longer and there are several exemplary references to that in previous parts of this study. It is beyond the scope of this project to make a detailed history review of the concept of privacy; yet, given that it is the one idea that had dominated regulatory and policy-making thinking with regard to IT technologies for a long time and, despite the fact that it may have lately been partially overshadowed by newer concepts of security or consent, it still remains among the pillars of IT regulation, it is worth summarizing the main trends about it. One more reason for doing so is that it will help us realize that the transition or, more precisely, the introduction of the proposed governance regime for cloud computing technologies alongside the rest of specific laws already in place for particular applications of them is no free fall from the sky; rather regulators and scholars have already suggested elements of the proposed regime in their discourse so far, just in a scattered manner. What needs to be done now is for competent regulatory and law-making bodies to gather all these ideas which are dispersed throughout literature and policy debate, bring them together, supplement them with the original perspectives that have been pre-

1171 See Chapter 9.
1172 See Chapter 6.

sented in previous chapters of this analysis and build up the much-needed fundamental common governance principles on cloud computing regulation.

To begin with, the four prevailing ways of defining privacy over the years since the concept was introduced as one of the main challenges with regard to any kind of interpersonal communication are[1173]:

- the non-interference concept[1174]
- the limited accessibility concept[1175]
- the privacy as information control concept[1176]
- a fourth concept incorporating various elements of the other three proposals but limiting the applicability of the idea of privacy to intimate or sensitive aspects of people's lives.

Each of these generic conceptions of privacy has found more or less welcoming ground across various jurisdictions and has served as the raw material for building the respective sets of laws on privacy regulation. It goes without saying that there was a varying degree in which each of these concepts had remained pure or undergone adaptations to reflect on each jurisdiction's views and long-held values on the issues relevant laws were set to settle each time. Out of all major jurisdictions and the main manifestations of them through time, there have been of course specific instances which stand out for their effectiveness, their outreach as well as their progressiveness. Among them, the German data privacy regime is often cited by many as one of the most successful[1177]. Although by the standards of a considerable number of scholars it is thought to be too rigid, one can hardly deny that the German privacy regulatory apparatus has traditionally featured a comprehensive, well-founded legislative platform with a solid constitutional footing and several progressive features, such as a legal requirement that organizations appoint internal privacy officers[1178]. Another of these elements exemplary of how German legal discourse has treated the notion of IT privacy with a clearly forward-thinking nature at certain mo-

1173 L. A. Bygrave (note 137).

1174 It is regarded by many as the oldest conceptualization of privacy. Originally, it was suggested in: Samuel D. Warren & Louis D. Brandeis, *The Right to Privacy*, IV Harvard Law Review 193–220 (1890.)

1175 A reference text for this concept of privacy is the following: Ruth Gavison, *Privacy and the Limits of Law*, 89 The Yale Law Journal 421–471 (1980.)

1176 L. A. Bygrave (note 137).

1177 Ulrich Dammann & Spiros Simitis (note 169).

1178 Anne Arendt, Ulrich Dammann & Spiros Simitis (note 742).

ments (although it did not prevail in the end) is the principle of 'systemic data protection' ('Systemdatenschutzprinzip')[1179]. Brought on the table as early as the beginning of the 1990s, this notion suggested the integration of data privacy concerns already in the design and development of information systems architecture, a line of thinking which surprisingly fits very well with many of the modern challenges posed by cloud computing technologies. Needless to say, promoters of that principle did not have in mind the cloud-based IT landscape we are faced with nowadays; even so, it is very interesting and useful to see that a regulatory framework such as the one described here would not be an unfounded or reckless move from a legislative point of view, just as it is no such one from a technical perspective. Regulatory thinking has already demonstrated remarkable forwardness and open-mindedness and it is not at all beyond its capacity to take the big leap and introduce a set of regulatory principles of common understanding such as the ones proposed in this study. Of course, what will make the big difference this time and what constitutes a substantial originality compared to the past is that the proposed cloud computing governance framework is based on a proactive and precautionary approach rather than on a corrective or remedial one.

h. Making a long-lasting governance regime a choice not a necessity

To sum things up, there have been numerous different approaches on privacy, security and other neighboring concepts that have been cited throughout this extensive analysis which has been attempting to discern

---

1179 For an analytical overview on the Systemdatenschutzprinzip and the ways it has lately been discussed or suggested that it could be utilized in the context of the German data protection regime, refer to: Martin Rost, *Standardisierte Datenschutzmodellierung*, 36 Datenschutz Datensich 433–438 (2012); Marit Hansen, *Datenschutz nach dem Summer of Snowden*, 38 Datenschutz Datensich 439–444 (2014); Volker Lüdemann, Alfred Scheerhorn, Christin Sengstacken & Daniel Brettschneider, *Systemdatenschutz im Smart Grid*, 39 Datenschutz Datensich 93–97 (2015); Steffen Kroschwald, Informationelle Selbstbestimmung in der Cloud. Datenschutzrechtliche Bewertung und Gestaltung des Cloud Computing aus dem Blickwinkel des Mittelstands (2016); S. Jandt, S. Kroschwald, A. Roßnagel & M. Wicker, *Datenschutzkonformes Cloud-Computing*, in Cloud-Services aus der Geschäftsperspektive, 207–266 (Helmut Krcmar, Jan Marco Leimeister, Alexander Roßnagel & Ali Sunyaev eds., 2016.)

among the whole lot and bring together only the ones crucial or relevant to cloud computing. There may be equally many others less relevant to the focus point of this project but still totally important approaches to different aspects of IT regulation. A significant number of them are also clearly progressive, inspired by liberal teachings in the fields of philosophy, human rights, economics or other fields. And all these progressive approaches together make a clear point towards the direction of a liberal governmentality[1180].

There have already been indications that particular regulatory bodies are beginning to realize the importance of regulating IT technologies not with a view to correcting any harm done as quickly as possible but with the aim of preventing it from happening as efficiently as it gets[1181]. One could say that on the regulatory front which focuses on how cloud networks should be designed things are already half a step ahead[1182], with the notion of 'privacy by design' quickly gaining ground. In this context, "privacy is to be thought-through ahead of time, that is, 'designed', 'set', 'planned'."[1183] It involves techniques and technologies that fashion privacy in new forms and 'packaging' and they even come up with ways to commercialize the various levels of it, beyond the basic one, as commodities[1184]. As its supporters champion, privacy by design may apply to "IT systems, accountable business practices, and physical design and networked infrastructure,"[1185] bringing to surface its remarkably wide and growing scope.

This is almost certainly the most advanced and forward-thinking specimen of IT-related regulatory approach that has been conceptualized so far. Yet, for the time being, it is limited on the technical design aspect of the

1180 Kristina Irion (note 220).

1181 Jean-Christophe Graz & Andreas Nölke, Transnational private governance and its limits, vol. 51 (2008.)

1182 Elen Stokes (note 888).

1183 R. K. Lippert & K. Walby (note 1147).

1184 Peter Hustinx, *Privacy by design. Delivering the promises*, 3 IDIS 253–255 (2010); A. Cavoukian, Privacy by Design; The 7 Foundational Principles, available at: https://www.ipc.on.ca/wp-content/uploads/Resources/7foundationalprinciples.pdf.

1185 R. K. Lippert & K. Walby (note 1147).

whole matter[1186]. The time is now to benefit from this future-oriented thinking that is gradually gaining strength on the technology or technical regulation front and expand its spirit to the entire spectrum of cloud computing regulation[1187]. Agreeing or researching and bringing together the best of what EU or US law and practice has to offer with regard to handling specific aspects of the cloud phenomenon and fortifying all these with the decisive yet clearly science- and fact-based ideas that have been analyzed on the course of this analysis will not be some reckless act but rather a strategic step ahead. Most importantly, it will give a decisive push towards the direction of cultivating a long-lasting, coherent and generic governance regime that it can come up with answers to many more challenges than the already existing ones which will be a choice and not necessity.

i. Can the transatlantic divide on privacy be bridged? Why the extensive use of cloud computing technologies makes the call for convergence an urgent one?

Having extensively analyzed the issue of cloud computing regulation with a particular focus on privacy regulation in the cloud from the perspectives of EU and US law, we have already reached the conclusion that better regulation on these issues does not necessarily mean that one law (or legal culture) should succumb to the other. Instead, it is more of a process whereby the two jurisdictions will agree on common goals or shared weaknesses and venture on seeking ways in which they could pursue the former or tackle the latter.

For starters, it can be argued without reservation that differences between the two systems of laws are often overstated, while mutual interests, especially on the part of law subjects and the civil society of are overlooked. As a matter of fact, none of the two regimes in its present form is perfect: EU law still provides ground for intrusions on privacy in the name of national security, and thus may be less protective than it is often as-

1186 For an indicative example of how old the observation of greater technical in comparison to legal advancement in the field of IT is refer to: Aron Mefford, *Lex Informatica: Foundations of Law on the Internet*, 5 Indiana Journal of Global Legal Studies 211–237 (1997.)

1187 M. Gillen (note 415).; David S. Wall (note 661).

sumed. At the same time, existing legal safeguards in the US are clearly insufficient in light of the revealed technological capacities of agencies such as the NSA over the last years, yet those revelations have prompted all three branches of government in the States to reassess NSA practices and relevant regulations in place, while they have also mobilized civil society[1188]. And as anxiety about privacy increases in the US, concerns about national security have dramatically risen in Europe following the series of terrorist attacks in several European cities over the last years. At the end of the day, the EU and the US may well be converging more than diverging with respect to national security surveillance and the great majority of measures taken in that front typically involve surveillance of data and communications largely hosted and facilitated by cloud computing.

Nobody denies that thanks to the relevant body of EU law, the CJEU has developed extensive case law in the field of privacy and data protection, establishing itself and the European Union as the leading jurisdiction in the field[1189]. However, at the same time, the EU data protection regime features a number of weaknesses and derogations which dilute its overall capacity to protect privacy rights[1190]. For starters, the EU data protection framework permits member states to restrict the rights granted to data subjects in the Data Protection Regulation for broad reasons of national security, defense or public security[1191]. This is a natural consequence of the division of competences between the EU and member states: the EU has only restricted authority to legislate in the field of security, and has already adopted a considerable range of measures coordinating law enforcement activities of the member states, or establishing EU counter-terrorism and security policies[1192]. However, under Article 4.2 TEU, "national security

1188 See also Chapter 3.

1189 See also Chapter 3 and 4.

1190 David Cole & Federico Fabbrini (note 32).

1191 Such reasons as grounds for restricting the applicability of the General Data Protection Regulation are to be found in several provisions of the GDPR, most notably in: cl. 16 pream. and Art. 23 Regulation (EU) 2016/679 (GDPR) (note 25).

1192 V. Mitsilegas, European union and internal security. Guardian of the people? (2014); Tridimas, T., & Gutierrez-Fons, J. A. (note 217); Alexander Roßnagel, *Datenschutzfragen des Cloud Computing*, in Wolken über dem Rechtsstaat? Recht und Technik des Cloud Computing in Verwaltung und Wirtschaft, 19–52 (Alexander Roßnagel ed., 2015.)

remains the sole responsibility of each Member State."[1193] As a result, this contradiction creates potential room for undermining of the overall protections granted by the Regulation which cannot be so easily quantified a priori given that the measures which may put it in question could as well stem from national and not European law. What is more, although there are minimum common rules for personal privacy established in the ECHR[1194], Europe's other major text regulating fundamental rights and freedoms besides the body of EU law, national rules demonstrate significant variations, with certain states providing advanced protection for privacy, while others lag behind. The GDPR aspires to cure this imbalance, yet the loopholes it potentially leaves for national legislators to divert from its core provisions still allow suspicion as to whether the status quo of privacy will be unanimous throughout the Union to flourish[1195].

Second, European data protection law is unlikely to place any serious obstacles to surveillance operations of EU member states conducted outside the EU (including infrastructure facilities, such as storage installations empowering cloud services). In accordance with the principle of loyal cooperation enshrined in Article 4(3) EU Treaty[1196], EU law sets limits to the actions of the EU member states' intelligence agencies in other EU member states[1197]. On the contrary though, it remains silent on member states' surveillance outside the EU[1198]. The picture does not get any clearer by the ECHR either, as neither that set of rules imposes significant limits on surveillance outside a member state's borders.

1193 The Treaty on European Union (TEU), C 115/13, 2008.

1194 Federico Fabbrini, Fundamental rights in Europe (2014.)

1195 On the broader issue of room for national derogations to the rules of the GDPR, see W. Gregory Voss, *Looking at European Union Data Protection Law Reform Through a Different Prism. The Proposed EU General Data Protection Regulation Two Years Later*, 17 Journal of Internet Law 1–3 (2014); Rothenberg, M., Jacobs, D., *Updating the Law of Information Privacy: The New Framework of the European Union*, 36 Harv. J. L. & Pub. Pol 606–652 (2013); V. Chang, Delivery and Adoption of Cloud Computing Services in Contemporary Organizations (2015); S. Meachem, *Cloud With a Chance of Regulation*, 57 ITNOW 18–21 (2015); Alexander Roßnagel ed. (note 285).

1196 "Pursuant to the principle of sincere cooperation, the Union and the Member States shall, in full mutual respect, assist each other in carrying out tasks which flow from the Treaties."; The Treaty on European Union (TEU), C 115/13, 2008.

1197 David Cole & Federico Fabbrini (note 32).

1198 David Cole & Federico Fabbrini (note 32); V. Mitsilegas (note 1192).

Equal obscurity remains on the European Court of Human Rights (ECtHR) front. Europe's top court for fundamental rights violations has repeatedly interpreted Article 8 ECHR, which grants a right to private and family life, as incorporating a right to data protection[1199] as well. Nevertheless, the ECtHR has never directly dealt with the case of surveillance operations exercised outside Europe and against foreign persons[1200]. Consequently, the ECtHR has yet to extend any Article 8 ECHR protection to a foreign national outside the jurisdiction or control of a contracting state.

In conclusion, while the EU Charter of Fundamental Rights and the EU data protection legislation undoubtedly establish a comprehensive framework to safeguard privacy in the era of digital communications and the cloud, states still have discretion with respect to national security surveillance[1201]. Consequently, while strong protections are in place within the geographical margins of EU law as well as in many cases with considerable elements of externality, neither EU law nor the ECHR for the time being seem to be able to constrain EU member states' surveillance of foreign nationals beyond their borders. This grey zone though leaves enough room for undermining people's privacy rights, especially when it comes to operations targeting data which are being handled via cloud computing, where the link for determining jurisdiction always stands on thin air, as we already discussed[1202].

Turning to the US, one has to admit that US law does not have any kind of systematized body of rules remotely resembling the General Data Protection Regulation, while existing constitutional precedents tend to give the government a relatively free reign with respect to data collection, particularly when it is done in the context of surveillance operations such as the NSA programs. But on further reflection, differences between the US and the EU may not be as stark as commonly thought. Especially when one focuses on the issue of surveillance activities.

Following US constitutional law, the US government has since long formulated two doctrines as legal basis for the constitutionality of its agencies' surveillance activities. The first stipulates that the Fourth Amend-

1199 L. A. Bygrave (note 137).

1200 David Cole & Federico Fabbrini (note 32).

1201 Maria Tzanou, *The EU as an emerging 'Surveillance Society'. The function creep case study and challenges to privacy and data protection*, 4 ICL Journal (2010.)

1202 See also Chapter 6.

ment does not protect information that individuals share with "third parties."[1203] As a result, the Fourth Amendment does not prevent the US government or any of its agents from obtaining such information, as long as they do so from the third party with whom the individual has shared such details.

Second, US courts have ruled that at least in certain cases the Fourth Amendment does not govern US officials' search of a foreign national's home abroad[1204]. This ruling, academic analysis finds, also includes search and seizure operations aimed at digital data of foreigners which are maintained on facilities away from US jurisdiction[1205].

To sum up, US law recognizes and protects privacy, both as a constitutional, Fourth Amendment matter, and as a statutory matter.[1206] For the most part, though US privacy laws are most protective when the government seeks to collect information within the US, about US citizens or permanent residents, nothing is explicitly stipulated with reference to digital surveillance operations aiming foreign nationals abroad; the only exception to this rule is certain discussions which have been provoked by concerns that such surveillance might intercept communications of foreign nationals where US citizens were also involved.

In light of the analysis above as well as in several other parts of this study, it seems that the issue of efficient protection and regulation of privacy and cloud computing is not suitable for proclaiming outright winners or losers between EU and US law; on the contrary, both legal systems have their strong and weak points, while they both leave considerable room for uncertainty when it comes to the protection of data of subjects which are foreign to their jurisdiction and the instance affecting their data takes place outside their geographic area of competence as well.

There are a number of very strong policy arguments why data protection and overall cloud regulation should be better coordinated between Europe and America. It is beyond the scope of this study to consider political, defense or military reasons why better coordination in regulating the

---

1203 See also Chapter 3.

1204 David Cole & Federico Fabbrini (note 32).; see in particular: United States v. Verdugo-Urquidez, 494 U.S. 259, 259 (1990.)

1205 Christopher Slobogin, Privacy at risk. The new government surveillance and the Fourth Amendment (2007); Orin Kerr (note 231).

1206 See also Chapter 3.

cloud is desirable[1207]. But it needs to be pointed out that there are also strong economic interests for both the EU and the US to support a transatlantic coordination in the field of cloud computing regulation. The US and the EU are the biggest trading partners in the world[1208]. At the same time, the rise of digital economy creates powerful incentives for them to enhance interconnectivity between their markets as well as between the laws that deal with any issues they might arise. The field of cloud computing regulation is probably the fundamental regulatory discipline where this coordination should begin from.

1207 For extensive analysis on these reasons that make better coordination between EU and US on the issue of cloud regulation refer to: David Cole & Federico Fabbrini (note 32); Johannes Thimm, Inseparable, but not equal. Assessing U.S.-EU relations in the wake of the NSA surveillance affair, 4/2014 (2014.)

1208 Refer also to Chapter 3.

CHAPTER 11. Conclusion

a. The driving forces that make the need for cloud computing regulation a pressing one

Throughout this analysis, it has been stressed out that cloud computing, as a pioneering way of taking advantage of the best data processing technologies have to offer, calls for a fresh look into the regulatory tools governing the wider IT phenomenon. These new regulatory frameworks do not need to be viewed as a substitute for current laws but rather as their natural but urgent successor, an original take on the IT governance starting from the cloud phenomenon as the core element of information technology and dealing with it from a broad, generic perspective, thus laying the general legal principles upon which any specialized IT legislation could be safely and with continuity developed in the future.

There may well be critical voices of this idea, i.e. the need for a regulatory framework focusing on the cloud as the foundation of information technologies and communication; yet, numbers and data from both the computer and legal science fronts suggest otherwise. In fact, latest numerical data suggest that the range and abundance of uses of cloud computing are growing at an exponential rate over the years, fueled recently by the push given to data industry by big data-related applications. Actually, analysis of the types and diversity of big-data centered uses of cloud computing indicates that technology is evolving so fast that is it driving the cloud's evolution at a pace much faster than any regulatory attempt from the existing ones could possibly effectively tame[1209].

1209 Chaowei Yang, Qunying Huang, Zhenlong Li, Kai Liu & Fei Hu, *Big Data and cloud computing. Innovation opportunities and challenges*, 10 International Journal of Digital Earth 13–53 (2016); Divyakant Agrawal, Philip Bernstein, Elisa Bertino, Susan Davidson, Umeshwas Dayal, Michael Franklin, Johannes Gehrke, Laura Haas, Alon Halevy, Jiawei Han, H. V. Jagadish, Alexandros Labrinidis, Sam Madden, Yannis Papakonstantinou, Jignesh Patel, Raghu Ramakrishnan, Kenneth Ross, Cyrus Shahabi, Dan Suciu, Shiv Vaithyanathan & Jennifer Widom, *Challenges and Opportunities with Big Data 2011-1* Cyber Center Technical Reports (2011); Divyakant Agrawal, Sudipto Das & Amr El Abbadi, *Big data and cloud computing. Current state and future opportunities* 530–533

At the same time, statistical analysis on the research done so far on cloud computing and extensive literature review on available resources on the broad topic reveal that the legal aspects of the cloud phenomenon remain largely unexplored. This is not so much because there is not considerable output on the legal and ethical challenges posed by the cloud already but rather because many of its technical feasibilities remain at a nascent level but tend to gain attention and develop at lightning speed once they gain the research communities attention. In particular, according to content analysis conducted for 236 scholarly journal articles published between 2009 and 2014 with the aims of

- Identifying possible trends and changes in cloud computing over the six years of the survey,
- comparing publishing productivity of journals about the cloud computing subject, and
- guiding future research about cloud computing

the results of which were published in 2016, the majority of cloud computing research output is about "cloud computing adoption" (19%), followed by the "legal and ethical issues" of cloud computing (15%). However, at the same time it was observed that numerous technical aspects of the cloud, which had remained mostly unexplored until recently are picking up pace really fast once they attract researchers' and industry's attention. For example, technical issues such as "cloud computing for mobile applications" and the "energy consumption dimension of cloud computing", which were found to be among the least explored and researched topic areas at the beginning of the study, started growing at a remarkable pace once they became hot topics for the cloud industry and relevant to the existing or upcoming cloud-based applications[1210]. (4%) are the least attention grabbing themes in the literature. However, "cloud computing for

(2011); Mauro Andreolini, Michele Colajanni, Marcello Pietri & Stefania Tosi, *Adaptive, scalable and reliable monitoring of big data on clouds*, 79-80 Journal of Parallel and Distributed Computing 67–79 (2015); Marcos D. Assunção, Rodrigo N. Calheiros, Silvia Bianchi, Marco A.S. Netto & Rajkumar Buyya, *Big Data computing and clouds. Trends and future directions*, 79-80 Journal of Parallel and Distributed Computing 3–15 (2015.)

1210 Merve Bayramusta & V. Aslihan Nasir, *A fad or future of IT? A comprehensive literature review on the cloud computing research*, 36 International Journal of Information Management 635–644 (2016). For further information regarding the vast research questions and opportunities around the cloud which still remain unexploited, refer also to: Marc Fouquet, Heiko Niedermayer & Georg

mobile applications" and "energy consumption dimension of cloud computing" themes have become popular in the last two years, so they are expected to be trendy topics of the near future. Another important finding was that the majority of the articles indexed during the study were published by engineering, information systems or technical journals such as "IT Professional Magazine", "International Journal of Information Management" and "Mobile Networks and Applications" which means that legal aspects of the cloud have until largely been collateral points of research focused on cloud computing and there is still ample room for dedicated legal analysis on cloud computing[1211].

At the same time, technical research into more advanced ways to monitor cloud environments is evolving at full speed paving already the way for applications and tools that can be deployed to track activity or optimize use of cloud networks in ways totally novel to what is known for the time being and what has been taken into account by regulators when writing existing laws for cloud-enabled applications[1212].

Carle, *Cloud computing for the masses*, in Proceedings of the 1st ACM workshop on User-provided networking challenges and opportunities, 31 (Paulo Mendes ed., 2009); Rekha Saluja, *Cloud Computing: Challenges and New Developments*, 5 International Journal of Science, Engineering and Computer Technology 173–176 (2015); Nabil Sultan, *Cloud computing. A democratizing force?*, 33 International Journal of Information Management 810–815 (2013); Mladen A. Vouk, *Cloud Computing – Issues, Research and Implementations*, 16 CIT 235–246 (2008.)

1211 Merve Bayramusta & V. Aslihan Nasir (note 1210). For further details on the multiple research aspects posed by cloud computing and its widespread use actors sectors of economy refer to: Gerald Münzl, Michael Pauly & Martin Reti eds., Cloud Computing als neue Herausforderung für Management und IT (2015.)

1212 Guilherme Da Cunha Rodrigues, Rodrigo N. Calheiros, Vinicius Tavares Guimaraes, Glederson Lessa dos Santos, Márcio Barbosa de Carvalho, Lisandro Zambenedetti Granville, Liane Margarida Rockenbach Tarouco & Rajkumar Buyya, *Monitoring of cloud computing environments*, in Proceedings of the 31st Annual ACM Symposium on Applied Computing, 378–383 (Sascha Ossowski ed., 2016). For additional resources on the future trends in technical tools for monitoring and managing cloud resources and networks, refer also to: Georgios Tselentis, Towards the future internet. Emerging trends from European research (2010); Jesús Montes, Alberto Sánchez, Bunjamin Memishi, María S. Pérez & Gabriel Antoniu, *GMonE. A complete approach to cloud monitoring*, 29 Future Generation Computer Systems 2026–2040 (2013.)

For all these reasons, it is firmly believed that the systematic analysis and collection under the same project of best practices, current trends and proposals for a sound cloud computing regulation that was attempted throughout the course of this study is an important one and could serve as the starting point for regulators to put together in the near future much more sound and better coordinated rules for the cloud-enabled IT landscape of today and tomorrow.

b. Overview of solutions and suggestions towards the development of sound cloud computing regulation regimes

The following is a summary of the proposals made throughout this study towards achieving cloud computing regulatory frameworks that will be more in line with the speed and frequency in which IT is evolving nowadays and will also provide for greater certainty for legal subjects on a cross-jurisdictional basis. It should be reiterated that the outcomes of this analysis are based on the preconditions set for it already in its introductory chapter. Moreover, given that the project is essentially a comparative analysis between norms and trends of two jurisdictions aiming not in proclaiming winners and losers but rather in bringing together best practices from and for both of them, some of the following propositions may not struck readers coming from one of the two schools of legal thought (i.e. the EU and US one) as absolutely original or ground-breaking. Yet it needs to be born in mind that this work has been meant as a synthesizing effort between the two jurisdictions it focuses on and, consequently, ideas which may be standard practice in one jurisdiction can be essentially new approaches for the other and vice versa.

The summary of the proposals made over previous chapters of this analysis is structured under three categories, i.e. normative, governance and policy ones.

i. Normative proposals

As normative are coined proposals which stem from theory of law and, ultimately, push towards the direction of cloud computing rules that will not be understood simply as an additional set of laws for IT but rather as a set of fundamental principles that will serve as the foundation of IT law:

- Currently, it is not uncommon that technological advancement may bypass regulatory prudence in the time between the initialization the conceptualization phase for a law and the time it is concluded causing a vicious circle. An exit from this pattern can only be achieved if cloud computing regulation deviates from the norm currently followed by IT laws that are largely ad-hoc formulated and takes a more technologically abstract yet intra-jurisdictionally systematic direction. In other words, cloud computing regulation should not serve as a cure to technological implementations that may go wrong but should change its focus on making sure that the margin for accidents from cloud-enabled technological applications (presently known or even forthcoming ones) is limited to the biggest extent possible[1213].
- Cloud regulation laws should refrain from undue restrictions. Experience and history indicate that in dynamic phenomena, such as cloud computing, restrictive approaches usually either hinder progress or are simply rendered invalid via a workaround. Consequently, it does not seem meaningful to try to control what will happen next in a sector by forbidding certain things from happening. The key to better regulation is definitely not greater or unjustified restrictions[1214].
- The legislators' mindset should be towards fostering a predictable, minimalist, consistent and simple legal environment. In fact, many scholars agree that this should not be just the wish pursued with every new adopted legislation but rather the primary goal future laws should serve: ensuring that the regulated environment in which law subjects will be let to act will be a simple-to-understand and opaque one[1215].
- Given the prevailing legal doctrine regarding IT technologies and the data tasks effectuated through them, the essential elements of an effective regulatory regime for the cloud should be transparency, availability and accountability. Transparency is an important element in the struggle to meet security, privacy or trust obligations, since it brings to the forefront the (contractual) will of all cloud actors (be them users, service providers, inspecting authorities etc.) to fulfil the globally accepted privacy principles that will make up for a sound and secure cloud environment. Availability arises as a prerequisite since in a sound governance framework for the cloud availability for reporting and inspec-

1213 For more refer to Chapter 4.

1214 For more refer to Chapter 5.

1215 *Id.* See also Chapter 4.

tion of cloud actors is of prime importance as an assurance for application of the commonly accepted privacy and security requirements. Finally, accountability is an important factor arising directly from one of the main legal challenges with regard to cloud computing: namely that commitments from parties to the cloud life cycle must be clear and enforceable in practice. This, in consequence, stimulates trust throughout the cloud cycle and further intensifies the bonds between providers and users of cloud services[1216].

- Laws for the cloud, primarily those focusing on determining competent jurisdiction, should be developed in the future having the theory of reasonableness in mind. This, according to Lowenfeld suggests that any set of rules developed with the aim of providing answers to the broad issue of jurisdiction, at the end of the day, attempts to strike a compromise between legal certainty and flexibility. The rules that may, at any time, be adopted "need to be clear and definite enough to lead to an acceptable degree of legal certainty, but also flexible enough to cover unforeseen and complex situations, which suggests the need for a 'safety valve' that allows jurisdiction not to be asserted even when technically it could be"[1217]. This concept is intended to help resolve particular situations, typical among which are those when there is a jurisdictional conflict between regulators in two sovereign states[1218].
- Regulators tasked with developing laws for the cloud should work bearing the external and internal perspective of every IT phenomenon about to be regulated in mind. According to them, the external perspective brings to surface physical reality, and the internal perspective exposes virtual reality. For instance, accessing a website on a browser can be interpreted as either sending a request to a remote server that sends back text and pictures (physical reality), or getting access to a place where certain information is hosted (virtual reality). An internal and an external viewer form two strikingly different understandings of the same thing. When it comes to plain users, there can be those who have an understanding of both realities simultaneously; technically savvy users, with a certain level of awareness about technology can very efficiently follow the external view along with the internal. Nonetheless, the internet and cloud computing as its main facilitator

1216 For more refer to Chapter 7.
1217 Dan Svantesson (note 548).
1218 For more refer to Chapter 6.

necessitate a choice between these two representations of reality. A user may be aware of both realities at the same time, but will have to choose to accept only one at a time when trying to understand online experiences. On the contrary, while regulators, alone or with the assistance of specialized advisors, may well be able to distinguish between the two versions of the cloud reality, they cannot act so in extremis as plain users: they need to come up with a set of rules of law which will serve the interests, respond to challenges and, ultimately, strike a balance between both perceptions of the cloud computing phenomenon in order for it to provide thorough and not partial answers[1219].

- There are lots of different ways to deploy the same kind of infrastructure and this means that the (regulatory) challenges coming with one type of cloud environment will not necessarily be the same with those of another. For instance, a great deal of issues regarding privacy raised by public clouds are non-existent or they are satisfactorily tackled when the same resources are utilized to set up a private cloud computing network. However, the technical expertise, the mechanical skills and the very materials (i.e. pieces of hardware) that are necessary in order to build up either a public (with just the standard protection features) or a private (with as advanced protection features as possible) cloud ecosystem are, in essence, the same. In both cases, and in every other in between, one will need pieces of the same kind of infrastructure, the same kind of information science and IT engineering knowledge that will permit one to put those pieces of hardware into meaningful working arrangements and, of course, even the features that will differentiate them and make them stand apart from each other will be based on the same technical principles and scientific intel that makes the overall concept of cloud computing technology possible. Consequently, it becomes evident that, despite the great variety in which cloud services and networks appear on the market and the substantial differences which might exist between all these variations of cloud environments, there is a common underlying connecting tissue that binds them all, and that is the knowledge (of informatics, computing engineering and other disciplines) related to them which is one and the same. With these in mind, the challenge is not to homogenize IT laws or pulverize jurisdictional particularities. It rather is to set common

1219 For more refer to Chapter 6.

goals and establish rules that will contribute to their achievement. The path towards achieving these goals can and will expectedly be different, both because cloud computing manifests itself through various different arrangements and because two or more identical cloud networks in different environments will naturally be treated in differentiated manners according to the legal culture in each environment. However, as long as the same purposes are pursued and, ultimately, materialize, the path and the means need not be identical[1220].

- Rules developed with the goal of regulating the cloud apart from putting emphasis on clearing out which cloud actor is tasked with what specific duties at each time throughout a cloud network's workflow, should also provide clear rules for shedding light on the issue of superiority between conflicting rules affecting the same areas of cloud-related activity putting an end to the insecurities that still so manifestly exist despite an already wide range of legal tools attempting to deal with all outstanding issues in the wider field of IT[1221].
- It is strongly recommended that a future regulatory framework for cloud computing should be based on a definition that will not only describe what cloud computing does, from a technical perspective, but also explain its dual nature as a concept, i.e. that it is not just about the external manifestations we see of it but also about the way the underlying technology and hardware are organized around certain actors to construct, all together, a dynamic and continuously changing business workflow. In this way, the subsequent rules will not only reflect on the external but also on the internal aspect of cloud computing dealing with the whole range of cloud-related issues calling for regulatory arrangement[1222].
- While laws on the applications made possible thanks to cloud computing technologies usually adopt a punitive or repressive approach trying to describe in what way harmful effects from malpractice with these applications could be limited, cloud computing regulation should adopt a primarily proactive approach focusing on who is charged with what functions and duties in that context throughout the cloud network. In this manner, it is expected that affected entities will be better aware of their duties and the preparations required to live up to depending on the

1220 For more refer to Chapter 8.
1221 For more refer to Chapter 9.
1222 Id.

role(s) they are playing within a cloud network, thus increasing the chances for smooth and transparent function of the cloud market and minimizing the odds for harmful events or spillovers thereof[1223].

- IT and cloud computing are perfect case studies to start off from Hayek's position on the regulatory state and, after combining it with the principles of the theory on knowledge and the law, to arrive in a modern formula that will guarantee the production of equally or, even better, more efficient regulation in the future. Specifically, and contrary to the voices putting forward the irrelevance of obsolescence of it, the regulatory state itself can still be justified as one of the key mechanisms for aggregating local knowledge. Similarly, in the field of cloud computing regulation achieving the optimal results is not a question of choosing who, among competent potential regulators, does better or the best laws. Rather, what it is really needed is to coordinate among all these competent regulators, to agree on elementary common principles that will define all the pieces of laws they may bring out and to make sure that, in the end, they will all work towards the same end product: a pragmatic and as timeless as possible regime of sound governance instead of an ever anxious to catch up with new standards regime of governing[1224].
- In the field of cloud computing, as in many other fields, improving regulation is not only a matter of replacing existing laws with new ones because older rules have been found to have become obsolete. Laws and overall legal certainty are also improved by putting in place basic regulation that will help us interpret and apply pre-existing legislation in a more coherent and in touch with technological reality manner. In addition, improvement is also achieved by agreeing on the fundamental concepts and principles that should be at the core of all executive laws across different jurisdictions in order for law subjects to enjoy, as much as possible, comparable levels of protection with reference to an issue which is of a genuinely borderless nature[1225].
- Insisting that the body of laws governing the cloud in one jurisdiction can be totally sealed against the expectations of its subjects falling under the competence of different legal orders but being potentially affected by the said body of rules as well, directly or indirectly, does

1223 Id. See also Chapter 4.
1224 For more refer to Chapter 10.
1225 Id.

more harm than good. Most importantly, it degrades the quality of the overall learning system through which constant law modification and update is possible. In the end, if IT laws are to remain relevant and improve their livability in view of the lightning speed at which the phenomena they address are changing, they need to prioritize towards a governance regime that will conserve legal cohesion in an as broader as possible area of application. Cloud computing regulation, as the body of rules that will govern the foundations of IT, is the ideal starting point for this new regulatory perspective to be set in motion[1226].

- Cloud computing regulators need to work towards rules governing the cloud that will not only focus on settling the issues arising out of each particular application of cloud technologies only but rather they will aim to be of a long-lasting and generic nature, as much as possible, so that the further-reaching goals of legal security and coherence of protection for all types of law subjects within the broader IT sector are achieved. This proposal for drafting cloud computing laws with a teleological mindset, if put forward across jurisdictions, helps us to further elaborate on the nature of cloud computing laws, which need to be inspired by a spirit of proportionality as well so that frictions and collisions among legal orders are softened as much as possible. Useful experience from other fields of law where cross-jurisdictional alignment has already been achieved to a substantial degree (for instance, from the field of trade law or the law of the sea) can also assist this process of integrating the teleological and proportionality methods deep into cloud computing law-making. Last but not least, given that the cloud terrain still is at this moment only loosely and case-based regulated, it is a unique opportunity to work on cloud regulation inspired by the teleological reasoning right from the beginning facilitating the establishment of a regime of governance over one of jurisdictionally fragmented governing in the sector[1227].
- Substantial integration of the spirit of the 'Systemdatenschutzprinzip' in future laws for the cloud. Brought on the table as early as the beginning of the 1990s, this notion suggested the integration of data privacy concerns already in the design and development of information systems architecture, a line of thinking which surprisingly fits very well

1226 Id.
1227 Id.

with many of the modern challenges posed by cloud computing technologies[1228].

ii. Governance proposals

As governance proposals are coined those that do not explicitly need additional regulations but could already fit with existing IT laws; however, they imperatively must be taken into account when cloud computing laws are designed in the future:

- The GDPR invests a lot on a priori over a posteriori regulation, which is in principle of course better. Notwithstanding, it still interprets a priori protection as a range of procedures and checklists data controllers have to go through before any specific data processing and not as some clearly formulated, aim-oriented general principles which will make clear the level of protection that is to be maintained at all times during a data processing cycle irrespective of how this will be achieved by any given data controller. In other words, what we need for a data protection regime looking to the future is not more forms or compliance questionnaires; the real challenge is to let everyone know under what quality standards data are expected to be processed and let them then decide how to achieve them, knowing that, should they fail, equally clear repercussions will be faced[1229].
- Pre-cloud facilities were designed with a primary objective to get the data processing done in a clearly laid-out and secure manner. Cloud-based facilities are constructed with the primary aim of getting data processing done in an as user-friendly as possible manner and with a priority on optimizing economies of scale for the provider but also the user of the cloud infrastructure. This change of focus resulted in the security of the processing not being possible to be taken for granted anymore. From a status quo where it was enough to know what role each of the actors participating in a data processing sequence held in order to be able to identify their responsibilities and duties, we are today in a situation where the data processing workflow is geographically and resource-wise dynamic and spread-out across the cloud facility, hence

1228 Id.

1229 For more refer to Chapter 4.

calling for a different approach that will guarantee security and transparency throughout the processing workflow[1230].
- It is suggested that the cloud industry be reorganized based on an end to end accountability approach. This approach will lead the greater sector to be arranged over a continuum or spectrum of parties, of whom only those that indeed process data at some point through the data life cycle will be considered as potentially culpable. Additionally, this accountability will not be vague nor will it only be affirmed when a wrongdoing occurs. It will, instead, have varying degrees of obligations and liabilities, directly analogous to the position of the party in the cloud cycle, the scope it is supposed to be serving and the processes for which it is fair to be held responsible. This approach would not only bring the actual responsible parties to the forefront of culpability but it would also contribute to the quest for achieving a more appropriate balance between commercial and privacy considerations in light of the complex and dynamic nature of today's cloud computing industry[1231].
- Effective data protection in today's cloud-dominated IT landscape cannot be guaranteed by legal instruments alone. Instead, a mixture of up-to-date, proactively oriented and precautionary regulations along with suitable technological assets and the series of specialized laws already in place is the key to achieving the best possible level of integrity, safety and security in the vast amount of cloud-facilitated applications. As data processing becomes pervasive, privacy enhancing technologies are increasingly important and an indispensable tool in the effort towards establishing a sound system of governance with regard to cloud computing and the entire environment of applications around it. Actually, the idea that technological support is indispensable in sealing data against the risks they face from technology-assisted processing is so strongly supported that in certain areas of computing it appears as a sine qua non. Specifically, in ubiquitous computing, it appears to be "a misperception to believe that it is possible to secure personal privacy and informational self-determination without technologies that provide anonymity, pseudonymity and transparency in a user-controlled way without hampering the user in his or her everyday business". Such

1230 Id.
1231 For more refer to Chapter 6.

technologies are already available and they could not only be used in reinforcing generic cloud computing laws of the nature and scope that have been analyzed in previous chapters, but they could also make possible privacy-friendly settings in cloud-based systems and applications, facilitate the much promoted opt-in principle, make possible the configuration of personalized user-settings for routine data processing, speed up and optimize automatic deleting processes, permit the deployment of personalized identity management or transmit systems, organize, aggregate and document declarations of consent that any data subject may have issued for certain types of data processes etc[1232].

iii. Policy proposals

The last set of recommendations includes policy proposals, i.e. specific measures that can be taken within each jurisdiction as well as on a cross-jurisdictional basis towards bringing the suggestions from two previous categories into effect:

- Future privacy laws should stipulate broad categories of uses and services involving data, certain of which will also be permissible without or with only limited, standardized safeguards. For riskier applications involving data, future regulatory schemes should articulate ground rules for how data users will determine the dangers of a particular data use or service and determine thereafter what measures best avoid or mitigate them[1233].
- EU data protection law creates for itself an ever-wider space of material and territorial scope. The same can generally be said for any jurisdiction, in principle: every legal order is inherently striving to impose itself as much as possible over others wishing to secure for its subjects an as extended as possible (physical as well as material) vital space of legal security. This, however, respectively increases the chances for conflicts among jurisdictions. Therefore, the need for coordination among different legal orders grows even more important so that frictions and jurisdictional uncertainty are avoided, as much as possible. Shifting the focus from data processing as a particular activity to cloud

1232 For more refer to Chapter 10.

1233 For more refer to Chapter 4.

enabled processes involving data in general and developing cloud computing regulation rules through this generic perspective will offer a much more suitable ground for common understanding among different legal orders[1234].

- The binary distinction between controllers and processors, sitting right now at the heart of the regulatory scheme utilized to decide on cloud-related issues, is unsuitable for a cloud computing environment and should be abolished. Alternatively, a wholly new principle of end to end accountability needs to be introduced, one that would run through the cloud business chain and will constantly hold the different actors accountable for their share of duties in the broader task of making sure the cloud cycle runs smoothly[1235].
- The relationship between the two pools of laws, i.e. the already existing and abundant one of laws regulating cloud-based applications and the currently nascent or almost non-existent but needed one of rules regulating the cloud per se, should not be hierarchical but rather complimentary: enriching the latter should be done in a way that will further boost the efficiency of the former[1236].
- In every law-making process governments or, in general, legislative authorities, have a certain range of mechanisms available to detect legal and regulatory issues related to the subject matter of the laws they are about to design. As it is commonly admitted, what issues do finally make it onto the legal and regulatory agenda greatly depends on the prevailing political economy in which an issue, in this case cloud computing, emerges and diffuses; accordingly, these conditions may vary across countries. As far as the cloud is concerned, although the two jurisdictions under examination in this study (i.e. EU and the US) may be following distinctly separate routes in the way they handle IT and, in particular, data-related issues, in both of them there is a strong momentum in civil society for taking decisive measures and adopting laws that will clear out the current blurry picture when it comes to regulating cloud technologies. This unanimous call for action should be heard by regulators and, apart from being a call for them to act, it can also serve as a perfect tool in working on producing rules for the cloud that will be based on common principles and will, therefore, be possible to

1234 For more refer to Chapter 6.

1235 Id.

1236 For more refer to Chapter 9.

be presented to both jurisdictions with an increased likelihood of being met favorably and embraced by all affected actors[1237].

- Any concept for data protection and technology-assisted cloud computing regulation needs to be designed by having two target groups in mind: producers of the respective technologies, who need to be legally obliged to ensure actual availability of the said technology, and users, that is, the various actors within the cloud workflow, with the aim of forcing them to actually put these measures in practice. Both target groups need to have clear guidelines from regulators for the development and application of privacy-friendly technologies. At the same time, making official the adoption of such technologies, as an indispensable asset towards the establishment of the new governance-oriented regime in the field of cloud computing, will encourage actors of these groups to actually invest resources and effort in developing and implementing such technologies. It is up to regulators' bravery to make the body of cloud computing laws as relevant as possible at this point, by going as far as concretizing future-oriented criteria for the design of technology that may be even directly derived from cloud computing regulation. What is more, cloud computing laws could even provide business and growth opportunities or even incentivize the use of such technologies[1238].

c. Future challenges – insights for further research

As it has been demonstrated, big data constitute the latest wave in the tsunami-like development of modern information technologies. Being a phenomenon which has been around only for a handful of years, they have grown exponentially and managed to play a decisive role in the final shaping and spirit of IT laws as new as the EU's GDPR. However, technological progress is relentless and, just as the world tries to process all the challenges big data have brought about, further waves of change are already looming on the horizon. The Internet of Things (IoT), the growth of which was, to a large extent, propelled by the success of big data, is quickly expanding in multiple directions beyond personal data. And just as the range

1237 Id.

1238 For more refer to Chapter 10.

of IoT applications multiplies so does its interrelation with the cloud[1239] and the challenges raised[1240]. For instance, soon it will become clear that it is not only important that the data collected on the cloud via IoT installations are safe and sealed from malpractice but that the metadata that will be produced as the output of processing activities carried out on the cloud are equally reliable, solid and accurate[1241]. Moreover, the proliferation of IoT applications and systems already challenges long-held legal perceptions in the field of IT, such as the illegality of hacking; there are already voices indicating that in the face of the diversity of IoT installations and the wide range of dangers that may be associated to them, even hacking should be considered a possibility under regulated circumstances[1242].

In conclusion, the issues dealt with on the course of this research are so dynamic that they could turn it into a never-ending project, should we wish to cover every single aspect and type of challenges cloud computing poses for IT law. Without being able, in the duration and with the constraints of a single PhD term, to provide answers to all questions, it is hoped that the points raised and the solutions proposed throughout this analysis will serve as a driving force for more pragmatic and more durable IT laws in the future, in an effort to maximize the benefits from the galloping advancement of technology for all types of actors, from users to service providers to regulators to the law itself and the security and sentiment of safety it should convey to its subjects.

1239 Everton Cavalcante, Jorge Pereira, Marcelo Pitanga Alves, Pedro Maia, Roniceli Moura, Thais Batista, Flavia C. Delicato & Paulo F. Pires, *On the interplay of Internet of Things and Cloud Computing. A systematic mapping study*, 89-90 Computer Communications 17–33 (2016.)

1240 Jatinder Singh, Thomas Pasquier, Jean Bacon, Hajoon Ko & David Eyers, *Twenty Security Considerations for Cloud-Supported Internet of Things*, 3 IEEE Internet Things J. 269–284 (2016); Christopher Rees, *Who owns our data?*, 30 Computer Law & Security Review 75–79 (2014); Niels Fallenbeck & Claudia Eckert (note 932); Birgit Vogel-Heuser, Thomas Bauernhansl & Michael ten Hompel eds., Handbuch Industrie 4.0 Bd.4 (2017.)

1241 For an example of beyond the norm cloud-based application which poses unprecedented regulatory challenges with regard to massive data exchanges and processing refer to: Fruzsina Molnár-Gábor & Jan O. Korbel, *Regulierung neuer Herausforderungen in den Naturwissenschaften – Datenschutz und Datenaustausch in der translationalen genetischen Forschung*, in Messen und Verstehen in der Wissenschaft. Interdisziplinäre Ansätze, 151–171 (Marcel Schweiker, Joachim Hass, Anna Novokhatko & Roxana Halbleib eds., 2017.)

1242 Ido Kilovaty, *Freedom to Hack* SSRN Journal (2017.)

List of case law

Court of Justice of the European Union

Maximillian Schrems v Data Protection Commissioner	C-362/14
Weltimmo s.r.o. v Nemzeti Adatvédelmi és Információszabadság Hatóság	C-230/14
Google Spain SL, Google Inc. v Agencia Española de Protección de Datos (AEPD), Mario Costeja González	C-131/12
Pammer v Reederei Karl Schlüter GmbH & Co and Hotel Alpenhof v Heller	C-585/08 and C-144/09
Yassin Abdullah Kadi and Al Barakaat International Foundation v Council of the European Union and Commission of the European Communities	C-402/05 P and C-415/05

US Courts

US Supreme Court

Jose Ernesto Medellin v. State of Texas	552 US 491 (2008)
Lawrence v. Texas	539 US 558 (2003)
Reno v. American Civil Liberties Union	521 US 844 (1997)
O'Connor v. Ortega	480 US 709 (1987)
United States v. Miller	425 US 435 (1976)
Katz v. United States	389 US 347 (1967)
Hoffa v. United States	385 US 293 (1966)
International Shoe Co. v. Washington	326 US 310 (1945)
Olmstead v. United States	277 US 438 (1928)

Lower US courts

United States v. D'Andrea	648 F.3d 1 (1st Cir. 2011)
Maes v. Folberg	504 F. Supp. 2d 339, 347 (N.D. Ill. 2007)
Muick v. Glenayre Elecs.	280 F.3d 741, 743 (7th Cir. 2002)

Other national courts

Italy

Sentenza nella cause penale contro Google Italy s.r.l.	n. 1972/2010

List of laws and statutes

(categorized as per legal order and type of instrument)

EU laws and statutes

Consolidated version of the Treaty on European Union (TEU)	2008/C 115/01
Charter of Fundamental Rights of the European Union (CFREU)	2012/C 326/02
Regulation of the European Parliament and of the Council on the protection of natural persons with regard to the processing of personal data and on the free movement of such data, and repealing Directive 95/46/EC (General Data Protection Regulation) (GDPR)	Regulation (EU) 2016/679
Council Regulation on jurisdiction and the recognition and enforcement of judgments in civil and commercial matters (Brussels I)	Regulation (EC) No 44/2001
Directive of the European Parliament and of the Council on the protection of individuals with regard to the processing of personal data and on the free movement of such data (Data Protection Directive) (DPD)	Directive 95/46/EC

US laws and statutes

United States of America: Constitution

Stored Communications Act (SCA)	18 U.S.C. § 2701 et seq.
United States of America: Uniting and Strengthening America by Providing Appropriate Tools Required to Intercept and Obstruct Terrorism Act of 2001 (USA PATRIOT Act)	Pub.L. 107–56
Foreign Intelligence and Surveillance Act (FISA)	50 U.S.C. §§ 1801-11, 1821-29, 1841-46, 1861-62, 1871
Electronic Communications Privacy Act (ECPA)	Pub.L. 99–50
Communications Decency Act (CDA)	47 U.S.C. § 230
Health Insurance Portability and Accountability Act (HIPAA)	Pub.L. 104–191, 110 Stat. 1936
Fair Credit Reporting Act (FCRA)	15 U.S.C. § 1681
Digital Millennium Copyright Act (DMCA)	Pub.L. 105-304

United Nations

UN General Assembly, Universal Declaration of Human Rights (UDHR)	217 A (III)

Council of Europe

Council of Europe, European Convention for the Protection of Human Rights and Fundamental Freedoms, as amended by Protocols Nos. 11 and 14 (ECHR)	ETS 5
Council of Europe, Convention for the Protection of Individuals with regard to the Automatic Processing of Individual Data	ETS 108

Bibliographical index

Audio or Video Documents

Larry Ellison, Larry Ellison on cloud computing (2009), available at: https://www.youtube.com/watch?v=0FacYAI6DY0.

Books

P. E. Agre & M. Rotenberg, Technology and Privacy: The New Landscape (1998): MIT Press.

Antony Anghie & C.G Weeramantry, Legal visions of the 21st century: essays in honour of judge Christopher Weeramantry (op. 1998). The Hague [etc.]: Kluwer Law International.

Anne Arendt, Ulrich Dammann & Spiros Simitis, Bundesdatenschutzgesetz (2011). Baden-Baden: Nomos-Verl.Ges.

I. Augsberg, Informationsverwaltungsrecht: Zur kognitiven Dimension der rechtlichen Steuerung von Verwaltungsentscheidungen (2014): Mohr Siebeck.

Aharon Barak & Sari Bashi, Purposive Interpretation in Law (2011). Princeton: Princeton University Press.

Christian Baun, Marcel Kunze, Jens Nimis & Stefan Tai, Cloud Computing (2011). Berlin, Heidelberg: Springer Berlin Heidelberg.

C. J. Bennett, Regulating Privacy: Data Protection and Public Policy in Europe and the United States (1992): Cornell University Press.

Colin J. Bennett & Charles D. Raab, The governance of privacy. Policy instruments in global perspective (2006). Cambridge, Mass.: MIT Press.

Donald H. Berman & Carole D. Hafner, Representing teleological structure in case-based legal reasoning: the missing link (1993): ACM.

M. Bovens, The Quest for Responsibility: Accountability and Citizenship in Complex Organisations (1998): Cambridge University Press.

S. Brenner, Law in an Era of Smart Technology (2007): Oxford University Press.

Stephen G. Breyer, Breaking the vicious circle. Toward effective risk regulation, vol. 1992 (1993). Cambridge, Mass.: Harvard University Press.

R. Brownsword, E. Scotford & K. Yeung, The Oxford Handbook of Law, Regulation and Technology (2017): OUP Oxford.

Eoghan Casey, Handbook of digital forensics and investigation (2010). London: Academic.

V. Chang, Delivery and Adoption of Cloud Computing Services in Contemporary Organizations (2015): IGI Global.

H. M. Collins, Tacit and explicit knowledge (2013). Chicago, London: The University of Chicago Press.

N. Cox, Technology and Legal Systems (2016): Taylor & Francis.

P. P. Craig & G. de Búrca, EU law. Text, cases, and materials (2015). Oxford, United Kingdom, New York, NY: Oxford University Press.

Frank B. Cross, Theory and practice of statutory interpretation (2012). Stanford: Stanford University Press.

Ulrich Dammann & Spiros Simitis, Bundesdatenschutzgesetz (2014). Baden-Baden: Nomos.

Hans Delfs & Helmut Knebl, Introduction to cryptography. Principles and applications, 2007: 1 (2007). Berlin: Springer.

J. Domingue, D. Fensel & J. A. Hendler, Handbook of Semantic Web Technologies (2011): Springer Berlin Heidelberg.

Ronald Dworkin, Law's empire (1986). Cambridge, Mass.: Belknap Press.

D. Dyzenhaus & T. Poole, Law, Liberty and State: Oakeshott, Hayek and Schmitt on the Rule of Law (2015): Cambridge University Press.

H.S.P.L.C.E.L.P. Eeckhout & P.L.T. Tridimas, Yearbook of European Law 2009, v. 28 (2010): Oxford University Press, USA.

Evelyn Ellis, The principle of proportionality in the laws of Europe (1999). Oxford, Portland, Or.: Hart Pub.

Thomas Erl, Richardo Puttini & Zaigham Mahmood, Cloud computing. Concepts, technology, & architecture (2013). Upper Saddle River, NJ: Prentice Hall.

Federico Fabbrini, Fundamental rights in Europe (2014). Oxford: Oxford University Press.

Elgar Fleisch & Friedemann Mattern, Das Internet der Dinge. Ubiquitous Computing und RFID in der Praxis : Visionen, Technologien, Anwendungen, Handlungsanleitungen (2005). Berlin: Springer.

M. Friedewald & R. J. Pohoryles, Privacy and Security in the Digital Age: Privacy in the Age of Super-Technologies (2016): Taylor & Francis.

Brett M. Frischmann, Michael J. Madison & Katherine Jo Strandburg, Governing knowledge commons (2014). New York: Oxford University Press.

Lon L. Fuller, The morality of law (1965). New Haven, Conn., London: Yale University Press.

Borivoje Furht & Armando Escalante, Handbook of cloud computing (2010). New York: Springer.

Peter Gola, Christoph Klug, Rudolf Schomerus & Barbara Körffer, Bundesdatenschutzgesetz. Kommentar (2010). München: C. H. Beck.

Jack L. Goldsmith & Tim Wu, Who controls the Internet? Illusions of a borderless world (2008). New York, NY: Oxford University Press.

Jean-Christophe Graz & Andreas Nölke, Transnational private governance and its limits, vol. 51 (2008). London, New York: Routledge.

Adam Greenfield, Everyware. The dawning age of ubiquitous computing (2006). Berkeley, CA: New Riders.

H. L. A. Hart, The concept of law (1998). Oxford: Clarendon Press.

Friedrich A. von Hayek, The road to serfdom (2005). Princeton, N.J.: Recording for the Blind & Dyslexic.

Uta Kohl, Jurisdiction and the Internet. A study of regulatory competence over online activity (2010). Cambridge: Cambridge University Press.

E. Kosta, Consent in European Data Protection Law (2013): Brill.

Steffen Kroschwald, Informationelle Selbstbestimmung in der Cloud. Datenschutzrechtliche Bewertung und Gestaltung des Cloud Computing aus dem Blickwinkel des Mittelstands (2016). Wiesbaden: Springer Vieweg.

Christopher Kuner, Transborder Data Flows and Data Privacy Law (2013). Oxford University Press.

L. Lessig, Code and other laws of cyberspace (1999): New York: Basic books.

Edward H. Levi & Frederick F. Schauer, An introduction to legal reasoning (2013). Chicago: The University of Chicago Press.

Ling Liu & M. Tamer Özsu, Encyclopedia of database systems (2009). New York: Springer.

Andreas F. Lowenfeld, International litigation and the quest for reasonableness. Essays in private international law (1996). Oxford, New York: Clarendon Press; Oxford University Press.

Christopher T. Marsden, Internet Co-Regulation. European Law, Regulatory Governance and Legitimacy in Cyberspace (2011). Cambridge: Cambridge University Press.

Viktor Mayer-Schönberger & Kenneth Cukier, Big data. A revolution that will transform how we live, work, and think (2013). Boston: Houghton Mifflin Harcourt.

McGraw-Hill, McGraw-Hill Dictionary of Scientific and Technical Terms (2003): McGraw-Hill.

Jens Meierhenrich, Oliver Simons & Friedrich Balke, The Oxford Handbook of Carl Schmitt, vol. 1 (2015): Oxford University Press.

Christopher Millard, Cloud Computing Law (2013). New York: Oxford University Press.

V. Mitsilegas, European union and internal security. Guardian of the people? (2014). [Place of publication not identified]: Palgrave Macmillan.

Andrew Murray, The regulation of cyberspace. Control in the online environment (2007). Milton Park, Abingdon [UK], New York, NY: Routledge-Cavendish.

Nordic Council of Ministers, Information Security in Nordic Countries (1993): Nordic Council of Ministers.

Christof Paar & Jan Pelzl, Understanding cryptography. A textbook for students and practitioners (2010). Berlin [u.a.]: Springer.

John G. Palfrey & Urs Gasser, Born digital. Understanding the first generation of digital natives (2010). New York: BasicBooks.

John G. Palfrey & Urs Gasser, Interop. The promise and perils of highly interconnected systems (2012). New York: Basic Books.

Siani Pearson, Taking account of privacy when designing cloud computing services (2009): IEEE Computer Society.

Siani Pearson & George Yee, Privacy and security for cloud computing (2013). London, New York: Springer.

Norman Pelzl, Methodische Entwicklung von zukunftsorientierten Geschäftsmodellen im Cloud-Computing, Band 88 (2016). Lohmar: Eul Verlag.

Stefan Poslad, Ubiquitous computing. Smart devices, environments and interactions (2009). Chichester, U.K.: Wiley.

Hans Christian Röhl, Wissen, zur kognitiven Dimension des Rechts, vol. 9 (2010). Berlin: Duncker & Humblot.

Alexander Rossnagel, Allianz von Medienrecht und Informationstechnik? Ordnung in digitalen Medien durch Gestaltung der Technik am Beispiel von Urheberschutz, Datenschutz, Jugendschutz und Vielfaltschutz; Dokumentation der Stiftungstagung (zugleich EMR-Workshop), der Alcatel SEL Stiftung für Kommunikationsforschung, des Instituts für Medienrecht (EMR), der Landeszentrale für politische Bildung (LpB) Baden-Württemberg, am 10. Mai 2001 im Landtag Baden-Württemberg, Stuttgart, Bd. 24 (2001). Baden-Baden: Nomos.

Alexander Roßnagel, Datenschutz in einem informatisierten Alltag (2007). Berlin: Friedich-Ebert-Stiftung.

Alexander Roßnagel, Tom Sommerlatte & Udo Winand, Digitale Visionen. Zur Gestaltung allgegenwärtiger Informationstechnologien (2008). Berlin, Heidelberg: Springer-Verlag.

Andreas Schedler, Larry Jay Diamond & Marc F. Plattner, The self-restraining state. Power and accountability in new democracies (1999). Boulder, Colo.: Lynne Rienner Publishers.

Gunnar Folke Schuppert & Andreas Vosskuhle, Governance von und durch Wissen, Bd. 12 (2008). Baden-Baden, Berlin: Nomos; Wissenschaftszentrum für Sozialforschung.

S. Scoglio, Transforming Privacy: A Transpersonal Philosophy of Rights (1998): Praeger.

V. Sharma, Information Technology Law and Practice (2011): Universal Law Publishing.

Anne-Marie Slaughter, A New World Order (2009). Princeton: Princeton University Press.

Christopher Slobogin, Privacy at risk. The new government surveillance and the Fourth Amendment (2007). Chicago: University of Chicago Press.

S. S. Smith, Web-based Instruction: A Guide for Libraries (2006): American Library Association.

E. Thomas Sullivan & Richard S. Frase, Proportionality principles in American law. Controlling excessive government actions (2009). Oxford, New York: Oxford University Press.

Dan Jerker B. Svantesson, Private international law and the internet (2012). Alphen aan den Rijn, Frederick, MD: Kluwer Law International; Sold and distributed in North, Central and South America by Aspen Publishers.

Peter P. Swire & Robert E. Litan, None of your business. World data flows, electronic commerce, and the European privacy directive (1998). Washington, D.C.: Brookings Institution Press.

D. Tambini, D. Leonardi & C. T. Marsden, Codifying Cyberspace: Communications Self-regulation in the Age of Internet Convergence (2008): Routledge.

Georgios Tselentis, Towards the future internet. Emerging trends from European research (2010). Amsterdam: IOS Press.

Mariana Valverde, Law's Dream of a Common Knowledge (2009). Princeton: Princeton University Press.

Ian Watson, The universal machine. From the dawn of computing to digital consciousness (2012). New York: Copernicus Books.

Bill Williams, The economics of cloud computing (2012). Indianapolis, Ind.: Cisco Press.

Hongji Yang & Xiaodong Liu, Software reuse in the emerging cloud computing era (2012). Hershey, PA: Information Science Reference.

Liang-Jie Zhang & Qun Zhou, CCOA: Cloud Computing Open Architecture (2009): IEEE.

K. S. Ziegler, Human Rights and Private Law: Privacy as Autonomy (2007): Bloomsbury Publishing.

Tomasz Zurek & Michał Araszkiewicz, Modeling teleological interpretation (2013): ACM.

Books, Edited

Michael Backes & Peng Ning eds., Computer security – ESORICS 2009. 14th European Symposium on Research in Computer Security, Saint-Malo, France, September 21-23, 2009: proceedings, vol. 5789 (2009). Berlin [etc.]: SpringerLink.

Giorgio Bongiovanni, Giovanni Sartor & Chiara Valentini eds., Reasonableness and Law, vol. 86 (2009). Dordrecht: Springer Netherlands.

Martin Gilje Jaatun, Gansen Zhao & Chunming Rong eds., Cloud computing. First international conference, CloudCom 2009, Beijing, China, December 1-4, 2009: proceedings, vol. 5931 (2009). Berlin, New York: Springer.

Helmut Krcmar, Jan Marco Leimeister, Alexander Roßnagel & Ali Sunyaev eds., Cloud-Services aus der Geschäftsperspektive (2016). Wiesbaden: Gabler.

Steffen Kroschwald ed., Informationelle Selbstbestimmung in der Cloud. Datenschutzrechtliche Bewertung und Gestaltung des Cloud Computing aus dem Blickwinkel des Mittelstands (2016). Wiesbaden: Springer Vieweg.

Gerald Münzl, Michael Pauly & Martin Reti eds., Cloud Computing als neue Herausforderung für Management und IT (2015). Berlin [Germany], Heidelberg [Germany]: Springer-Verlag.

Alexander Roßnagel ed., Datenschutzaufsicht nach der EU-Datenschutz-Grundverordnung. Neue Aufgaben und Befugnisse der Aufsichtsbehörden (2017). Wiesbaden: Springer Fachmedien Wiesbaden.

Marcel Schweiker, Joachim Hass, Anna Novokhatko & Roxana Halbleib eds., Messen und Verstehen in der Wissenschaft. Interdisziplinäre Ansätze (2017). Wiesbaden: Springer Fachmedien Wiesbaden.

John R. Vacca ed., Security in the private cloud (2017). Boca Raton: Taylor & Francis, a CRC title, part of the Taylor & Francis imprint, a member of the Taylor & Francis Group, the academic division of T&F Informa, plc.

Birgit Vogel-Heuser, Thomas Bauernhansl & Michael ten Hompel eds., Handbuch Industrie 4.0 Bd.4 (2017). Berlin, Heidelberg: Springer Berlin Heidelberg.

Conference Proceedings

2008 Grid Computing Environments Workshop.

2009 ICSE Workshop on Software Engineering Challenges of Cloud Computing.

2012 IEEE 4th International Conference on Cloud Computing Technology and Science (CloudCom).

IEEE INFOCOM 2010 – IEEE Conference on Computer Communications.

International Workshop on Computational Autonomy (2003): Springer Berlin Heidelberg.

2012 International Conference on Computer Science and Electronics Engineering (2012): IEEE.

2012 International Conference on Computing, Electronics and Electrical Technologies (ICCEET) (2012): IEEE.

ACM ed., Controlling data in the cloud: outsourcing computation without outsourcing control (2009): ACM.

Jameela Al-Jaroodi & Shahram Latifi eds., ITNG 2010. Information Technology New Generations: proceedings of the Seventh International Conference on Information Technology :12-14, April 2009, Las Vegas, Nevada, USA (2010). Los Alamitos, Calif., Piscataway, N.J.: IEEE Computer Society; IEEE.

Solon Barocas & Helen Nissenbaum eds., On Notice: The Trouble with Notice and Consent (2009).

Elizabeth Chang ed., 24th IEEE International Conference on Advanced Information Networking and Applications (AINA), 2010. 20 – 23 April 2010, Perth, Australia; proceedings (2010). Piscataway, NJ, Piscataway, NJ: IEEE.

IEEE ed., An audit logic for accountability (2005): IEEE.

IEEE ed., 2010 19th IEEE International Workshop on Enabling Technologies. Infrastructures for Collaborative Enterprises (2010). [Place of publication not identified]: IEEE.

KIIT University ed., 2015 International Conference on Computational Intelligence & Networks (CINE).

Paulo Mendes ed., Proceedings of the 1st ACM workshop on User-provided networking challenges and opportunities (2009). New York, NY: ACM.

Sascha Ossowski ed., Proceedings of the 31st Annual ACM Symposium on Applied Computing (2016). New York, NY: ACM.

Alexander Roßnagel ed., Wolken über dem Rechtsstaat? Recht und Technik des Cloud Computing in Verwaltung und Wirtschaft, vol. 33 (2015). Baden-Baden: Nomos.

IEEE Staff ed., 2011 IEEE International Conference on Services Computing (2011). [Place of publication not identified]: IEEE.

Adrian Vermeule ed., Local and Global Knowledge in the Administrative State (2013).

Gabriela Zanfir ed., What Happens in the Cloud Stays in the Cloud, or Why the Cloud's Architecture Should Be Transformed in 'Virtual Territorial Scope' (2013).

Liang-Jie Zhang ed., World Conference on Services-I, 2009 (2009). Piscataway, NJ: IEEE.

Contribution in Legal Commentary

Daniel Halberstam, Constitutionalism and Pluralism in Marbury and Van Gend, in: U of Michigan Public Law Working Paper (2008).

Contributions

Bu-Qing Cao, Bing Li & Qi-Ming Xia, A Service-Oriented Qos-Assured and Multi-Agent Cloud Computing Architecture, in Cloud computing. First international conference, CloudCom 2009, Beijing, China, December 1-4, 2009: proceedings, 644–649 (Martin Gilje Jaatun, Gansen Zhao & Chunming Rong eds., 2009).

Deyan Chen & Hong Zhao, Data Security and Privacy Protection Issues in Cloud Computing, in 2012 International Conference on Computer Science and Electronics Engineering, 647–651 (2012).

Guilherme Da Cunha Rodrigues, Rodrigo N. Calheiros, Vinicius Tavares Guimaraes, Glederson Lessa dos Santos, Márcio Barbosa de Carvalho, Lisandro Zambenedetti Granville, Liane Margarida Rockenbach Tarouco & Rajkumar Buyya, Monitoring of cloud computing environments, in Proceedings of the 31st Annual ACM Symposium on Applied Computing, 378–383 (Sascha Ossowski ed., 2016).

Tharam Dillon, Chen Wu & Elizabeth Chang, Cloud Computing: Issues and Challenges, in 24th IEEE International Conference on Advanced Information Networking and Applications (AINA), 2010. 20 – 23 April 2010, Perth, Australia; proceedings, 27–33 (Elizabeth Chang ed., 2010).

Luciana Duranti, Adam Jansen, Giovanni Michetti, Mumma Courtney, Daryll Prescott, Corinne Rogers & Thibodeau Kenneth, Preservation as a Service for Trust, in Security in the private cloud, 47–72 (John R. Vacca ed., 2017).

Niels Fallenbeck & Claudia Eckert, IT-Sicherheit und Cloud Computing, in Handbuch Industrie 4.0 Bd.4, 137–171 (Birgit Vogel-Heuser, Thomas Bauernhansl & Michael ten Hompel eds., 2017).

Marc Fouquet, Heiko Niedermayer & Georg Carle, Cloud computing for the masses, in Proceedings of the 1st ACM workshop on User-provided networking challenges and opportunities, 31 (Paulo Mendes ed., 2009).

Ines Houidi, Marouen Mechtri, Wajdi Louati & Djamal Zeghlache, Cloud Service Delivery across Multiple Cloud Platforms, in 2011 IEEE International Conference on Services Computing, 741–742 (IEEE Staff ed., 2011).

Yashpalsinh Jadeja & Kirit Modi, Cloud computing – concepts, architecture and challenges, in 2012 International Conference on Computing, Electronics and Electrical Technologies (ICCEET), 877–880 (2012).

S. Jandt, S. Kroschwald, A. Roßnagel & M. Wicker, Datenschutzkonformes Cloud-Computing, in Cloud-Services aus der Geschäftsperspektive, 207–266 (Helmut Krcmar, Jan Marco Leimeister, Alexander Roßnagel & Ali Sunyaev eds., 2016).

Xiaolong Jin & Jiming Liu, From Individual Based Modeling to Autonomy Oriented Computation, in International Workshop on Computational Autonomy, 151–169 (2003).

Andrea de Mauro, Marco Greco & Michele Grimaldi, What is big data? A consensual definition and a review of key research topics, in AIP Conference Proceedings, Volume 1644, Issue 1, 97–104 (2015).

Fruzsina Molnár-Gábor & Jan O. Korbel, Regulierung neuer Herausforderungen in den Naturwissenschaften – Datenschutz und Datenaustausch in der translationalen genetischen Forschung, in Messen und Verstehen in der Wissenschaft. Interdisziplinäre Ansätze, 151–171 (Marcel Schweiker, Joachim Hass, Anna Novokhatko & Roxana Halbleib eds., 2017).

Siani Pearson & Andrew Charlesworth, Accountability as a Way Forward for Privacy Protection in the Cloud, in Cloud computing. First international conference, CloudCom 2009, Beijing, China, December 1-4, 2009: proceedings, 131–144 (Martin Gilje Jaatun, Gansen Zhao & Chunming Rong eds., 2009).

Siani Pearson, Vasilis Tountopoulos, Daniele Catteddu, Mario Sudholt, Refik Molva, Christoph Reich, Simone Fischer-Hubner, Christopher Millard, Volkmar Lotz, Martin Gilje Jaatun, Ronald Leenes, Chunming Rong & Javier Lopez, Accountability for cloud and other future Internet services, in 2012 IEEE 4th International Conference on Cloud Computing Technology and Science (CloudCom), 629–632.

Deepak Puthal, B.P.S. Sahoo, Sambit Mishra & Satyabrata Swain, Cloud Computing Features, Issues, and Challenges: A Big Picture, in 2015 International Conference on Computational Intelligence & Networks (CINE), 116–123 (KIIT University ed.).

Alexander Roßnagel, Datenschutzfragen des Cloud Computing, in Wolken über dem Rechtsstaat? Recht und Technik des Cloud Computing in Verwaltung und Wirtschaft, 19–52 (Alexander Roßnagel ed., 2015).

Vijay Sarathy, Purnendu Narayan & Rao Mikkilineni, Next Generation Cloud Computing Architecture: Enabling Real-Time Dynamism for Shared Distributed Physical Infrastructure, in 2010 19th IEEE International Workshop on Enabling Technologies. Infrastructures for Collaborative Enterprises, 48–53 (IEEE ed., 2010).

Wei-Tek Tsai, Xin Sun & Janaka Balasooriya, Service-Oriented Cloud Computing Architecture, in ITNG 2010. Information Technology New Generations: proceedings of the Seventh International Conference on Information Technology :12-14, April 2009, Las Vegas, Nevada, USA, 684–689 (Jameela Al-Jaroodi & Shahram Latifi eds., 2010).

Cong Wang, Qian Wang, Kui Ren & Wenjing Lou, Privacy-Preserving Public Auditing for Data Storage Security in Cloud Computing, in IEEE INFOCOM 2010 – IEEE Conference on Computer Communications, 1–9.

Kaiqi Xiong & Harry Perros, Service Performance and Analysis in Cloud Computing, in World Conference on Services-I, 2009, 693–700 (Liang-Jie Zhang ed., 2009).

Lamia Youseff, Maria Butrico & Dilma Da Silva, Toward a Unified Ontology of Cloud Computing, in 2008 Grid Computing Environments Workshop, 1–10.

Cheng Zeng, Xiao Guo, Weijie Ou & Dong Han, Cloud Computing Service Composition and Search Based on Semantic, in Cloud computing. First international conference, CloudCom 2009, Beijing, China, December 1-4, 2009: proceedings, 290–300 (Martin Gilje Jaatun, Gansen Zhao & Chunming Rong eds., 2009).

Internet Documents

M. Arif, A history of cloud computing, available at: http://www.computerweekly.com/feature/A-history-of-cloud-computing (18 February 2015).

M. Armbrust, A. Fox, R. Griffith, A. Joseph D., R. Katz H., A. Konwinski, G. Lee, D. Patterson A., A. Rabkin, A. Stoica & M. Zaharia, Above the Clouds: A Berkeley View of Cloud Computing, available at: http://www.eecs.berkeley.edu/Pubs/TechRpts/2009/EECS-2009-28.html (2 March 2015).

Article 29 Working Party, Working document on determining the international application of EU data protection law to personal data processing on the Internet by non-EU based websites, available at: http://ec.europa.eu/justice/data-protection/article-29/documentation/opinion-recommendation/index_en.htm.

Article 29 Working Party, Opinion 3/2009 on the Draft Commission Decision on standard contractual clauses for the transfer of personal data to processors established in third countries, under Directive 95/46/EC (data controller to data processor), available at: http://ec.europa.eu/justice/data-protection/article-29/documentation/opinion-recommendation/index_en.htm.

Article 29 Working Party, Opinion 03/2013 on purpose limitation, available at: http://ec.europa.eu/justice/data-protection/article-29/documentation/opinion-recommendation/index_en.htm (3 February 2015).

Ozalp Babaoglu, M. Jelasity, Anne Marie Kermarrec, Alberto Montresor & Maarten van Steen, Operating Systems Review (ACM), available at: http://dl.acm.org/citation.cfm?doid=1151374.1151379.

Francesca Bosco, Assessing Europe's cyber challenges, available at: http://policyreview.info/articles/news/assessing-europes-cyber-challenges/355 (4 July 2016).

Tobias Bräutigam, The Land of Confusion. International Data Transfers between Schrems and the GDPR.

A. Cavoukian, Privacy by Design; The 7 Foundational Principles, available at: https://www.ipc.on.ca/wp-content/uploads/Resources/7foundationalprinciples.pdf.

Centre for Information Policy Leadership, Data Protection Accountability: The Essential Elements A Document for Discussion, available at: http://www.huntonfiles.com/files/webupload/CIPL_Galway_Accountability_Paper.pdf (19 March 2015).

European Commission, Unleashing the Potential of Cloud Computing in Europe, available at: http://eur-lex.europa.eu/LexUriServ/LexUriServ.do?uri=COM:2012:0529:FIN:EN:PDF (20 November 2014).

Robert Gellman, Privacy in the Clouds: Risks to Privacy and Confidentiality from Cloud Computing, available at: https://www.worldprivacyforum.org/2011/11/resource-page-cloud-privacy/ (20 April 2015).

Chris Hoofnagle, COMPARATIVE STUDY ON DIFFERENT APPROACHES TO NEW PRIVACY CHALLENGES, IN PARTICULAR IN THE LIGHT OF TECHNOLOGICAL DEVELOPMENTS. B.1 – UNITED STATES OF AMERICA, available at: http://ec.europa.eu/justice/policies/privacy/docs/studies/new_privacy_challenges/final_report_country_report_B1_usa.pdf (2 May 2016).

Hunton Privacy Blog, Article 29 Working Party Clarifies Purpose Limitation Principle; Opines on Big and Open Data, available at: https://www.huntonprivacyblog.com/2013/04/09/article-29-working-party-clarifies-purpose-limitation-principle-opines-on-big-and-open-data/ (5 November 2015).

International Working Group on Data Protection in Telecommunications, Working Paper on Cloud Computing – Privacy and data protection issues. "Sopot Memorandum", available at: http://ec.europa.eu/justice/data-protection/article-29/documentation/opinion-recommendation/index_en.htm#h2-3 (3 February 2015).

Xenofon Kontargyris, From effective to efficient regulation of ICT (2): the big leap towards embracing vertical, apart from horizontal, interdisciplinarity, available at: http://www.juwiss.de/88-2016/ (13 September 2017).

Xenofon Kontargyris, From effective to efficient regulation of ICT: time to build the backbone of information technology legislation, available at: http://www.juwiss.de/66-2016/.

D. Linthicum, MSDN Documentation. Service Oriented Architecture (SOA), available at: https://msdn.microsoft.com/en-us/library/bb833022.aspx (4 November 2015).

J. Locke, The Roots of Cloud Computing, available at: http://www.servercloudcanada.com/2013/10/the-roots-of-cloud-computing/ (11 January 2017).

McAlpine C., Weigh Legal Risks of Cloud Computing, available at: http://www.baselinemag.com/c/a/Legal/Weigh-Legal-Risks-of-Cloud-Computing-869422 (19 February 2016).

Peter Mell & Timothy Grance, The NIST Definition of Cloud Computing. Recommendations of the National Institute of Standards and Technology, available at: http://csrc.nist.gov/publications/nistpubs/800-145/SP800-145.pdf (4 November 2015).

National Telecommunications & Information Administration (NTIA), PRIVACY AND SELF-REGULATION IN THE INFORMATION AGE, available at: https://www.ntia.doc.gov/report/1997/privacy-and-self-regulation-information-age (4 May 2016).

R. Peeva, File Hosting vs. Cloud Computing, available at: http://www.websitepulse.com/blog/file-hosting-vs-cloud-computing (4 November 2015).

Antonio Regalado, Who Coined 'Cloud Computing'?, available at: https://www.technologyreview.com/s/425970/who-coined-cloud-computing/ (11 January 2017).

Reidenberg, J. R., Schwartz, P. M., Data Protection Law and On-line Services: Regulatory Responses.

Reilly, D., Wren, C., & Berry, T., Cloud computing: Forensic challenges for law enforcement. In Internet Technology and Secured Transactions (ICITST).

Neil Robinson, Hans Graux, Maarten Botterman & Lorenzo Valeri, RAND Europe: Review of the European Data Protection Directive, available at: http://www.rand.org/pubs/technical_reports/TR710.html (13 February 2015).

Paul M. Schwartz, Legal Access to Cloud Information. Data Shards, Data Localization, and Data Trusts.

Jonathan Stuart Ward & Adam Barker, Undefined By Data. A Survey of Big Data Definitions, available at: http://arxiv.org/pdf/1309.5821.

Journal Articles

Divyakant Agrawal, Philip Bernstein, Elisa Bertino, Susan Davidson, Umeshwas Dayal, Michael Franklin, Johannes Gehrke, Laura Haas, Alon Halevy, Jiawei Han, H. V. Jagadish, Alexandros Labrinidis, Sam Madden, Yannis Papakonstantinou, Jignesh Patel, Raghu Ramakrishnan, Kenneth Ross, Cyrus Shahabi, Dan Suciu, Shiv Vaithyanathan & Jennifer Widom, Challenges and Opportunities with Big Data 2011-1 Cyber Center Technical Reports (2011).

Divyakant Agrawal, Sudipto Das & Amr El Abbadi, Big data and cloud computing. Current state and future opportunities 530–533 (2011).

Robert B. Ahdieh, The Visible Hand: Coordination Functions of the Regulatory State, 09 Emory University School of Law, Public Law and Legal Theory Research Paper Series 578–649 (2009).

Michael Akehurst, Jurisdiction in International Law, 46 Brit. Y. B. Int'l L. 145–258 (1972).

Robert Alexy, On the Structure of Legal Principles, 13 Ratio Juris 294–304 (2000).

Ricardo Alonso, Wouter Dessein & Niko Matouschek, When Does Coordination Require Centralization?, 98 American Economic Review 145–179 (2008).

Alfred Aman, A Global Perspective on Current Regulatory Reform: Rejection, Relocation, or Reinvention?, 2 2 Indiana Journal of Global Legal Studies 429 (1995) 429–464 (1995).

Mauro Andreolini, Michele Colajanni, Marcello Pietri & Stefania Tosi, Adaptive, scalable and reliable monitoring of big data on clouds, 79-80 Journal of Parallel and Distributed Computing 67–79 (2015).

Damon C. Andrews & John M. Newman, Personal Jurisdiction and Choice of Law in the Cloud, 73 Md. L. Rev. 313–388 (2013).

Stephanos Androutsellis-Theotokis & Diomidis Spinellis, A survey of peer-to-peer content distribution technologies, 36 ACM Comput. Surv. 335–371 (2004).

Kevin D. Ashley & Edwina L. Rissland, Law, learning and representation, 150 Artificial Intelligence 17–58 (2003).

Marcos D. Assunção, Rodrigo N. Calheiros, Silvia Bianchi, Marco A.S. Netto & Rajkumar Buyya, Big Data computing and clouds. Trends and future directions, 79-80 Journal of Parallel and Distributed Computing 3–15 (2015).

Nicholas Bagley & Richard L. Revesz, Centralized Oversight of the Regulatory State, 106 Columbia Law Review 1260–1330 (2006).

Kenneth A. Bamberger & Deirdre K. Mulligan, Privacy on the Books and on the Ground, 63 Stanford Law Review 247–316 (2011).

Merve Bayramusta & V. Aslihan Nasir, A fad or future of IT? A comprehensive literature review on the cloud computing research, 36 International Journal of Information Management 635–644 (2016).

Patricia L. Bellia, Federalization in Information Privacy Law, 118 Yale Law Journal 868–890 (2009).

Trevor Bench-Capon & Giovanni Sartor, A model of legal reasoning with cases incorporating theories and values. AI and Law, 150 Artificial Intelligence 97–143 (2003).

Y. Benkler, Internet regulation: a case study in the problem of unilateralism, 11 European Journal of International Law 171–185 (2000).

Paul Schiff Berman, Cyberspace and the State Action Debate: The Cultural Value of Applying Constitutional Norms to 'Private' Regulation, 71 University of Colorado Law Review 1263–1310 (2000).

Paul Schiff Berman, Global Legal Pluralism, 80 S. Cal. L. Rev. 1155–1238 (2006).

Paul Schiff Berman, The New Legal Pluralism, 5 Annual Review of Law and Social Science 225–242 (2009).

J. Bing, Data Protection, jurisdiction and the choice of law Privacy Laws & Policy Reporter 92–98 (1999).

Julia Black, Constructing and contesting legitimacy and accountability in polycentric regulatory regimes, 2 Regulation & Governance 137–164 (2008).

D. Scott Blake, Let's Be Reasonable: Fourth Amendment Principles in the Digital Age, 5 SEVENTH CIRCUIT REV. 491–531 (2010).

P. Blume, Transborder data flow: is there a solution in sight?, 8 International Journal of Law and Information Technology 65–86 (2000).

Martin Boodman, The Myth of Harmonization of Laws, 39 The American Journal of Comparative Law 699–724 (1991).

Scott Brewer, Exemplary Reasoning. Semantics, Pragmatics, and the Rational Force of Legal Argument by Analogy, 109 Harvard Law Review 923–1028 (1996).

Grainne de Burca, The EU, the European Court of Justice and the International Legal Order after Kadi. Harvard International Law Journal, 1 Fordham Law Legal Studies Research 1–51 (2009).

Rajkumar Buyya, Chee Shin Yeo, Srikumar Venugopal, James Broberg & Ivona Brandic, Cloud computing and emerging IT platforms. Vision, hype, and reality for delivering computing as the 5th utility, 25 Future Generation Computer Systems 599–616 (2009).

L. A. Bygrave, Privacy protection in a global context–a comparative overview, 47 Scandinavian Studies in Law 319–348 (2004).

Lee A. Bygrave, Aytomated Profiling, 17 Computer Law & Security Review 17–24 (2001).

Eve M. Caudill & Patrick E. Murphy, Consumer Online Privacy. Legal and Ethical Issues, 19 Journal of Public Policy & Marketing 7–19 (2000).

Everton Cavalcante, Jorge Pereira, Marcelo Pitanga Alves, Pedro Maia, Roniceli Moura, Thais Batista, Flavia C. Delicato & Paulo F. Pires, On the interplay of Internet of Things and Cloud Computing. A systematic mapping study, 89-90 Computer Communications 17–33 (2016).

Anupam Chander & Uyen P. Le, Breaking the Web. Data Localization vs. the Global Internet Emory Law Journal, Forthcoming 53 (2014).

Andrew Charlesworth, Clash of the Data Titans? US and EU Data Privacy Regulation, 6 European Public Law 253–274 (2000).

Jiahong Chen, How the best-laid plans go awry. The (unsolved) issues of applicable law in the General Data Protection Regulation, 6 International Data Privacy Law 310–323 (2017).

Fa-Chang Cheng & Wen-Hsing Lai, The Impact of Cloud Computing Technology on Legal Infrastructure within Internet—Focusing on the Protection of Information Privacy, 29 2012 International Workshop on Information and Electronics Engineering 241–251 (2012).

Annalisa Ciampi, The Potentially Competing Jurisdiction of the European Court of Human Rights and the European Court of Justice, 28 Yearbook of European Law 601–609 (2009).

David Cole & Federico Fabbrini, Bridging the Transatlantic Divide? The United States, the European Union, and the Protection of Privacy Across Borders. iCourts Working Paper Series, No. 33, 2015 International Journal of Constitutional Law (2015).

David Couillard, Defogging the Cloud: Applying Fourth Amendment Principles to Evolving Privacy Expectations in Cloud Computing, 93 Minnesota Law Review 2205–2239 (2009).

Frank B. Cross, Law and trust, 93 The Georgetown Law Journal 1457–1545 (2005).

Dara Hallinan, Michael Friedewald, Paul McCarthy, Citizens' Perceptions of Data Protection and Privacy in Europe, 28 Computer Law and Security Review 263–272 (2012).

Jennifer C. Daskal, The Un-Territoriality of Data, 125 Yale Law Journal 326–398 (2015).

Primavera De Filippi, Primavera De Filippi & Luca Belli, Law of the Cloud v Law of the Land: Challenges and Opportunities for Innovation, 3 European Journal of Law and Technology 156–173 (2012).

Lothar Determann, What Happens in the Cloud: Software as a Service and Copyrights, 29 Berkeley Technology Law Journal 1096–1129 (2015).

Dias, Renata Dalle Molle Araujo, The Potential Impact of the EU General Data Protection Regulation on Pharmacogenomics Research, 36 Med. & L. 43–58 (2017).

Hoang T. Dinh, Chonho Lee, Dusit Niyato & Ping Wang, A survey of mobile cloud computing. Architecture, applications, and approaches, 13 Wirel. Commun. Mob. Comput. 1587–1611 (2013).

Colin S. Diver, Statutory Interpretation in the Administrative State, 133 University of Pennsylvania law review 549–599 (1985).

Benoit Dupont, Cybersecurity Futures: How Can We Regulate Emergent Risks? Technology Innovation Management Review 6–11 (2013).

Baudouin. Dupret, Legal pluralism, plurality of laws, and legal practices, 1 European Journal of Legal Studies (2007).

Luciana Duranti & Corinne Rogers, Trust in digital records. An increasingly cloudy legal area, 28 Computer Law & Security Review 522–531 (2012).

Clarence A. Dykstra, The Quest for Responsibility, 33 The American Political Science Review 1–25 (1939).

M. J. Eger, Emerging Restrictions on Transnational Data Flows: Privacy Protection or Non-Tariff Trade Barriers, 10 Law & Pol 1055–1105 (1978).

William N. Eskridge & Philip P. Frickey, Statutory Interpretation as Practical Reasoning, 42 Stanford Law Review 321–384 (1990).

John A. Ferejohn & Barry R. Weingast, A positive theory of statutory interpretation, 12 International Review of Law and Economics 263–279 (1992).

Ian Foster, Yong Zhao, Ioan Raicu & Shiyong Lu, Cloud Computing and Grid Computing 360-Degree Compared," IEEE Grid Computing Environments (GCE08) 2008, co-located with IEEE/ACM Supercomputing 2008 2012 ACM/IEEE 13TH INTERNATIONAL CONFERENCE ON GRID COMPUTING 1–10.

Susan Freiwald & Patricia Bellia, The Fourth Amendment Status of Stored E-mail: The Law Professors' Brief in Warshak v. United States Journal Articles 559–588 (2007).

A. Froomkin, Of Governments and Governance, 14 Berkeley Technology Law Journal 618–633 (1999).

Lon L. Fuller, Positivism and Fidelity to Law. A Reply to Professor Hart, 71 Harvard Law Review 630–672 (1958).

Amir Gandomi & Murtaza Haider, Beyond the hype. Big data concepts, methods, and analytics, 35 International Journal of Information Management 137–144 (2015).

Ruth Gavison, Privacy and the Limits of Law, 89 The Yale Law Journal 421–471 (1980).

Wesley Gee, Internet Tracking: Stalking or a Necessary Tool for Keeping the Internet Free, 20 CommLaw Conspectus 223–252 (2011).

Tom Geller, In privacy law, it's the U.S. vs. the world, 59 Commun. ACM 21–23 (2016).

M. Gillen, Internet Co-Regulation: European Law, Regulatory Governance and Legitimacy in Cyberspace, 20 International Journal of Law and Information Technology 147–149 (2012).

J. Goldring, Globalisation, National Sovereignty and the Harmonisation of Laws, 3 Uniform Law Review – Revue de droit uniforme 435–451 (1998).

Graham Greenleaf, Global Data Privacy Laws: Forty Years of Acceleration. UNSW Law Research Paper No. 2011-36 Privacy Laws and Business International Report 11–17 (2011).

Graham Greenleaf, The Influence of European Data Privacy Standards Outside Europe: Implications for Globalisation of Convention 108, 2 International Data Privacy Law 68–92 (2012).

John Griffiths, What is Legal Pluralism?, 18 The Journal of Legal Pluralism and Unofficial Law 1–55 (1986).

Dieter Grimm, Proportionality in Canadian and German Constitutional Jurisprudence, 57 University of Toronto Law Journal 383–397 (2007).

Neil Gunningham & Joseph Rees, Industry Self-Regulation: An Institutional Perspective, 19 Law & Policy 363–414 (1997).

Marit Hansen, Datenschutz nach dem Summer of Snowden, 38 Datenschutz Datensich 439–444 (2014).

Tor-Inge Harbo, The Function of the Proportionality Principle in EU Law, 16 European Law Journal 158–185 (2010).

Carol Harlow, Global Administrative Law: The Quest for Principles and Values, 17 Eur J Int Law 187–214 (2006).

Ibrahim Abaker Targio Hashem, Ibrar Yaqoob, Nor Badrul Anuar, Salimah Mokhtar, Abdullah Gani & Samee Ullah Khan, The rise of "big data" on cloud computing. Review and open research issues, 47 Information Systems 98–115 (2015).

Friedrich A. von Hayek, The Use of Knowledge in Society, 35 The American Economic Review 519–530 (1945).

Alden Heintz, The Dangers of Regulation, 29 J Communication 129–134 (1979).

Paul de Hert & Vagelis Papakonstantinou, The new General Data Protection Regulation. Still a sound system for the protection of individuals?, 32 Computer Law & Security Review 179–194 (2016).

Mireille Hildebrandt, Profiling and the rule of law, 1 IDIS 55–70 (2008).

Dennis D. Hirsch, In Search of the Holy Grail: Achieving Global Privacy Rules Through Sector-Based Codes of Conduct, 74 Ohio State Law Journal 1030–1069 (2013).

D. Hofman, Duranti L. & E. How, Trust in the Balance. Data Protection Laws as Tools for Privacy and Security in the Cloud, 10 Algorithms 47 (2017).

W. K. Hon, C. Millard & I. Walden, The problem of 'personal data' in cloud computing: what information is regulated? -The cloud of unknowing, 1 International Data Privacy Law 211–228 (2011).

W. K. Hon, C. Millard & I. Walden, Who is responsible for 'personal data' in cloud computing? --The cloud of unknowing, Part 2, 2 International Data Privacy Law 3–18 (2012).

W. Kuan Hon, Julia Hörnle & Christopher Millard, Data Protection Jurisdiction and Cloud Computing. When are Cloud Users and Providers Subject to EU Data Protection Law? The Cloud of Unknowing, Part 3, 26 International Review of Law, Computers & Technology (2012).

W. Kuan Hon & Christopher Millard, Data Export in Cloud Computing. How Can Personal Data Be Transferred Outside the EEA? The Cloud of Unknowing, Part 4, 9 SCRIPT-ed (2011).

W. Kuan Hon, Christopher Millard & Ian Walden, The Problem of 'Personal Data' in Cloud Computing – What Information is Regulated? The Cloud of Unknowing, Part 1, 1 International Data Privacy Law 211–228 (2011).

J. Hoover, Compliance in the Ether: Cloud Computing, Data Security and Business Regulation, 8 Journal of Business & Technology Law 255–273 (2013).

Gerrit Hornung, Regulating privacy enhancing technologies: seizing the opportunity of the future European Data Protection Framework, 26 Innovation: The European Journal of Social Science Research 181–196 (2013).

Peter Hustinx, Privacy by design. Delivering the promises, 3 IDIS 253–255 (2010).

Kristina Irion, Government Cloud Computing and the Policies of Data Sovereignty, 4 Policy and Internet 40–71 (2012).

Paul T. Jaeger, Jimmy Lin & Justin M. Grimes, Cloud Computing and Information Policy: Computing in a Policy Cloud?, 5 Journal of Information Technology & Politics 269–283 (2008).

Paul T. Jaeger, Jimmy Lin, Justin M. Grimes & Shannon N. Simmons, Where is the cloud? Geography, economics, environment, and jurisdiction in cloud computing, 14 First Monday (2009).

David R. Johnson, Susan P. Crawford & John G. Palfrey, The accountable net: Peer production of internet governance, 9 Berkman Center for Internet & Society at Harvard Law School Virginia Journal of Law and Technology 1–32 (2004).

David R. Johnson & David G. Post, Law And Borders--The Rise of Law in Cyberspace, 48 Stanford Law Review 1367–1402 (1996).

Richard Jones, Legal Pluralism and the Adjudication of Internet Disputes, 13 International Review of Law, Computers & Technology 49–68 (1999).

Amin Jula, Elankovan Sundararajan & Zalinda Othman, Cloud computing service composition. A systematic literature review, 41 Expert Systems with Applications 3809–3824 (2014).

Margot Kaminski, Why trade is not the place for the EU to negotiate privacy Internet Policy Review (2015).

Sean P. Kanuck, Information Warefare: New Challenges for Public International Law, 37 Harv. Int'l LJ 272–568 (1996).

Orin Kerr, The Case for the Third-Party Doctrine, 107 Michigan Law Review 561–601 (2009).

Orin S. Kerr, The Problem of Perspective in Internet Law, 91 Georgetown Law Journal 357–405 (2003).

Orin S. Kerr, The Fourth Amendment and New Technologies: Constitutional Myths and the Case for Caution, 102 Michigan Law Review 102–183 (2004).

Orin S. Kerr, The Fourth Amendment and the Global Internet, 67 Stanford Law Review 285–329 (2014).

Orin S. Kerr, The Next Generation Communications Privacy Act, 162 University of Pennsylvania law review 373–419 (2014).

Ido Kilovaty, Freedom to Hack SSRN Journal (2017).

Won Kim, Cloud computing architecture, 9 IJWGS 287–303 (2013).

Nancy J. King & V. T. Raja, What Do They Really Know About Me in the Cloud? A Comparative Law Perspective on Protecting Privacy and Security of Sensitive Consumer Data, 50 Am Bus Law J 413–482 (2013).

Benedict Kingsbury, The Concept of 'Law' in Global Administrative Law, 20 Eur J Int Law 23–57 (2009).

Benedict Kingsbury, Nico Krisch & Richard Stewart, The Emergence of Global Administrative Law, 68 Law and Contemporary Problems 15–62 (2005).

Alfred Kobsa, Privacy-enhanced personalization, 50 Commun. ACM 24–33 (2007).

B.-J. Koops, The trouble with European data protection law, 4 International Data Privacy Law 250–261 (2014).

Jonathan G. S. Koppell, Pathologies of Accountability. ICANN and the Challenge of "Multiple Accountabilities Disorder", 65 Public Administration Review 94–108 (2005).

N. Krisch, The Pluralism of Global Administrative Law, 17 European Journal of International Law 247–278 (2006).

Nir Kshetri, Privacy and security issues in cloud computing. The role of institutions and institutional evolution, 37 Telecommunications Policy 372–386 (2013).

W. Kuan Hon & C. Millard, Cloud Computing vs. Traditional Outsourcing – Key Differences, 23 Computers & Law (2012).

C. Kuner, Data Protection Law and International Jurisdiction on the Internet (Part 1), 18 International Journal of Law and Information Technology 176–193 (2010).

C. Kuner, Data Protection Law and International Jurisdiction on the Internet (Part 2), 18 International Journal of Law and Information Technology 227–247 (2010).

Christopher Kuner, Internet Jurisdiction and Data Protection Law: An International Legal Analysis (Part 1), 18 International Journal of Law and Information Technology 176–202 (2010).

Christopher Kuner, Internet Jurisdiction and Data Protection Law: An International Legal Analysis (Part 2), 18 International Journal of Law and Information Technology 227–257 (2010).

Michèle Lamont, Rethinking Expertise. By Harry Collins and Robert Evans. Chicago. University of Chicago Press, 2007. Pp. 153. $37.50, 115 American Journal of Sociology 569–571 (2009).

Stefanie Leimeister, Markus Böhm, Christoph Riedl & Helmut Krcmar, The Business Perspective of Cloud Computing: Actors, Roles and Value Networks ECIS 2010 Proceedings (2010).

Philip Leith, The socio-legal context of privacy, 2 IJC 105–136 (2006).

Lawrence Lessig, Law Regulating Code Regulating Law, 35 Loyola University Chicago Law Journal 1–14 (2003).

Lawrence Lessig & Paul Resnick, Zoning speech on the Internet: A legal and technical model, 98 Michigan Law Review 395–431 (1999).

R. K. Lippert & K. Walby, Governing Through Privacy. Authoritarian Liberalism, Law, and Privacy Knowledge, 12 Law, Culture and the Humanities 329–352 (2016).

E. Douglas Litowitz, Internal versus external perspectives in law: toward mediation, 26 Florida State University Law Review 127–150 (1998).

Volker Lüdemann, Alfred Scheerhorn, Christin Sengstacken & Daniel Brettschneider, Systemdatenschutz im Smart Grid, 39 Datenschutz Datensich 93–97 (2015).

Marcel Machill, Thomas Hart & Bettina Kaltenhäuser, Structural development of Internet self-regulation, 4 INFO 39–55 (2002).

Giandomenico Majone, Policy Harmonization. Limits and Alternatives, 16 Journal of Comparative Policy Analysis: Research and Practice 4–21 (2014).

Earl M. Maltz, Statutory Interpretation and Legislative Power: The Case for a Modified Intentionalist Approach, 63 Tul. L. Rev. 1–28 (1988).

F. A. Mann & Académie de droit international de La Haye., The doctrine of international jurisdiction revisited after twenty years, 186 Recueil des cours = Collected courses 9–116 (1984).

Sean Marston, Zhi Li, Subhajyoti Bandyopadhyay, Juheng Zhang & Anand Ghalsasi, Cloud computing — The business perspective, 51 Decision Support Systems 176–189 (2011).

Viktor Mayer-Schonberger & Yann Padova, Regime Change: Enabling Big Data through Europe, XVII The Columbia Science & Technology Law Review 315–335 (2016).

S. Meachem, Cloud With a Chance of Regulation, 57 ITNOW 18–21 (2015).

Aron Mefford, Lex Informatica: Foundations of Law on the Internet, 5 Indiana Journal of Global Legal Studies 211–237 (1997).

Raul Mendez, Google case in Italy, 1 International Data Privacy Law 137–139 (2011).

Sally Engle Merry, Legal Pluralism, 22 Law & Society Review 869–896 (1988).

Ralf Michaels, Global Legal Pluralism, 5 Annual Review of Law & Social Science (2009).

L. Moerel, Back to basics: when does EU data protection law apply?, 1 International Data Privacy Law 92–110 (2011).

Jesús Montes, Alberto Sánchez, Bunjamin Memishi, María S. Pérez & Gabriel Antoniu, GMonE. A complete approach to cloud monitoring, 29 Future Generation Computer Systems 2026–2040 (2013).

Menno Mostert, Annelien L. Bredenoord, Biesaart, Monique C I H & Delden, Johannes J M van, Big Data in medical research and EU data protection law. Challenges to the consent or anonymise approach, 24 European Journal of Human Genetics 956–960 (2016).

Milton Mueller, ICANN and Internet governance: sorting through the debris of “self-regulation”, 1 info 497–520 (1999).

Richard Mulgan, 'Accountability'. An Ever-Expanding Concept?, 78 Public Administration 555–573 (2000).

Nancy J. King, V.T. Raja, What Do They Really Know About Me in the Cloud? A Comparative Law Perspective on Protecting Privacy and Security of Sensitive Consumer Data, 50 American Business Law Journal 413–482 (2013).

Michael R. Nelson, The Cloud, the Crowd, and Public Policy, 25 Issues in science and technology 71–76 (2009).

Eva Nieuwdorp, The pervasive discourse, 5 Comput. Entertain. 13 (2007).

John T. Noonan, THE CONCEPT OF LAW. By H. L. A. Hart. Oxford: Oxford University Press, 1961. Pp. viii, 263. 21s, 7 Am. J. Juris. 169–177 (1962).

Olof Nyrén, Magnus Stenbeck & Henrik Grönberg, The European Parliament proposal for the new EU General Data Protection Regulation may severely restrict European epidemiological research, 29 European Journal of Epidemiology 227–230 (2014).

David W. Opderbeck, Encryption Policy and Law Enforcement in the Cloud, 49 Connecticut Law Review (2017).

Mike P. Papazoglou & Willem-Jan van den Heuvel, Service oriented architectures. Approaches, technologies and research issues, 16 The VLDB Journal 389–415 (2007).

Siani Pearson & Nick Wainwright, An interdisciplinary approach to accountability for future internet service provision, 1 IJTMCC 52–72 (2013).

Nicholas Platten, Protectors of Privacy: Regulating Data in the Global Economy – By A.L. Newman, 48 JCMS: Journal of Common Market Studies 453–454 (2010).

Reinhard Posch, Neue Herausforderungen für eine Informations- und Datensicherungsstrategie, 2014 Strategie und Sicherheit (2014).

Henry Prakken, An exercise in formalising teleological case-based reasoning. Artificial Intelligence and Law, 10 Artificial Intelligence and Law 113–133 (2002).

Charles D. Raab & Paul de Hert, The Regulation of Technology: Policy Tools and Policy Actors TILT Law & Technology Working Paper Series (2007).

Joseph Raz, Legal Principles and the Limits of Law, 81 The Yale Law Journal 823–854 (1972).

Chris Reed, How to Make Bad Law: Lessons from Cyberspace, 73 The Modern Law Review 903–932 (2010).

Christopher Rees, Who owns our data?, 30 Computer Law & Security Review 75–79 (2014).

Joel Reidenberg, Lex Informatica: The Formulation of Information Policy Rules through Technology, 76 Tex. L. Rev. 553–593 (1997).

Joel Reidenberg, Resolving Conflicting International Data Privacy Rules in Cyberspace, 52 Stan. L. Rev. 1315–1371 (1999).

Joel Reidenberg, Technology and Internet Jurisdiction, 153 University of Pennsylvania law review 1951–1974 (2005).

Gustavo Ribeiro, No Need to Toss a Coin: Conflicting Scientific Expert Testimonies and Intellectual Due Process, 12 Law, Probability and Risk 1–44 (2013).

Richard B. Stewart, The Global Regulatory Challenge to U.S. Administrative Law, 37 N.Y.U. J. Int 695–762 (2006).

William Jeremy Robison, Free at What Cost? Cloud Computing Privacy Under the Stored Communications Act, 98 Georgetown Law Journal 1195–1239 (2010).

Martin Rost, Standardisierte Datenschutzmodellierung, 36 Datenschutz Datensich 433–438 (2012).

Rothenberg, M., Jacobs, D., Updating the Law of Information Privacy: The New Framework of the European Union, 36 Harv. J. L. & Pub. Pol 606–652 (2013).

John Mark Michael Rumbold & Barbara Pierscionek, The Effect of the General Data Protection Regulation on Medical Research, 19 Journal of medical Internet research e47 (2017).

Sabino Cassese, Administrative Law without the State – The Challenge of Global Regulation, 37 N.Y.U. J. Int 663–694 (2005).

Rekha Saluja, Cloud Computing: Challenges and New Developments, 5 International Journal of Science, Engineering and Computer Technology 173–176 (2015).

Amedeo Santosuosso & Alessandra Malerba, Legal Interoperability as a Comprehensive Concept in Transnational Law, 6 Law, Inn Tech 51–73 (2014).

G. Sartor & Viola de Azevedo Cunha, M., The Italian Google-Case. Privacy, Freedom of Speech and Responsibility of Providers for User-Generated Contents, 18 International Journal of Law and Information Technology 356–378 (2010).

Giovanni Sartor, Doing justice to rights and values: teleological reasoning and proportionality. Artificial Intelligence and Law, 18 Artif Intell Law 175–215 (2010).

Andrej Savin, Profiling and Automated Decision Making in the Present and New EU Data Protection Frameworks SSRN Journal (2014).

Heinz-Dieter Schmelling, Motivation. Wie verhält sich die IT-Sicherheit zum IT-Outsourcing?, 40 Datenschutz und Datensicherheit – DuD 635–639 (2016).

Klaus Schmidt & Alejandro Laje, The Proportionality and Solidarity Principles and Their Impact on Privacy Laws in German Jurisprudence, 5 Laws 27–38 (2016).

T. Schultz, Carving up the Internet. Jurisdiction, Legal Orders, and the Private/Public International Law Interface, 19 European Journal of International Law 799–839 (2008).

Paul Schwartz, Information Privacy in the Cloud, 161 University of Pennsylvania law review 1623–1662 (2013).

Paul Schwartz, The EU-U.S. Privacy Collision: A Turn to Institutions and Procedures, 126 Harvard Law Review 1966–2009 (2013).

Paul M. Schwartz, Preemption and Privacy. UC Berkeley Public Law Research Paper, 118 Yale Law Journal 904-947 (2009).

Paul M. Schwartz & Daniel J. Solove, The PII Problem: Privacy and a New Concept of Personally Identifiable Information, 86 New York University Law Review 1814–1894 (2011).

Jatinder Singh, Thomas Pasquier, Jean Bacon, Hajoon Ko & David Eyers, Twenty Security Considerations for Cloud-Supported Internet of Things, 3 IEEE Internet Things J. 269–284 (2016).

Daniel J. Solove, A Taxonomy of Privacy, 154 University of Pennsylvania law review 477–560 (2006).

Alexander Somek, The Concept of 'Law' in Global Administrative Law: A Reply to Benedict Kingsbury, 20 Eur J Int Law 985–995 (2009).

Dawn Song, Elaine Shi, Ian Fischer & Umesh Shankar, Cloud Data Protection for the Masses Computer 39–45 (2012).

John F. Sowa, Top-level ontological categories, 43 International Journal of Human-Computer Studies 669–685 (1995).

Elen Stokes, Regulating Technologies: Legal Futures, Regulatory Frames and Technological Fixes by Roger Brownsword and Karen Yeung (eds), 73 The Modern Law Review 682–689 (2010).

S. Subashini & V. Kavitha, A survey on security issues in service delivery models of cloud computing, 34 Journal of Network and Computer Applications 1–11 (2011).

Clare Sullivan, Protecting digital identity in the cloud: Regulating cross border data disclosure, 30 Computer Law & Security Review 137–152 (2014).

Nabil Sultan, Cloud computing. A democratizing force?, 33 International Journal of Information Management 810–815 (2013).

Cass R. Sunstein, ON ANALOGICAL REASONING, 106 Harvard Law Review 741–791 (1993).

Dan Svantesson, Protecting Privacy on the 'Borderless' Internet – Some Thoughts on Extraterritoriality and Transborder Data Flow, 19 Bond Law Review 168–187 (2007).

Hassan Takabi, James B. D. Joshi & Gail-Joon Ahn, Security and Privacy Challenges in Cloud Computing Environments IEEE Security & Privacy 24–31 (2010).

Brian Z. Tamanaha, Understanding Legal Pluralism: Past to Present, Local to Global, 30 Sydney L. Rev. 375–411 (2008).

Omer Tene & Jules Polonetsky, Privacy in the Age of Big Data: A Time for Big Decisions, 64 Stan. L. Rev. Online 63–69 (2011).

Omer Tene & Jules Polonetsky, Judged by the Tin Man: Individual Rights in the Age of Big Data, 11 J. on Telecomm. & High Tech. L. 351–368 (2013).

Y. Tian, Current Issues of Cross-Border Personal Data Protection in the Context of Cloud Computing and Trans-Pacific Partnership Agreement. Join or Withdraw, 34 Wisconsin International Law Journal 367–408 (2016).

Tridimas, T., & Gutierrez-Fons, J. A., EU Law, International Law, and Economic Sanctions against Terrorism: The Judiciary in Distress?, 32 Fordham International Law Journal 660–730 (2008).

Hans-Heinrich Trute, Law and Knowledge – Remarks on a Debate in German Legal Science, 32 Ewha Journal of Social Sciences 34 (2016).

Edwin Tucker, The Morality of Law, by Lon L. Fuller, 40 40 Indiana Law Journal 270 (1965) 270–279 (1965).

Maria Tzanou, The EU as an emerging 'Surveillance Society'. The function creep case study and challenges to privacy and data protection, 4 ICL Journal (2010).

W. Gregory Voss, European Union Data Privacy Law Developments, 70 Business Lawyer 253–260 (2014/2015).

W. Gregory Voss, Looking at European Union Data Protection Law Reform Through a Different Prism. The Proposed EU General Data Protection Regulation Two Years Later, 17 Journal of Internet Law 1–3 (2014).

Mladen A. Vouk, Cloud Computing – Issues, Research and Implementations, 16 CIT 235–246 (2008).

David S. Wall, Digital Realism and the Governance of Spam as Cybercrime, 10 Eur J Crim Policy Res 309–335 (2004).

Huaiqing Wang, Matthew K. O. Lee & Chen Wang, Consumer privacy concerns about Internet marketing, 41 Commun. ACM 63–70 (1998).

Burke T. Ward & Janice C. Sipior, The Internet Jurisdiction Risk of Cloud Computing, 27 Information Systems Management 334–339 (2010).

Robert Ware, The strategic use of American cyberlaw and cyberspace jurisprudence, 48 Managerial Law 303–321 (2006).

Samuel D. Warren & Louis D. Brandeis, The Right to Privacy, IV Harvard Law Review 193–220 (1890).

Rolf H. Weber, Accountability in the Internet of Things, 27 Computer Law & Security Review 133–138 (2011).

Webster, J., & Watson, R. T., Analyzing the past to prepare for the future: Writing a literature review., 26 MIS quarterly 13–23 (2002).

Christof Weinhardt, Arun Anandasivam, Benjamin Blau, Nikolay Borissov, Thomas Meinl, Wibke Michalk & Jochen Stößer, Cloud Computing – A Classification, Business Models, and Research Directions, 1 Bus. Inf. Syst. Eng. 391–399 (2009).

A. E. Whitley, P. L. Willcocks & W. Venters, Privacy and Security in the Cloud: A Review of Guidance and Responses, 22 Journal of International Technology and Information Management 75–92 (2013).

James Q. Whitman, The Two Western Cultures of Privacy. Dignity versus Liberty, 113 The Yale Law Journal 1151–1221 (2004).

Jonathan B. Wiener, The regulation of technology, and the technology of regulation, 26 Technology in Society 483–500 (2004).

Andrew Keane Woods, Against Data Exceptionalism, 68 Stanford Law Review 729–789 (2016).

Chaowei Yang, Qunying Huang, Zhenlong Li, Kai Liu & Fei Hu, Big Data and cloud computing. Innovation opportunities and challenges, 10 International Journal of Digital Earth 13–53 (2016).

Zachary NJ Peterson, Mark Gondree, Robert Beverly, A position paper on data sovereignty: the importance of geolocating data in the cloud Proceedings of the 3rd USENIX conference on Hot topics in cloud computing (2011).

Dimitrios Zissis & Dimitrios Lekkas, Addressing cloud computing security issues, 28 Future Generation Computer Systems 583–592 (2012).

Lecture

Dimitra Kamarinou, Christopher Millard & Jatinder Singh, Machine Learning with Personal Data (2016).

Legal Commentary

Dutch Lawyers ed., Privacy for the Homo Digitalis. Proposal for a New Regulatory Framework for Data Protection in the Light of Big Data and the Internet of Things (2016): Wolters Kluwer.

Newspaper Articles

Ibrahim Hasan, New EU data protection regulation Law Society Gazette (2016).

C. Tuna, Ellison and Benioff Spar Over Cloud Credentials Wall Street Journal (2010).

Press Releases

eHealth Governance Initiative, DISCUSSION PAPER ON SEMANTIC AND TECHNICAL INTEROPERABILITY (2012).

Digital Agenda in the Europe 2020 strategy (2012).

Reports or Gray Literature

Response to the UK Ministry of Justice's Call for Evidence on the European Commission's Data Protection Proposals (2012).

DER HESSISCHE DATENSCHUTZBEAUFTRAGTE, Key data protection points for the trilogue on the General Data Protection Regulation (2015).

Luciana Duranti, Trust in online records and data. Integrity in Government through Records Management: Essays in Honour of Anne Thurston.

European Commission, Working Paper No. 2: Data protection laws in the EU: The difficulties in meeting the challenges posed by global social and technical developments (2010).

European Parliament, Report on the First Report on the implementation of the Data Protection Directive (95/46/EC) (COM(2003) 265 – C5-0375/2003 – 2003/2153(INI)) (2004).

Primavera De Filippi & Internet Policy Review, Foreign clouds in the European sky: how US laws affect the privacy of Europeans (2013): HIIG – Alexander von Humboldt Institute for Internet and Society.

Inc. Gartner, Cloud Computing Confusion Leads to Opportunity (2008).

Urs Gasser, Cloud Innovation and the Law: Issues, Approaches, and Interplay (2014).

Graham Greenleaf, Major Changes in Asia Pacific Data Privacy Laws: 2011 Survey (2012).

Douwe Korff, EC Study on Implementation of Data Protection Directive 95/46/EC (2008).

Francesca Musiani & Internet Policy Review, Decentralised internet governance: the case of a 'peer-to-peer cloud' (2014): HIIG – Alexander von Humboldt Institute for Internet and Society.

Tim O'Reilly & John Battelle, Web Squared: Web 2.0 Five Years On.

Older Adults and Technology Use (2014).

Neil Robinson, Lorenzo Valeri, Jonathan Cave, Tony Starkey, Hans Graux, Sadie Creese & Paul P. Hopkins, The Cloud: Understanding the Security, Privacy and Trust Challenges. Prepared for Unit F.5, Directorate-General Information Society and Media, European Commission (2012).

Osvaldo Saldias & Internet Policy Review, Cloud-friendly regulation: The EU's strategy towards emerging economies (2013): HIIG – Alexander von Humboldt Institute for Internet and Society.

Johannes Thimm, Inseparable, but not equal. Assessing U.S.-EU relations in the wake of the NSA surveillance affair, 4/2014 (2014). Berlin.

A. van Cleeff, W. Pieters & R. J. Wieringa, Security Implications of Virtualization: A Literature Study, vol. 3: IEEE.

Daniel J. Weitzner, Harold Abelson, Tim Berners-Lee, Chris Hanson, James Hendler, Lalana Kagal, Deborah L. McGuinness, Gerald Jay Sussman & K. Krasnow Waterman, Transparent Accountable Data Mining: New Strategies for Privacy Protection (2006).

Willcocks, Leslie P., Venters, Will and Whitley, Edgar A., Cloud and the future of business: from costs to innovation: part two: challenges (2012). London.

M. Zhou, R. Zhang, W. Xie, W. Qian & A. Zhou, Security and Privacy in Cloud Computing: A Survey: IEEE.

Special Issue

Graham Greenleaf ed., Global Data Privacy Laws: 89 Countries, and Accelerating. Special Supplement, Issue 115 (2012).